Learning Desktop Publishing
WordPerfect® 6 for Windows™

Blanc/Dembo/Brown

DDC Publishing

Acknowledgments

A special thanks to our husbands, Harold Dembo, Alan Blanc and Larry Brown, who have given us encouragement and support while they watched us work at the computer long into the night, and to our children, Pamela and Jaime for their input, understanding and everlasting patience.

We also wish to thank Cynthia Belis and Rochelle Pollack who have given us support and encouragement during the development of this book.

To the professional staff at DDC, thank you for your expertise, professionalism and coordinating efforts in editing this book and keeping us focused:

Managing Editor
Kathy Berkemeyer
Chicago, IL

Design and Layout
Jeff Kurek
New York, NY

Technical Editor
Sally Hargrave
Carol Stream, IL

Graphic Designer
Cynthia Harmon
New York, NY

Editor
Rebecca Fiala
Chicago, IL

Director of Publications
Don Gosselin
New York, NY

Copyright © 1994 by DDC Publishing, Inc.

Published by DDC Publishing, Inc.

All rights reserved, including the right to reproduce this book or portions thereof in any form whatsoever. For information, address DDC Publishing, Inc., 14 East 38th Street, New York, New York 10016.

First Dictation Disc Printing
Catalog No. F9

ISBN: 1-56243-191-9
UPC: 7-15829-15012-5

10 9 8 7 6 5 4 3 2 1

Printed in the United States of America

WordPerfect® is a registered trademark of WordPerfect Corporation.

All registered trademarks, trademarks, and service marks contained in this book are the property of their respective companies.

Table of Contents

INTRODUCTION

WELCOME TO WORDPERFECT FOR WINDOWS DESKTOP PUBLISHING!
- Desktop Publishing Defined
- How to Use This Book
- About the Data Disk

LESSON 1: WORDPERFECT BASICS
Exercises 1-6 2-27

- Mouse Terms and Actions
- WordPerfect 6 for Windows Screen
- View Bars
- Default Settings
- View Modes
- Reveal Codes
- Undelete/Undo
- Print
- Paper Size and Orientation
- Print Preview
- Help

LESSON 2: TEXT ALIGNMENTS & FONTS
Exercises 7-18 28-65
Summary Exercises A, B

- Text Alignment
- Justification
- Indents
- Font Face
- Font Style
- Font Size
- Font Appearance
- Font Position and Relative Size
- Wingdings
- Font Shading

LESSON 3: CHARACTER & LINE SPACING
Exercises 19-22 66-81
Summary Exercises A, B

- Kerning
- Word and Letterspacing
- Leading
- Line Height

LESSON 4: COLUMNS
Exercises 23-26 82-101
Summary Exercises A, B, C

- Regular Newspaper
- Newspaper with Custom Widths
- Balanced Newspaper
- Parallel

LESSON 5: GRAPHIC BOXES
Exercises 27-38 102-155
Summary Exercises A, B, C, D

- Create a Figure Box
- Create a Text Box
- Rotate a Text Box
- Change Print Quality
- Edit a Graphics Box
- Anchor Types
- Size, Position and Rotate Graphics Box
- Change Graphics Box Contents
- Borders and Fills
- Text Wrap Options
- Captions
- Scale, Rotate and Flip an Image
- Watermarks

Continued...

Table of Contents

LESSON 6: GRAPHIC LINES
Exercises 39-42 156-179
Summary Exercises A, B, C, D

- Create and Edit Lines
- Copy, Delete and Shade Lines
- Paragraph, Page Borders and Fills
- Shading

LESSON 7: SPECIAL ENHANCEMENTS
Exercises 43-53 180-239
Summary Exercises A, B, C, D, E

- Reverse Text
- Drop Cap
- Special Characters
- Bullets and Numbers
- TextArt
- Draw

LESSON 8: MULTIPLE-PAGE DOCUMENTS
Exercises 54-56 240-261
Summary Exercises A, B

- Headers and Footers
- Multiple Headers and Footers
- Page Numbers
- Widow and Orphan Protection
- Hyphenation

LESSON 9: TABLES and CHARTS
Exercises 57-74 262-329
Summary Exercises A, B

- Create a Table
- Text and Table Alignments
- Edit a Table
  - Insert and Delete Columns and Rows
  - Change Column Widths
  - Join and Split Cells
  - Position a Table
- Table Enhancements
  - Lines, Borders, Fills
- Tables within Documents
- Tables with Graphics
- Create a New Chart
- Edit a Chart
- Explode a Pie Chart
- Create a Chart from a Table
- Chart Enhancements
  - Legends
  - Data Labels
  - Color and Line Styles

LESSON 10: TEMPLATES and STYLES
Exercises 75-80 330-355
Summary Exercises A, B

- Use a Template
- Use Pre-Defined Styles
- Create and Save a Style
- Quick Create
- Edit Styles
- Retrieve Styles

Log of Exercises

	Document Name	Page
LESSON 1		
1	--	--
2	--	--
3	CODES	13
4	--	--
5	CODES (R3)	22
6	--	--
LESSON 2		
7	RSVP	29
8	CONGRATS	31
9	COMPANY	33
10	FLOWER*/FLOWER1	35-37
11	JACKET*/JACKET1	40-41
12	RSVP (R7)	45
13	FOOD	47-49
14	JACKET1 (R11)	50-51
15	FOOD (R13)	53
16	CONGRATS (R8)	55-57
17	FOOD (R13, 15)	60-61
18	SALE	62-63
2A	BICYCLE*/BICYCLE1	64
2B	COMPUTE*/COMPUTE1	65
LESSON 3		
19	FLOWER1(R10)	68-69
20	GOLF*/GOLF1	72-73
21	SALE (R18)	75
22	HERE	77
3A	FISH*/FISH1	78-79
3B	BOOK*/BOOK1	80-81
LESSON 4		
23	COCOA	85-86
24	GOODBYE	89-90
25	COOK	93
26	RESUME	95
4A	LIST	96-97
4B	RACE	98-99
4C	WORKTIPS	100-101

	Document Name	Page
LESSON 5		
27	IMAGES	104-105
28	TEXTBOX	108-109
29	IMAGES (R27)	111
30	PICTURE	114-115
31	HORSE	119-120
32	FLOWLET	122-123
33	BORDERS	126-127
34	BIRDS	131-133
35	CONGRAT1 (R8, 16)	135
36	PETS	141-143
37	WISH	144-145
38	PAPER	146-147
5A	CONDOR	148-149
5B	ROAR	150-151
5C	ROAR1	152-153
5D	COCOA1	154-155
LESSON 6		
39	INN	158-159
40	FOOD (R13, 15, 17)	162-163
41	GRAYLET	165-166
42	COMPANY (R9)	168-169
6A	COOK (R25)	170-171
6B	CONDOR (5A)	172-173
6C	SPECIES*/SPECIES1	174-175
6D	JACKET*/JACKET2	176-178
LESSON 7		
43	BOOK*/BOOK2	182-183
44	SPECIES1 (R6C)	184-185
45	FLOWLET (R32)/FLOWER2	188-189
46	FLOWER3	192-193
47	MUSIC	196-197
48	TRONICS/FISHY	202-204
49	GLASS/CAMERA/LUGGAGE/CAT/THINGS	210-211
50	FLOWERPOT/REPEAT	214-215
51	WORDS	220-221
52	ANNOTATE	224-225
53	AIRPLANE/GROUP	228-229
7A	FISH*/FISH2	230-231
7B	RSVP (R7, 12)	232-233

Continued...

Log of Exercises

	Document Name	Page
7C	MAGAZINE	234-235
7D	WORDS (R51)/ SUNLET/ FLOWER1(R10,19)/ FLOWPOT (R50)/ PLANTER	236-237
7E	AIRPLANE (R53)/ LUGGAGE(R49)/ GLASS (R49)/ WELCOME	238-239

LESSON 8

	Document Name	Page
54	COMPLND*/ COMPLND1	244-245
55	SAVE*/SAVE1	249-251
56	SAVE1 (R55)	254-255
8A	MARSH*/MARSH1	256-259
8B	COMPLND1 (R54)	260-261

LESSON 9

	Document Name	Page
57	REVIEW	264-265
58	ATBAT	266-267
59	NUMBER	270-271
60	RMS	272-273
61	WINGDING	274-275
62	REVIEW (R57)	278-279
63	RMS (R60)	282-283
64	ATBAT (R58)	286-287
65	ATBAT (R58, 64)	292-293
66	IS	294-295
67	BUY	296-297
68	SUN	300-301
69	SUN (R68)	304-305
70	ANIMAL	306-307
71	FLOWER4	311-313
72	FLOWER4 (R71)	315-317
73	SUN (R68, 69)	320-321
74	FUND	324-325
9A	FLOWLET(R32)/ FLOWER5	326-327
9B	BOND	328-329

LESSON 10

	Document Name	Page
75	FAX1/MEMO4	331-33
76	WATCH*/WATCH1	336-337
77	GOLFPG	340-341
78	FILM	344-345
79	GOLFPG/GOLFPG1	347
80	FILM (R78)/FILM1	350-351
10A	CERTIF2/BUSCARD1	352-353
10B	FISHFOOD	354-355

INTRODUCTION

Desktop Publishing provides you with the ability to change ordinary typewritten text into attractive, professional-looking documents using design elements. Design elements include font faces, font styles, font sizes, graphics, lines, and spacing techniques.

WordPerfect 6 for Windows contains many features commonly found in page layout software programs used by graphic designers. True desktop publishing requires a design background to effectively create newsletters, flyers, advertisements, brochures, menus, stationery, invitations, etc.* *LEARNING DESKTOP PUBLISHING USING WORDPERFECT 6 FOR WINDOWS* introduces you to those features found in the software that will enable you to create your own attractive documents.

It is assumed you are familiar with the fundamental word processing features of WordPerfect 6 for Windows.

Each lesson in this book explains WordPerfect concepts, provides numerous exercises to apply those concepts, and illustrates the necessary keystrokes or mouse actions to complete the application.

HOW TO USE THIS BOOK

Each exercise contains four parts:

1. CONCEPTS:

- Explain the WordPerfect concept being introduced.
- Graphic symbols are used to call your attention to the following:

 *Quick Feature Access*

 *Exercise Objectives*

 *Cautions and Warnings*

 *Tips for using a feature or completing an exercise.*

---

*For a quick reference to design principles, refer to *GRAPHIC DESIGN FOR DESKTOP PUBLISHING* by J. Schwartzman, a Quick Reference Guide published by DDC.

Continued...

INTRODUCTION

2. EXERCISE DIRECTIONS

- Tells you how to complete the exercise.

Some exercise directions will include "disk" and "keyboard" icons. If you are using a file which has been saved on the data disk (see data disk explanation below), follow the directions next to the disk icon. If you do not have the data disk, follow the directions next to the keyboard icon.

 Open **FLOWER** (filename). Save As **FLOWER1** (to keep original file intact).

or

 Type the exercise as shown.

3. EXERCISES

- Apply the concept that was introduced.

4. KEYSTROKE/MOUSE PROCEDURES

- Outline the keystrokes or mouse actions required to complete the exercise.

Keystrokes and mouse actions are provided only when a new concept is introduced. Therefore, if you forget the keystroke and/or mouse procedures for completing a task, use WordPerfect's Help feature or the book's index to locate the page where the keystroke and/or mouse procedures are provided. WordPerfect 6 for Windows screens and icons are provided, when necessary, to clarify lesson concepts.

ABOUT THE DATA DISK

A data disk may be purchased from the publisher. The data disk contains text files used in some of the exercises. Using the data disk allows you to complete the exercise without keyboarding lengthy text. If, however, you do not purchase the disk, you will create the exercises as directed. As noted above, exercise directions will include "disk" and "keyboard" icons.

Lesson 1 • WordPerfect Basics

EXERCISE

- **MOUSE TERMS AND ACTIONS** - **THE WORDPERFECT 6 FOR WINDOWS SCREEN**
- **VIEW BARS**

CONCEPTS:

- This book emphasizes basic desktop publishing features. It is assumed that you are familiar with the basic features of WordPerfect 6 for Windows.

- The keystrokes/mouse actions to perform basic word processing tasks used in this book are listed at the end of this exercise as a review.

Mouse Terms and Actions

- The following mouse terminology and their corresponding actions are described below and will be used throughout the book:

Point	Move the mouse (on the tabletop) so the mouse pointer points to a specific item.
Click	Quickly press and release the mouse button.
	NOTE: Use the left mouse button unless otherwise instructed.
Double-click	Press the mouse button twice in rapid succession.
Drag	Press and hold down the mouse button while moving the mouse.

The WordPerfect 6 for Windows Screen

- When WordPerfect 6 for Windows is accessed, the following screen displays:

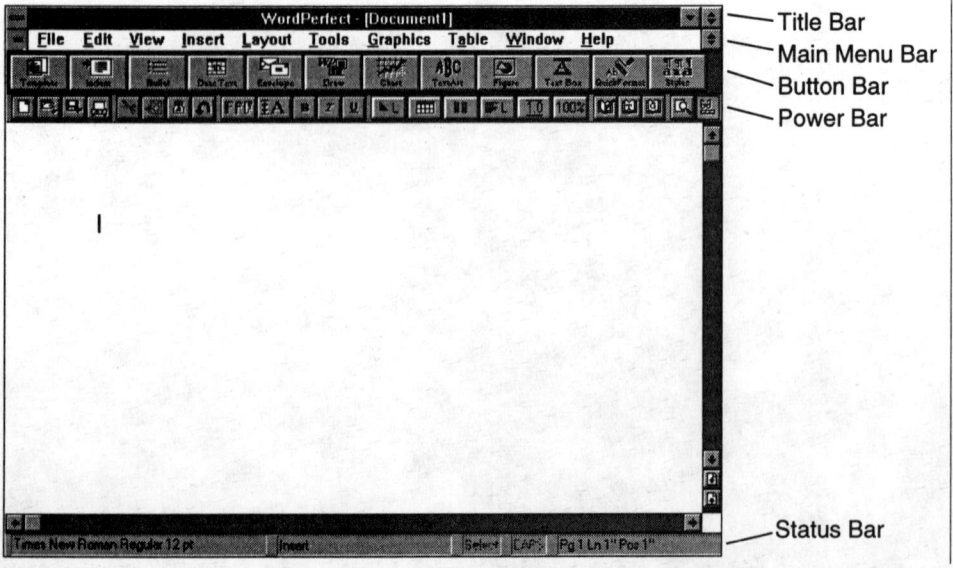

2

View Bars

- There are many different bars available in WordPerfect 6 for Windows. The bars that generally display when WordPerfect is accessed (unless changes were made when WordPerfect was installed) are the: Title Bar, Menu Bar, Button Bar, Power Bar, and Status Bar. Note the illustration on bottom of previous page.

- Using the View menu, you can choose to view or not view the following bars: Button Bar, Power Bar, Ruler Bar, and Status Bar. In addition, you can choose to hide all of the bars in the WordPerfect work area.

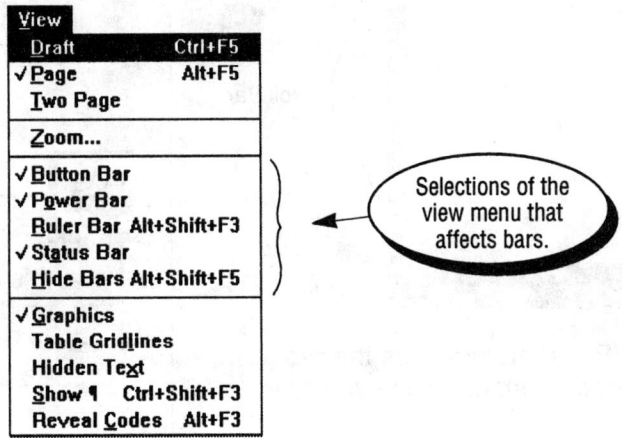

Lesson 1 ■ Exercise 1

- The WordPerfect Bars (including Feature and Scroll Bars) are described below. Note the WordPerfect for Windows screen below which includes the ruler and feature bars:

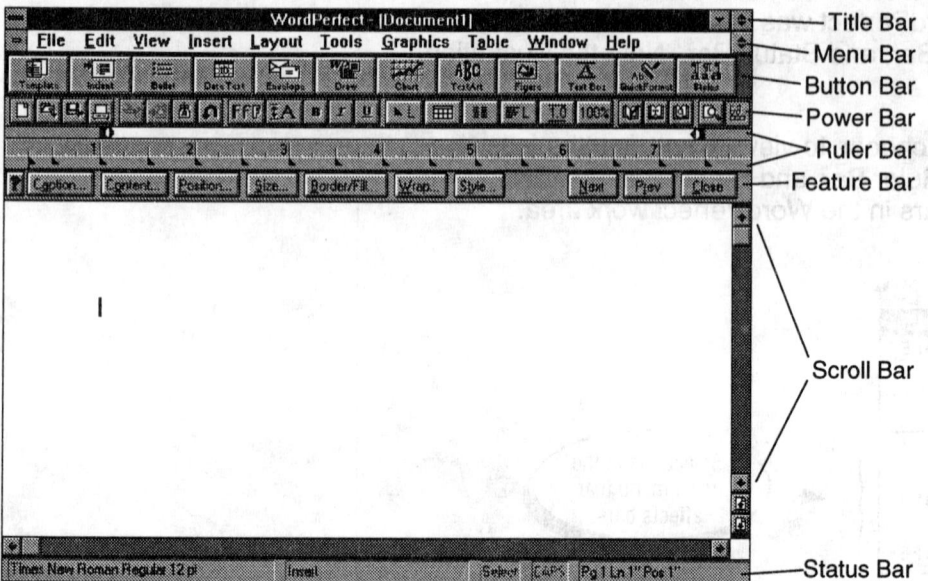

In this exercise, you will hide and display view bars.

- **Title Bar**, located at the very top of the WP screen indicates the program name, the directory and the name of the document on which you are working:

    WordPerfect - [C:\wpwin6.0\l1e1]

- **Menu Bar,** located below the title bar, contains a group of selections that allows you to perform most WordPerfect tasks. Within each main menu item, there are numerous sub-menu commands which are listed in a pull-down menu.

- **Button Bar,** contains icons (symbols or graphic images that represents a command or function) that will quickly execute features, programs and macros. The Button Bar is similar to the power bar. One difference is that while you can create a new Button Bar, you can only change buttons on the existing Power Bar.

- **Power Bar,** located below the Button Bar, contains buttons that represent the most frequently used editing and layout features.

- **Ruler Bar**, (not necessarily displayed when you access WordPerfect) lets you quickly set and move tabs, margins, make paragraph adjustments, position columns, and move columns and margins in tables.

- **Feature Bar,** appears when certain features (such as Graphics) are used. A feature bar offers quick access to commands that are associated with the feature you are using.

- **Scroll Bars,** appear at the right and/or bottom of a window. The vertical scroll bar is used to move your document forward and backward so you can see that part of the document that does not appear on the screen.

- **Status Bar**, located at the bottom of the screen, displays information about your document. The status bar will sometimes display messages and warnings.

EXERCISE DIRECTIONS:

1. Select <u>V</u>iew from the main menu.
2. Display the Button and Power Bar. If they are already displayed, skip to step 3.

   Note the checkmark next to each after they have been selected.
3. Hide the Power Bar.
4. Hide all Bars (Select <u>V</u>iew, <u>H</u>ide Bars, OK)

   ▪ *NOTE:* All the bars disappear from the screen giving you maximum amount of screen for work area.

5. Press ESC to restore all bars.
6. Hide the Status Bar (<u>V</u>iew, St<u>a</u>tus Bar)
7. Display the Ruler Bar (<u>V</u>iew, <u>R</u>uler Bar)
8. Display the Status Bar.
9. Hide the Ruler Bar.
10. Restore Power Bar.
11. Close the document window.

VIEW BARS

1. Click <u>V</u>iew .... `Alt` + `V`
2. Click the bar to display or hide:

   NOTE: A checkmark appears next to bars that are selected.

   <u>B</u>utton Bar .... `B`
   P<u>o</u>wer Bar .... `O`
   <u>R</u>uler Bar .... `R`
   St<u>a</u>tus Bar .... `A`

HIDE BARS

Alt + Shift +F5

1. Click <u>V</u>iew .... `Alt` + `V`
2. Click <u>H</u>ide Bars .... `H`
3. Click **OK**

RESTORE BARS

Escape

1. Click <u>V</u>iew .... `Alt` + `V`
2. Click <u>H</u>ide Bars .... `H`

   NOTE: Even though "bars are hidden," you can still use the mouse on the non-visible menu bar at the top of the screen.

Lesson 1 • WordPerfect Basics

EXERCISE 2

■ DEFAULT SETTINGS ■ VIEW MODES

CONCEPTS:

Default Settings

- **Defaults** are automatic settings in a computer program. Think of defaults as the settings that are in effect if you do nothing.

- Settings such as margins, tabs, line spacing, type style, type size and text alignment are automatically set by the WordPerfect program.

Selected Default Settings

Layout Feature	Default Setting
each margin	1"
line spacing	single
tabs	every 1/2"
justification	left
Preferences	
Button Bar	WordPerfect
Power Bar	Default
Status Bar	Default
Keyboard	WPWin 6.0 keyboard
Menu Bar	WPWin 6.0 menu
Fonts	
if Windows driver is installed	Times New Roman, 12 pt.
if WordPerfect driver is installed	Courier, 12 pt.

This book uses the default preferences. *DO NOT MAKE CHANGES TO THE PREFERENCES UNLESS INSTRUCTED TO DO SO.*

- Default settings can be changed temporarily, but when you start a new document, the settings are returned to their original values.

- To change default settings temporarily, access the desired feature and make the desired change. For example, to change line spacing from single space to double space, choose Layout, Line, Spacing, type 2, and choose OK.

- Many default settings can be changed permanently (creating new default settings). Three features that are used to change default settings are Preferences, Initial Style Codes and Initial Fonts.

- The **Preference** options let you customize WordPerfect to fit your needs. Preferences have standard default settings that fit most situations. Before changing a default, note the original setting so you can return to it if desired.

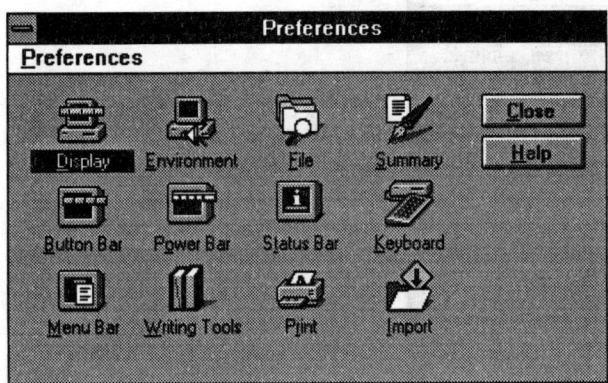

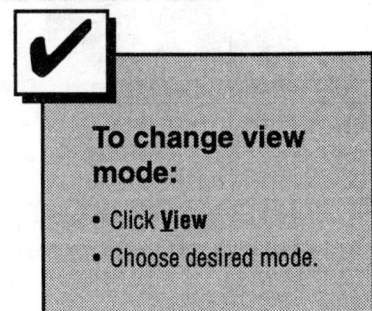

To change view mode:
- Click **V**iew
- Choose desired mode.

- Every new document contains an **Initial Style** code at the beginning of the document. You cannot delete this code, but you can edit it. You can use the Initial Style code to define a format that can be used with each new document you create. For example, you can change default settings, margins, font, tab setting, justifications, etc., to settings that you want to use for most documents. The default Initial Style code contains no settings.

- WordPerfect starts every document with a default font. The default font is changed by using the Initial Fonts feature. The original default font is Times New Roman 12 point if WordPerfect was installed using the Windows printer driver; or Courier 12 point if installed using the WordPerfect printer driver.

Page View Modes

- Documents can be viewed in three different modes: Draft, Page and Two Page.

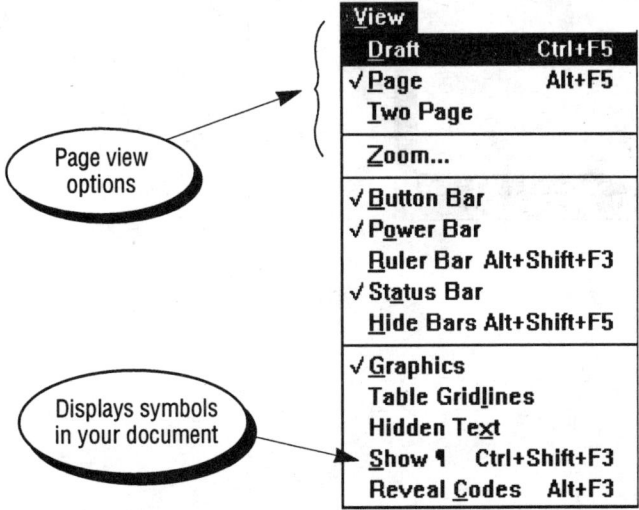

Lesson 1 ■ Exercise 2   7

Lesson 1 ■ Exercise 2

- **Page mode** displays a WYSIWYG (What You See is What You Get) view of your document.

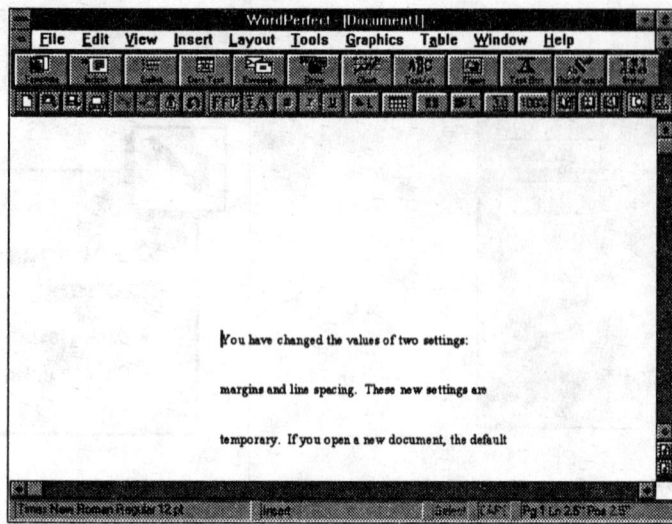

- **Draft mode** is near WYSIWYG. However, features such as headers, footers, watermarks, and some formatting features are not displayed. In addition, top and bottom margins are not displayed. Information is displayed more quickly as you move through your document in Draft mode.

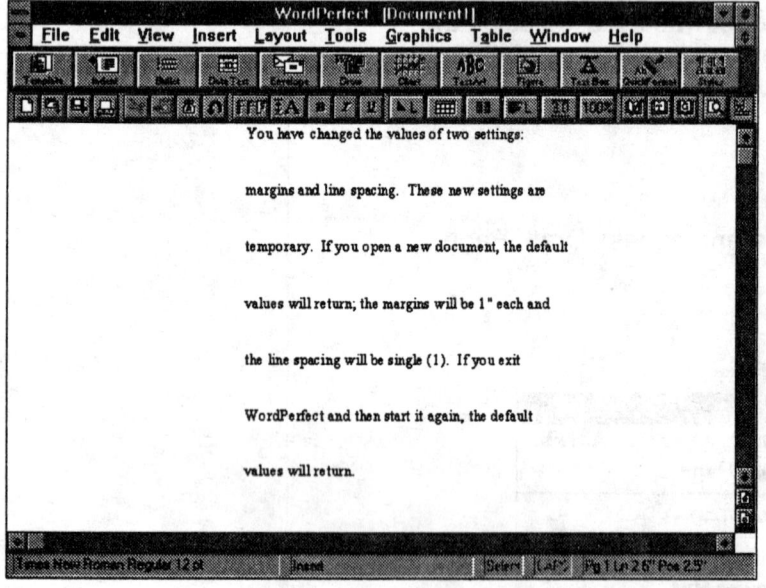

When using graphics, deselecting the Graphics option in the View menu will also help speed up your work.

- **Two Page mode** displays two consecutive pages side by side.

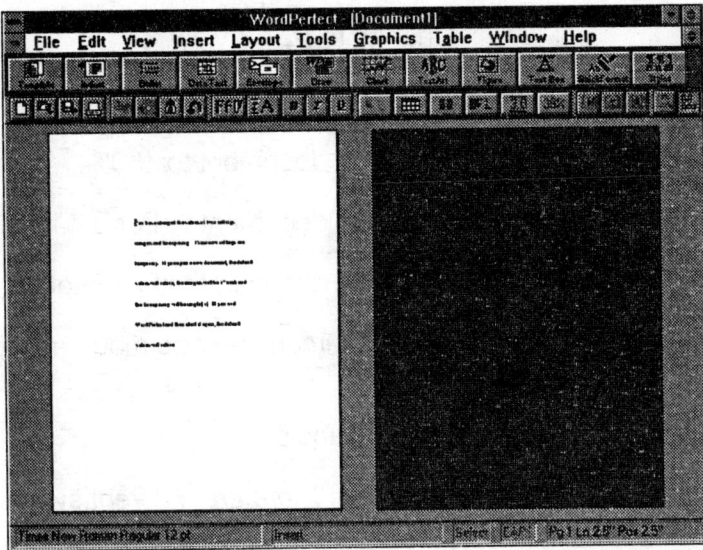

NOTE: The right page is displayed as gray because there is not a second page in this document.

- In addition, you can use *Show Symbols* to display the following symbols in your document.

    ¶   Hard Return Symbol
    →   Tab
    ■   Space

- The **Zoom** option lets you specify the size of your screen display. You can Zoom between 25% and 400%, or you can choose the following options:

Margin Width	Displays a full line with minimal white space on the sides.
Page Width	Displays the width of the page, including the margins.
Full Page	Displays all margins, including the top and bottom.

Zoom View at 200%

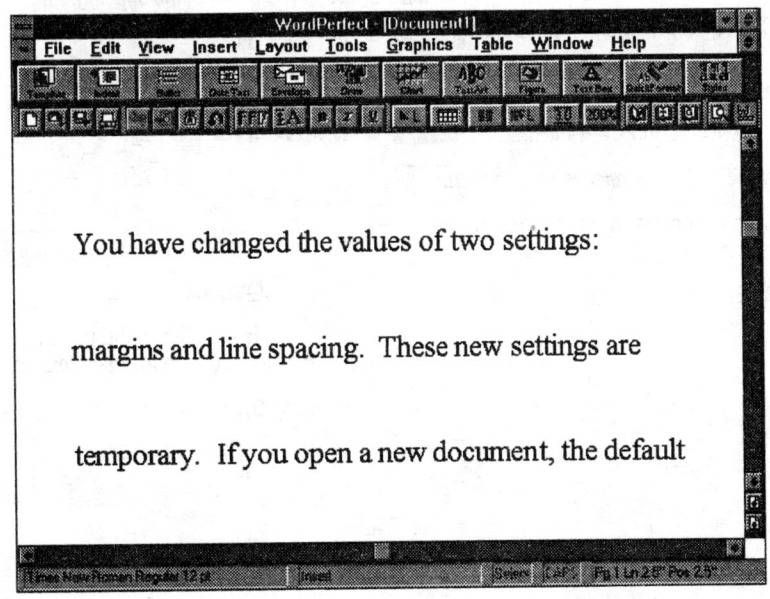

In this exercise, you will change the default settings for margins and line spacing, and you will view the document using different view modes.

Lesson 1 ■ Exercise 2

Lesson 1 ■ Exercise 2

EXERCISE DIRECTIONS:

1. Start with a clear screen.
2. Change the left, right, top and bottom margins to 2.5".
   - NOTE: The status indicators, **Ln 2.5"** and Pos **2.5"** reflect the new margins settings.
3. Change line spacing to 3 (triple spacing).
4. Type the exercise as shown.
5. Change to **Draft** view.
   - NOTE: The top margin is no longer displayed.
6. Change to **Two Page** view.
   - NOTE: Two pages appear on the screen. One page is shaded because there is nothing on it.
7. Change to **Page** view.
   - NOTE: The top margin reappears.
8. Zoom the document to 150%.
9. Zoom the document to Page Width.
10. Zoom the document to Full Page.
11. View document in Page mode and Zoom to 100%.
12. Show symbols.
    - NOTE: There are different symbols for paragraphs, tabs, spaces, right justify a line, etc.
13. Close the document window.

CHANGE VIEW MODES

Draft: Ctrl + F5; Page: Alt + F5

1. Click **V**iew .... `Alt` + `V`
2. Click a view option:
   - **D**raft .... `D`
   - **P**age .... `P`
   - **T**wo Page .... `T`

SHOW SYMBOLS

Ctrl+Shift+F3

1. Click **V**iew .... `Alt` + `V`
2. Click **S**how ¶ .... `S`

ZOOM

- Using Menu Bar -

1. Click **V**iew .... `Alt` + `V`
2. Click **Z**oom .... `Z`
3. Select a zoom option:
   - 50% .... `5`
   - 75% .... `7`
   - 100% .... `1`
   - 150% .... `0`
   - 200% .... `2`
   - Margin Width .... `A`
   - Page Width .... `W`
   - Full Page .... `F`
   - Other .... `O`
4. Click **OK** .... `Enter`

- Using Power Bar -

1. Click 100% on Power bar ......
   NOTE: Do not release mouse button
2. Drag the pointer to the desired option (same as above).
3. Release mouse button.

LINE SPACING

- Click Line spacing .... `1.0` button on Power Bar
- Select desired line spacing.

OR

1. Click **L**ayout .... `Alt` + `L`
2. Click **L**ine .... `L`
3. Click **S**pacing .... `S`
3. Type desired line spacing.
4. Click **OK**

MARGINS

Ctrl + F8

1. Click **L**ayout .... `Alt` + `L`
2. Click **M**argins .... `M`
3. Type desired left, right, top and/or bottom margin in the appropriate text box.
4. Click **OK**

You have changed the values of two settings:

margins and line spacing. These new settings are

temporary. If you open a new document, the default

values will return; the margins will be 1" each and

the line spacing will be single (1). If you exit

WordPerfect and then start it again, the default

values will return.

Lesson 1 ▪ WordPerfect Basics

EXERCISE 3

REVEAL CODES

CONCEPTS:

- Certain WordPerfect commands cause **hidden codes** to be inserted in a document. When you turn the **Reveal Codes** screen on, the document window is divided into two parts. The top part is the normal editing screen, and the bottom part displays the same text along with the codes contained in the text.

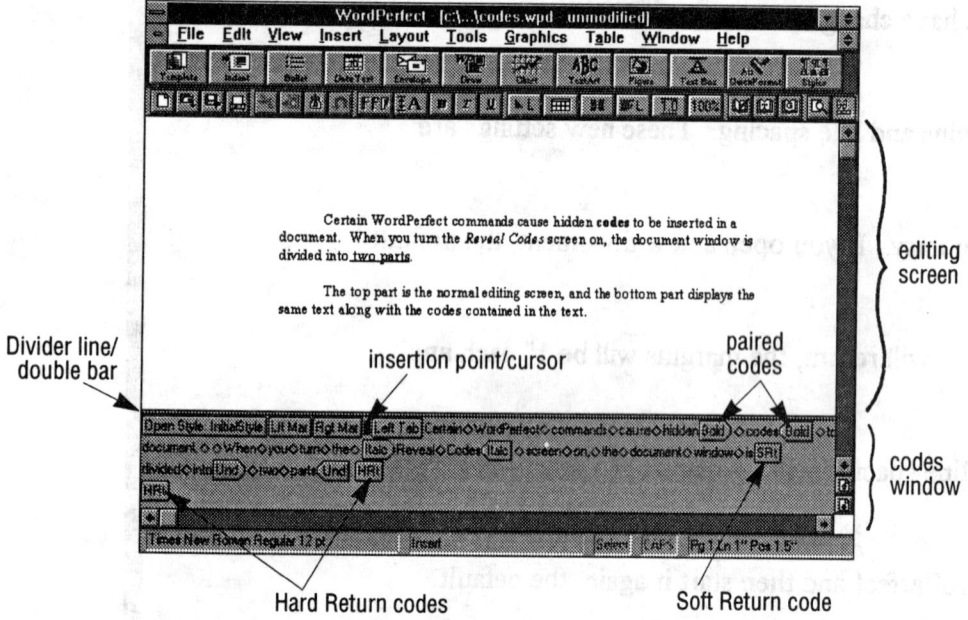

To Reveal Codes:
- Click **View**
- Click **Reveal Codes**

OR

Press **Alt + F3**

OR

Drag horizontal bar down to where Reveal Codes should begin.

To increase size of reveal codes screen:

Drag the double bar separating the text screen from the Reveal Codes screen upward.

- It is useful to know where codes are located when editing a document, working with graphics, or deleting codes that are not needed.

- Some codes represent commands that affect the formatting of text, while other codes represent graphics boxes or lines or other features. Codes appear within rectangular boxes in the Reveal Codes screen.

- Some codes are single codes that are inserted where the command is issued and affect text following the code, like line spacing and margin settings. Other codes are paired and affect only the portion of the document between the beginning code and ending code, for example, bold and underline.

- The first code in a document is the Open Style:Initial Style Code. This code cannot be deleted but it can be changed using Initial Codes Style.

- The cursor (insertion point) appears as a red rectangle in the Reveal Codes screen, and spaces appear as diamonds.

To delete a code:
- Move cursor (insertion point) in front of code.
- Press **Delete key**

OR

Use the mouse pointer to drag the code out of the Reveal Codes window.

- Some codes do not show the settings for a feature unless the cursor is in front of the code, for example [Lft Mar]. When you move the cursor in front of the code, it expands to display the command setting well as the command's name.

- Notice in the illustration on previous page that [Hrt], a hard return code, appears whenever you press [Enter]. On the right side of the Reveal Codes screen, [Srt], a soft return code, appears wherever WordPerfect automatically wraps text to the next line.

- WordPerfect automatically displays the Reveal Codes screen at 25% of the document window size.

In this exercise, you will create a short paragraph. You will reveal codes and identify and delete some of the codes.

EXERCISE DIRECTIONS:

1. Start with a clear screen.
2. Set 1.5" left and right margins.
3. Begin the exercise at the top of your screen.
4. Type the exercise on the right as shown.
5. Reveal Codes.
6. Press Ctrl + Home twice.
    - *NOTE: The cursor moves to the right of the Open Style: Initial Style Code.*
7. Press End.
    - *NOTE: The cursor moves to the end of the Reveal Codes screen (on the current line) and displays codes in the right of the document. Notice the [SRt] code, indicating a "soft return."*
8. Press Home.
    - *NOTE: The cursor moves to the beginning of the Reveal Codes screen.*
9. Expand the [Lft Mar] code.
10. Press the right arrow key several times and notice how the cursor moves around within the Reveal Codes screen.
11. Change the size of the Reveal Codes screen.
12. Delete the bold and underline codes.
13. Turn Reveal Codes off.
14. Save the file; name it **CODES**.
15. Close the document window.

Lesson 1 ▪ Exercise 3

Certain WordPerfect commands cause hidden **codes** to be inserted in a document. When you turn the *Reveal Codes* screen on, the document window is divided into _two parts_.

The top part is the normal editing screen, and the bottom part displays the same text along with the codes contained in the text.

REVEAL CODES/DELETE A CODE

Alt + F3

Drag horizontal bar down to where Reveal Codes should begin.

OR

1. Click **View** .... `Alt` + `V`
2. Click **Reveal Codes** .... `C`
3. Place insertion point (cursor) to the left of code to delete.

OR

Point to and click on code to delete.

4. Press **Delete** .... `Del`

EXIT REVEAL CODES

Alt + F3

Drag divider line up or down into document window.

EXPAND A CODE

Move insertion point (cursor) in front of code to expand or click on the code.

NOTE: Only codes that contain settings can be expanded.

Lesson 1 ▪ Exercise 3

Lesson 1 • WordPerfect Basics

EXERCISE 4
UNDO/UNDELETE

CONCEPTS:

- **Undo** lets you reverse your last editing action. **Undelete** restores any of your last three deletions. While you can *Undelete* deletions at any location, Undo restores information in its original location.

- You can undo an action a second time (or more) in order to restore your previous undo action, that is, you can *undo* an *undo*. However, you cannot undo cursor movements; you can't, for example, return to your previous location.

- The Undelete dialog box offers you the option to rotate through the last three deletions and restore the deletion you want. You can use Undelete to move text by deleting text, moving the insertion point and then undeleting the text. This action is similar to **cut** and **paste**. You cannot mix the two actions, that is, you cannot *paste* deleted text and you cannot *Undelete* cut or copied text.

To undo text:
- Click Undo button

OR

- Press **Ctrl + Z**

OR

- Click **E**dit
- Click **U**ndo

To Undelete text:
- Press **Ctrl + Shift + Z**

OR

- Click **E**dit
- Click U**n**delete
- Click **R**estore

In this exercise, you will create a short paragraph and then use the undo and undelete features on some of the text you created.

EXERCISE DIRECTIONS:

1. Start with a clear screen.
2. View the document screen at 150%.
3. Set left and right margins to 1.5"
4. Set line spacing to 2.
5. Type the exercise as shown.
6. Delete the first sentence.
7. Undo the action.
8. Undo the action again.
   - NOTE: *The first sentence disappears again.*
9. Undo the action again (sentence will reappear).
10. Delete "marvelous" in the second paragraph.
11. Position your insertion point immediately before "information." Then, undelete "marvelous".
12. Delete "correct" in the second paragraph.
13. Delete "after ruining a document by accidentally performing an incorrect editing action."
14. Position your insertion point immediately before "material" in the second paragraph. Then, undelete "correct".
    - NOTE: *You must cycle through the corrections by clicking the Previous Button in the Undelete dialog box until "correct" appears. Then, click the Restore Button.*
15. Undelete the last the sentence.
16. Close the document window. Do not save the file.

In this exercise you are going to compare the undo and undelete features.

The undo feature lets you reverse your last editing action, while the undelete feature lets you return any one (or all) of your last three deletions at the cursor's current location.

This is marvelous information that can help you recover deleted data and restore correct material after ruining a document by accidentally performing an incorrect editing action.

UNDELETE

Ctrl + Shift + Z

1. Click **Edit**.................... Alt + E
2. Click **U**n**delete**............... N
   Select option:
3. Click **Restore**
   to restore last deletion........ R

OR

Click **Next** or **Previous**........... P or N
to cycle through last 3 deletions

Click **Restore**.................... R

UNDO (an action)

Ctrl + Z

1. Click **Edit**.................... Alt + E
2. Click **U**ndo.................... U

Lesson 1 ■ Exercise 4

Lesson 1 ▪ WordPerfect Basics

EXERCISE 5

▪ PAPER SIZE AND ORIENTATION ▪ PRINT PREVIEW

CONCEPTS:

- WordPerfect lets you print part or all of a document that is in the screen window. You can print a page of the document, the full document, selected pages of a document, multiple pages or one or more blocks of text within the document. A document may be printed from the disk, without retrieving it to the screen.

- After accessing Print, a dialog box appears asking you to indicate whether you wish to print the full document (more than one page) the current page, multiple pages (which you designate) or a document on disk. You may also indicate the number of copies you desire to print.

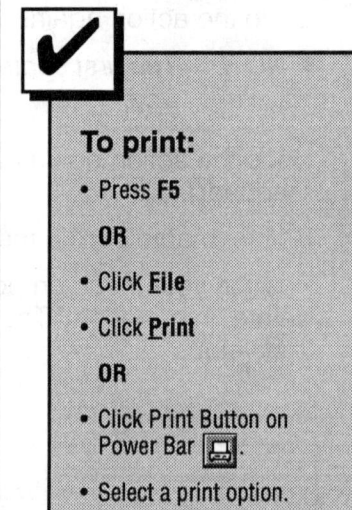

To print:
- Press **F5**

  OR
- Click **File**
- Click **Print**

  OR
- Click Print Button on Power Bar.
- Select a print option.

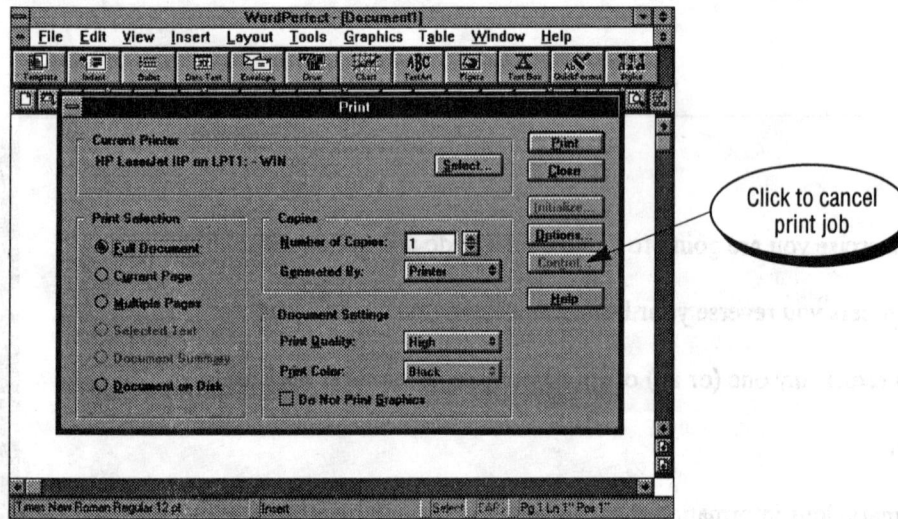

Click to cancel print job

- When printing all pages in a multiple page document, you must select Full Document, not the Page option. The insertion point may be on any page in the document when selecting this option.

- To print selected pages (pages 2 and 3, pages 3 through 5, etc.), select the Multiple Pages option, select Print, then enter the page range you wish to print in the Page(s) text box.

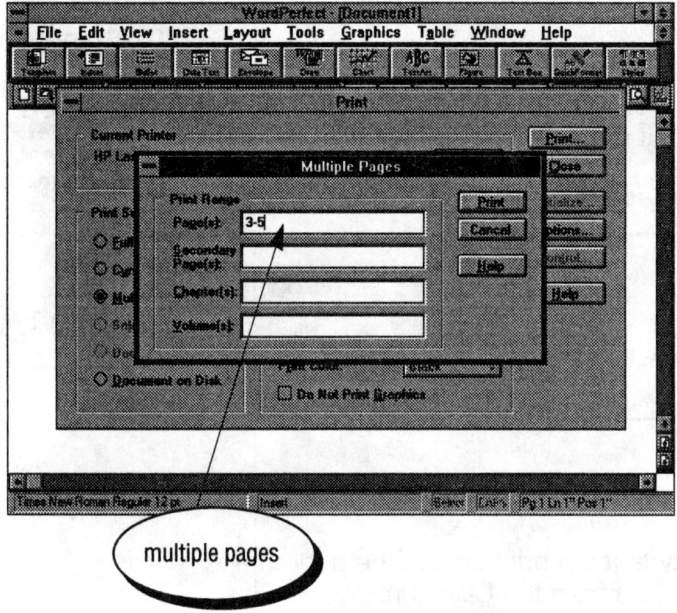

multiple pages

TYPE	TO PRINT
3	page 3
1,3,5	Pages 1, 3 and 5
4-	Page 4 to end of document
-2	The beginning of document through page 2
2-6	Pages 2 through 6
1-2,6	Pages 1, 2 and 6
2,5,9-11	Pages 2,5, and 9 through 11

- You can cancel an individual print job or all print jobs while they are printing by selecting Control from the Print dialog box, then Cancel Print Job.

Lesson 1 ▪ Exercise 5

Paper Size and Orientation

- Most documents are printed on standard 8.5" x 11" paper. However, other paper sizes are used to create newsletters, brochures, menus, tables, flyers, and announcements.

- Text printed across the width of a page (8.5" x 11" paper) is referred to as **portrait orientation**. Text printed across the long side of a page is referred to as **landscape orientation**. Portrait orientation is the default.

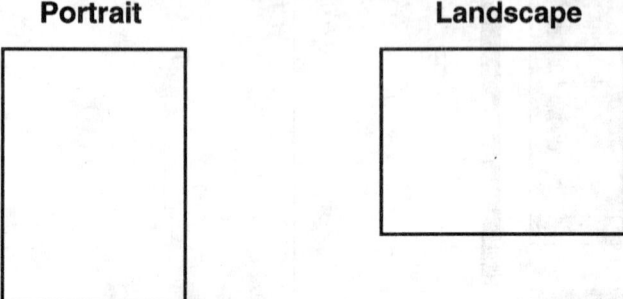

To change paper size and orientation:

- Position insertion point at top of new page.
- Click **Layout**
- Click **Page**
- Click **Paper Size**

- You may change the paper size and the way text will print across the page (orientation) by selecting Page, then Paper Size from the Layout main menu.

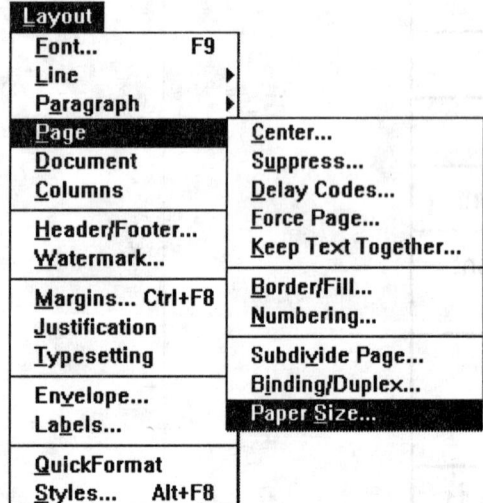

- The choices in the Paper Definitions list box depend on the printer you are using.

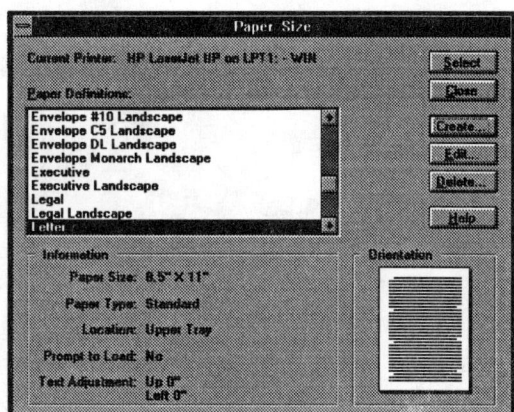

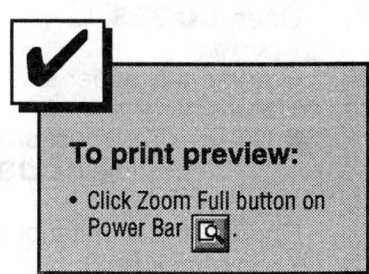

To print preview:
- Click Zoom Full button on Power Bar.

- The Information section of the dialog box provides information about the paper size selection you make. The Orientation preview window lets you see how your selected paper definition will be printed. Note that the selections provided are for the typical documents you might prepare in an office: a letter using various size stationery and different size envelopes.

- To create paper sizes other than those provided, you must select Create and indicate the size of paper you desire in Create Paper Size dialog box. To use this paper size setting again, enter a name for it in the Name box. The name will then be listed among the choices provided in the Paper Definitions dialog box.

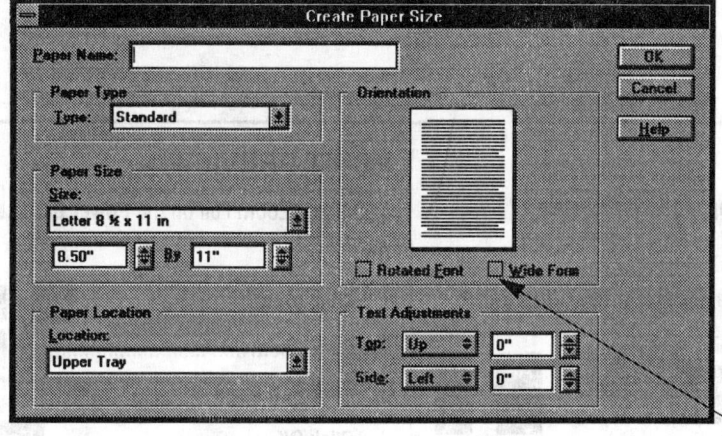

Click to print in landscape

In this exercise, you will open a file created earlier, practice changing the paper size and orientation, and print one copy.

- To print in landscape orientation, you must click in the Wide check box.

Print Preview

- In addition to the view modes outlined in Exercise 2, WordPerfect lets you quickly preview your document before printing it by clicking the Page Zoom Full button on the Power Bar .

Lesson 1 ■ Exercise 5

Lesson 1 ▪ Exercise 5

EXERCISE DIRECTIONS:

1. Open **CODES**.

2. Change the paper size to 5" x 7".

   ▪ *NOTE: You must create a new paper size; name it* **CODES**.

3. Change the orientation to landscape (click Wide check box).

4. Select the CODES paper size.

5. Print one copy. Respond to printer messages as needed.

6. Close the document; save the changes.

PRINT

Click Print button on Power Bar............ 🖨

OR

1. Click **F**ile .... Alt + F
2. Click **P**rint .... P

CHANGE PAPER SIZE AND ORIENTATION

1. Click **L**ayout .... Alt + L
2. Click **P**age .... P
3. Click Paper **S**ize .... S

4. Select a paper definition in the list box

   OR

   To create a paper size other than those listed:

   a. Click C**r**eate .... Alt + R
   b. Click **N**ame box............. Alt + N
   c. Type name of new paper size setting.
   d. Click horizontal paper size dimension text box (left box) and type horizontal paper size.
   e. Click vertical paper size dimension text box (right box) and type vertical paper size.

   To change to Landscape orientation:

   Click **W**ide Form check box.... Alt + W

5. Click OK .... Enter
6. Click **C**lose or Select .... Alt + C

PRINT PREVIEW

Click Page Zoom Full on the Power Bar .... 🔍

OR

1. Click **V**iew. .... Alt + V
2. Click **Z**oom .... Z
3. Click **F**ull Page .... F
4. Click OK. .... Enter

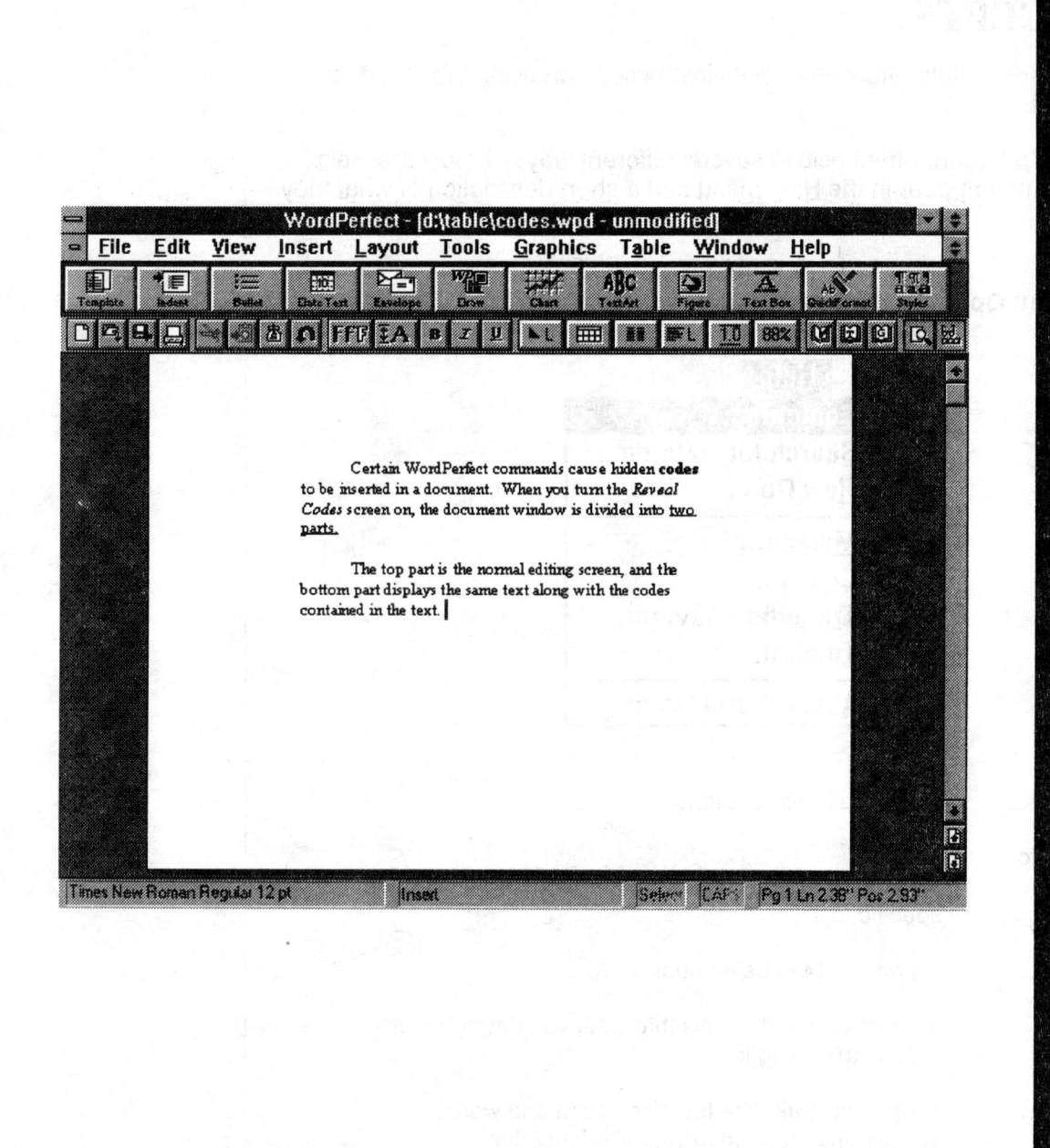

Lesson 1 • WordPerfect Basics

EXERCISE 6

HELP

CONCEPTS:

- WordPerfect Help offers immediate instructions on using WordPerfect features.

- The **Help** feature offers help in several different ways. Below are Help options that appear in the Help menu and a short description of what they do.

Help Menu Options and Descriptions

```
Help
Contents...
Search for Help on...
How Do I...
Macros...
Coach...
Transition Advisor...
Tutorial...
About WordPerfect...
```

Contents...	A list of all Help sections
Search for Help on...	An index that you can search through to get help about a specific topic.
Macros...	An on-line Macros manual.
Coach...	Interactive mini-tutorials that walk you through a procedure as you are using it.
Advisor...	Helps you make the transition from one word processing program to WordPerfect 6 for Windows.
Tutorial...	An interactive guide through WordPerfect basics.

Help Buttons and Descriptions

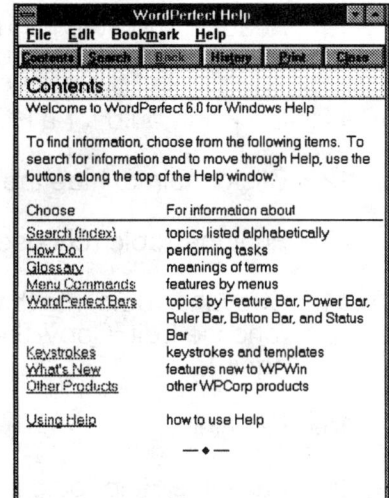

Contents	Returns you to the Contents screen where you can quickly move to a specific area of Help.
Search	Moves you to the Search screen where you can search for a specific Help topic.
Back	Returns you to the last topic used.
History	Displays the last 40 Help topics opened. Double-clicking will reopen a topic.
Print	Prints the current Help topic
Close	Closes the Help window.

Other Help Features

Glossary	A Help feature, accessed from Contents, that has definitions for WordPerfect terms.
Context Sensitive Help	Help that is available for a specific feature while you are using that feature.
Help: What Is?	This is case sensitive Help that is available anywhere in the document window.
Pop-up Terms	Help terms that are marked with a dotted underline. When you move the pointer onto such a term, the pointer turns into a hand.
Hint Topic (light bulb)	Gives tips about the active Help topic.
Always on Top	Ensures that Help stays open and is displayed on top of other windows. Allows you to keep Help instructions visible while you follow the instructions.
Copy Help into Document Window	Allows you to copy a Help topic to the Clipboard and then paste it into a document window.
Print Help Topics	Allows you to print a Help topic.

To get help while using that feature:
- Press **F1**

To get help while anywhere in document window:
- Press **Shift + F1**
- When pointer turns to ⃕⃔, click on item you want help on.

You may want to resize your document window so you can easily access all of your document when Help on Top is turned on.

In this exercise, you will practice using the Help menu.

Lesson 1 ■ Exercise 6

EXERCISE DIRECTIONS:

1. Start with a clear screen.
2. Access Help, Contents.
3. Choose Glossary.
4. Click J (the J key illustration at top of screen).
5. Click on jump term (the definition for jump term appears).
6. Click again (the definition disappears).
7. Click Back (you return to Glossary).
8. Click Back again (you return to Contents).
9. Click Using Help (at the bottom of list).
10. Read through the information about Using Help.
11. Click lightbulb for a Hint about Using Help.
12. Click again to hide the hint.
13. Print the Topic (choose File, Print Topic).
14. Copy the Topic into the document window (choose Edit, Copy, then choose Copy again).
15. Exit Help.
16. Paste the Help topic into your document (choose Edit, Paste).
17. Scroll to the top of the document.
18. Zoom view to 150%.
19. Close the document; do not save it.

HELP

F1

1. Click **H**elp.................................... Alt + H
2. Click a help option:

   Contents... C
   Search for Help On......................... S
   How Do I.. H
   Macros... M
   C**o**ach... O
   Transition Advisor........................... R
   Tutorial... T
   About WordPerfect......................... A

EXIT HELP

Double-click control menu box................. ▩

OR

1. Click **F**ile.. Alt + F
2. Click E**x**it....................................... X

Lesson 2 ▪ Text Alignments & Fonts

EXERCISE

▪ CENTER LINE ▪ CENTER PAGE TOP TO BOTTOM (VERTICALLY CENTER)

CONCEPTS:

Center Line

▪ WordPerfect lets you center a single line of text between the left and right margins, on a tab, or in a column by selecting Line, Center from the Layout main menu, or by clicking the *right* mouse button anywhere in the document window and selecting Center. Text may be centered *before* or *after* typing.

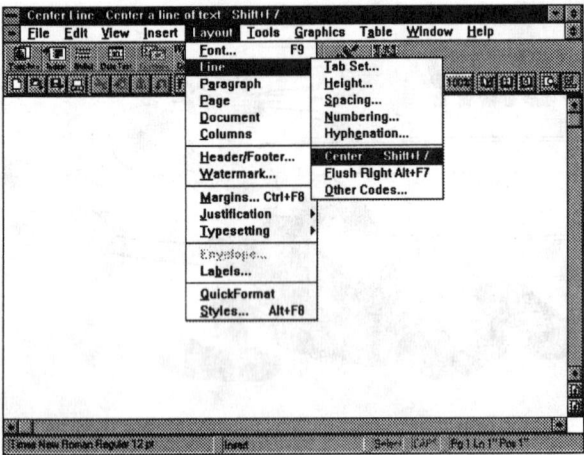

-OR-

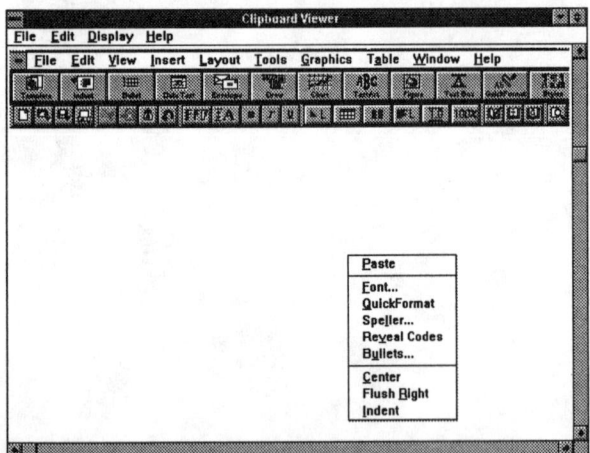

Center Page Top to Bottom (Vertically Center)

▪ Text may be centered vertically on a page (center page from top to bottom). If there are hard returns before or after the centered text, WordPerfect includes them in the vertical centering. Therefore, to center text vertically without additional blank lines, start the text at the top of the screen.

To center text:
- Click right mouse button.
- Click **Center**
  OR
- Click **Layout**
- Click **Line**
- Click **Center**

To center page vertically:
- Click **Layout**
- Click **Page**
- Click **Center**
- Click **Current Page**

To preview centered text:
- Click **View**
- Click **Zoom**
- Click **Full page**
  OR
- Select Page Zoom Full on the Power Bar.

The proofreaders' mark for centering is:] [

In this exercise, you will create an announcement and center text horizontally and vertically.

EXERCISE DIRECTIONS:

1. Start with a clear screen.
2. Use the default margins.
3. Center the page from top to bottom (vertically center).
4. Create the announcement below as indicated.
5. Preview your work.
6. Print one copy.
7. Save the exercise; name it **RSVP**.
8. Close the document window.

CELEBRATE

ON THE HUDSON

This New Year's Eve, there is no more elegant, more beautiful spot than the Hudson River Cafe. Dance with the Statue of Liberty in view to the sounds of our live band and DJ.

Enjoy a six-course Hudson Valley feast and a spectacular dessert to be remembered as the last memory of the year.

NEW YEAR'S EVE DINNER DANCE

Call for reservations 212-876-9888. Our courteous staff will be glad to assist you at any time. We are located at Four World Financial Center.

HUDSON RIVER CLUB

CENTER LINE

Shift + F7

CENTER NEW TEXT

1. Place insertion point at beginning of line to be centered.
2. Click **L**ayout .... `L`
   Click **L**ine .... `L`
   Click **C**enter .... `C`

OR

Click *right* mouse button anywhere in document window

Click **C**enter .... `C`

3. Keyboard text .... *text*
4. Press Enter .... `Enter`
   to return to left margin.

CENTER EXISTING TEXT

1. Select text to center.
2. Click **L**ayout .... `L`
   Click **L**ine .... `L`
   Click **C**enter .... `C`

OR

Click *right* mouse button anywhere in document window

Click **C**enter .... `C`

3. Press Enter .... `Enter`
   to return to left margin.

CENTER PAGE TOP TO BOTTOM (Vertically Center)

NOTE: Text will not appear vertically centered on the screen, but will appear centered on the page when previewed.

1. Place insertion point anywhere on page.
2. Click **L**ayout .... `Alt` + `L`
3. Click **P**age .... `P`
4. Click **C**enter .... `C`
5. Click Current **P**age .... `P`

OR

Click .... `S`
Current and **S**ubsequent Pages.

6. Click OK .... `Enter`

Lesson 2 ■ Exercise 7

Lesson 2 ▪ Text Alignments & Fonts

EXERCISE 8

▪ FLUSH RIGHT ▪ CENTER PAGE TOP TO BOTTOM

CONCEPTS:

- **Flush right** is a feature that aligns a single line or part of a line of text at the right margin. You may choose flush right *before* or *after* typing text by selecting Line, Flush Right from the Layout main menu or by clicking the *right* mouse button anywhere in the document window and selecting Flush Right.

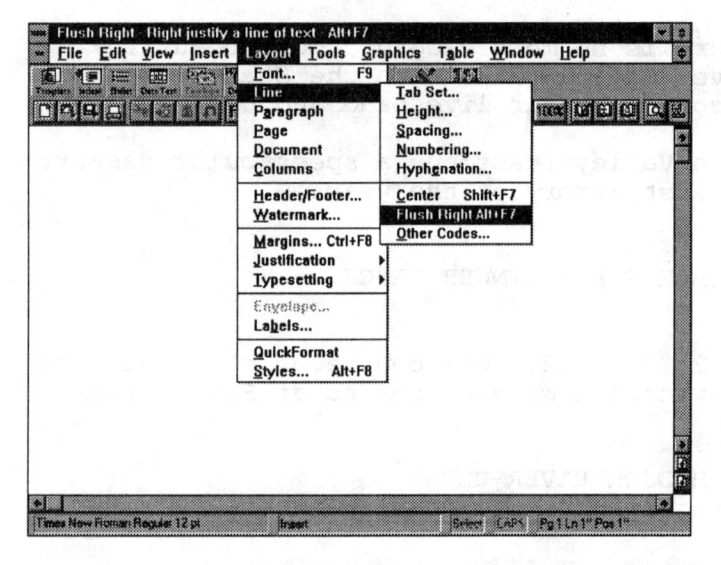

-OR-

To flush right text:
- Click **Layout**
- Click **Line**
- Click **Flush Right**

To align a partial or full line of existing text at the right margin, make sure the line ends with a hard return.

In this exercise, you will create an announcement containing right-aligned text.

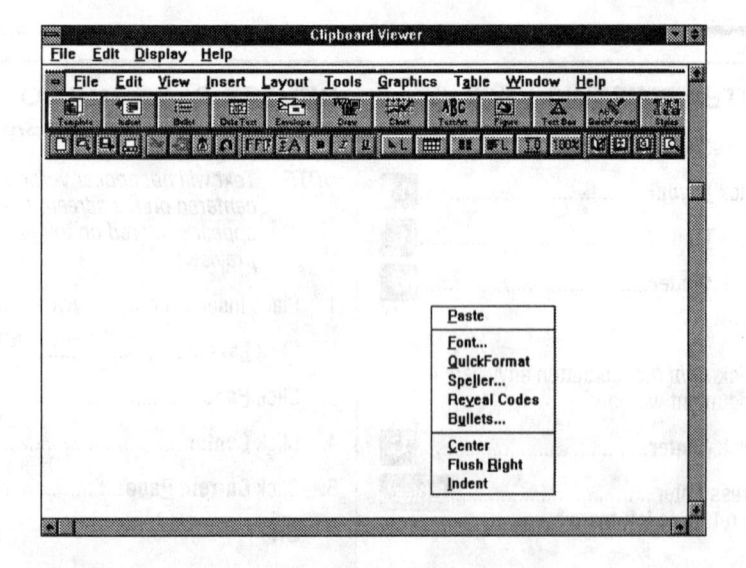

- Right alignment is particularly useful when typing dates or creating invitations, menus or business flyers.

EXERCISE DIRECTIONS:

1. Start with a clear screen.
2. Use the default margins.
3. Center the page from top to bottom.
4. Center and right align text, as indicated.
5. Print one copy.
6. Save the exercise; name it **CONGRATS**.
7. Close the document window.

```
                    MORITZ & CHASE
                  1603 East 7th Street
                  Astoria, OR 94101

Is Pleased to Announce that the following Associates will become
members of the firm on

                    January 1, 1995


DENVER                                        Steven M. Jones

NEW YORK                                    Arthur J. Williams

SAN FRANCISCO                              Roberta W. Asher
                                               Donna Newman

WASHINGTON, D.C.                             Pamela T. Blanco

and that the following Of Counsel will become members of the firm
on

                    January 1, 1995


LONDON                                   Raymond T. Sedgewick

LOS ANGELES                               Angela Tsacoumis
                                          Roberto Vasquez
```

FLUSH RIGHT

Alt + F7

RIGHT ALIGN NEW TEXT

1. Place insertion point at beginning of text to flush right.
2. Click **L**ayout .... Alt + L
   Click **L**ine L
   Click **F**lush Right .... F

   OR

   Click *right* mouse button anywhere in document window.

   Click **F**lush **R**ight .... R

3. Type text .... *text*
4. Press Enter .... Enter
   to return to left margin.

RIGHT ALIGN EXISTING TEXT

1. Select text to make flush right.
2. Click **L**ayout .... Alt + L
   Click **L**ine L
   Click **F**lush Right .... F

   OR

   Click *right* mouse button anywhere in document window.

   Click **F**lush **R**ight .... R

3. Press Enter .... Enter
   to return to left margin.

Lesson 2 ■ Exercise 8

Lesson 2 ▪ Text Alignments & Fonts

EXERCISE 9

JUSTIFICATION (LEFT, CENTER, RIGHT, FULL, ALL)

Justify

CONCEPTS:

- **Justification** lets you align all text that follows the justification code until another justification code is entered. WordPerfect provides five alignment options:

    Left All lines are even at the left margin, but are ragged at the right margin (the default).

    xxxxxxxxx
    xxxxxxx
    xxxxx
    xxxxx

    Center All lines are centered between the margins.

    xxxxx
    xxxxxxxx
    xxxx

    Right All lines are ragged at the left margin, but even at the right margin.

    xxxxxxxxx
    xxxxxxx
    xxxxx
    xxxxx

    Full All lines are even at the left and right margins, except for the last line of the paragraph.

    xxxxxxxxxxxxxxxx
    xxxxxxxxxxxxx
    xxxxx

    All All lines are even at the left and right margins, including the last line of the paragraph.

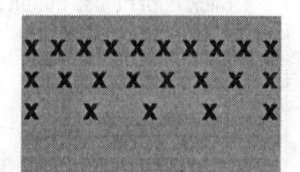

    x x x x x x x x x x
    x x x x x x x x
    x   x   x   x   x

- Justification should be used to affect blocks of text, not individual lines. Text may be justified *before* or *after* typing text.

- WordPerfect applies *left* justification to your text by default.

To justify text:
- Click Justification Button on Power Bar.

OR

- Click **L**ayout
- Click **J**ustification
- Select Justification option.

When you change justification of existing text, all text following the code will be changed. Do not be alarmed. Insert another justification code to return your text to the desired justification option.

In this exercise, you will create an announcement using center, left, right, full, and all justification.

EXERCISE DIRECTIONS:

1. Start with a clear screen.
2. Center the page from top to bottom.
3. Type each section of text on the right, changing the justification alignment appropriately.
4. Print one copy.
5. Preview your document.
6. Save the exercise; name it **COMPANY**.
7. Close the document window.

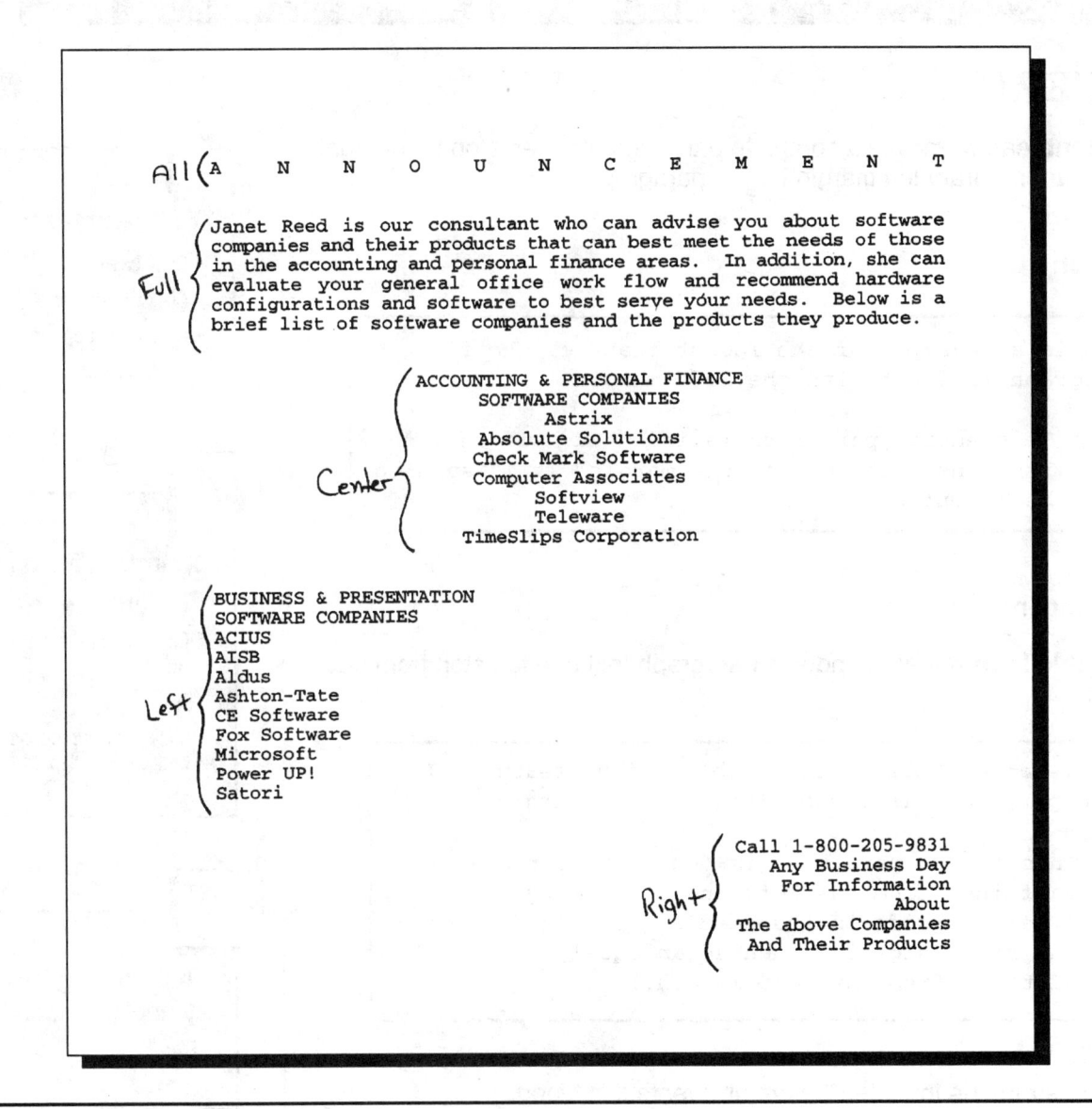

All — A N N O U N C E M E N T

Full — Janet Reed is our consultant who can advise you about software companies and their products that can best meet the needs of those in the accounting and personal finance areas. In addition, she can evaluate your general office work flow and recommend hardware configurations and software to best serve your needs. Below is a brief list of software companies and the products they produce.

Center —
```
            ACCOUNTING & PERSONAL FINANCE
                 SOFTWARE COMPANIES
                       Astrix
                  Absolute Solutions
                  Check Mark Software
                  Computer Associates
                       Softview
                       Teleware
                 TimeSlips Corporation
```

Left —
```
BUSINESS & PRESENTATION
SOFTWARE COMPANIES
ACIUS
AISB
Aldus
Ashton-Tate
CE Software
Fox Software
Microsoft
Power UP!
Satori
```

Right —
```
                          Call 1-800-205-9831
                             Any Business Day
                             For Information
                                        About
                          The above Companies
                          And Their Products
```

JUSTIFY

Shift + F8 L, J

1. Place insertion point at beginning of text to receive justification change (*new text*).

   OR

   Select text to receive justification change (*existing text*).

2. Click **L**ayout .... `Alt` + `L`
3. Click **J**ustification .... `J`

   OR

   Click Justification Button .... on Power Bar.

4. Click a justification option:

   Left .... `L`
   Right .... `R`
   C**e**nter .... `E`
   Full .... `F`
   All .... `A`

Lesson 2 ■ Exercise 9

Lesson 2 ▪ Text Alignments & Fonts

EXERCISE 10
▪ INDENT

left indent

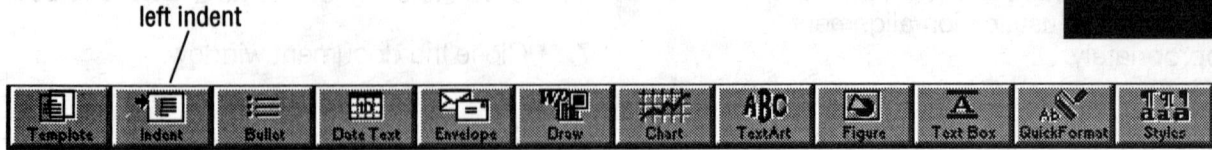

CONCEPTS:

- The **Indent** feature moves a complete paragraph one tab stop to the right and sets a temporary left margin for the paragraph.

Left Indent

```
This is an example of the Indent feature. The first
paragraph is flush with the left margin.

    This entire paragraph is indented half an inch
    from the left edge of the margin. It is said to
    be indented.
```

Double Indent

- The **Double Indent** feature indents paragraph text one tab stop from both margins.

```
This is an example of the Double Indent feature. The
first paragraph is flush with the left margin.

    This entire paragraph is double indented a
    half inch from the left and right margins.
    (The left side is indented one tab stop;
    the right side is indented an equal
    distance from the left margin.)
```

- Paragraphs may be indented *before* or *after* text is typed.

- Since text is indented to a tab setting, accessing the Indent feature once will indent text .5" to the right (or left and right); accessing it twice will indent text 1", etc.

To indent text:
- Click **L**ayout
- Click **P**aragraph
- Click indent option.

To indent from left margin:
- Click Indent Button on Button Bar
OR
- Click the *right* mouse button and select **I**ndent.

The proofreaders' symbol for indenting is: ⌐

In this exercise, you will create a flyer using the indent and double indent features.

- The indent feature is accessed by selecting Paragraph from the Layout main menu.

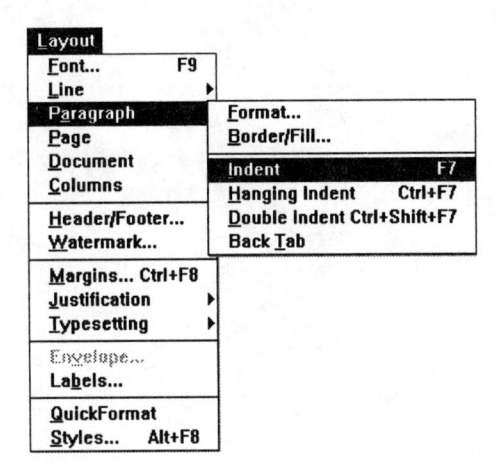

- To indent from the left margin only, you may click the Indent button on the Button Bar or click the right mouse button and select Indent.

- The indent mode is ended by a hard return.

EXERCISE DIRECTIONS:

1. Start with a clear screen.
2. Center the page from top to bottom.
3. Use the default margins (1" on the left and right).
4. Open **FLOWER** from the data disk; save as **FLOWER1**.

    or

    Type the exercise as shown.

5. Preview your document.
6. Print one copy.
7. Close the file; save the changes.

    or

    Save the file; name it **FLOWER1**.

8. Close the document window.

Lesson 2 ■ Exercise 10

INDENT/DOUBLE INDENT

F7/Ctrl + Shift + F7

Click Indent Button.............................
on Button Bar once for each .5"
indentation (from *left* margin).

OR

1. Click *right* mouse button.
2. Select Indent (from *left* margin).

OR

1. Place insertion point where indention should begin.
2. Click **L**ayout .... Alt + L
3. Click P**a**ragraph .... A
4. Click **I**ndent I

OR

Click **D**ouble Indent .... D

NOTE: Repeat steps 1-3 until desired indentation is achieved.

To end indent mode:

Press Enter...................................... Enter

Center → The Perennial Potter
14 Highway 37
Middletown, NJ
908-555-5555

Justification All → O n e - D a y   S a l e   —   J u l y   2 1 ,   1 9 9 5

It is another new year and by now you are ready to add to your existing garden. This year we have over 75 perennial plants to choose from. There are all sizes and types to suit your needs.

Justification Full / **Indent .5"** →

We have perennials that can be grown in full sun or in partial shade. We even have some that require full shade and some that require full sun.

We have perennials that will survive temperatures below 50 degrees and perennials that need at least 40 degrees to survive.

We have perennials that bloom in early spring and perennials that bloom in the late fall.

Center → Below is a sampling of some of our favorites:

Double Indent .5" → DELPHINIUM: One of the tallest of our perennials, the delphinium comes in brilliant colors such as blue, purple, white, pink and lavender. The plants grow as tall as 72" in full sun. [.5"]

Double Indent 1" → PLATYCODON: The "Balloon Flower" is a medium sized perennial that comes in violet, white and pink. The plants grow as tall as 36" in full sun to partial shade. [1"]

Justification Full

Double Indent 1.5" → COREOPSIS: These daisy-like perennials come in yellow and pink. The plants grow as tall as 24" in full sun to partial shade. [1.5"]

Double Indent 2" → SEDUM: This ground cover comes in pink, red, yellow and white. The plants grow up to 6" tall and spread quickly in full sun. [2"]

Justification All → FROM   TALL   TO   SHORT,   WE   HAVE   THE   PERENNIAL   FOR   YOU!

Lesson 2 ▪ Exercise 10

Lesson 2 ▪ Text Alignments & Fonts

EXERCISE 11

▪ HANGING INDENT ▪ FIRST LINE INDENT

CONCEPTS:

Hanging Indent

- When all the lines in a paragraph are indented except the first line, a **hanging indent** is created.

```
This paragraph is an example of a "hanging indent."
    Note that all the lines in the paragraph are
    indented except the first line.  This is an
    effective way of emphasizing paragraph text.
```

- This method will indent the second and succeeding lines of the paragraph to the first tab stop.

- A hanging indent is selected from the Layout main menu.

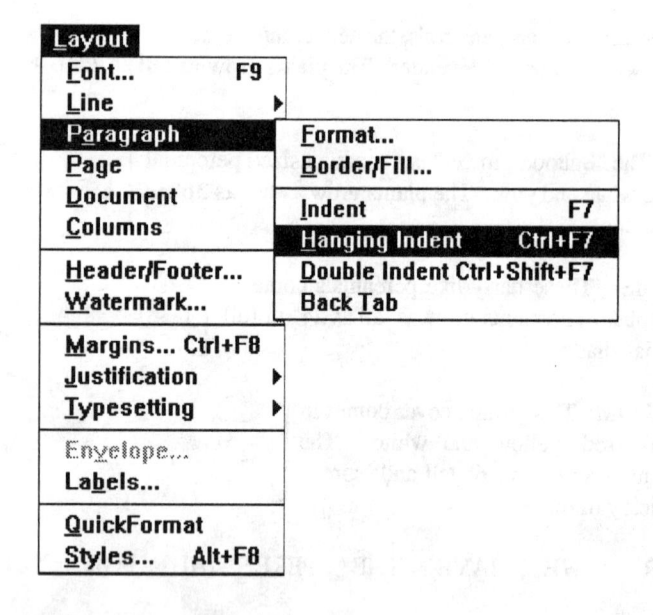

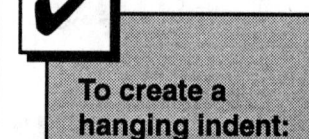

```
Layout
  Font...        F9
  Line           ▶
  Paragraph      ▶   Format...
  Page               Border/Fill...
  Document
  Columns            Indent            F7
                     Hanging Indent    Ctrl+F7
  Header/Footer...   Double Indent     Ctrl+Shift+F7
  Watermark...       Back Tab

  Margins... Ctrl+F8
  Justification  ▶
  Typesetting    ▶

  Envelope...
  Labels...

  QuickFormat
  Styles...   Alt+F8
```

✓

To create a hanging indent:
- Click **L**ayout
- Click **P**aragraph
- Click **H**anging Indent

38

First Line Indent

- A **first line indent** lets you set the amount of space each paragraph indents. Each time you press the Enter key, the insertion point automatically begins at the indented setting. This feature eliminates the need to use the Tab key to indent each new paragraph. You also have the option of setting the amount of spacing between paragraphs.

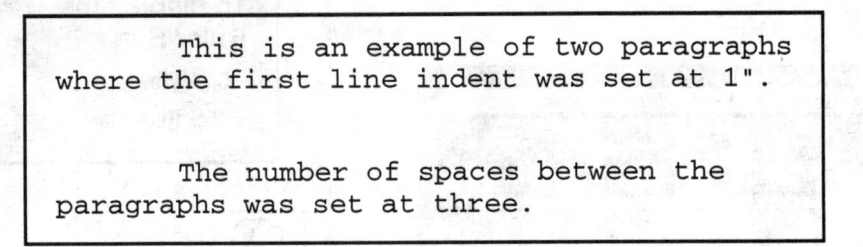

```
          This is an example of two paragraphs
     where the first line indent was set at 1".


          The number of spaces between the
     paragraphs was set at three.
```

> **To create a first line indent:**
> - Click **L**ayout
> - Click P**a**ragraph
> - Click **F**ormat

- A first line indent is selected from the Layout main menu.

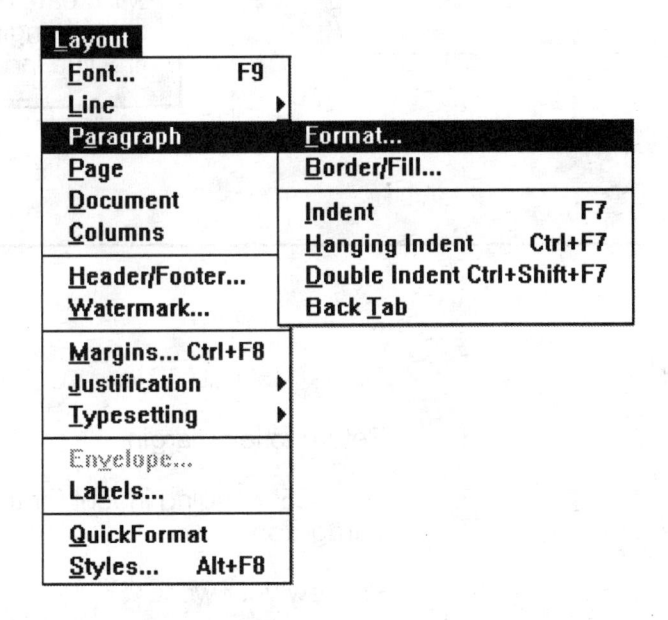

```
Layout
  Font...           F9
  Line              ▶
  Paragraph         ▶  Format...
  Page                 Border/Fill...
  Document             Indent            F7
  Columns              Hanging Indent    Ctrl+F7
  Header/Footer...     Double Indent Ctrl+Shift+F7
  Watermark...         Back Tab
  Margins... Ctrl+F8
  Justification     ▶
  Typesetting       ▶
  Envelope...
  Labels...
  QuickFormat
  Styles...  Alt+F8
```

- In the Paragraph Format dialog box which follows, you enter the amount you wish each paragraph to indent in the First Line Indent text box. You may also add extra spacing between paragraphs by entering the *number of Enters* in the Spacing between Paragraphs text box.

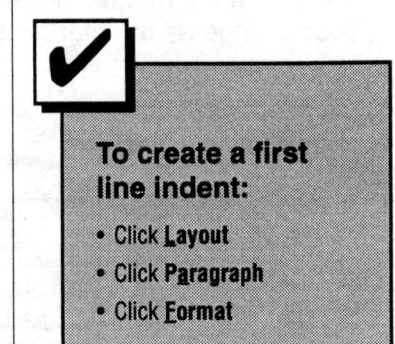

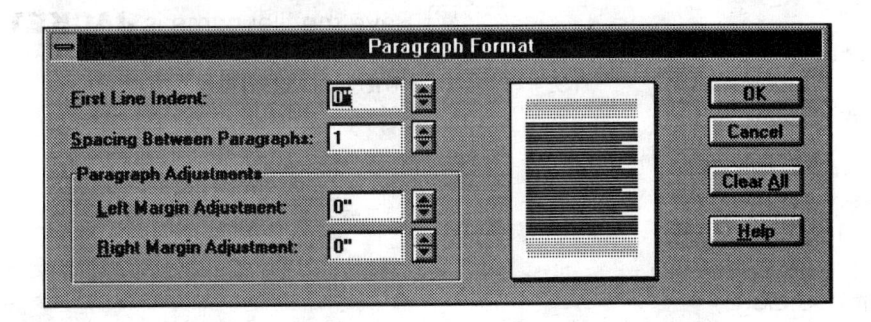

```
                    Paragraph Format
  First Line Indent:         [0"]                        [ OK     ]
  Spacing Between Paragraphs:[1]                         [ Cancel ]
  ┌Paragraph Adjustments─────────────                    [ Clear All ]
  │  Left Margin Adjustment:  [0"]                       [ Help   ]
  │  Right Margin Adjustment: [0"]
```

Lesson 2 ▪ Exercise 11   39

Lesson 2 • Exercise 11

- First line indents may also be set by dragging the **first line indent marker** (the top left triangle) *right* on the Ruler Bar to the desired first line indent position. As the marker is being moved, the Status Bar displays the exact position of the marker. Again, this method allows you to see the effect of your change as the marker is moved.

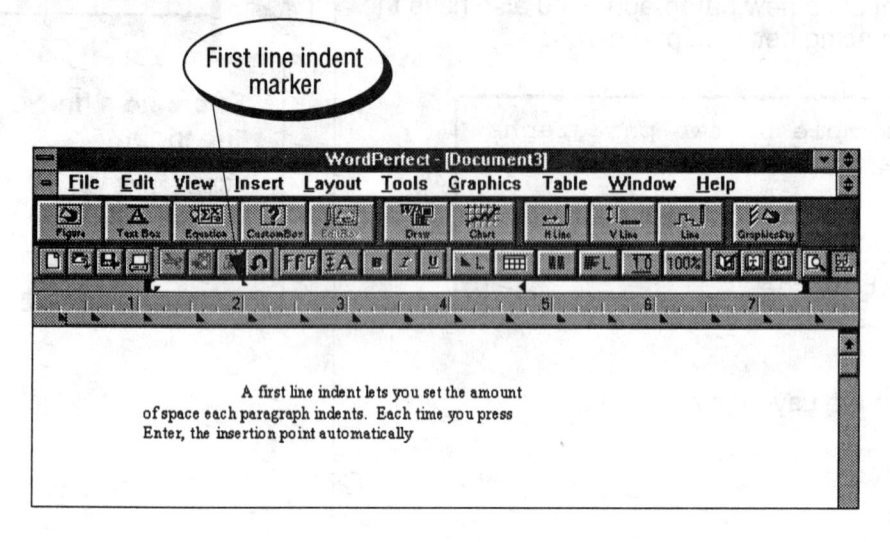

> You must display the Ruler Bar if you wish to drag the first line indent marker. **To display the Ruler Bar:**
> - Click **V**iew
> - Click **R**uler Bar

> In this exercise, you will create of flyer using hanging and first line indents.

EXERCISE DIRECTIONS:

1. Start with a clear screen.
2. Center the page from top to bottom.
3. Use the default margins (1" on the left and right)
4. Display the Ruler Bar.
5. Open **JACKET** from the data disk; save as **JACKET1**.

   or

   Type the exercise as shown.
6. Use a .5" hanging indent for the first paragraph.
7. For the second, third, and fourth paragraphs set a .5" first line indent and set the spacing between paragraphs to six. (Set these changes in the Paragraph Format dialog box.)
8. Return to left margin.
9. Use a .5" hanging indent for the final paragraph.
10. Preview your work.
11. Print one copy.
12. Close the file; save the changes.

    or

    Save the file; name is **JACKET1**.
13. Close the document window.

[Hanging Indent .5"] NOW AVAILABLE: Authentic baseball team jackets personalized with your own name. Harold's Sportswear Store now carries the genuine article. Our jackets are exactly the same as the ones worn by every baseball team.

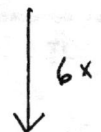

↓ 6x

The jackets are personalized for you absolutely free. Choose your favorite team and have your name on the jacket. You can look like a professional baseball player in your authentic jacket!

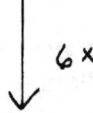

↓ 6x

And the price is right. Just $149.99 plus $5.50 for shipping and handling. Remember, there is no charge for personalizing the jacket with your name.

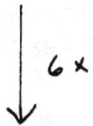

↓ 6x

Each jacket is made by the same company that makes the jackets for the professional baseball team members. They fit the same. They have the same logo. They even have the same label inside as the professional team jacket.

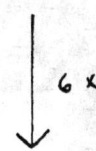

↓ 6x

[Hanging Indent .5"] WHAT ARE YOU WAITING FOR? Be the first in your neighborhood to own the official baseball team jacket. To order your authentic jacket, call Harold's Sportswear Store today. Dial 1-800-555-BALL. You can charge the jacket and receive it within one week.

HANGING INDENT

Ctrl + F7

1. Click **L**ayout .... Alt + L
2. Click **P**aragraph .... A
3. Click **H**anging Indent .... H

To end hanging indent:

Press Enter .... Enter

FIRST LINE INDENT

1. Place insertion point where indentation should begin.
2. Click **L**ayout .... Alt + L
3. Click **P**aragraph .... A
4. Click **F**ormat .... F
5. Click **F**irst Line Indent text box.
6. Enter first line indent amount.

   OR

   Click increment arrows to select a first line indent amount.

7. Click **OK** .... Enter

OR

Using Ruler Bar:

1. Place insertion point where indentation should begin.
2. Drag first line indent marker *right* to desired first line indent position.

PARAGRAPH SPACING

1. Place insertion point where indentation begins.
2. Click **L**ayout .... Alt + L
3. Click **P**aragraph .... A
4. Click **F**ormat .... F
5. Click **S**pacing Between Paragraphs .. S
6. Enter paragraph spacing amount.
7. Click **OK** .... Enter

RETURN TO PREVIOUS SETTINGS

1. Place insertion point where reset adjustments should begin.
2. Click **L**ayout .... Alt + L
3. Click **P**aragraph .... A
4. Click **F**ormat .... F
5. Click **C**lear All .... A
6. Click **OK** .... Enter

Lesson 2 ▪ Text Alignments & Fonts

EXERCISE 12

CHANGE FONT FACE, FONT STYLE, AND FONT SIZE

CONCEPTS:

- A font is a complete set of characters in a specific face, style and size. Each set includes upper- and lowercase letters, numerals and punctuation. A font that might be available to you in WordPerfect is: **Arrus BLK BT**.

- A font face (often called "typeface" or just "font") is the design of a character. Each design has a name and is intended to convey a specific feeling. WordPerfect's Font Face list box names the fonts available for your printer.

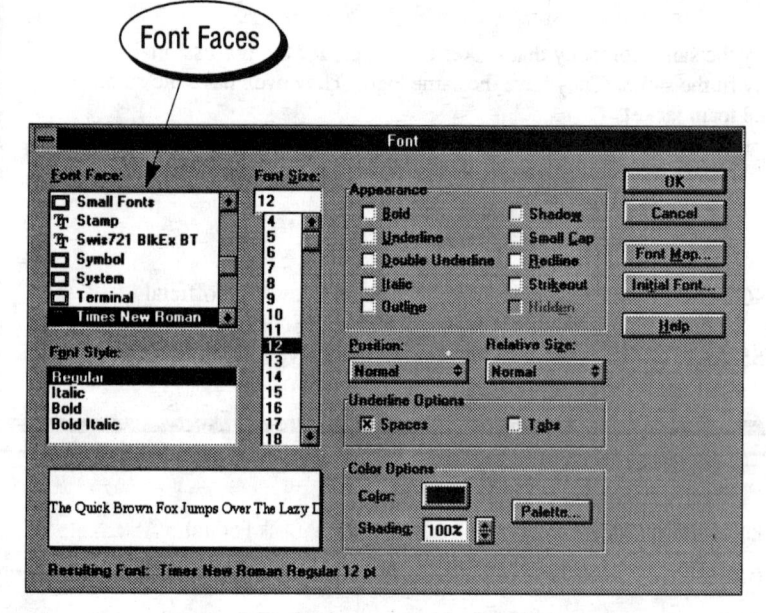

To change a font face, size, or style:
- Click **L**ayout
- Click **F**ont
- Select desired option.

The fonts that are available to you depend on your printer's capabilities.

In the Font dialog box, selected fonts are displayed in the Preview window at the lower left side and are described in the Resulting Font line.

- You should select font faces that will make your document attractive and communicate its particular message. As a rule, use no more than two or three font faces in any one document.

FONT FACES:

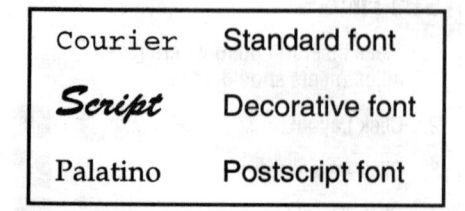

Courier	Standard font
Script	Decorative font
Palatino	Postscript font

In this exercise, you will change the font faces, font styles and font sizes of an announcement previously created.

42

- There are basically three types of typefaces: serif, sans serif, and script. A **serif** face has lines, curves or edges extending from the ends of the letter: **T**, while a **sans serif** (without lines) face is straight-edged: **T**, and **script** looks like handwriting: *T*.

SERIF FONT FACE:

Times New Roman

SANS SERIF FONT FACE:

Helvetica

SCRIPT FONT FACE:

Brush Script MT

- A serif typeface is typically used for document text because it is more readable. Sans serif is often used for headlines or technical material. Script typefaces are used for formal invitations and announcements.
- **Font style** refers to the slant and weight of letters, such as Bold and Italic.

FONT STYLES:

> Times New Roman Regular
> *Times New Roman Italic*
> **Times New Roman Bold**
> ***Times New Roman Bold Italic***

The Font Style box lists the styles or weights specially designed and available for the selected font. You may also apply attributes such as bold and italic, outline and small cap through the Appearance panel of the Font dialog box (This will be covered in the next exercises).

- Fonts are also categorized as monospaced (fixed-pitch) or proportional.

FONT SPACING:

> COURIER--MONOSPACED
> PALATINO--PROPORTIONAL

Monospaced fonts, such as Courier, allot the same horizontal space on the line for each character -- an **I** takes as much space as an **M**.
Proportional fonts, such as Times Roman, allot less space for letters such as **I** and more space for letters such as **M**.

Lesson 2 ■ Exercise 12

- **Font size** generally refers to the height of the font, usually measured in points.

FONT SIZE:

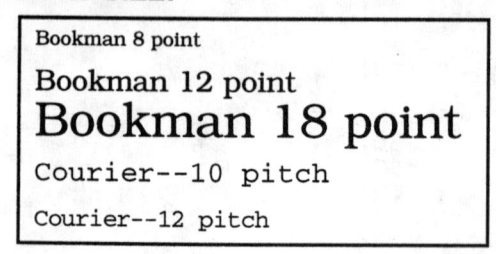

> Bookman 8 point
>
> Bookman 12 point
>
> ## Bookman 18 point
>
> Courier--10 pitch
>
> Courier--12 pitch

There are 72 points to an inch. However, monospaced font size may be expressed in characters per inch, such as Roman 10cpi. Use 10 to 12 point type size for document text and larger sizes for headings and headlines. Font size may be changed from the Power Bar [fA], or by clicking the right mouse button anywhere in the document window and selecting font.

- You can change fonts *before* or *after* typing text. Font Face may be changed from the Power Bar [frv], or by clicking the *right* mouse anywhere in the document window and selecting **Font**.

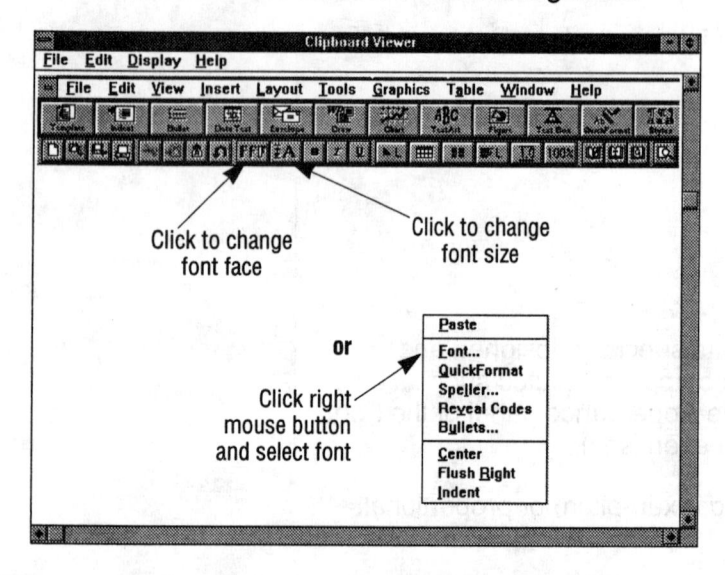

Click to change font face

Click to change font size

or

Click right mouse button and select font

Paste
Font...
QuickFormat
Spe**l**ler...
Re**v**eal Codes
B**u**llets...
Center
Flush **R**ight
Indent

-OR-

by selecting **Font** from the **L**ayout main menu.

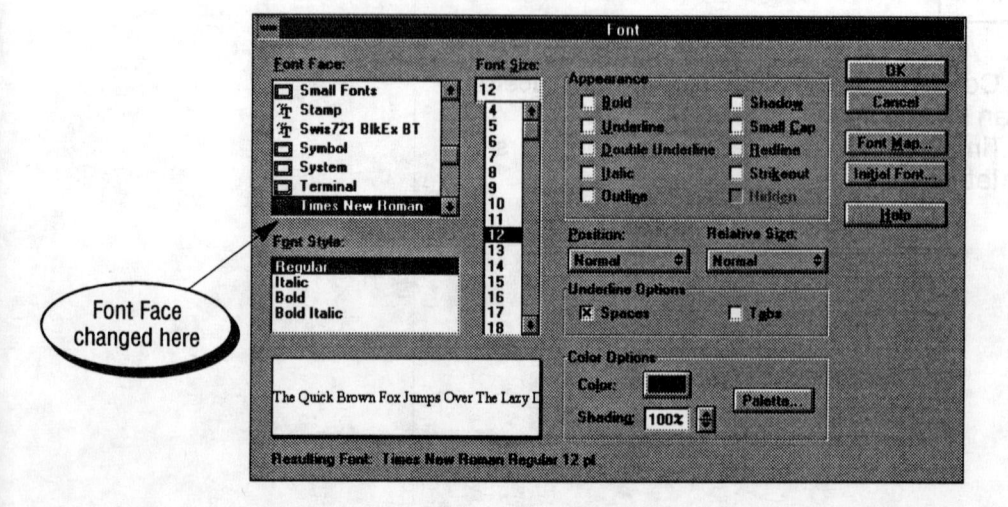

Font Face changed here

EXERCISE DIRECTIONS:

1. Start with a clear screen.
2. Open **RSVP**.
3. Make the font face, font size, and font style changes indicated on the exercise.
4. Center all text, as shown.
5. Preview your document.
6. Print one copy.
7. Close the file; save the changes.

CELEBRATE } serif 60pt bold

ON THE HUDSON } sans serif 35pt

This New Year's Eve, there is no more elegant, more beautiful spot than the Hudson River Cafe. Dance with the Statue of Liberty in view to the sounds of our live band and DJ.

Enjoy a six-course Hudson Valley feast and a spectacular dessert to be remembered as the last memory of the year.
} sans serif 10pt

NEW YEAR'S EVE DINNER DANCE } sans serif 28pt

Call for reservations 212-876-9888. Our courteous staff will be glad to assist you at any time. We are located at Four World Financial Center.
} sans serif 10pt

HUDSON RIVER CLUB } sans serif 28pt

CHANGE FONT FACE, FONT SIZE, AND FONT STYLE

—USING DIALOG BOX—

F9

OR

Click *right* mouse anywhere in the document window and select Font.

1. Place insertion point where font change will begin (before typing).

    OR

    Select text to receive font change (after typing).

2. Click **L**ayout .... Alt + L
3. Click **F**ont .... F

    NOTE: At Font dialog box, currently selected font is displayed in Preview window and described in resulting font line.

4. In **F**ont Face list, highlight .... F
   desired font
5. In F**o**nt Style box, highlight .... O
   desired style
6. In Font **S**ize box, highlight .... S
   desired size

—USING POWER BAR (FONT FACE AND FONT SIZE ONLY)—

Place insertion point where font change will begin (before typing).

OR

Select text to receive font change (after typing).

To change font face:

Click Font Face Button .... [FfF]

Select desired font from list.

To change font size:

Click Font Size Button .... [≡A]

Select desired size from list.

Lesson 2 ■ Exercise 12

Lesson 2 ▪ Text Alignments & Fonts

EXERCISE 13

FONT APPEARANCE (BOLD UNDERLINE, DOUBLE UNDERLINE, ITALIC)

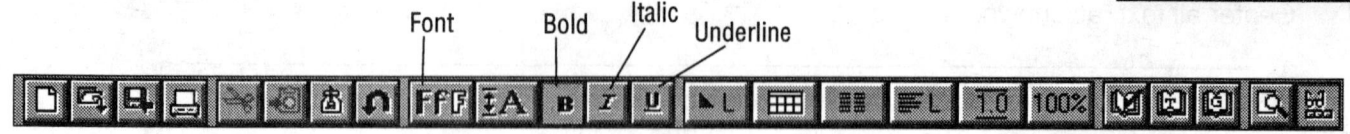

Font — Bold — Italic — Underline

CONCEPTS:

- **Bold**, underline, double underline and *italic* are features used to emphasize or enhance text and are referred to as **appearance attributes**. These features work as on/off toggle switches. You must choose the command to turn on the feature; then choose the command to turn off the feature.

- The appearance of a font face is changed in the Font dialog box:

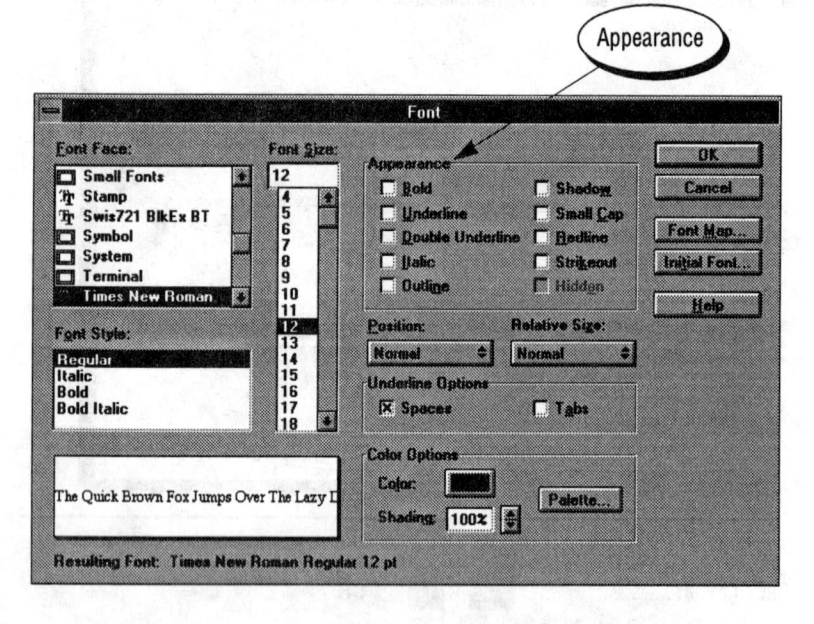

-OR-

by using the using the style buttons shown above (There is no double underline button in the Power Bar.).

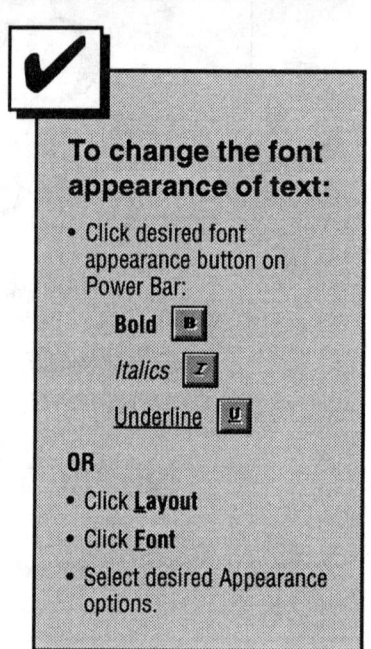

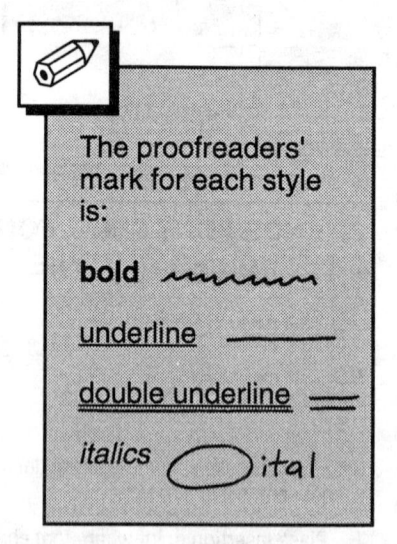

To change the font appearance of text:

- Click desired font appearance button on Power Bar:

    Bold [B]

    Italics [I]

    Underline [U]

OR

- Click **Layout**
- Click **Font**
- Select desired Appearance options.

The proofreaders' mark for each style is:

bold ⁓⁓⁓⁓

underline ⎯⎯

double underline ⎯⎯

italics ⓘⓣⓐⓛ

46

- Font style also adds bold and italics to a font face, but not all font faces have these styles added. They can be added, however, as an appearance attribute.

- Text may be emphasized *before* or *after* typing.

NOTE: *Other appearance attributes (outline, shadow, small cap, redline, strikeout and hidden text) will be covered in the next lesson.*

After bolding, underlining, double underlining or italicizing desired text, you must turn off the feature by repeating the procedure you used to turn on the feature.

In this exercise, you will create a menu using varied font sizes and appearances.

EXERCISE DIRECTIONS:

1. Start with a clear screen.
2. Center the page top to bottom.
3. Using a serif font face, type the menu on page 49, applying alignments, font appearances, and font sizes as indicated.
4. Preview your document.
5. Print one copy.
6. Save the file; name it **FOOD**.
7. Close the document window.

APPEARANCE CHANGES

BOLD   Ctrl + B

UNDERLINE   Ctrl + U

ITALICS   Ctrl + I

DOUBLE
UNDERLINE   not applicable

1. Place insertion point before text to receive appearance change (*new text*)

   OR

   Select/highlight text to receive appearance change (*existing text*).

2. Click **L**ayout .... Alt + L
3. Click **F**ont .... F

   OR

   Double-click Font Face Button on Power Bar

4. Click in box to select desired appearance change (s).
5. Click **OK** .... Enter

   OR

   Click desired appearance button on Power Bar:

   Bold .... B

   Italics I

   Underline .... U

   NOTE: Double Underline must be selected on **F**ont dialog box.

RETURN TO NORMAL OR TURN FEATURE OFF

1. Place insertion point where appearance change will end (new text).

   OR

   Select text to return to normal (existing text).

2. Click **L**ayout .... Alt + L

   OR

   Click *right* mouse button.

3. Click **F**ont L
4. Click box to deselect appearance change.
5. Click **OK** .... Enter.

   OR

   Click selected appearance button on Power Bar to turn feature off:

   Bold .... B

   Italics I

   Underline .... U

   NOTE: Double Underline must be deselected on **F**ont dialog box.

The Sherwood Forest Inn {18pt bold}

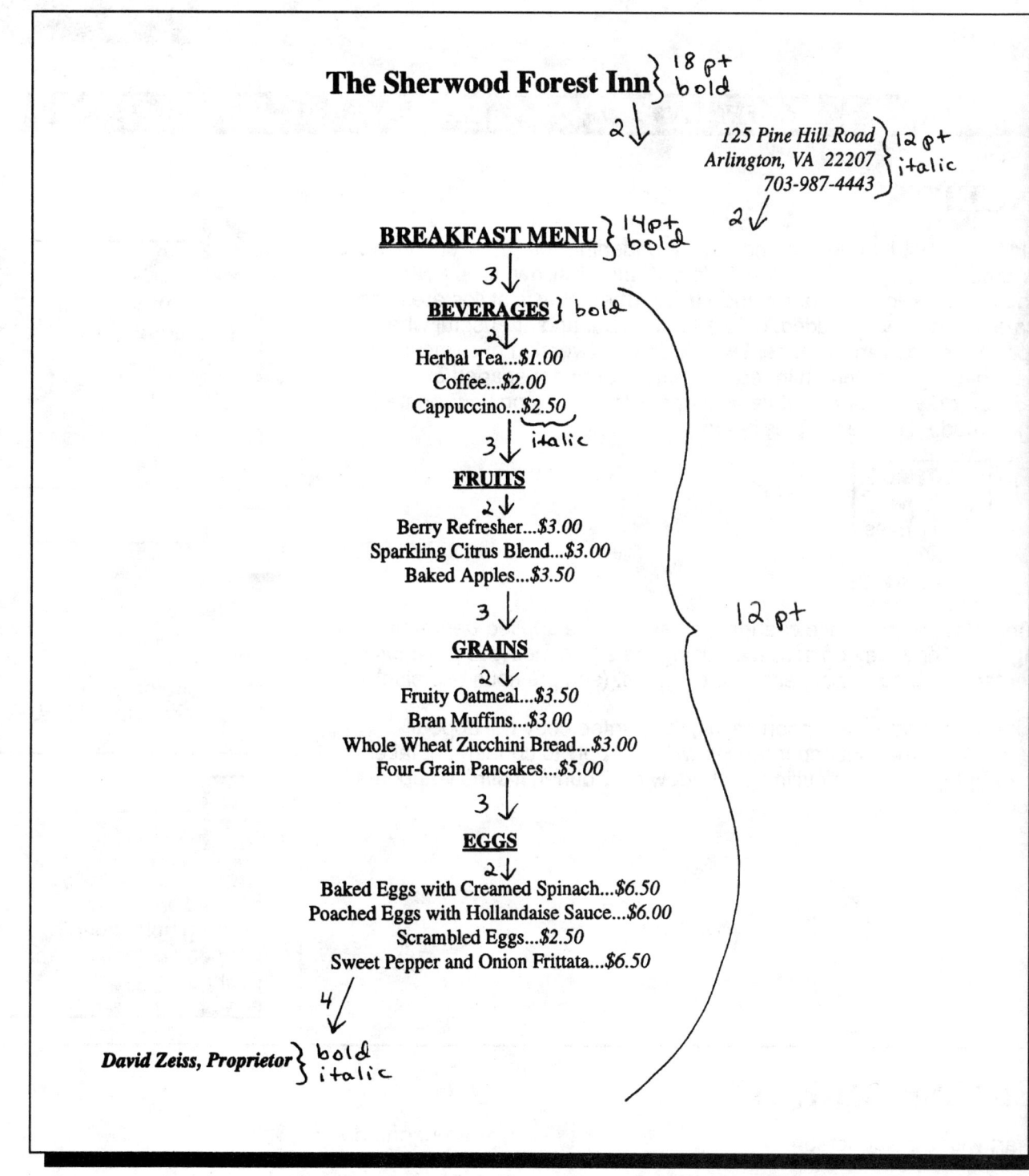

125 Pine Hill Road {12pt italic}
Arlington, VA 22207
703-987-4443

BREAKFAST MENU {14pt bold}

BEVERAGES {bold}

Herbal Tea....$1.00
Coffee...$2.00
Cappuccino...$2.50

FRUITS

Berry Refresher....$3.00
Sparkling Citrus Blend...$3.00
Baked Apples...$3.50

GRAINS

Fruity Oatmeal...$3.50
Bran Muffins...$3.00
Whole Wheat Zucchini Bread...$3.00
Four-Grain Pancakes...$5.00

EGGS

Baked Eggs with Creamed Spinach...$6.50
Poached Eggs with Hollandaise Sauce...$6.00
Scrambled Eggs...$2.50
Sweet Pepper and Onion Frittata...$6.50

David Zeiss, Proprietor {bold italic}

Lesson 2 ▪ Text Alignments & Fonts

EXERCISE 14

FONT APPEARANCE (OUTLINE, SHADOW, SMALL CAPS, REDLINE AND STRIKEOUT)

CONCEPTS:

- In addition to bold, underline and double underline, WordPerfect provides other emphasis styles. These include **outline**, **shadow**, **small caps**, redline and strikeout. **Redline** and **strikeout** emphasis styles are used to indicate text has been added, deleted or moved, and are useful when comparing the current document with a different version of a document. Redline displays on screen in red but usually appears shaded or underlined or with a series of vertical bars (depending on your printer) when printed. Note examples below:

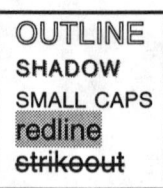

    OUTLINE
    SHADOW
    SMALL CAPS
    redline
    strikeout

- Like the other appearance changes, these may be applied *before* or *after* typing text. They may be accessed using the same methods previously presented for the other appearance changes. (see previous exercise).

- If your printer does not support italics, the printed copy will appear underlined. Some font appearances will not apply to certain font faces. For example, if you use outline or shadow on Courier, it simply appears bolded.

To change the text font appearance:
- Click **L**ayout
- Click **F**ont
- Click desired Appearance option.

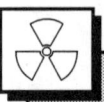

The fonts and font appearances that are available to you depend on your printer's capabilities.

In this exercise, you will create a flyer using bold, double underline, italics, and shadow.

EXERCISE DIRECTIONS:

1. Start with a clear screen.
2. Open **JACKET1**.
3. Make font size and appearance changes as indicated in the exercise.
4. Preview your document.
5. Print one copy.
6. Close your file; save the changes.
7. Close the document window.

[Handwritten annotations shown in italics below]

NOW AVAILABLE: *— 14pt bold and shadow* Authentic baseball team jackets personalized with your own name. Harold's Sportswear Store *— bold* now carries the genuine article. Our jackets are *exactly* *— italic* the same as the ones worn by every baseball team.

The jackets are personalized for you *absolutely free* *— italic*. Choose your favorite team and have your name on the jacket. You can look like a professional baseball player in your authentic jacket!

And the price is right. Just $149.99 plus $5.50 *— underline* for shipping and handling. Remember, there is *no charge* *— italic* for personalizing the jacket with your name.

Each jacket is made by the same company that makes the jackets for the professional baseball team members. They fit the same. They have the same logo. They even have the same label inside as the professional team jacket.

WHAT ARE YOU WAITING FOR? *— 14pt bold and shadow* Be the *first* *— italic* in your neighborhood to own the official baseball team jacket. To order your authentic jacket, call **Harold's Sportswear Store** *— bold* today. Dial **1-800-555-BALL** *— bold and outline*. You can charge the jacket and receive it within one week.

APPEARANCE CHANGES

Outline/Shadow/Small Caps/Redline/Strikeout

1. Place insertion point before text to receive appearance change (new text)

   OR

   Select/highlight text to receive appearance change (existing text).

2. Click **L**ayout .... `Alt` + `L`

   OR

   Click *right* mouse button anywhere in document window.

3. Click **F**ont .... `F`

4. Click in box to select desired appearance change.

5. Click **OK** .... `Enter`

NOTE: Outline, Shadow, Small Caps, Redline and Strikeout must be selected on Font menu.

RETURN TO NORMAL OR TURN FEATURE OFF

1. Place insertion point where appearance change will end (new text).

   OR

   Select/highlight text to return to normal (existing text).

2. Click **L**ayout .... `Alt` + `L`

   OR

   Click *right* mouse button anywhere in document window.

3. Click **F**ont .... `F`

4. Click box to deselect appearance change.

5. Click **OK** .... `Enter`

Lesson 2 ▪ Text Alignments & Fonts

EXERCISE 15
REMOVE FONT APPEARANCE

CONCEPTS:

Remove Font Appearance Changes

■ If you decide you would like to remove the font appearance change you applied to text, select/highlight the text where style is to be removed and repeat the procedure used to apply the appearance change. You can also remove font appearance changes by deleting the codes that were inserted when the styles were applied.

To delete a code in Reveal Codes mode:

- Use the mouse pointer to click on the code and press the Delete key,

OR

- Use the mouse pointer to drag the code out of the Reveal Codes window.

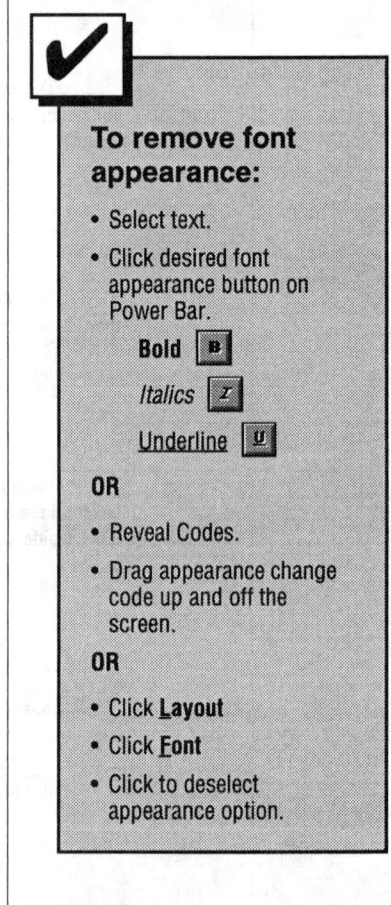

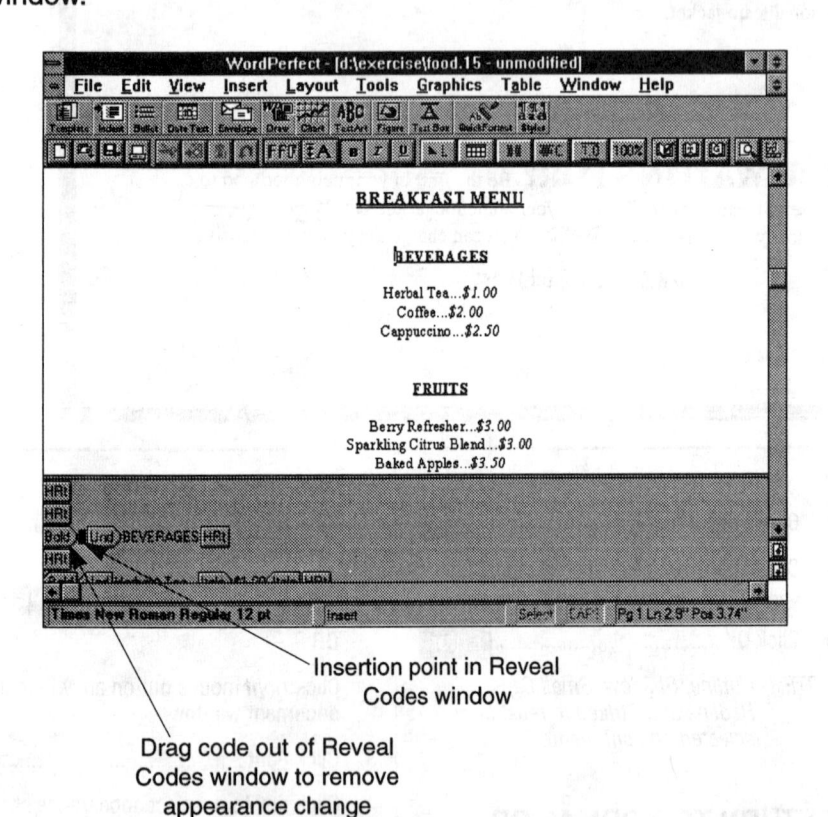

Insertion point in Reveal Codes window

Drag code out of Reveal Codes window to remove appearance change

---

To remove font appearance:

- Select text.
- Click desired font appearance button on Power Bar.

    Bold B

    Italics I

    Underline U

OR

- Reveal Codes.
- Drag appearance change code up and off the screen.

OR

- Click **L**ayout
- Click **F**ont
- Click to deselect appearance option.

In this exercise, you will delete appearance changes from a previously saved menu.

EXERCISE DIRECTIONS:

1. Start with a clear screen.
2. Open **FOOD.**
3. Make the revisions as indicated.
4. Preview your document.
5. Print one copy.
6. Close your file; save the changes.
7. Close the document window.

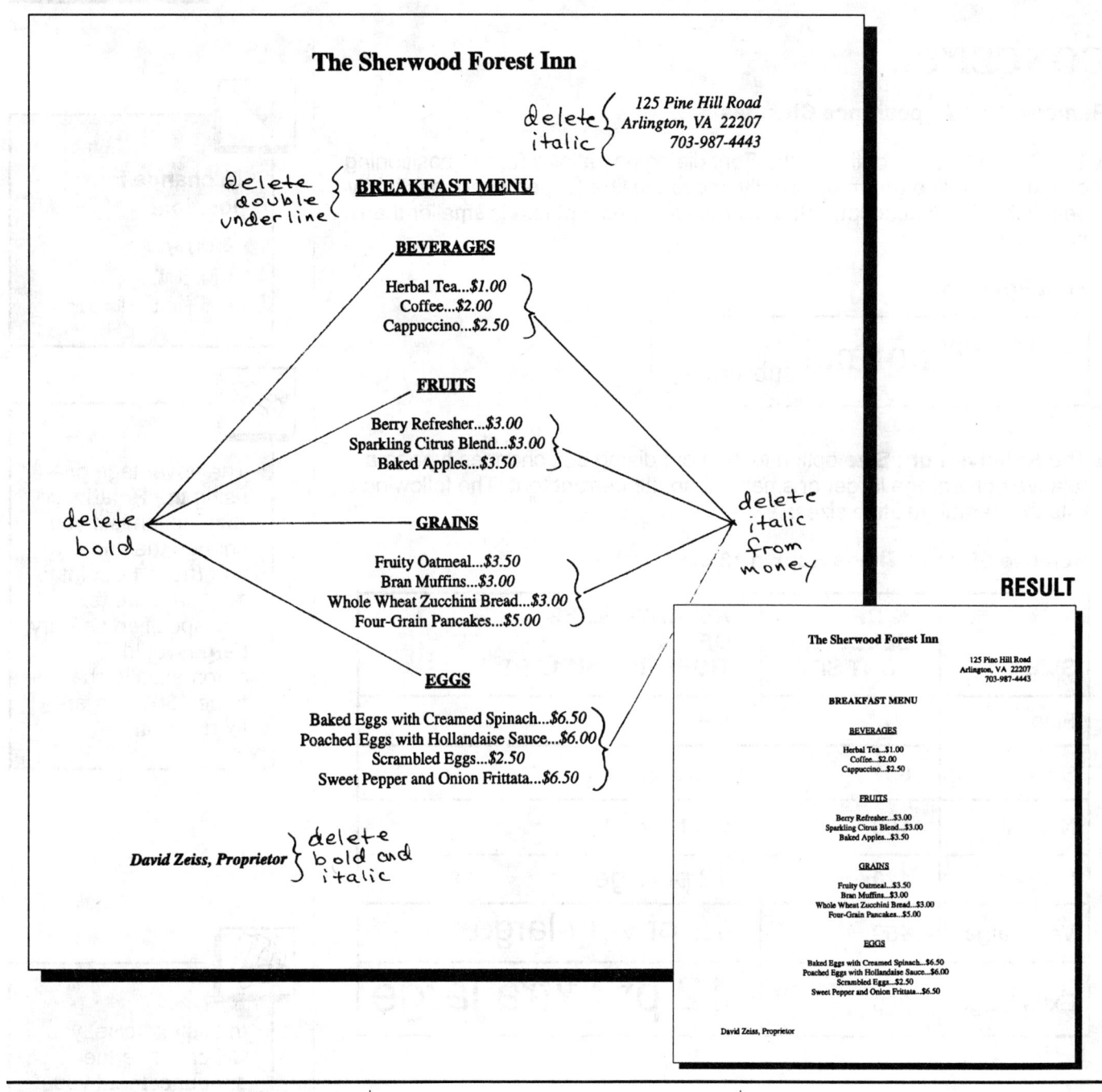

The Sherwood Forest Inn

delete italic { *125 Pine Hill Road*
Arlington, VA 22207
703-987-4443

delete double underline { **BREAKFAST MENU**

BEVERAGES

Herbal Tea...$1.00
Coffee...$2.00
Cappuccino...$2.50

FRUITS

Berry Refresher...$3.00
Sparkling Citrus Blend...$3.00
Baked Apples...$3.50

GRAINS

Fruity Oatmeal...$3.50
Bran Muffins...$3.00
Whole Wheat Zucchini Bread...$3.00
Four-Grain Pancakes...$5.00

EGGS

Baked Eggs with Creamed Spinach...$6.50
Poached Eggs with Hollandaise Sauce...$6.00
Scrambled Eggs...$2.50
Sweet Pepper and Onion Frittata...$6.50

delete bold (on left)
delete italic from money (on right)

David Zeiss, Proprietor } *delete bold and italic*

RESULT

REMOVE FONT APPEARANCE

1. Select/highlight text to return to normal.
2. Click *right* mouse button anywhere in document window.

   OR

   Click **L**ayout .... `Alt` + `L`

3. Click **F**ont .... `F`
4. Click appearance change to remove.

   OR

   Click Bold Button ....

Click Italic Button ....

Click Underline Button ....

Lesson 2 ▪ Exercise 15   53

Lesson 2 ▪ Text Alignments & Fonts

EXERCISE 16

CHANGE FONT POSITION AND RELATIVE FONT SIZE

CONCEPTS:

Remove Font Appearance Changes

- The **Font Position** option in the Font dialog box allows for the positioning of text on the line (normal), slightly above the line (superscript), or slightly below the line (subscript). Superscript and subscript text is smaller than normal text.

Font Position

^{superscript} normal $_{subscript}$

- The **Relative Font Size** option in the Font dialog box changes type to a relative percentage larger or smaller than the current font. The following lists the default relative sizes:

Relative Sizes of Times Roman 12 pt

SIZE	% OF SELECTED FONT SIZE	RELATIVE SIZES OF TIMES ROMAN 12 PT
Fine	60	12 pt fine
Small	80	12 pt small
Normal	100	12 pt normal
Large	120	12 pt large
Very Large	150	12 pt very large
Extra Large	200	12 pt extra large

To change font position:
- Click **L**ayout
- Click **F**ont
- Click **P**osition list box

The advantage of using the **Relative Size** option is if you change the current font (from 12 point to 10 point), the text you specified as **V**ery **L**arge would automatically change to be 150% larger—to 15 point.

In this exercise, you will enhance the announcement you created in an earlier exercise by changing font faces and font sizes.

- The Position and Relative Size are changed in the Font dialog box.

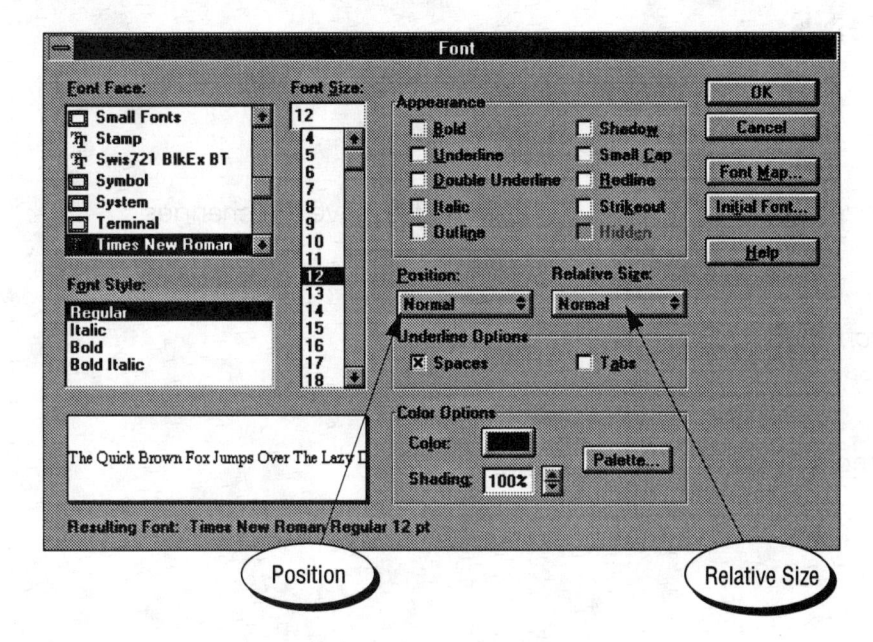

Position

Relative Size

Lesson 2 ▪ Exercise 16

EXERCISE DIRECTIONS:

1. Start with a clear screen.
2. Open **CONGRATS**.
3. Change the font face and font size to a 12 point serif font.

   ▪ NOTE: *Since this is a formal announcement, the font face chosen communicates a professional tone.*

4. Change the relative font sizes and font appearances as indicated.
5. Preview your document.
6. Print one copy.
7. Close the file; save the changes.

CHANGE FONT POSITION AND RELATIVE SIZE

—USING DIALOG BOX—

F9

OR

Click *right* mouse button anywhere in the document window and select Font.

1. Place insertion point where font change will begin (before typing).

   OR

   Select text to receive font change (after typing).

2. Click **Layout** .... `Alt` + `L`
3. Click **Font** .... `F`

   NOTE: *At Font dialog box, currently selected font is displayed in Preview window and described in resulting font line.*

4. In **P**osition box, highlight `P` desired position.
5. In Relative Size box, highlight `Z` desired size.

MORITZ & CHASE {very large bold}

1603 East 7th Street {superscript}
Astoria, OR 94101 {bold}

Is Pleased to Announce that the following Associates will become members of the firm on {small italic}

January 1, 1995

DENVER	Steven M. Jones
NEW YORK	Arthur J. Williams
SAN FRANCISCO	Roberta W. Asher
	Donna Newman
WASHINGTON, D.C.	Pamela T. Blanco

{bold / normal}

and that the following Of Counsel will become members of the firm on {small italic}

January 1, 1995

LONDON	Raymond T. Sedgewick
LOS ANGELES	Angela Tsacoumis
	Roberto Vasquez

{bold / normal}

Lesson 2 ▪ Exercise 16   57

Lesson 2 ▪ Text Alignments & Fonts

EXERCISE 17

ORNAMENTAL FONT FACES

CONCEPTS:

- **Wingdings** is an ornamental font face collection that is used to enhance a document. Below is the Wingding collection of fonts.

> **To add a Wingding to text:**
> - Select Wingding font face.
> - Select letter or character corresponding to desired Wingding.
> - Select previous font face after Wingding is chosen.

> If you add a Wingding font and your existing text becomes unreadable, simply change back to your original font at the point where the change must be made.

> A Wingding font face must be available with your printer.

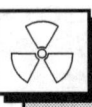

- The upper- and lowercase of the letter and character key provide different Wingdings. To choose a Wingding, you must select the Wingding font face and then press the corresponding keyboard letter or character shown in the chart above.

- Another source of ornamental fonts is the special character sets called the Iconic Symbols. This will be covered in Lesson 8 (Special Enhancements).

- Wingdings can be used to:

    Separate items on a page:

    > Wingdings
    > ◆❖❖◆
    > Graphics

    Emphasize items on a list:

    > ☺puppy
    > ☺kitten

    Enhance a page:

    > 📖📖📖📖📖📖📖📖
    > MYSTERY BOOK SALE
    > 📖📖📖📖📖📖📖📖

    Add an in-line graphic:

    > Save your document on 💾.

- A Wingding font face is chosen on the Font dialog box.

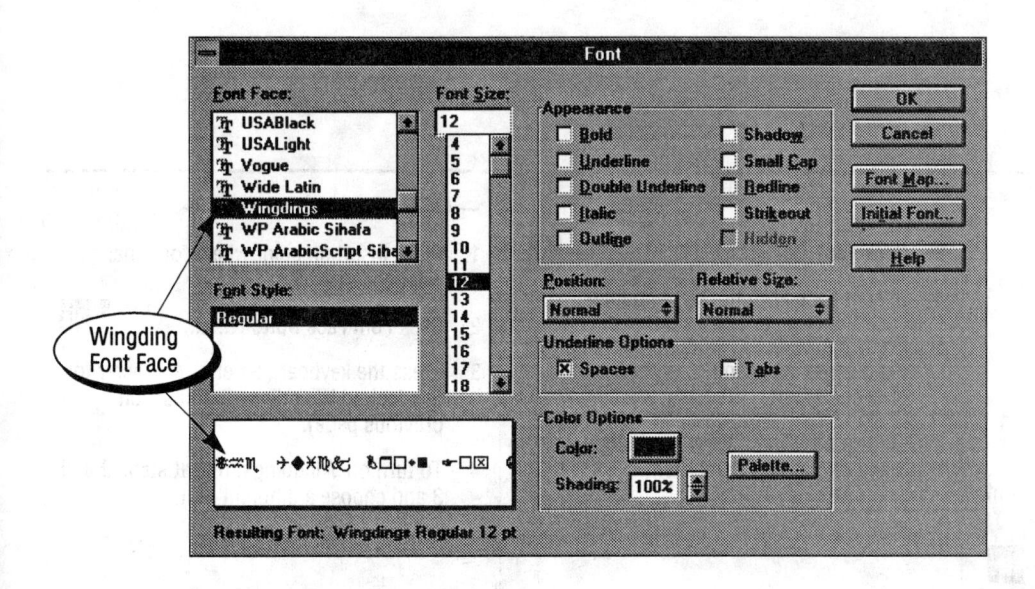

In WordPerfect 6.0a and later versions, Iconic Symbols can be accessed through the Font menu.

In this exercise, you will add Wingdings to separate portions of a menu created earlier.

Lesson 2 ▪ Exercise 17   59

Lesson 2 ▪ Exercise 17

EXERCISE DIRECTIONS:

1. Start with a clear screen.
2. Open **FOOD**.
3. Enhance the document with Wingdings (one or more or any combination) where indicated on the right.
4. Change font face, size and appearance as indicated.
5. Insert a blank line where indicated.
6. Preview your document.
7. Print one copy.
8. Close your file; save the changes.
9. Close the document window.

ADD WINGDINGS

—USING DIALOG BOX—

F9

OR

Click *right* mouse anywhere in the document window and select Font.

1. Place insertion point where Wingding font will begin.
2. Click **L**ayout .... Alt + L
3. Click **F**ont .... F
4. In Font Face list, choose Wingdings.
5. Press the keyboard letter or character for the desired Wingding (See chart on previous page).
6. To turn off Wingdings, repeat steps 2 and 3 and choose a different font.

—USING POWER BAR—

1. Place insertion point where font change will begin.
2. Click Font Face Button ....
3. Press the keyboard letter or character for the desired Wingding (See chart on previous page).
4. To turn off Wingdings, repeat steps 2 and 3 and choose a different font.

The Sherwood Forest Inn {24pt}

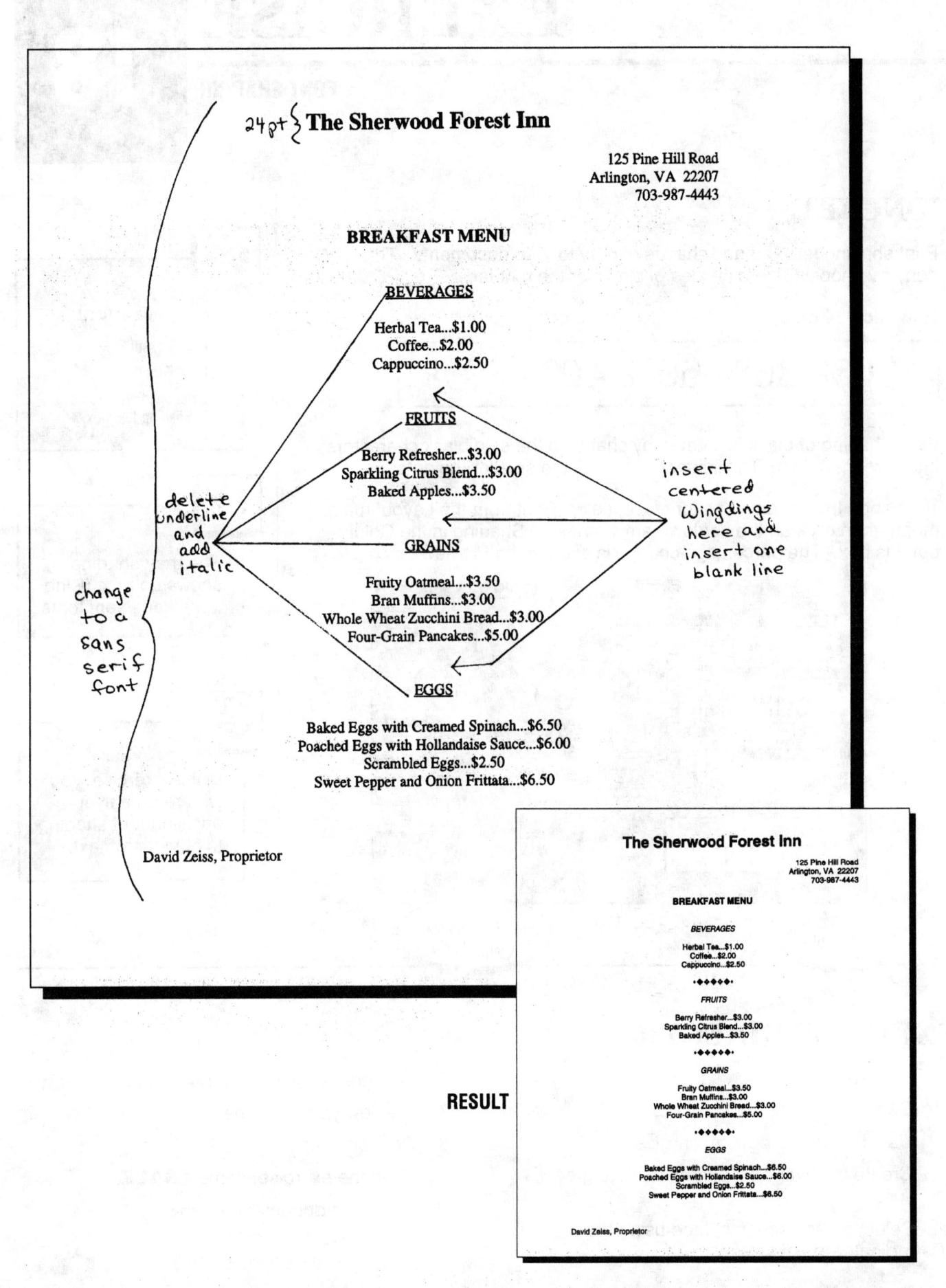

125 Pine Hill Road
Arlington, VA 22207
703-987-4443

BREAKFAST MENU

BEVERAGES

Herbal Tea...$1.00
Coffee...$2.00
Cappuccino...$2.50

FRUITS

Berry Refresher...$3.00
Sparkling Citrus Blend...$3.00
Baked Apples...$3.50

GRAINS

Fruity Oatmeal...$3.50
Bran Muffins...$3.00
Whole Wheat Zucchini Bread...$3.00
Four-Grain Pancakes...$5.00

EGGS

Baked Eggs with Creamed Spinach...$6.50
Poached Eggs with Hollandaise Sauce...$6.00
Scrambled Eggs...$2.50
Sweet Pepper and Onion Frittata...$6.50

David Zeiss, Proprietor

[Handwritten annotations:]
- 24pt } (for title)
- change to a sans serif font
- delete underline and add italic (for section headings)
- insert centered Wingdings here and insert one blank line (between sections)

RESULT

Lesson 2 ■ Exercise 17

Lesson 2 ▪ Text Alignments & Fonts

EXERCISE 18
FONT SHADING

CONCEPTS:

- Font shading lets you add shades of gray to your documents. This is done by choosing percentages of black for the font face.

Helvetica 24 pt:

> 100% 80% 60% 40% 20%

- Gray shading of black is created by changing the sold black characters into screened dots. The lighter the shade, the smaller the dots.

- To change the shading of a font face, select Font from the Layout main menu, then click on the up/down arrows next to Shading in the Color options box. The percentage change is seen in the Preview box.

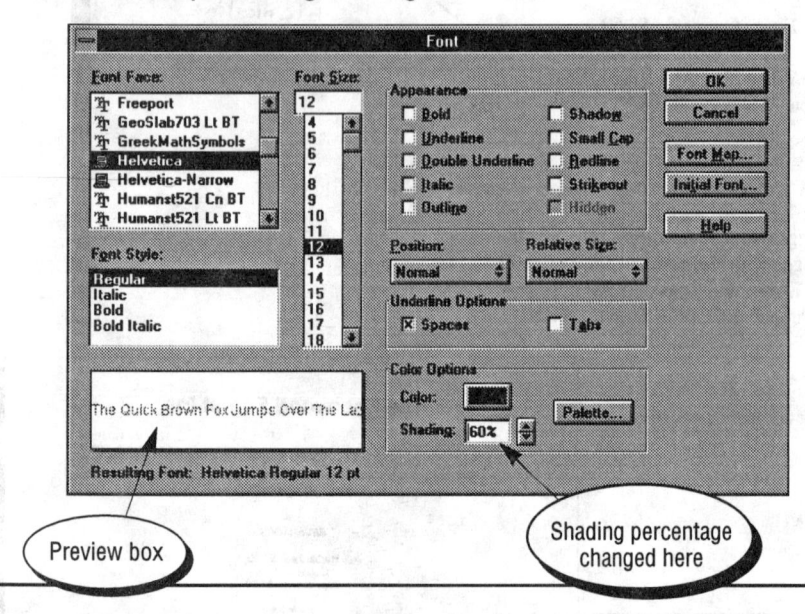

(Font dialog box shown with Preview box and Shading percentage changed here callouts)

To shade a font:
- Click **Layout**
- Click **Font**
- Enter shading percentage in Shading text box.

The gray shading shows up best using large sans serif fonts.

In this exercise, you will create a flyer applying font shading to portions of text.

EXERCISE DIRECTIONS:

1. Start with a clear screen.
2. Center the page from top to bottom.
3. Use .5" top and bottom margins.
4. Create the flyer on the right, centering each line.
5. Select a sans serif font face using the indicated point sizes.
6. Use gray shading and bold as indicated.
7. Preview your document.
8. Print one copy.
9. Save the exercise; name it **SALE**.
10. Close the document window.

Sample Flyer

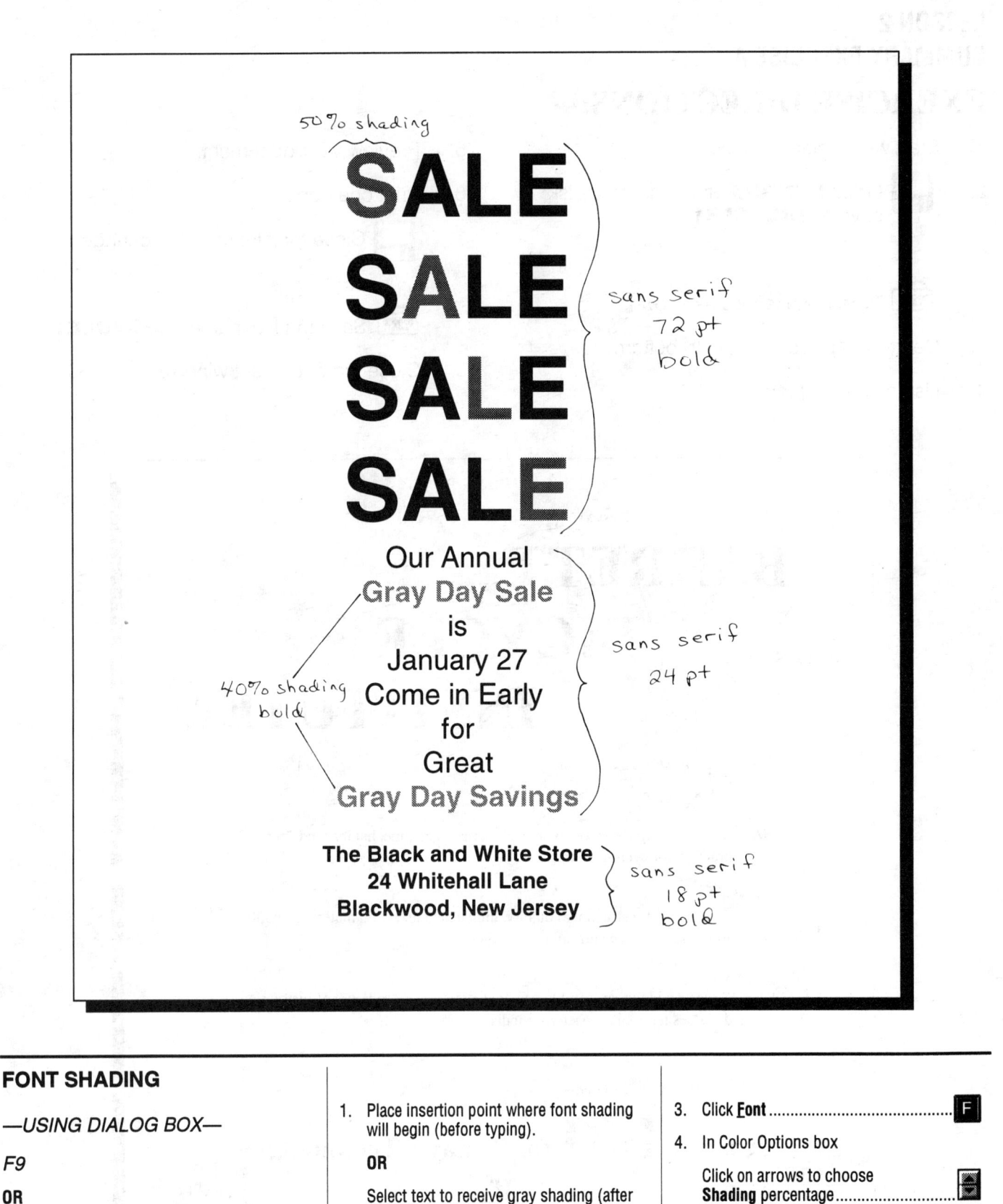

SALE *(50% shading)*

SALE

SALE

SALE

sans serif, 72 pt, bold

Our Annual
Gray Day Sale
is
January 27
Come in Early
for
Great
Gray Day Savings

sans serif, 24 pt
40% shading, bold

The Black and White Store
24 Whitehall Lane
Blackwood, New Jersey

sans serif, 18 pt, bold

FONT SHADING

—USING DIALOG BOX—

F9

OR

Click *right* mouse anywhere in the document window and select Font

1. Place insertion point where font shading will begin (before typing).

   OR

   Select text to receive gray shading (after typing).

2. Click **L**ayout .... `Alt` + `L`

3. Click **F**ont .... `F`

4. In Color Options box

   Click on arrows to choose **Shading** percentage ....

   OR

   Type desired percent

5. Click **OK** .... `Enter`

Lesson 2 ■ Exercise 18

LESSON 2
SUMMARY EXERCISE A
EXERCISE DIRECTIONS:

1. Start with a clear screen.
2. Open **BICYCLE** from the data disk; save as **BICYCLE1**.

   or

   Type the exercise as shown.
3. Center the page from top to bottom.
4. Use a serif font face.
5. Preview your document.
6. Print one copy.
7. Close the file; save the changes.

   or

   Save the file; name it **BICYCLE1**.
8. Close the document window.

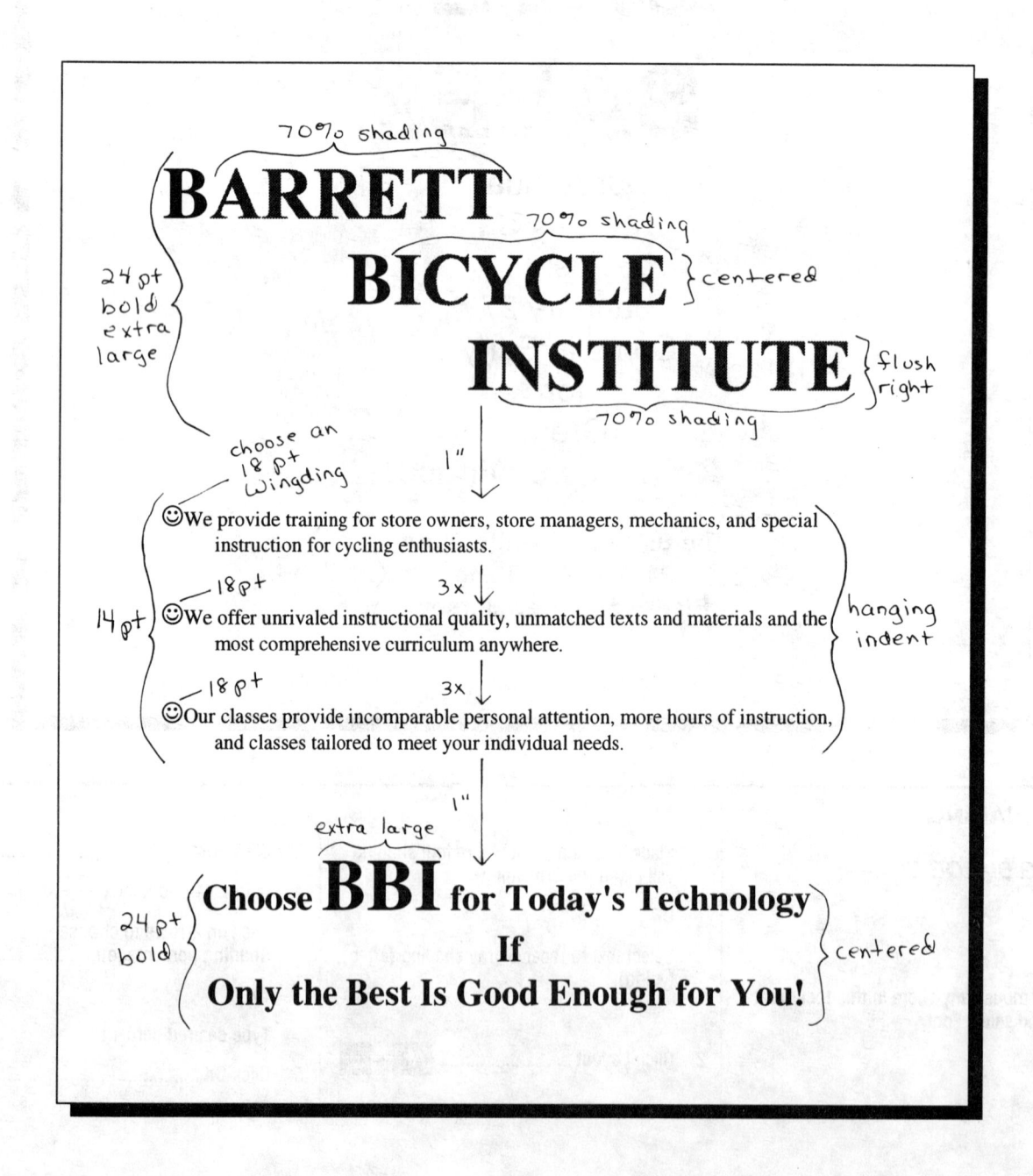

70% shading

BARRETT

70% shading

BICYCLE {centered}

24 pt bold extra large

INSTITUTE {flush right}

70% shading

choose an 18 pt Wingding

↓ 1"

☺ We provide training for store owners, store managers, mechanics, and special instruction for cycling enthusiasts.

— 18 pt   3x ↓

14 pt ☺ We offer unrivaled instructional quality, unmatched texts and materials and the most comprehensive curriculum anywhere.

{ hanging indent

— 18 pt   3x ↓

☺ Our classes provide incomparable personal attention, more hours of instruction, and classes tailored to meet your individual needs.

↓ 1"

extra large

Choose **BBI** for Today's Technology
If
Only the Best Is Good Enough for You!

24 pt bold   {centered}

LESSON 2
SUMMARY EXERCISE B
EXERCISE DIRECTIONS:

1. Start with a clear screen.
2. Open **COMPUTE** from the data disk; save as **COMPUTE1**.

   or

   Type the exercise as shown.
3. Center the page from top to bottom.
4. Use a sans serif font face.
5. Preview your document.
6. Print one copy.
7. Close the file; save the changes.

   or

   Save the file; name it **COMPUTE1**.
8. Close the document window.

COMPUTER TRAINING, INC. } 24pt bold, large, centered

2↓

❖**Computer Classes**❖ } 24pt bold, centered (Choose a Wingding)

3↓

Each month we offer new computer classes to the public. Whether you wish to use the computer for personal or business use, we have the right course for you. We offer courses on software, hardware, preventive maintenance, and computer repair. Our knowledgeable trainers are computer certified. } 14 pt Full Justification

4↓

2 West 17th Street ❖ Suite 23 ❖ New York City
212-555-2121
} 18 pt centered (superscript bold)

4↓

Whether you are considering a new purchase or want to make the most of what you have...helping you succeed is our business. } 14 pt centered 60% shading

Lesson 2 ■ Exercise B

Lesson 3 ▪ Character and Line Spacing

EXERCISE 19

KERNING

CONCEPTS:

▪ **Kerning** adjusts the space between certain letters based on their shape and slant to make them more pleasing to the eye.

No Kerning: **VAULT**
Kerning: **VAULT**

▪ **Automatic Kerning** makes spacing adjustments for predefined pairs of letters. The letter pairs are dependent on the font chosen. Automatic Kerning is chosen in the Typesetting dialog box.

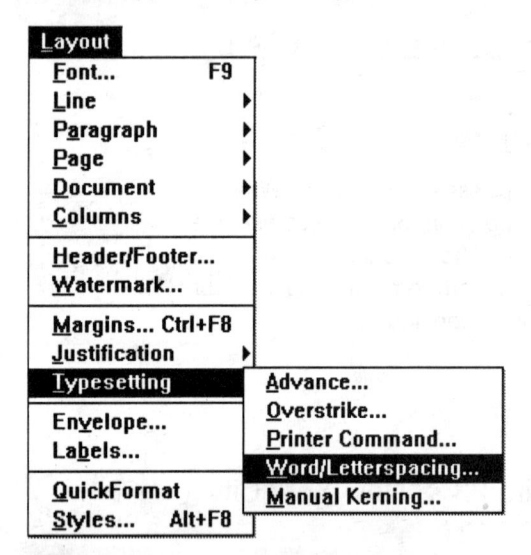

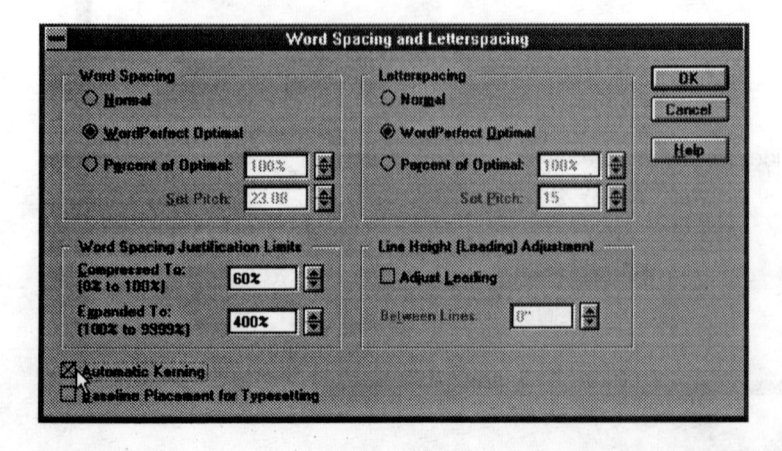

✓ To automatically kern:
- Click **L**ayout
- Click **T**ypesetting
- Click **W**ord/Letterspacing
- Click **A**utomatic Kerning

✓ To manually kern:
- Click **L**ayout
- Click **T**ypesetting
- Click **M**anual Kerning

✏️ Spacing gaps between certain letters become exaggerated as font size increases.

👉 In this exercise, you will manually and automatically kern portions of a previously saved flyer.

66

- **Manual Kerning** allows you to make spacing adjustments between any two characters. Manual Kerning is chosen in the Manual Kerning dialog box.

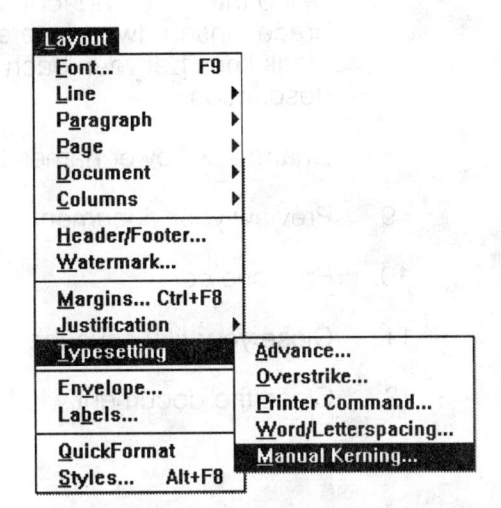

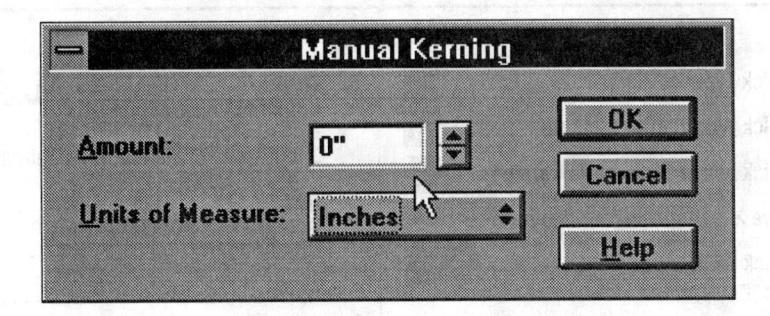

- To increase the space between two characters, a positive number is placed in the Amount box. To decrease the space between two characters, a negative number is placed in the Amount box. You have to experiment until the right positive or negative number is found.

- Reveal Codes will show the amount of space kerned between two characters.

Lesson 3 ■ Exercise 19

Lesson 3 ■ Exercise 19

EXERCISE DIRECTIONS:

1. Start with a clear screen
2. Open **FLOWER1**
3. Change the point sizes in the first line.
4. Bold the first four lines and the last line.
5. Manually kern the first two letters of each word on line 1 (The Perennial Potter) so the second letter of each word begins under the first letter.
6. Automatically kern the body text beginning with "It is . . ." through the last paragraph.
7. Using the Wingding font and the { (open brace); insert two centered *flowers* in the blank lines between each flower description.
8. Change all flower names to bold italic.
9. Preview your document.
10. Print one copy.
11. Close your file; save the changes.
12. Close the document window.

AUTOMATIC KERNING

1. Place insertion point where kerning is to begin (before or after typing).
2. Click **L**ayout .... Alt + L
3. Click **T**ypesetting .... T
4. Click **W**ord/Letter Spacing .... W
5. Click box for **A**utomatic Kerning .... A

   An X appears in the box.

6. Click **OK** .... Enter

To end automatic kerning:

1. Place insertion point where kerning is to end (before or after typing).
2. Click **L**ayout .... Alt + L
3. Click **T**ypesetting .... T
4. Click **W**ord/Letter Spacing .... W
5. Click box for **A**utomatic Kerning .... A

   The X is removed from the box.

6. Click **OK** .... Enter

MANUAL KERNING

1. Place insertion point between the pair of letters to kern.
2. Click **L**ayout .... Alt + L
3. Click **T**ypesetting .... T
4. Click **M**anual Kerning .... M
5. Click .... Alt + U
   Units of Measurement

   Choose one of the following options:

   Inches I
   Centimeters C
   Points .... P
   Millimeters .... M
   1200ths 1

6. Click **A**mount .... Alt + A
7. Click arrows or enter a specific amount (positive or negative)
8. Click **OK** .... Enter

The Perennial Potter
14 Highway 37
Middletown, NJ
908-555-5555

One-Day   Sale   —   July   21,   1995

It is another new year and by now you are ready to add to your existing garden. This year we have over 75 perennial plants to choose from. There are all sizes and types to suit your needs.

We have perennials that can be grown in full sun or on partial shade. We even have some that require full shade and some that require full sun.

We have perennials that will survive temperatures below 50 degrees and perennials that need at least 40 degrees to survive.

We have perennials that bloom in early spring and perennials that bloom in the late fall.

Below is a sampling of some of our favorites:

DELPHINIUM: One of the tallest of our perennials, the delphinium comes in brilliant colors such as blue, purple, white, pink and lavender. The plants grow as tall as 72" in full sun.

❀❀

PLATYCODON: The "Balloon Flower" is a medium sized perennial that comes in violet, white and pink. The plants grow as tall as 36" in full sun to partial shade.

❀❀

COREOPSIS: These daisy-like perennials come in yellow and pink. The plants grow as tall as 24" in full sun to partial shade.

❀❀

SEDUM: This ground cover comes in pink, red, yellow and white. The plants grow up to 6" tall and spread quickly in full sun.

FROM   TALL   TO   SHORT,   WE   HAVE   THE   PERENNIAL   FOR   YOU!

Lesson 3 ▪ Character and Line Spacing

EXERCISE 20

WORD SPACING AND LETTERSPACING

CONCEPTS:

▪ The **Word Spacing and Letterspacing** features let you adjust the spacing between words and letters in your document.

Letterspacing:

Optimal:
It is not the time nor the place
80% of Optimal:
It is not the time nor the place
120% of Optimal:
It is not the time nor the place

Word Spacing

Optimal:
It is not the time nor the place
80% of Optimal:
It is not the time nor the place
120% of Optimal:
It is not the time nor the place

Combined Word Spacing and Letterspacing

Optimal:
It is not the time nor the place
Words and Letters 80% of Optimal
It is not the time nor the place
Words and Letters 120% of Optimal:
It is not the time nor the place

To Change Word/Letterspacing:
- Click **L**ayout
- Click **T**ypesetting
- Click **W**ord/Letterspacing

Not all printers support the Word Spacing and Letterspacing feature.

A tighter Word/Letterspacing (less than 100%) allows you to fit more words on a page.

- Word/Letterspacing is chosen in the Typesetting dialog box.

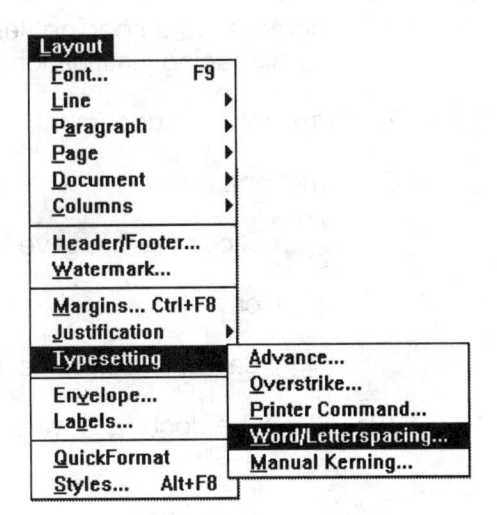

[Layout menu showing Font... F9, Line, Paragraph, Page, Document, Columns, Header/Footer..., Watermark..., Margins... Ctrl+F8, Justification, Typesetting (with submenu: Advance..., Overstrike..., Printer Command..., Word/Letterspacing..., Manual Kerning...), Envelope..., Labels..., QuickFormat, Styles... Alt+F8]

- The **Word Spacing Justification Limits** feature lets you adjust spacing in text where the justification was set to *full*. Minimum and maximum limits for spacing are set.

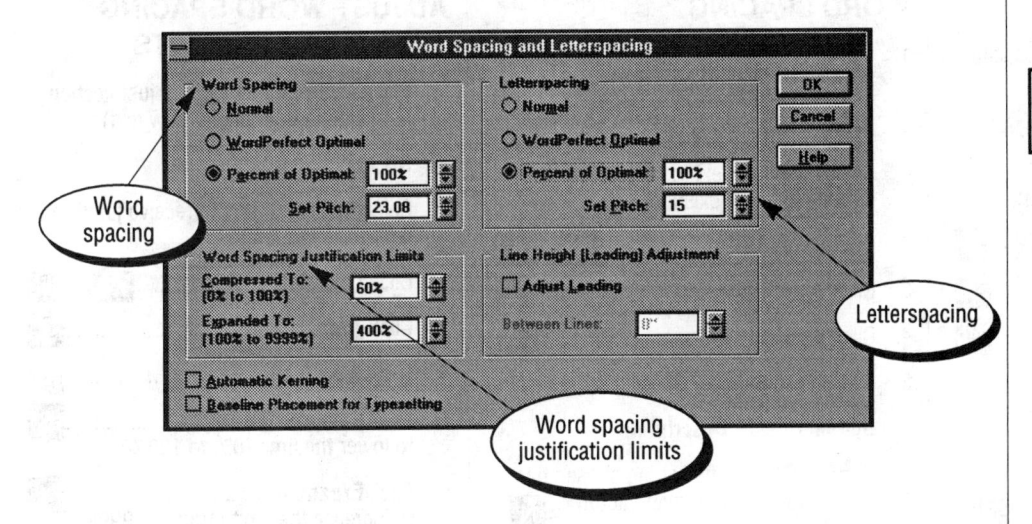

[Word Spacing and Letterspacing dialog box:
- Word Spacing: Normal, WordPerfect Optimal, Percent of Optimal: 100%, Set Pitch: 23.08
- Letterspacing: Normal, WordPerfect Optimal, Percent of Optimal: 100%, Set Pitch: 15
- Word Spacing Justification Limits: Compressed To: (0% to 100%) 60%, Expanded To: (100% to 9999%) 400%
- Line Height (Leading) Adjustment: Adjust Leading, Between Lines
- Automatic Kerning, Baseline Placement for Typesetting
- OK, Cancel, Help]

Labels: Word spacing, Letterspacing, Word spacing justification limits

---

✏️ Increase the Compressed To setting to increase spacing between words if words appear too close together.

✏️ Decrease the Expanded To setting to decrease spacing between words if words appear too far apart.

☢️ You will see no different when the Word Spacing Justification Limits are changed if your printer does not support this feature.

👉 In this exercise, you will create a flyer using the Word Spacing and Letterspacing features to adjust portions of text.

Lesson 3 ▪ Exercise 20

EXERCISE DIRECTIONS:

1. Start with a clear screen.
2. Center the page from top to bottom.
3. Set 2" left and right margins and .5" top and bottom margins.
4. 💾 Insert **GOLF** from data disk; save as **GOLF1**.

   or

   ⌨ Type the exercise as shown.
5. Use a serif font face and change the point sizes, justification, and font appearance as shown.
6. Increase word spacing, letter spacing, and word spacing justification limits indicated.
7. Preview your document.
8. Print one copy.

   💾 Close the file; save the changes.

   or

   ⌨ Save the file; name it **GOLF1**.
10. Close the document window.

LETTERSPACING

1. Place insertion point where letterspacing change is to begin (new text).

   OR

   Select/highlight text to receive letterspacing change (existing text).
2. Click **L**ayout .... Alt + L
3. Click **T**ypesetting .... T
4. Click **W**ord/Letter Spacing .... W
5. Select desired Letterspacing option:

Option	Description	
Nor**m**al	The setting chosen by font manufacturer.	M
Word Perfect **O**ptimal	The setting chosen by WordPerfect Corp.	O
Pe**r**cent Optimal	To set your own spacing.	R
Set **P**itch	To specify number of characters per inch.	P

   NOTE: If Percent of Optimal is chosen, specify a spacing value and pitch setting.
   Less than 100%--reduces spacing; greater than 100%--increases spacing.
6. Click **OK** .... Enter

WORD SPACING

1. Place insertion point where word spacing change is to begin (new text).

   OR

   Select/highlight text to receive word spacing change (existing text).
2. Click **L**ayout .... Alt + L
3. Click **T**ypesetting .... T
4. Click **W**ord/Letter Spacing .... W
5. Select desired Word Spacing option:

Option	Description	
Nor**m**al	The setting chosen by font manufacturer.	N
Word Perfect **O**ptimal	The setting chosen by WordPerfect Corp.	W
Pe**r**cent Optimal	To set your own spacing.	E
Set **P**itch	To specify number of characters per inch.	P

   NOTE: If Percent of Optimal is chosen, specify a spacing value and pitch setting.
   Less than 100%--reduces spacing; greater than 100%--increases spacing.
6. Click **OK** .... Enter

ADJUST WORD SPACING JUSTIFICATION LIMITS

1. Place insertion point where justification limit setting is to begin (new text)

   OR

   Select/highlight text to receive justification limit (existing text)
2. Click **L**ayout .... Alt + L
3. Click **T**ypesetting .... T
4. Click **W**ord/Letter Spacing .... W
5. Click **C**ompressed To C
   to lower the limit (0% to 100%)
6. Click E**x**panded To X
   to increase the limit (100% to 9999%)
7. Click **OK** .... Enter

GO FOR IT
GOLF
SCHOOL

36pt bold
- GO FOR IT — increase word spacing 120%
- GOLF — increase letterspacing 150%
- SCHOOL — increase letterspacing 120%

centered

When you (24pt bold)

GO FOR IT (36pt bold) — increase word spacing 140%

go to the
leader
in
golf instruction

24pt bold

At our schools, you will learn the fundamentals of golf. We will instruct you on effective warm-up exercises. Our individual trainers will work with you on your grip and your swing. We will also instruct you on practical principles and the psychology of golf which we guarantee will improve your game.

If you sign up now, you will receive a free box of our GO FOR IT golf balls.

14pt Full justification — increase word spacing justification limits 800%

We have locations throughout
the United States
1-800-555-GOLF

24pt bold, centered — increase letterspacing 160%

Lesson 3 ■ Exercise 20   73

Lesson 3 ▪ Character and Line Spacing

EXERCISE 21
LEADING

CONCEPTS:

- **Leading** (pronounced *led-ding*) is the amount of white space between lines of type.

- Leading is changed to adjust text to fit on the page or to make text more readable.

- The amount of white space to be added or subtracted is specified in the Word Spacing and Letterspacing dialog box.

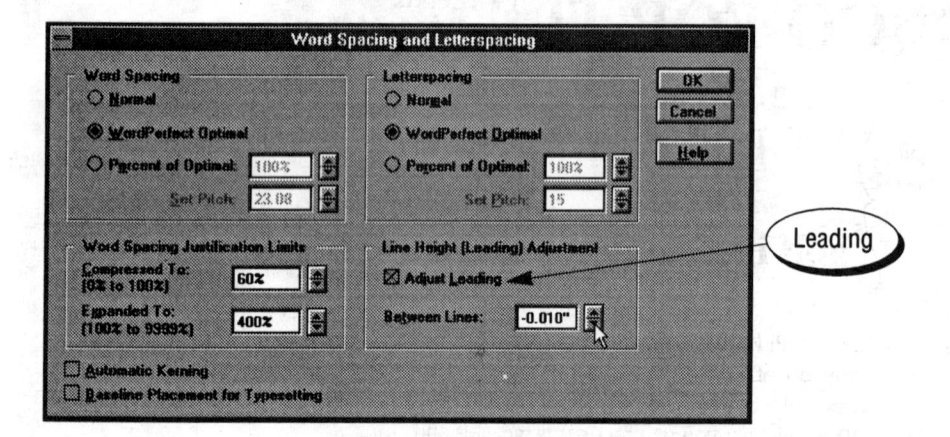

(Word Spacing and Letterspacing dialog box shown with "Leading" label pointing to the Line Height (Leading) Adjustment section)

To change Leading:
- Click **L**ayout
- Click **T**ypesetting
- Click **W**ord/Letterspacing
- Click Adjust **L**eading text box.

In this exercise, you will change the leading of portions of text of a previously created flyer.

- Reducing leading can reduce the readability while increasing leading can aid readability.

Without Leading Adjustment:

> To make text easy to read, fonts that are measured in points usually use leading that is 120% of the font's point size.
> For example a 10 point font frequently uses 12 point leading.

With Leading Adjustment (-.050"):

> To make text easy to read, fonts that are measured in points usually use leading that is 120% of the font's point size.
> For example a 10 point font frequently uses 12 point leading.

With Leading Adjustment (.050"):

> To make text easy to read, fonts that are measured in points
> usually use leading that is 120% of the font's point size.
> For example a 10 point font frequently uses 12 point leading.

EXERCISE DIRECTIONS:

1. Start with a clear screen.
2. Open **SALE**.
3. Change the leading as indicated on the right.
4. Preview your document.
5. Print one copy.
6. Close your file; save the changes.
7. Close the document window.

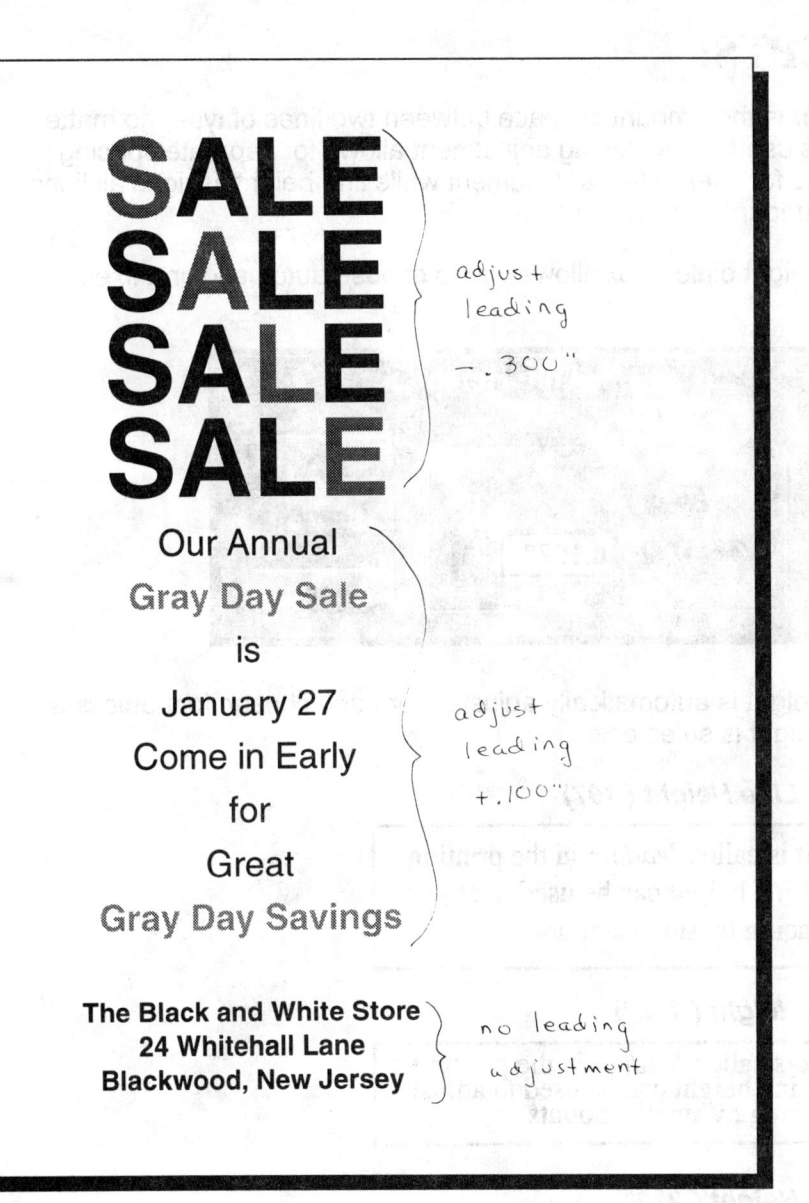

SALE
SALE
SALE
SALE

} adjust leading −.300"

Our Annual
Gray Day Sale
is
January 27
Come in Early
for
Great
Gray Day Savings

} adjust leading +.100"

**The Black and White Store
24 Whitehall Lane
Blackwood, New Jersey**

} no leading adjustment

ADJUST LEADING

1. Place insertion point where leading change is to begin (new text).

    OR

    Select/highlight text to receive leading change (existing text).

2. Click **L**ayout .... `Alt` + `L`
3. Click **T**ypesetting .... `T`
4. Click **W**ord/Letter Spacing .... `W`
5. Click Adjust **L**eading .... `L`, `Space`
6. Click Be**t**ween lines .... `T`
7. Select amount of leading adjustment.
8. Click **OK** .... `Enter`

Lesson 3 ■ Exercise 21

Lesson 3 ▪ Character and Line Spacing

EXERCISE 22
LINE HEIGHT

CONCEPTS:

- **Line height** is the amount of space between two lines of type, no matter what font is used. The leading adjustment allows for separate spacing adjustments for lines within a document while line height assigns all lines the same amount of space.

- The Line Height dialog box allows you to choose automatic or a fixed height.

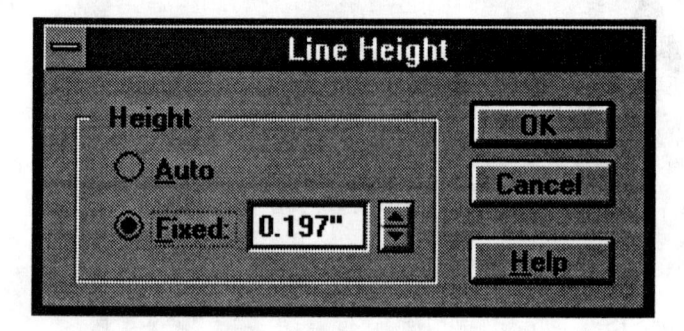

To change line height:
- Click **L**ayout
- Click **L**ine
- Click **H**eight

- The Line Height is automatically adjusted for each chosen font unless a fixed line height is selected.

Automatic Line Height (.197)

Line height is called *leading* in the printing industry. Line height can be used to adjust the line spacing by small amounts.

Fixed Line Height (.130")

Line height is called *leading* in the printing industry. Line height can be used to adjust the line spacing by small amounts.

Fixed Line Height (.230")

Line height is called *leading* in the printing industry. Line height can be used to adjust the line spacing by small amounts.

In this exercise, you will create an announcement using both fixed and automatic line heights.

EXERCISE DIRECTIONS:

1. Start with a clear screen.
2. Center the page from top to bottom.
3. Set .5" top and bottom margins.
4. Center the text at right using a bolded serif font and the point sizes indicated.
5. After selecting the first line's font and point size, set a fixed line height using the number shown in the fixed line height box.
6. Change to an automatic line height beginning with the 6 point "IT'S HERE" line.
7. Preview your document.
8. Print one copy.
9. Save the exercise; name it **HERE**.
10. Close the document window.

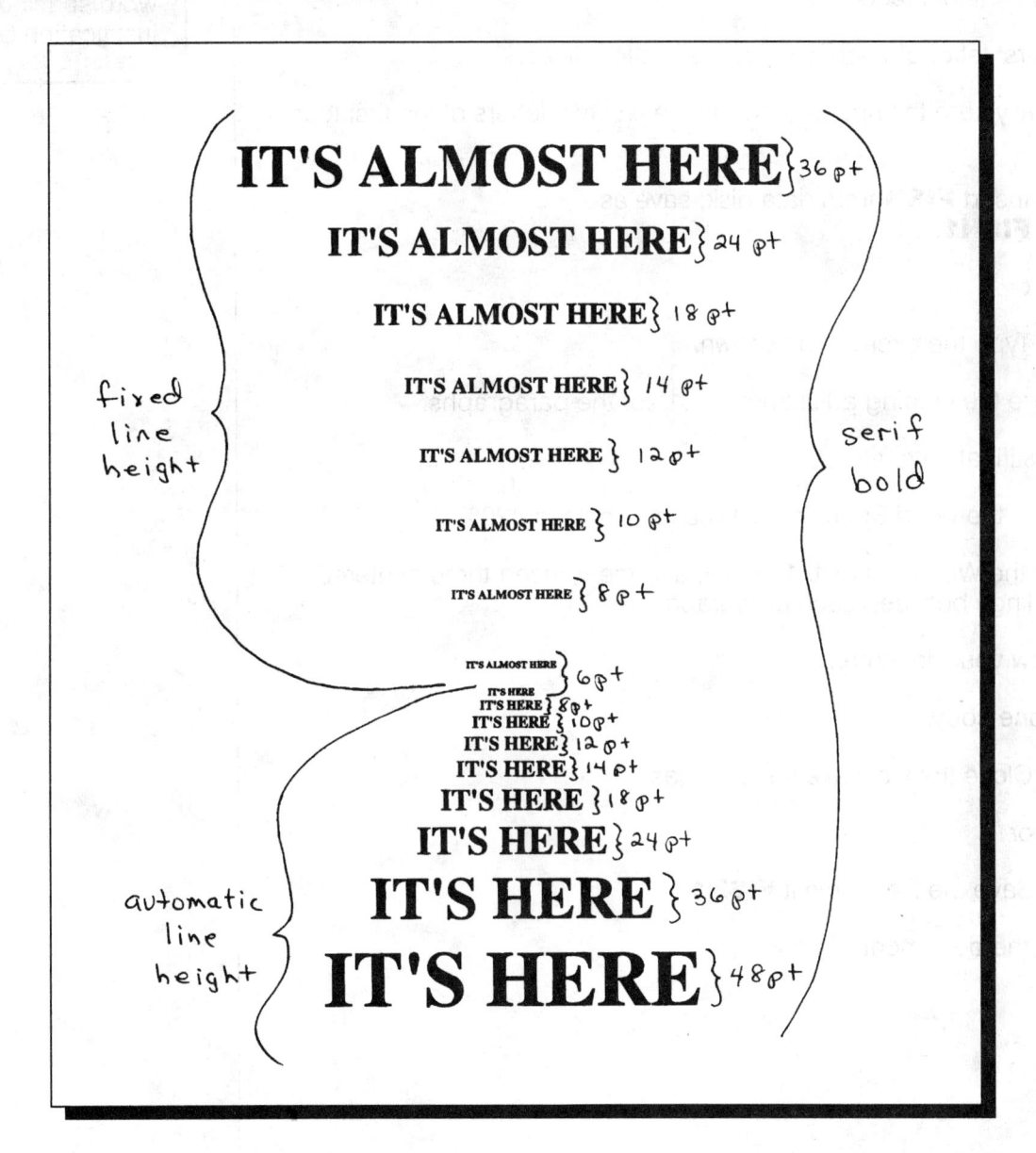

IT'S ALMOST HERE } 36 pt
IT'S ALMOST HERE } 24 pt
IT'S ALMOST HERE } 18 pt
IT'S ALMOST HERE } 14 pt
IT'S ALMOST HERE } 12 pt
IT'S ALMOST HERE } 10 pt
IT'S ALMOST HERE } 8 pt

{ fixed line height

{ serif bold

IT'S ALMOST HERE } 6 pt
IT'S HERE } 8 pt
IT'S HERE } 10 pt
IT'S HERE } 12 pt
IT'S HERE } 14 pt
IT'S HERE } 18 pt
IT'S HERE } 24 pt
IT'S HERE } 36 pt
IT'S HERE } 48 pt

{ automatic line height

ADJUST LINE HEIGHT

1. Place insertion point where line height change is to begin.

   OR

   Select/highlight text to receive line height change (existing text).

2. Click **L**ayout .... Alt + L
3. Click **L**ine L
4. Click **H**eight .... H
5. Click **A**uto or **F**ixed .... A or F

   NOTE: If Fixed is selected, type new line height or select amount of leading adjustment

6. Click **OK** .... Enter

LESSON 3
SUMMARY EXERCISE A

EXERCISE DIRECTIONS:

1. Start with a clear screen.
2. Center the page from top to bottom.
3. Set .5" top and bottom margins.
4. Use a serif font face.
5. Bold first letter of each word of the first four lines.
6. Manually kern the space between the first two letters of the first four lines.
7. Insert **FISH** from data disk; save as **FISH1**.

    or

    Type the exercise as shown.
8. Change the leading adjustment to .1" for the paragraphs.
9. Set justification to all.
10. Expand the Word Spacing Justification Limits to 420%.
11. Using the Wingding font, 18 point, and the v, insert three centered Wingdings between each paragraph.
12. Preview your document.
13. Print one copy.
14. Close the file; save the changes.

    or

    Save the file; name it **FISH1**.
15. Close the document window.

In this exercise, you will create a flyer using manual kerning and setting word spacing justification limits.

[72pt bold] [36pt] [manually kern]

Fish
Is
Super
Healthy

word spacing justification limits = expand to 420%

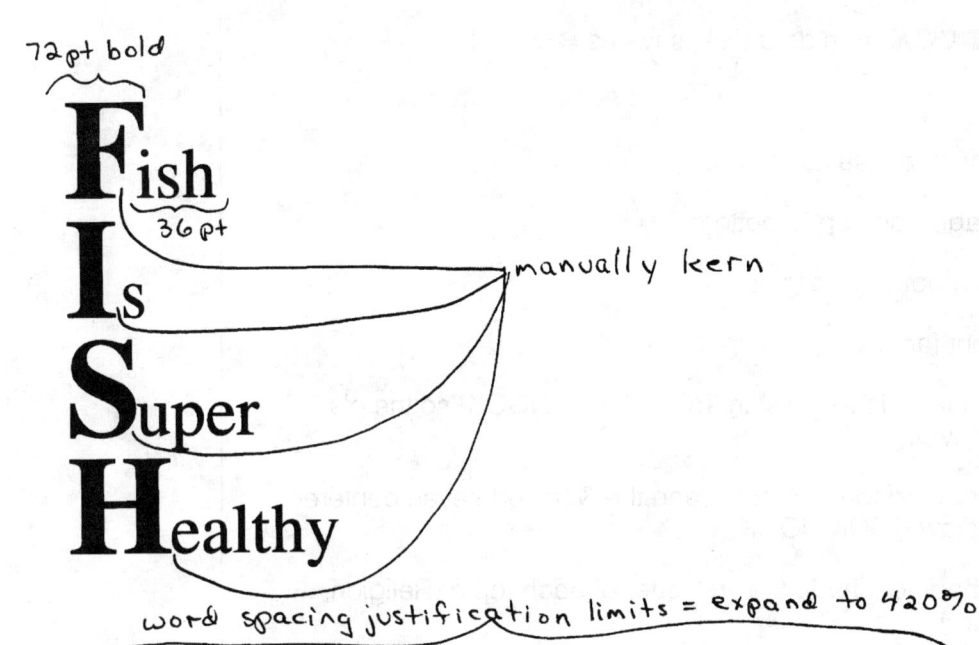

[18pt, .1" leading] [justify All]

If you are health-conscious or diet-conscious, fish is the way to go. You can never get bored with fish since there are so many varieties you can prepare in so many different ways.

❖❖❖

Whether you poach, steam, broil, pan fry, deep fry, stir fry, barbecue, saute, bake or smoke fish, it is still the food to eat.

❖❖❖

You can have salmon, sole, shark, snapper, halibut, haddock, smelts, swordfish, tuna, bluefish, carp, catfish, sardines, monkfish, mackerel, scrod, pompano, herring, trout, shad or turbot.

❖❖❖

You can serve fish as an hors d'oeurvre, appetizer or main dish.

LESSON 3
SUMMARY EXERCISE B

EXERCISE DIRECTIONS:

1. Start with a clear screen.
2. Open **BOOK** from data disk; save as **BOOK1**.

    or

    Type the exercise as shown.
3. Center the page from top to bottom.
4. Set .5" top and bottom margins.
5. Use a serif font face.
6. Manually kern the "double o's" in "BOOK" and "NOOK" so the o's overlap as shown.
7. Using the Wingding font, 24 point, and the &, insert seven centered Wingdings below BOOK NOOK.
8. Using 70% shading, shade the first letter of each topic (Religion, Education, etc.).
9. Manually kern the topics where necessary to even out spacing between letters.
10. Increase the letterspacing of the topics in order to extend the last line to the right margin.
11. Change the leading of the topics to -.2".
12. Preview your document.
13. Print one copy.
14. Close the file; save the changes.

    or

    Save the file; name it **BOOK1**.
15. Close the document window.

**Grand Opening
of the**

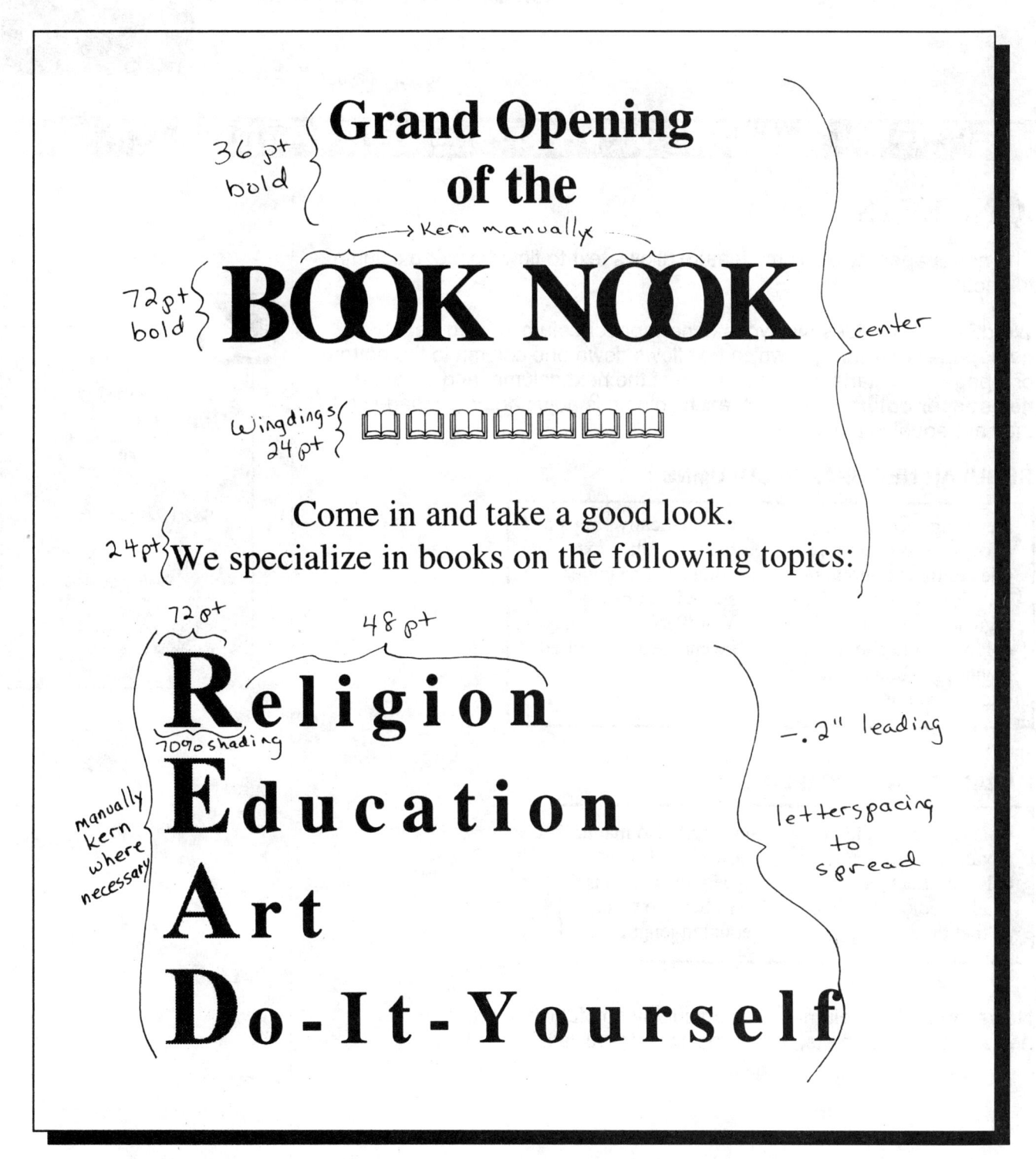

36 pt bold

→ Kern manually ←

BOOK NOOK

72 pt bold

center

Wingdings 24 pt: 📖 📖 📖 📖 📖 📖 📖

Come in and take a good look.
We specialize in books on the following topics:

24 pt

72 pt — 48 pt

Religion
70% shading

Education

manually kern where necessary

Art

Do-It-Yourself

−.2" leading

letterspacing to spread

Lesson 3 ▪ Exercise B

Lesson 4 ▪ Columns

EXERCISE 23
REGULAR NEWSPAPER COLUMNS

Column layout

CONCEPTS:

- The newspaper style column feature allows text to flow from one column to another.

- WordPerfect provides two types of newspaper columns: **regular newspaper columns,** in which text flows down one column to the bottom of a page then starts again at the top of the next column, and **balanced newspaper columns** in which each column is adjusted on the page so they are equal in length.

REGULAR NEWSPAPER COLUMNS

Newspaper columns allow text to flow from one column to another. This is an example of a regular newspaper column. When text reaches the bottom of one column, it automatically wraps to the top of the next column. The gutter space is set by WordPerfect, but may be changed, as desired.

BALANCED NEWSPAPER COLUMNS

This is an example of a balanced newspaper column. Each column is adjusted on the page so that they are equal in length. No matter how much text is typed, the columns will balance to be equal in length.

- Newspaper style columns are particularly helpful when creating newsletters, pamphlets, brochures, lists or articles.

To access Columns:

- Select **Layout**
- Select **Columns**
- Select **D**efine

OR

- Click Columns Define on Power Bar
- Specify number of columns you desire.

- The column feature is accessed by selecting Columns from the Layout main menu, then selecting Define.

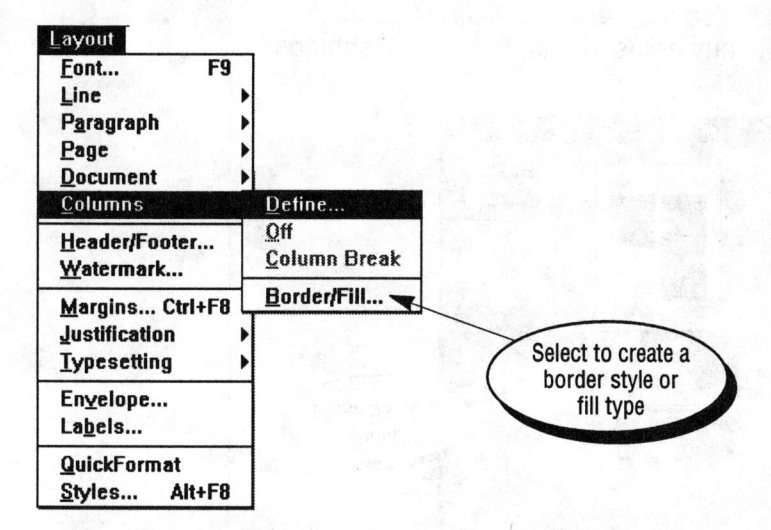

  Select to create a border style or fill type

- To create newspaper columns quickly without accessing the dialog box, click the Column Button on the Power Bar and specify the desired number of columns.

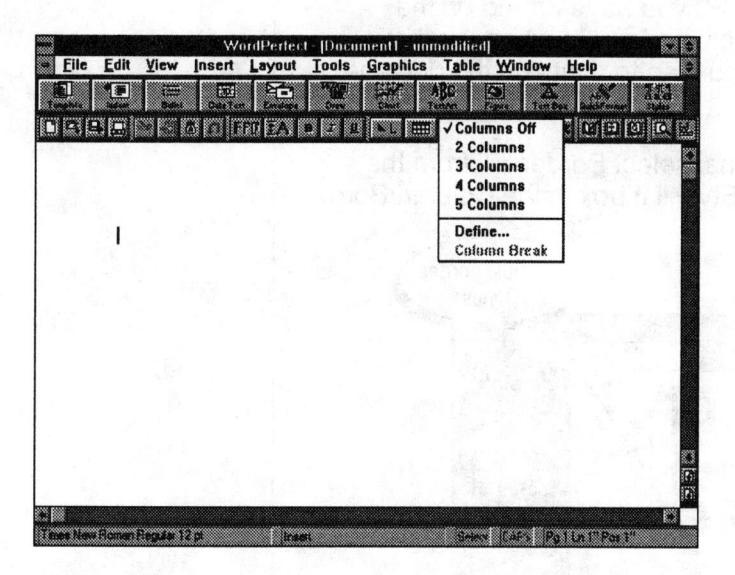

Lesson 4 ■ Exercise 23

- In the Columns dialog box which appears, define the number of columns and the column type you desire. You may also adjust the spacing between columns (sometimes called the *gutter* space), and the width of each column. If you choose not to make any adjustments, the default settings will apply.

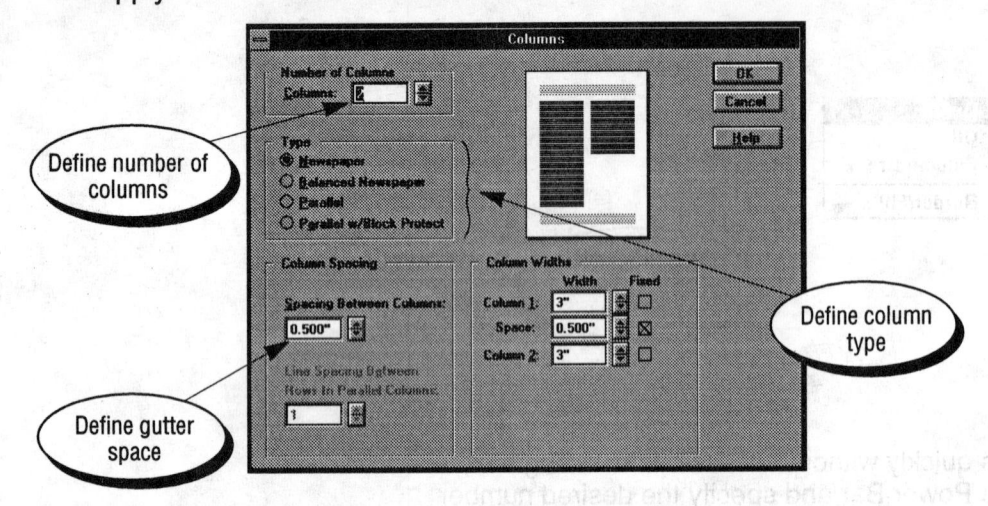

  Define number of columns
  Define gutter space
  Define column type

- After defining the columns and clicking OK, you have turned *on* the column feature. You must turn *off* the Column feature when you have completed your columnar document if you plan to continue the document without columns.

- To include a vertical line between columns, select Border/Fill from the drop-down menu, then click the Border Style list box in the Column Border dialog box.

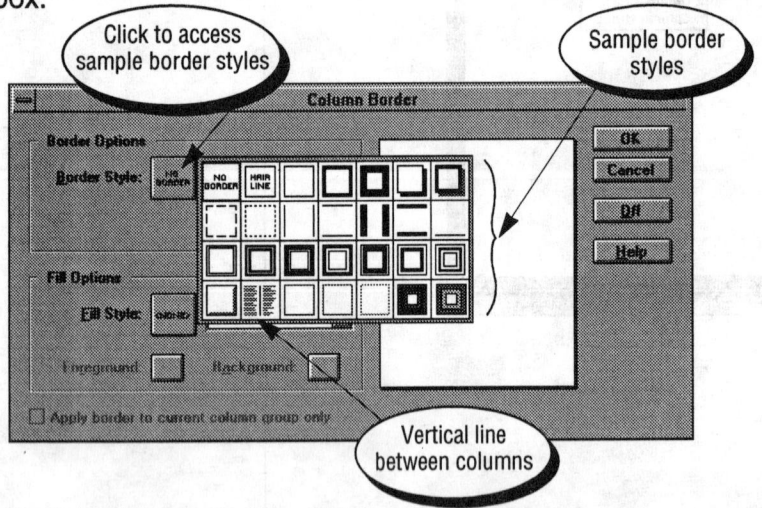

  Click to access sample border styles
  Sample border styles
  Vertical line between columns

Then, click the illustration showing a vertical line between columns from the samples which display.

- Columns may be created before or after typing text.

- You can retrieve text from a file into newspaper-style columns. When retrieving text from a file into columns, be sure your insertion point is within the column mode.

- Click the mouse in the desired column to move the insertion point quickly from column to column.

> In this exercise, you will create a two-column report using newspaper style columns.

84

EXERCISE DIRECTIONS:

1. Start with a clear screen.
2. Use the default margins.
3. Begin the exercise at the top of the screen. Type the title in sans serif 18 point bold as shown; press Enter twice.
4. Begin columns at Ln 1.51".
5. Set line spacing to 1.5".
6. Create the article on the right using a two column, *regular* newspaper style format. Use the default distance between columns.
7. Set column text to serif 14 point.
8. Insert a vertical line (border) between columns.
9. Full justify document text.
10. Spell check.
11. Preview your document.
12. Print one copy.
13. Save the exercise; name it **COCOA**.
14. Close the document window.

- NOTE: Since printers and typefaces available will vary, your text might run on to page two. If this occurs, adjust your line spacing or leading, or select another serif typeface so all text fits on one page.

CREATE TEXT COLUMNS (Newspaper)

1. Place insertion point where column is to begin.

   OR

   Select existing text to include in columns.

2. Click Column Button on Power Bar ..

   Click Define.

   OR

   Click **L**ayout .... `Alt` + `L`
   Click **C**olumns .... `C`
   Click **D**efine .... `D`

3. Click a Column Type:

   Newspaper .... `N`
   Balanced **N**ewspaper .... `B`
   *****P**arallel .... `P`
   Parallel w/Block Protect .... `A`

   *(Will be presented in Exercise 26)

5. Change none, either, or all of the following options as desired.

   a. Click **C**olumns .... `C`
   Type desired number of columns.
   b. Click **S**pacing Between Columns .... `S`
   Type desired distance.

6. Click **OK** .... `Enter`

INCLUDE VERTICAL LINE BETWEEN COLUMNS

1. Click **L**ayout .... `Alt` + `L`
2. Click **C**olumns .... `C`
3. Click **B**order/Fill .... `B`
4. Click Border Style list box.
5. Click a desired border style.
6. Click **OK** .... `Enter`

TURN OFF COLUMNS

1. Place insertion point where column is to be turned off.
2. Click **L**ayout .... `Alt` + `L`
3. Click **C**olumns .... `C`
4. Click O**f**f .... `F`

MOVE INSERTION POINT FROM COLUMN TO COLUMN

1. Click in desired column.

Lesson 4 ■ Exercise 23

CHOCOLATE

CHOCOLATE is probably the world's favorite food. You can drink it hot or cold, or eat it as a snack or as part of a meal. It is made into pies, cakes, cookies, candy, ice cream and even breakfast cereal. It is nourishing, energy-saving and satisfying.

Chocolate came to us from Mexico, by way of Europe. When the Spanish explorer Cortez arrived at the court of Montezuma, the Aztec Emperor, he found him drinking a cold, bitter drink called Chocolatl. It was made from seeds of the cacao tree, ground in water and mixed with spices. Montezuma gave Cortez the recipe and some cacao and vanilla beans. Cortez took them back to Spain, where the Spanish king and queen quickly improved the drink by adding sugar and having it served hot. For about a hundred years, chocolate was exclusively a royal Spanish treat. But once the secret leaked out, the upper classes in most of the European capitals were soon sipping hot chocolate. From Amsterdam, the Dutch settlers brought chocolate to the American colonies, and in 1765 a man named Baker started a chocolate mill near Boston.

A hundred years later, a man in Switzerland found a way to make solid sweet milk chocolate, and a great candy business was born. Chocolate companies like Nestle and Hershey need a lot of cacao beans. About one-third of the supply, over 350 thousand tons, is imported each year from the African country of Ghana. Ghana is the world's largest supplier of cacao beans. For many years, chocolate was made by hand. Now machines do most of the work.

THE CHOCOLATE FACTORY has been specializing in the finest chocolate products for over 50 years. Stop in and sample some of our outstanding chocolate delights.

NEXT EXERCISE!!

Lesson 4 ▪ Columns

EXERCISE 24

NEWSPAPER COLUMNS WITH CUSTOM WIDTHS

CONCEPTS:

- WordPerfect allows you to create columns with custom widths. As indicated in the Columns dialog box, the default width of a two-column table using default margins is 3"; the gutter space is .5". To change the column width, click the Column 1 and/or Column 2 text box and type the desired width.

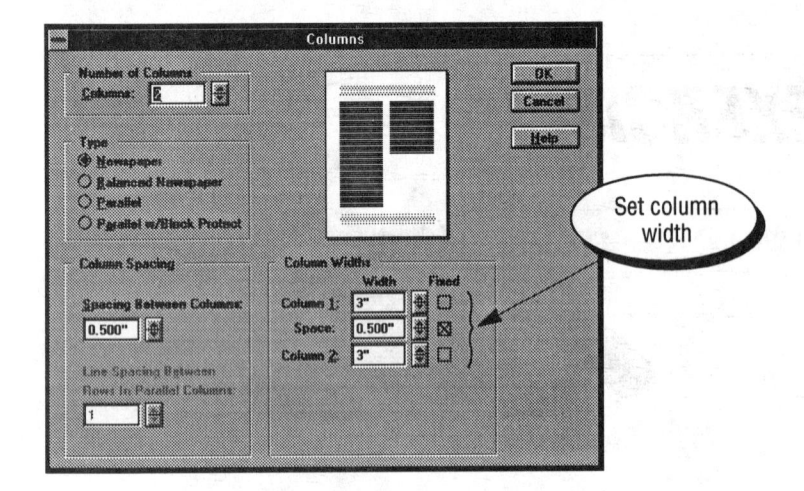

- Column widths may also be changed by dragging the left and right column width markers on the ruler bar. (Select <u>R</u>uler Bar from the <u>V</u>iew main menu).

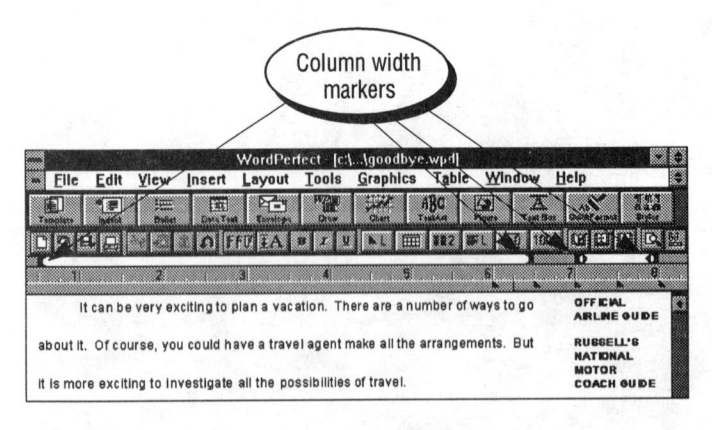

To change column width:

- Click **L**ayout
- Click **C**olumns
- Click **D**efine
- Click in **Column 1** and/or **Column 2** text box.
- Type desired width.

In this exercise, you will create an article using a two column newspaper style format in which the second column is narrower than the first. The text does not fill up the first column and requires you force the insertion point to the top of the second column. This is done by pressing Ctrl + ENTER when you are ready to move to the top of the second column. You will also change your line spacing back to single space when you begin the second column.

Remember to type the centered heading before you turn *on* the Columns feature.

88

EXERCISE DIRECTIONS:

1. Start with a clear screen.
2. Set .5" left and right margins.
3. Begin the exercise on Ln 1".

To create the heading:

4. Type the heading in sans serif 24 point bold italic.
   - Set the "V" to 56 points.
   - Kern the text to the right of the "V" to -0.120".
   - Set word spacing to 250% of optimal.

To make the &:

5. Type a "k".
   - Set the size to 72 point.
   - Change the font to Wingdings. (The k will change to an ampersand).
   - Change font shade to 40%.

6. Right align GUIDEBOOKS.
   - Set the size to 24 point bold.
   - Set the letter spacing to 200% of optimal.

To create the remaining exercise:

7. Begin the column text on Ln. 4.4".
8. Create a two-column, regular newspaper style format.
9. Change width of column one to 5"; change the width of column two to 1". Use the default distance between columns.
10. Set column one text to sans serif 12 point; set column two text to sans serif 10 point bold.
11. Full justify column 1 text.
12. Double space the first column; single space the second column.
13. Spell check.
14. Preview your document.
15. Print one copy.
16. Save the exercise; name it **GOODBYE.**
17. Close the document window.

# VACATION PLANNING & GUIDEBOOKS

It can be very exciting to plan a vacation. There are a number of ways to go about it. Of course, you could have a travel agent make all the arrangements. But it is more exciting to investigate all the possibilities of travel.

First, you can check the hundreds of guidebooks which can be purchased at bookstores. Then, you can send away to the government tourist offices in the country you are planning to visit. They will send you lots of free literature about the country --places to visit and a list of accommodations. The travel advertisements in your newspaper will tell you where the bargains are. After you have planned your trip by looking through the guidebooks listed to the right, ask your travel agent to do the actual booking.

Enjoy!

OFFICIAL AIRLINE GUIDE

RUSSELL'S NATIONAL MOTOR COACH GUIDE

STEAMSHIP GUIDE

HOTEL AND RESORT GUIDE

RESTAURANT, INN AND MUSEUM GUIDE

SIGHTSEEING GUIDE

FARM VACATIONS AND ADVENTURE TRAVEL GUIDE

CREATE COLUMNS with CUSTOM WIDTHS

1. Place insertion point where column is to begin.
2. Click **L**ayout .... Alt + L
3. Click **C**olumns C
4. Click **D**efine .... D
5. Click **Column 1** text box .... Alt + 1
6. Type desired width .... Enter
7. Click **Column 2** text box .... Alt + 2
8. Type desired width.

   NOTE: Repeat procedure for each additional column.

9. Click **OK** .... Tab , Enter

NEXT EXERCISE!!

Lesson 4 ▪ Columns

EXERCISE 25

BALANCED NEWSPAPER COLUMNS

CONCEPTS:

- Balanced newspaper columns adjust on the page as you type so that each column is equal in length.

BALANCED NEWSPAPER COLUMNS

> This is an example of a balanced newspaper column. Each column is adjusted on the page so that they are equal in length. No matter how much text is typed, the columns will balance to be equal in length.

- The procedure for creating balanced columns is the same as creating newspaper-style columns, except the column type must be changed to "Balanced Newspaper" in the Columns dialog box:

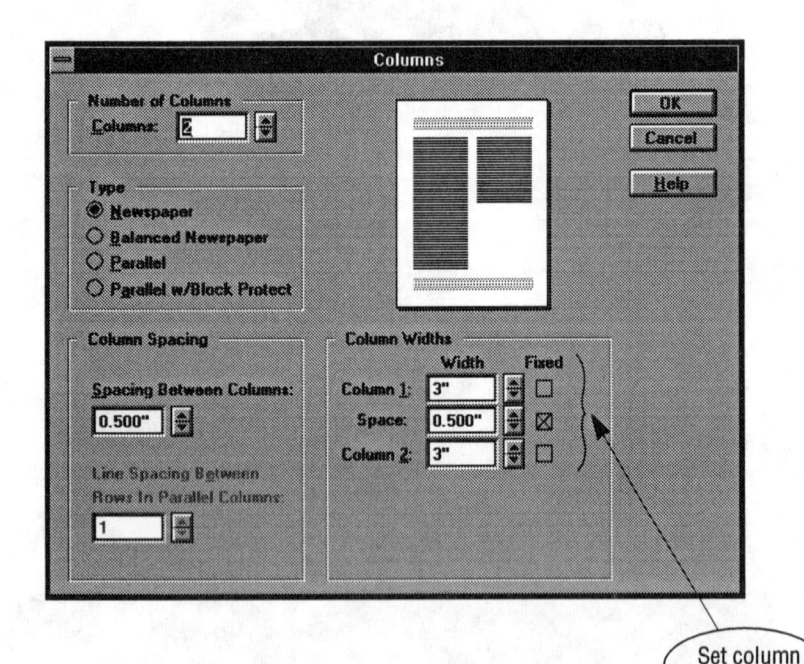

Set column widths

To create balanced newspaper columns:

- Click **L**ayout
- Click **C**olumns
- Click **D**efine
- Select **B**alanced Newspaper as the column Type in the Column dialog box.

The title should be centered before the column mode is turned on. Otherwise, the title will center in the first column.

In this exercise, you will create an article using a three column balanced newspaper column.

EXERCISE DIRECTIONS:

1. Start with a clear screen.
2. Set .5" left and right margins.
3. Begin the exercise on Ln 2"; center the heading.
4. Set the heading text to sans serif 18 point bold. Set the word and letter spacing to 200% of optimal. Press Enter twice after the heading.
5. Create the article on the right using a three column balanced newspaper style format. Use the default distance between columns.
6. Set the column text to serif 12 point and subheads to sans serif 14 point bold. Set letter spacing for subhead text to 85% of optimal.
7. Spell check.
8. Use any desired Wingding to precede the paragraphs below COOKING TIPS.
9. Center the page vertically (top to bottom).
10. Preview your document.
11. Print one copy.
12. Save the exercise; name it **COOK.**
13. Close the document window.

THE ART OF COOKING

Preparing a meal requires skill and patience. The results may mean the difference between eating just to exist and the satisfaction that comes from one of the major pleasures of life.

Cooking is an art. Every recipe should be prepared with tender, loving care and it should be one of the primary ingredients. A cook must develop a feeling for what each ingredient will do in a recipe.

QUALITY RAW MATERIALS
An outstanding meal must be prepared with high-quality raw materials, cooked simply but perfectly to enhance their natural flavor. It is important to plan your meal carefully. The menu should contain a contrast in textures, flavor and color. Salad should be served as a separate course. Use the best natural foods of the season and plan menus around them. Try not to use packaged frozen items if you can get them fresh. If you have a garden, use the fresh garden vegetables and fruit whenever you can.

It's a challenge to try to fit all the fruit--strawberries, raspberries, cantaloupes, watermelons, blueberries, blackberries, peaches, nectarines, cherries, and plums into the menu. You might want to use fresh herbs like dill, parsley, basil, or tarragon. Or, you might want to try a variety of garden lettuces and home-grown tomatoes like beefsteaks, plum and cherry-size.

COOKING TIPS
❖Never serve guests a dish which you have not prepared at least once before.
❖Do not serve too much on a plate.
❖The menu should contain a contrast in textures, flavor and color.

Are you getting hungry?

Lesson 4 ▪ Columns

EXERCISE 26

PARALLEL COLUMNS

CONCEPTS:

- WordPerfect's parallel Column feature allows text to move across the columns.

PARALLEL COLUMNS

Monday	Meeting with John Smith at 9:00 a.m.
Tuesday	Lunch appointment with Randy Grafeo to discuss merger.

- Parallel columns are particularly helpful when creating a list, script, itinerary, minutes of a meeting, or any other document in which text is read horizontally.

- The procedure for creating parallel columns is the same as creating newspaper style columns, except the column *Type* must be changed to Parallel in the Columns dialog box.

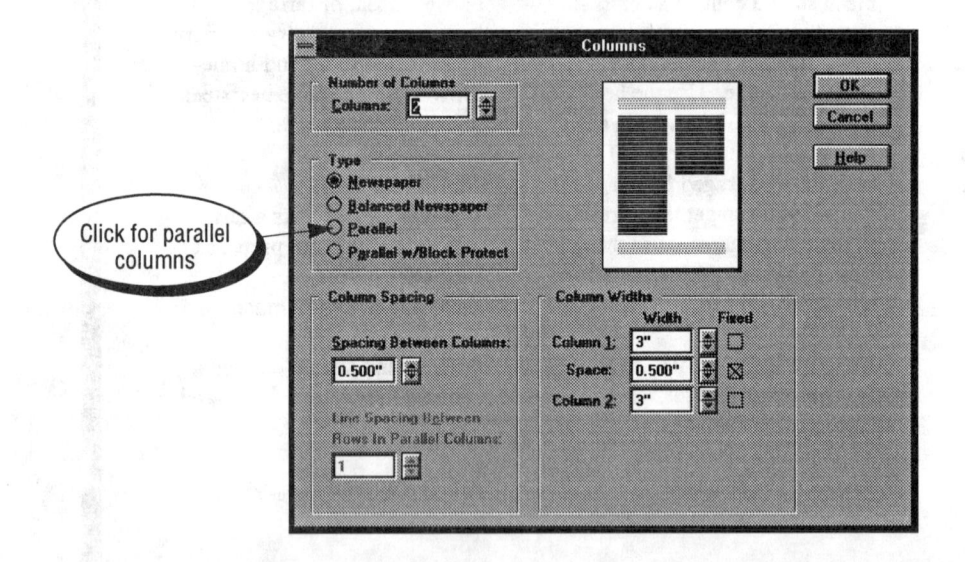

(Columns dialog box shown — "Click for parallel columns" points to the Parallel option under Type.)

- After text is entered in the first column, enter a hard page break (Ctrl + Enter) to force the insertion point to move to the next column. After text is entered in the second column, a hard page break must be entered to force the insertion point to the third column. A hard page break is also needed to move the insertion point back to the first column.

- Text cannot be retrieved into parallel columns.

✓ To create parallel columns:
- Select Parallel as the column Type in the Columns dialog box.

✏ Be sure to type right-aligned heading before you turn ON the column feature.

☞ In this exercise, you will create a resume using unequal parallel columns (the first column will be narrower than the second).

EXERCISE DIRECTIONS:

1. Start with a clear screen.
2. Set .5" left and right margins.
3. Begin the exercise on Ln 1".
4. Right align name and address information.
   - set name to all caps, sans serif 14 point bold; set first letter in each name to 24 point.
   - set letter spacing for the first and last name to 200% of optimal.
   - set address and phone information to 10 point italics.
   - Press Enter four times after the heading.
5. Create the exercise using a two column parallel style format starting on Ln 2.62".
6. Change the width of column one to 1.5"; change the width of column two to 5.5". Use the default distance between columns.
7. Type the text using serif 12 point.
8. Spell check.
9. Preview your document.
10. Print one copy.
11. Save the exercise; name it **RESUME**.
12. Close the document window.

JODY **A**BBATO
7652 Shore Road
Staten Island, NY 10314
Phone: (718) 654-5555
Fax: (718) 777-5555

CAREER OBJECTIVE:	To secure a responsible management position in a leading hotel chain with opportunities for growth.
EDUCATION	Sept. 1990-June 1994 *Cornell University*, School of Hotel Administration, Ithaca, NY 14850. Received a Bachelor of Science degree in Hotel Administration with a 3.5 overall average.
SKILLS	Keyboarding - 50 wpm IBM Personal Computer, knowledge of WordPerfect, Lotus, and Excel
EXPERIENCE	June 1994-August 1994 *Holiday Inn*, Richmond Avenue, Staten Island, NY 10314. Duties: Worked in accounting department as assistant to manager. June 1993-August 1993 *Marriott Hotel*, Broadway, New York, NY 10012. Duties: Data entry operator in accounting department.
ACTIVITIES	Vice President of Cornell University Management Society Member of Cornell University Student Senate Staff reporter for Cornell University *Management News*
REFERENCES	Dr. Stanley Simon, Professor of Management, Cornell University, Ithaca, NY 14850 (325) 456-8765. Ms. Maria Lopez, Manager, Holiday Inn, Richmond Avenue, Staten Island, NY 10314 (718) 876-3677.

Lesson 4 ■ Exercise 26

LESSON 4
SUMMARY EXERCISE A

EXERCISE DIRECTIONS:

1. Start with a clear screen.

2. Use the default margins.

3. Begin the exercise on Ln 1".

4. Center the heading; set it to serif 14 point bold. Press Enter three times.

5. Create the exercise using a three-column parallel style format. Use the default column widths and distance between columns.

6. Set column text to 12 point.

    - *NOTE:* *The font style used in this exercise is Engravers Gothic. You may, however, use any desired sans serif font. Don't confuse this font style with small caps, which looks very similar.*

7. After the Column feature is turned on, center the first column heading (NAME). Move the insertion point to the second column (Ctrl + Enter). Center the second column heading (ADDRESS). Move the insertion point to the third column and center RESPONSIBILITY.

8. After the last column item has been typed, turn *off* the column feature and type remaining text.

9. Spell check.

10. Preview your document.

11. Print one copy.

12. Save the exercise; name it **LIST**.

13. Close the document window.

In this exercise, you will create a name and address list using an equal parallel column format.

BUSINESS ASSOCIATION DIRECTORY

NAME	ADDRESS	RESPONSIBILITY
Adams, Brenda	765 West Avenue New York, NY 10098 222-555-5577	Convention
Appel, Peter	39 East 96 Street Brooklyn, NY 22224 728-555-5588	Publicity
Barnes, Desmond	20 West 66 Street New York, NY 20054 222-555-6666	Newsletter
Brady, Edward	21 Dolin Road Bronx, NY 20456 222-555-3333	Membership
Brown, Donna	2209 Broadway New York, NY 20299 222-555-2222	Political Action
Chou, David	76 River End Road Queens, NY 22322 728-555-0000	Convention/ Registration
Hussin, Ahmed	225 Racliff Street Bronx, NY 20456 222-555-1111	Membership
LeChamp, Renee	200 East 77 Street New York, NY 22023 222-555-8888	Newsletter
*Sovino, Rosemarie	76 Kings Highway Brooklyn, NY 22223 728-555-2323	Publicity

*In addition to Publicity, Rosemarie Sovino will be in charge of greeting guests and making sure they have the necessary registration materials to be admitted to seminars.

LESSON 4
SUMMARY EXERCISE B

EXERCISE DIRECTIONS:

1. Start with a clear screen.
2. Set .5" left and right margins and .3" top and bottom margins.
3. Begin the exercise at the top of the screen.
4. Right align the heading. Use a sans serif font in 36 point bold.
    - NOTE: The font style used in the heading is Swis721 BlkEx BT.

    Use a 40% shade for all but the first letter of each word.
5. Using the Wingding font and the letter "t", create a horizontal "line" of diamonds below the heading in 24 point. Press Enter once.
6. Right align "A Publication of....." in sans serif 18 point.
    - NOTE: The font style used is Humanst521 Cn BT.
    - Press Enter once.
    - Create the diamonds between words in 18 point.
7. Using the Wingding font and the letter "t", create a horizontal line of diamonds across the page (as shown) in 10 point. Press Enter twice.
8. Type the headline in serif 24 point bold. Press Enter once.
9. Type the author's name in sans serif 12 point. Press Enter twice.
10. Create two balanced newspaper columns. Set column text to serif 12 point.
11. Type and center subheading, "Weekly Training Pointers," in serif 18 point bold.
12. When you have completed the first two columns, turn off the column feature. Enter once.
13. Create 4 parallel columns. Set column widths as follows:

    Col 1:   1"

    Col 2:   1"

    Col 3:   2.4"

    Col 4:   1.25"

    Space between columns: .5"
14. Set column heading text to serif 10 point bold. Left align headings within the columns.
15. Left align column text; remove bold.
16. Spell check.
17. Preview your document.
18. Print one copy.
19. Save the exercise; name it **RACE**.
20. Close the document window.

A newsletter is a document used by an organization to communicate information about an event, news of general interest, or information regarding new products.

Newsletters consist of several parts:

NAMEPLATE- may include the name of the newsletter, the organization publishing the newsletter, the logo (a symbol or distinctive type style used to represent the organization.

DATELINE- includes the volume number, issue number and the date.

HEADLINE- title preceding each article.

BODY TEXT- the text of the article.

In this exercise, you will create a newsletter using two balanced newspaper columns, then change to four parallel columns. You will also use gray shading and Wingdings in the exercise.

RACING NEWS

A Publication of Cycling Clubs of America ♦♦♦♦♦ Summer 1994

200 Riders Join Unknown Coast Tour
by Miles Davis

On Friday, July 15th, the tenth annual Tour of the Unknown Coast bicycle race began under foggy skies. Over 200 professional riders turned out from all over the Northwest for this century competition billed as California's toughest. The course starts in the Victorian village of Ferndale and then proceeds up the Grizzly Bluff road, over the Blue Slide Hills and down into the Rio Dell. It continues along the Eel River, through Scotia, and then twists along the Avenue of the Giants, Rockefeller Forest and Bull Creek. After six miles of coastline, the route starts up the infamous, narrow 22 percent grade known to bicyclists as the *wall*. After dropping into Capetown, the course follows the mountainous coastal terrain, dubbed the endless hills, back into Ferndale.

Lars Engleman, Karl Schaffer and Grant LaMonde broke away from the pack going up Panther Gap, and moved into a 25-second lead. The stage was set for a LaMonde victory. He sprinted down the final grade to a 5-second lead over the breakaway group. LaMonde was immersed in the enthusiastic support of the crowd. I couldn't have done it without my teammates. Most people don't recognize cycling as a team sport," said LaMonde.

Weekly Training Pointers

In my last article, I discussed some ways that those with limited time to train might better use that time. Any good training schedule needs to contain the basic elements. These are intervals, long endurance rides, and some days committed to shorter, low gear spinning rides for recovery.

So, assuming you have a good endurance base of at least 1,000 miles in, and you are ready to begin adding intervals to your weekly program, let's take a look at a typical week.

DAY	WORKOUT TYPE	DISTANCE/SPEED/TIME	TARGET HEART RATE
MON.	Recovery	30-35 miles at constant, steady pace or 90 minutes of "spin" in low gears if you raced Sunday	75% of training effect rate
TUES.	Intervals	Diversify weekly. Select from timed repeats, time-trial simulations, hill climbing, and all-out sprints. Warm up with 10 mile spin; cool down with 5 mile spin.	Varied
WED.	Recovery	30-35 miles at constant, steady pace. Low gear spinning.	60-65% of training effect rate
THURS.	Endurance	60-70 miles at constant, steady pace. Pedal without stopping, i.e., no coasting.	Start at 60-70% of training effect rate
FRI.	Rest	Prepare the bike for weekend races. Take a short spin to loosen up your legs.	

Lesson 4 ■ Exercise B

LESSON 4
SUMMARY EXERCISE C

EXERCISE DIRECTIONS:

1. Start with a clear screen.

2. Use the default margins.

3. Center the page top to bottom.

4. Right-align the heading in sans serif 36 point bold. Unbold and italicize the second line.

5. Create the exercise using a three column, parallel style format.

6. Use the default column widths and distance between columns.

7. To create each tip:

   - Type and c*enter* each number in sans serif 100 point bold.

   - Change font to 12 point italic.

   - Press Enter once.

   - Set justification to *All* for subhead.

   - Type subhead.

   - Press Enter once.

   - Change font to serif.

   - Set justification to *Left* for paragraph text.

   - Type paragraph text.

   - Press Ctrl + Enter to advance to next column.

8. Type remaining tips using procedures outlined in step 7.

9. Preview your file.

10. Save the exercise; name it **WORKTIPS.**

11. Close the document window.

In this exercise, you will create a flyer using parallel columns. You will also gain practice using alignments and changing font faces, styles and sizes.

SIX TIPS FOR THE *WORKAHOLIC*

1
SLOW DOWN
Make a conscious effort to eat, talk, walk and drive more slowly. Give yourself extra time to get to appointments so you are not always rushing.

2
LEARN TO DELEGATE
Let others share the load-- you don't have to do everything yourself. You will have more energy and the end result will be better for everyone.

3
DRAW THE LINE
When you are already overloaded and need more personal time, do not take on any other projects. You will be just causing yourself more stress.

4
CUT YOUR HOURS
Be organized, but do not let your schedule run your life. Also, try to limit yourself to working eight hours a day--and not a minute more.

5
CARE FOR YOURSELF
Eat properly, get enough sleep and exercise regularly. Do what you can so that you are healthy, both mentally and physically.

6
TAKE BREAKS
Take frequent work breaks: Short walks or meditating for a few minutes can help you unwind and clear your head.

Lesson 5 ▪ Graphics Boxes

EXERCISE 27

CREATING A FIGURE BOX

CONCEPTS:

- **Graphics** are design elements, such as pictures (art), charts, and lines, used to make a visual statement. The ability to combine graphics and text enables you to create documents such as letterheads, newsletters, brochures and flyers in which pictures contribute to the effectiveness of the message.

- WordPerfect places each graphic image in a "box" which is referred to as a *graphics box*. A graphics box can contain a figure, text or an equation. (Text boxes will be covered in Exercise 28; equations will not be covered in this text). Note the two graphic boxes below.

FIGURE BOX

TEXT BOX

This is an example of a text box. Default border options are "thick" for top and bottom and none for the sides.

- The **Figure Box** is commonly used to place images, diagrams, or charts. By default, a figure box contains an image enclosed in a single-line border. You can resize and reposition the figure within your document, and frequently you can edit the figure itself.

- WordPerfect provides a selection of graphic image files which are often referred to as "clip art." These files include not only pictures, but also borders and watermarks (watermarks will be covered in Exercise 37).

- By default, these files are stored in the \WPWIN60\GRAPHICS directory. WordPerfect graphics are named with a .WPG extension.

- The clip art images that are part of the WordPerfect Program are illustrated in Appendix A. You can, however, purchase disks with other graphics and import them into your document.

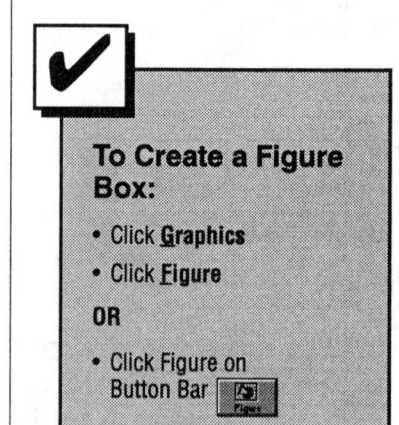

✔

To Create a Figure Box:

- Click **Graphics**
- Click **Figure**

OR

- Click Figure on Button Bar

- You select the desired graphic file from the Insert Image dialog box. You may use the View feature to preview a graphic before selecting it.

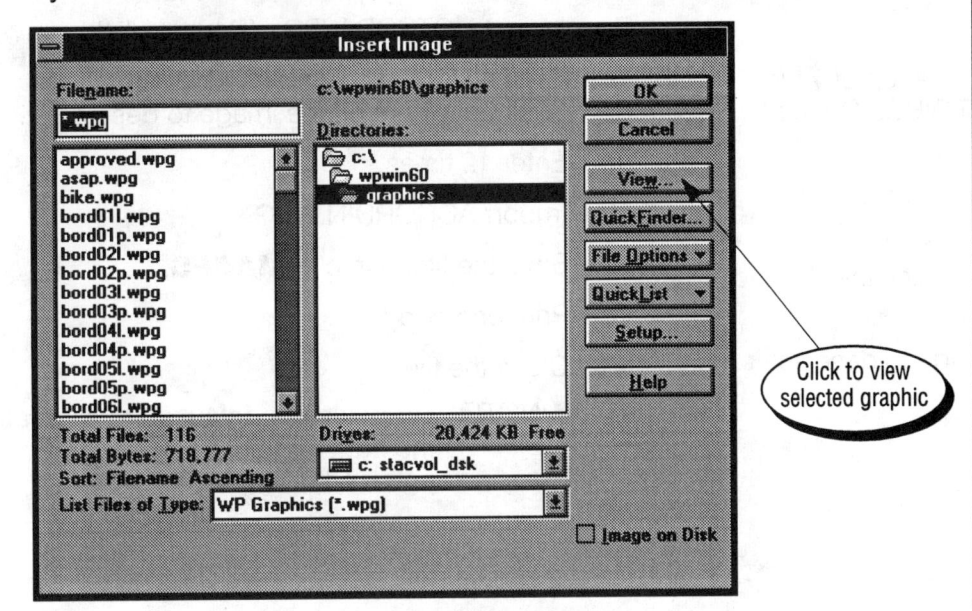

Click to view selected graphic

- When a graphic is first imported, it displays enclosed in a box with "sizing handles." The Graphics Feature Bar also appears, giving you access to the most commonly used graphics features.

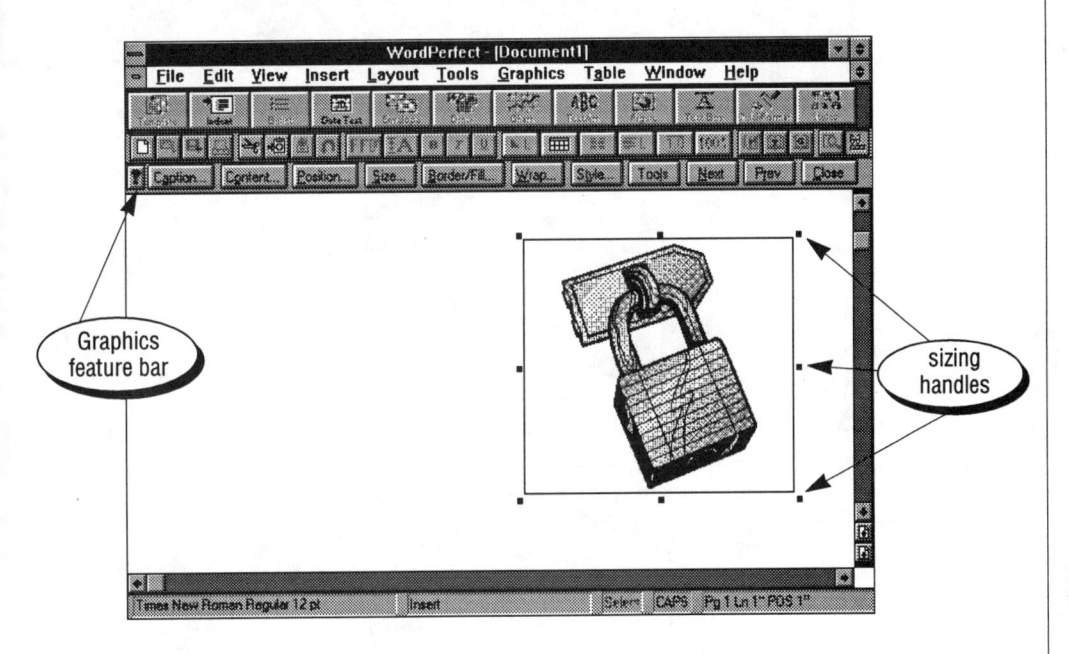

Graphics feature bar

sizing handles

- When the graphic figure first appears, it is aligned at the right margin and pre-sized by WordPerfect. (Note exercise illustration). The default size of a graphic varies, depending on the graphic selected.

- You can reduce, enlarge, stretch, move or delete the graphic figure when the sizing handles are displayed. The sizing handles indicate that the graphic is "selected" and is in an edit mode. You will learn to edit the graphic in the next exercise.

> In this exercise, you will create three graphics, using the default position and size.

Lesson 5 ▪ Exercise 27

EXERCISE DIRECTIONS:

1. Start with a clear screen.
2. With the insertion point at the top of your screen, select POINTOUT.WPG. Do not import it.
3. Click View to preview the image before importing it.
4. Import the image. (Double-click the desired graphic file).
5. Click anywhere off the image to deselect it (remove handles).
6. Enter 21 times.
7. Import HOTROD.WPG. (Double-click filename.)
8. Click anywhere off the image to deselect it.
9. Enter 12 times.
10. Import ACCORDIN.WPG.
11. Save the file; name it **IMAGES**.
12. Print one copy.
13. Close the file.
    - *NOTE:* Graphics are defaulted to align at the right margin. Each image is presized differently.

TO IMPORT A GRAPHIC

F11

1. Click Figure on Button Bar .... [Figure]

   OR

   Click **G**raphics .... Alt + G
   Click **F**igure .... F

2. Double-click desired graphic file.

   NOTE: Click Vie**w** .... Alt + W
   to preview image.

3. Click **OK**.

Lesson 5 ■ Exercise 27

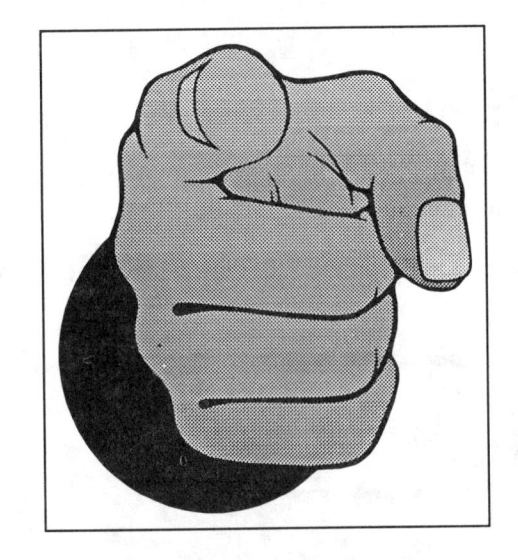

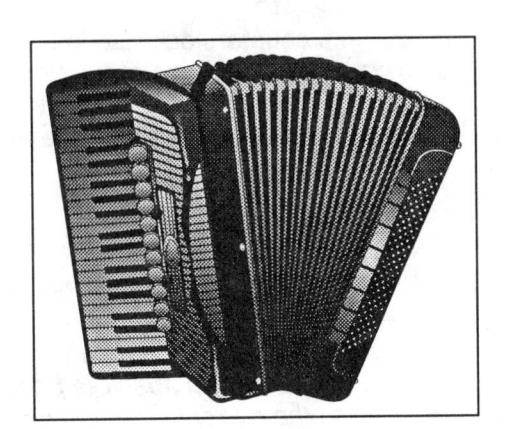

Lesson 5 ▪ Graphics Boxes

EXERCISE 28

▪ CREATE A TEXT BOX ▪ ROTATE A TEXT BOX

CONCEPTS:

- **The Text Box** is typically used for setting off special text such as tables, charts, sidebars and callouts.

- WordPerfect automatically applies a thick top and bottom border to the text box.

This is a text box. Default border options are "thick" for top and bottom and none for the sides.

- Like a graphics figure box, when the text box first appears, it is aligned at the right margin and presized by WordPerfect. (Note exercise).

- You can resize and reposition the text box within your document, and you can edit the text within the box. The Graphics Feature Bar enables you to specify position, size, and wrap options for your text box as you would for a figure box. You may also size and move the box on screen with the mouse. These topics will be covered in the next exercise.

- You may rotate the box contents counterclockwise in 90 degree increments. You may also want to set the size of the box to Size to Content. Sizing text to the content will size the box to the length of the text (providing that the text is not longer than the margins).

This box will be rotated 90 degrees.

NOTE: In this and subsequent exercises, you will be directed to begin text at a particular vertical location on the page. Use the Advance feature to accomplish this direction. The Advance feature is used to place text at an absolute position on a page or at a position relative to the current insertion point position. For these exercises, set **advance measurements from the Top of Page**. Note keystrokes below.

✓

To Create a Text Box:
- Click **Graphics**
- Click **T**ext

OR

- Click Text Box on Button Bar [Text Box].

☛ In this exercise, you will create two text boxes, one of which is rotated.

CONTINUED...

Lesson 5 ▪ Exercise 28

Lesson 5 ■ Exercise 28

EXERCISE DIRECTIONS:

1. Start with a clear screen.
2. Use the default margins.
3. With your insertion point at the top of the screen, create the first text box and type the text as shown. Use 14 point for the word "size" and any desired font for the word "style." Set line height (Layout, Line, Height) to 0.257". Do not click off handles.
4. Size the box to content. (Click Size, Size to Content for Width and Height option.)
5. Rotate the box 90 degrees.
6. Use the Advance feature to bring the insertion point to Ln 4.15" (from top of page).
7. Create the second text box and type the text as shown.
8. Use the Advance feature to bring the insertion point to Ln 6.11" (from top of page).
9. Create the third text box. Do not click off handles.
10. Size the box to content.
11. Rotate the box 180 degrees.
12. Use the Advance feature to bring the insertion point to Ln 7.29" (from top of page).
13. Create the fourth text box. Do not click off handles. Size the box to content.
14. Rotate the box 270 degrees.
15. Print one copy.
16. Save the file; name it **TEXTBOX**.
17. Close the document window.

CREATE A TEXT BOX

Alt+F11

1. Place insertion point where you want text box.
2. Click **G**raphics .... Alt + G
3. Click **T**ext Box .... T
   A text box appears with active insertion point.
4. Type text into box.
   Adjust box position, size and caption as you would a figure box, if desired.
5. Click **C**lose C

ROTATE TEXT BOX

1. Select text box to rotate.
   OR
   Click **G**raphics .... Alt + G
   Click **E**dit Box .... E
2. Click **S**ize .... Alt + Shift + S
3. Click Width: Si**z**e to Content I
4. Click Height: Si**z**e to Content .... Z
5. Click OK .... Enter
6. Click **C**ontent .... Alt + Shift + O
7. Select desired degree of rotation:
   No Rotation .... N
   90 Degrees 9
   180 Degrees 1
   270 Degrees 2
8. Click OK .... Enter
9. Click **C**lose .... Alt + Shift + C

ADVANCE

NOTE: You cannot advance text past a page break onto another page.

1. Click **L**ayout .... Alt + L
2. Click **T**ypesetting .... T
3. Click **A**dvance .... A
4. Choose a horizontal or vertical advance position.
5. Click horizontal or vertical text box.
6. Type a desired distance.
7. Click OK .... Enter

90-degree rotated text box

This text box will contain entered text. You can change the font SIZE and *style* while you are entering the text, or you can edit the box later and make the changes to the text at that time.

180-degree rotated text

270-degree rotated text

Lesson 5 ▪ Graphics Boxes

EXERCISE 29

CHANGE PRINT QUALITY

CONCEPTS:

- Resolution or (print quality) refers to the crispness of detail in an image. It is measured in dots per inch (DPI), that is, the number of dots that can be printed on a one-inch line. The higher the number of DPI, the better the resolution (or print quality) of a graphic image. Some printers have the ability to print more dots per inch than others, so they can produce a higher resolution image when printing at their highest quality. Most printers have the ability to print at different quality levels. Printers are a determining factor in the quality of your graphic image output. *If you are using a laser printer, you may not see a difference between high, medium and draft quality output.*

- WordPerfect's print quality feature lets you select from *high medium*, and *draft* quality. The higher the print quality (resolution), the longer it takes to print, dramatically so with graphics. Draft quality is used for rough draft printing; high quality is used for important final products.

High

Medium

Draft

To change print quality:

- Click **Print** button on Power bar

  OR

- Click **File**
- Click **Print**
- Click **Print Quality List Box**.
- Select desired quality level.

In this exercise, you will print one copy of a previously created graphic image using a different print quality.

- Print quality may be changed in the Print Dialog Box:

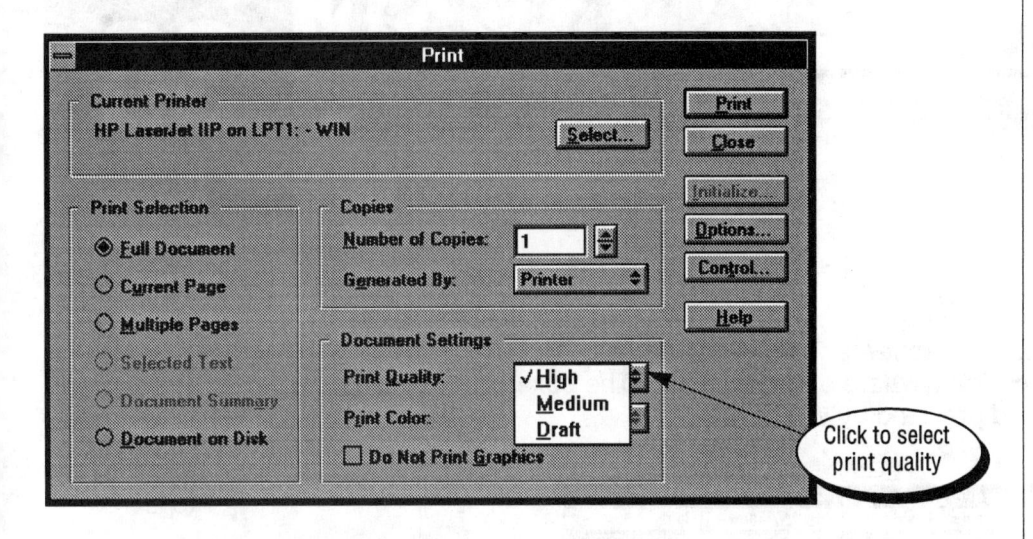

- Changing print quality does not leave a code in the document; however, print quality settings do stay with the document when it is saved.

EXERCISE DIRECTIONS:

- *NOTE: If you are using a laser printer, skip this exercise since you will not be able to see a difference in the output.*

1. Open **IMAGES**.
2. Change the print quality to Draft.
3. Print one copy.
4. Change the print quality to Medium.
5. Print one copy.
    - *NOTE: Compare the printouts in this exercise with the printout from Exercise 27. Note the difference in print qualities.*
6. Close the file; save the changes.

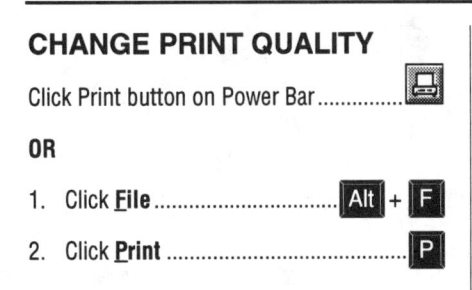

CHANGE PRINT QUALITY

Click Print button on Power Bar..............

OR

1. Click **File** .... Alt + F
2. Click **Print** .... P

3. Click **Print Quality** list box. .... Q
4. Select print quality option:
   - **High** .... H
   - **Medium** .... M
   - **Draft** .... D
5. Click **OK** .... Enter

Lesson 5 ▪ Exercise 29   111

Lesson 5 ▪ Graphics Boxes

EXERCISE 30

EDIT A GRAPHICS BOX: SIZE, POSITION (MOVE), DELETE, COPY

CONCEPTS:

- When a graphics box is created, it appears with sizing handles. (To remove the sizing handles, click anywhere off the graphic.) The box is aligned at the right margin and presized by WordPerfect.

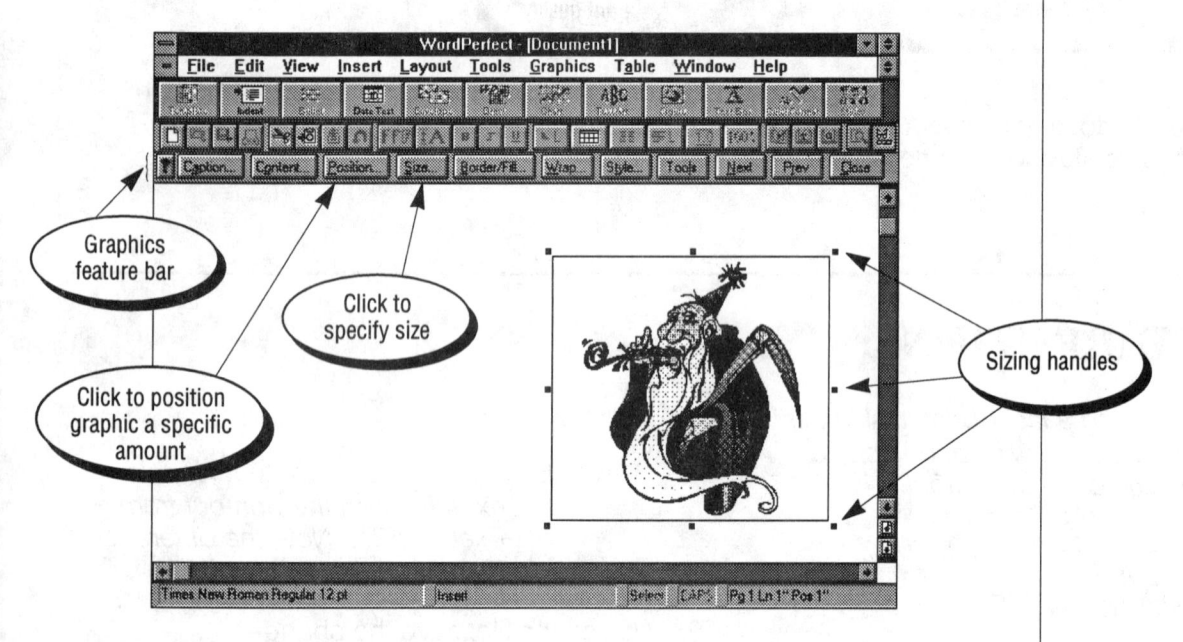

Selecting a Graphics Box

- The sizing handles must be displayed to edit the image or text box ; that is, to delete or copy it, or to change its size or position.

- Displaying the handles on a graphics box is referred to as *selecting* it.

Sizing a Graphics Box

- **To size a graphics box** using the mouse, point to one of the sizing handles. When the pointer becomes a double-headed arrow, drag the side or corner of the box to the desired size. Or, you may click the Size Button on the Feature Bar and specify the size of the box in the Box Size dialog box.

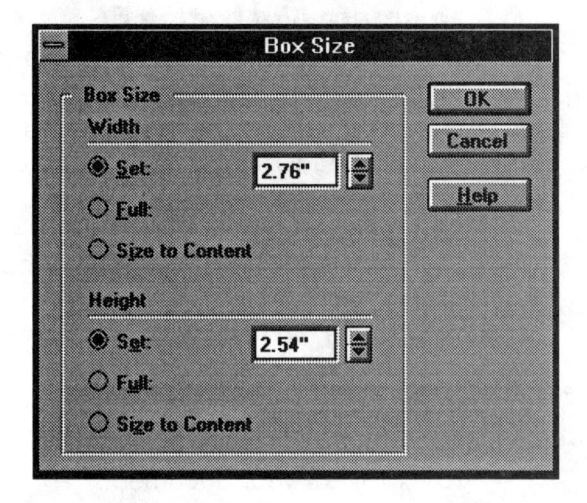

Positioning (Moving) a Graphics Box

- **To position a graphics box** using the mouse, point, click and hold down the mouse button within the selected box. When the pointer becomes a four-headed arrow, drag the box to the desired location. Or, you may click the Position Button on the Feature Bar and specify the desired horizontal or vertical position in the Box Position dialog box.

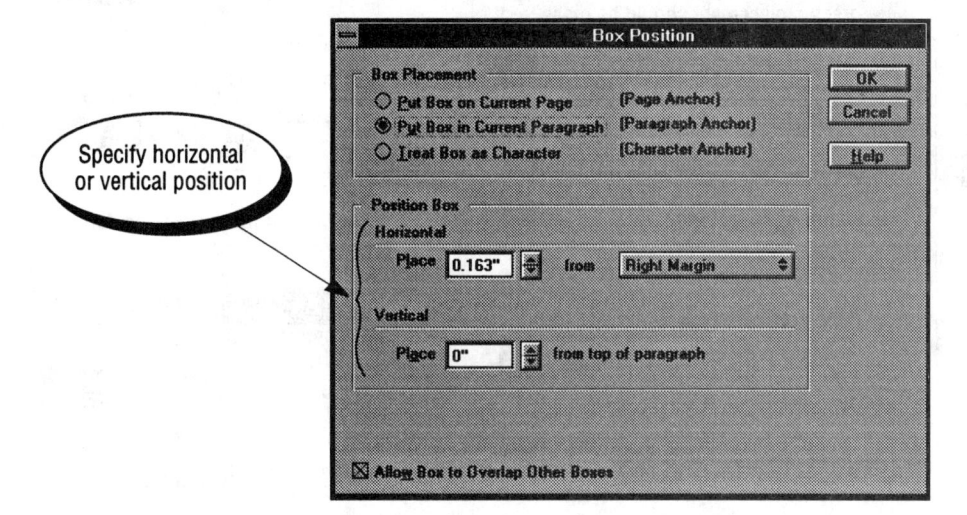

Specify horizontal or vertical position

Deleting a Graphics Box

- **To delete a graphics box**, select the box (so the sizing handles appear) and press the Delete key.

Copying a Graphics Box

- **To copy a graphics box**, select the box, select Copy from the Edit main menu. Position the insertion point where the copied box should appear. Then, select Paste from the Edit main menu. Use this feature when you wish to make an exact duplicate of the box size and content.

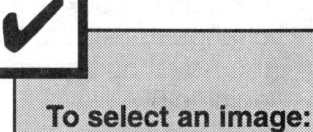

To select an image:
- Point to the image.
- Click once.

To Quick Copy a Graphic:
- Select the graphic.
- Press **Ctrl + C**
- Move insertion point to new location and click once.
- Press **Ctrl + V**

In this exercise, you will create several figure boxes and one text box. You will then align them left, right and center. You will also size, move, delete and copy them using both the mouse and the dialog boxes to do so.

Lesson 5 ■ Exercise 30

Lesson 5 ■ Exercise 30

EXERCISE DIRECTIONS:

To create illustration A:

1. Start with a clear screen.
2. With the insertion point at the top of your screen, create a figure box and import BUCK.WPG.
3. Position the box horizontally 3.5" from the left edge of the page; size it to 1" wide by 1" high. Use the Advance feature to bring your insertion point to 2.5".
4. Create a second figure box and import the graphic, CHEETAH.WPG.
5. Position the box 0" from the left margin and change the size to 2" wide by 2" high. Use the Advance feature to bring your insertion point to 5".
6. Create a third figure box and import the graphic, FATHRTME.WPG.
7. Change the size to 3" wide by 3" high.
8. Use the Advance feature to bring your insertion point to 8.47".
9. Create a text box and enter the text as shown. Change the width to 2.5" wide; use the default height. Position it 0" from Center of Paragraph.
10. Save the exercise; name it **PICTURE**. Do not close the document.

To create illustration B:

11. Select the first graphics box and delete it.
12. Select the second graphics box. *Using the mouse*, stretch it to extend between the left and right margins and move it to the top of the page.
13. Select the third graphics box and, *using the mouse*, move it to the center below the cheetah.
14. Select the text box and size it To Content (text will fit on one line).
15. Copy the box once and place it below the other as shown.
16. Preview your document.
17. Print one copy.
18. Close the file; save the changes.

SELECT A GRAPHICS BOX

Shift+F11

Click graphic.

OR

Click **G**raphics .... Alt + G

Click **E**dit Box .... E

DELETE A GRAPHICS BOX

1. Select graphic to delete.
2. Press Delete key.

POSITION A GRAPHICS BOX

1. Select the graphic.
2. Click **P**osition on .... Alt + Shift + P
   Graphic Feature Bar.

OR

Click right mouse button on graphic and choose **P**osition.

To Position Horizontally:

a. Click **H**orizontal Place
   text box .... Alt + L

b. Type desired horizontal measurement.

c. Click list box and select *from* where graphic placement should be measured:

- **L**eft Edge of Page L
- Left **M**argin .... M
- **R**ight Margin .... R
- **C**enter of Paragraph C

To Position Vertically:

a. Click **V**ertical Place
   text box .... Alt + A

b. Type desired vertical measurement.

3. Click OK .... Enter

SIZE A GRAPHICS BOX

1. Select the graphic.
2. Click **S**ize on .... Alt + Shift + S
   Graphics Feature Bar.

OR

Click right mouse button on graphic and choose **S**ize.

To set height and width:

a. Click **S**et (Width) text box .. Alt + S

b. Type desired width.

c. Click **S**et (Height) text box . Alt + E

d. Type desired height.

To have graphic fill page:

Click .... Alt + F, and/or Alt + U
Full for Width and Height

To have WordPerfect determine optimum width and height:

Click .... Alt + I, and/or Alt + Z
Size to Content for Width and Height.

3. Click OK .... Enter

COPY A GRAPHICS BOX

Ctrl + C, Ctrl + V

1. Select the graphic.
2. Click **E**dit .... Alt + E
3. Click **C**opy C
4. Click at location on page where copied graphic should appear.
5. Click **E**dit .... Alt + E
6. Click **P**aste .... P

ILLUSTRATION A

This is a text box which will be edited.

ILLUSTRATION B

This is a text box which will be edited.

This is a text box which will be edited.

Lesson 5 ■ Exercise 30   115

Lesson 5 ▪ Graphics Boxes

EXERCISE 31

COMBINE A GRAPHICS BOX WITH TEXT (ANCHOR TYPES)

CONCEPTS:

Change Graphics Box Position (Anchor Type)

- When a graphics box is combined with text, you must specify the way you want the graphic box to be anchored to the text. This option may be accessed by clicking the Position button on the Graphics Feature Bar.

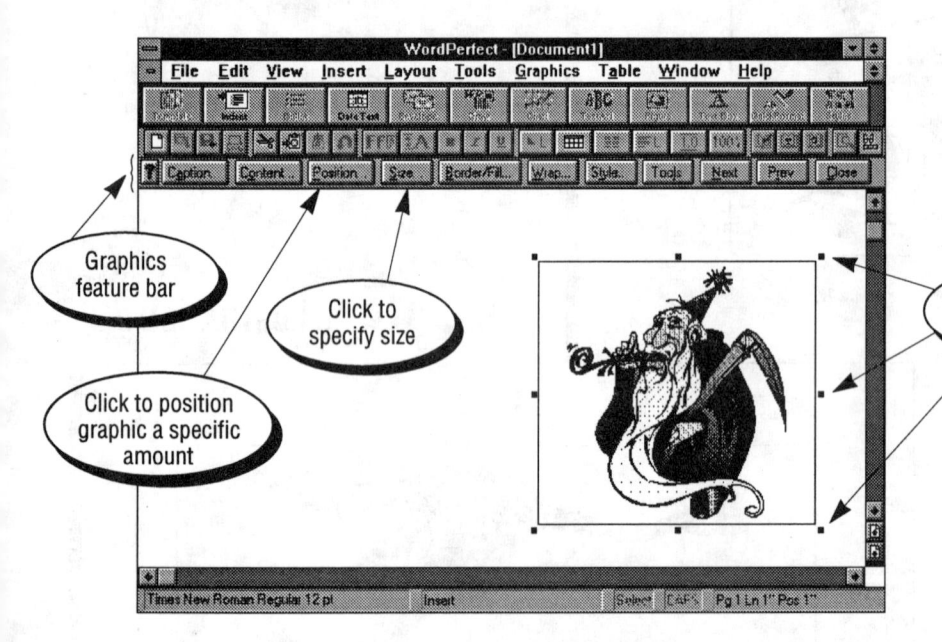

- In the Box Position dialog box which follows, you have three anchor options:

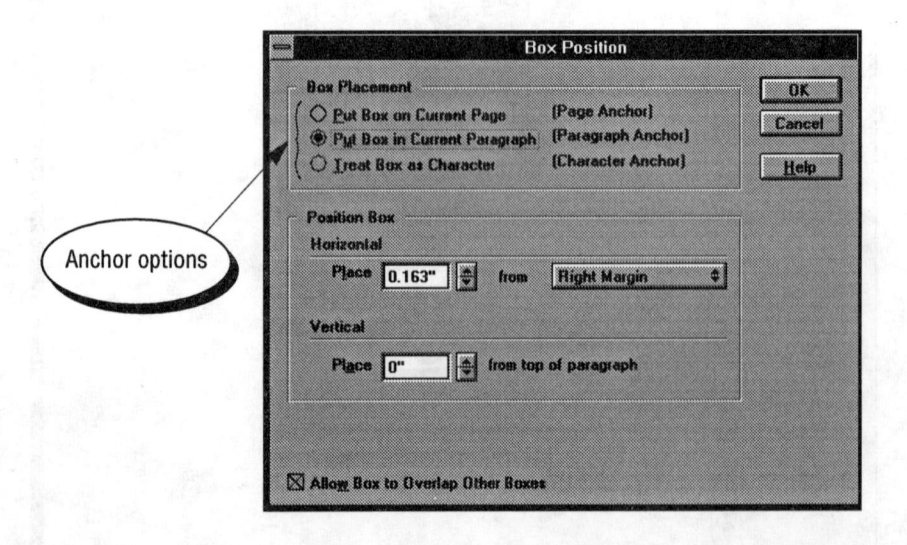

To change anchor position:
- Select the graphic.
- Click **Graphics**
- Click **Edit Box**
- Click the Position button on the Feature Bar [Position...]
- Make the necessary changes in the Box Position dialog box which follows.

Put Box on Current Page (*Page Anchor*) - permits text to be positioned at a fixed location on the page. The graphics box will remain in that position regardless of any changes made to the document. The graphics box can be horizontally positioned in relation to the margins, the columns (if columns are present), or the left edge of the paper.   Graphic boxes can be vertically positioned at the *top of page, top, bottom, or center of margins.* Note illustration below:

Horizontal position: left
Vertical Position: top

Horizontal position: right
Vertical Position: top

Horizontal Position: Center
Vertical Position: Center

Horizontal Position: Left
Vertical Position: Bottom

Horizontal Position: Right
Vertical Position: Bottom

Put Box in Current Paragraph *(Paragraph Anchor)* - permits the graphics box to stay with the paragraph preceding it. Then, if you add/delete material from the document or move the paragraph, the graphic box will move, too. This is the default. The box can be placed down from the top of the paragraph by specifying the desired amount of inches in the Vertical Place text box. The horizontal position is used to place the box at the left edge of the page, at the left or right margin, or in the center of a paragraph.   Note illustration below:

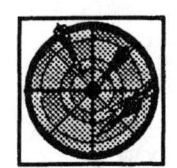

This paragraph anchor illustration has graphics boxes placed in two locations. The dartboard is positioned at the left margin horizontally, and 0.001" from the top of the paragraph vertically. The group graphic is positioned right horizontally (at 0" from the right margin) and 1" from the top of the paragraph vertically. The paragraph uses justified text.

Treat Box as Character *(Character Anchor)* - permits graphic boxes to stay with a character on a line. The box will move right and wrap if necessary as new text is added before the box. Since the character anchor box is automatically placed after the character to its left (at the location of the insertion point when created), the horizontal position is not used. However, the vertical position (Box Position) option allows you to align the top, center or bottom of the box with the line of text the box is on. Baseline is an imaginary line upon which characters sit. The baseline option is used to align the last line of text in a box, with the baseline of the line the box is on. Note illustration below:

> The vertical position of this graphics box is top.
>
> The vertical position of this graphics box is center.
>
> The vertical position of this graphics box is bottom.
>
> xx The vertical position of this graphics box is content baseline. The baseline of the last line of text in the box is aligned with the baseline of the first line of this paragraph.

Change the Graphics Box Contents

- The contents of a graphics box may be be changed to have the following contents:

Empty -	An empty graphics box used as a placeholder in a document.
Image -	A graphics image such as CHEETAH.WPG.
Text -	Regular text typed directly into the box or a text file may be retrieved into the box.
Equation -	An equation inserted into the box through the Equation Editor (This feature will not be covered).
Image on Disk -	An image you specify inserted only when the document is printed. The image will not appear on the screen. This is meant to minimize the size of your file when working with numerous graphics.
OLE Object -	An image or object created in another program. (Object linking and embedding).

To change graphics box contents:

- Select the graphic.
- Click **Graphics**
- Click **Edit Box**
- Click Content on the Graphics Feature Bar.
- Choose a content option from the Contents drop-down list.

In this exercise, you will create a paragraph using the Paragraph Anchor options to position the graphics box. You will also change the box contents.

EXERCISE DIRECTIONS:

1. Start with a clear screen.
2. Set left margin to 1" and right margin to 4".

To create illustration A:

3. Create the paragraph on the right.
4. Import HORSE_J.WPG.
5. Size the graphic to 1" wide by 1" tall.
6. Use the default (Paragraph Anchor) type.
7. Horizontally position the graphic 0" *from left margin*; vertically position the graphic .5" from the *top of paragraph*.
8. Print one copy.

To create illustration B:

9. Select the graphic.
10. Change the horizontal position to 0" *from right margin*; and the vertical position to 1" from *top of paragraph*.
11. Change the graphics box contents to empty; confirm deletion.
12. Print one copy.
13. Save the file; name it **HORSE**.
14. Close the document window.

ANCHOR AND POSITION A GRAPHIC

1. Select the graphic.
2. Click **Position** on ...... [Alt] + [Shift] + [P]
   Graphics Feature Bar
3. Click Box Placement option:

   P**u**t Box in Current Page .... [P]
   (Page Anchor)

   P**u**t Box in Current Paragraph .... [U]
   (Paragraph Anchor)

   Treat Box as Character .... [T]
   (Character Anchor)

4. Set horizontal and vertical placement options.
5. Click **OK** .... [Enter]

CHANGE BOX CONTENTS

1. Select the graphic.
2. Click **Co**ntent on ...... [Alt] + [Shift] + [O]
   Graphics Feature Bar
3. Select a content option from the **Content** drop down list:

   Empty .... [E]

   Image .... [I]

   Text .... [T]

   E**q**uation .... [Q]

   Image on **D**isk .... [D]

   OLE Object .... [O]

4. Click **OK** .... [Enter]

ILLUSTRATION A

This paragraph examines how graphics boxes are positioned when the paragraph anchor type is used. Create the box at the beginning of the paragraph so WordPerfect will recognize where the paragraph starts. The Horizontal Position is used to place the box right, left, center or full (width of paragraph). The Vertical Position is used to place the box down a set amount from the top of the paragraph.

ILLUSTRATION B

This paragraph examines how graphics boxes are positoned when the paragraph anchor type is used. Create the box at the beginning of the paragraph so WordPerfect will recognize where the paragraph starts. The Horizontal Position is used to place the box right, left, center or full (width of paragraph). The Vertical Position is used to place the box down a set amount from the top of the paragraph.

NEXT EXERCISE!!

Lesson 5 ▪ Graphics Boxes

EXERCISE 32

▪ ANCHOR, SIZE, AND POSITION GRAPHICS BOXES ▪ ROTATE TEXT BOXES

CONCEPTS:

- If you want the graphics box to remain in a certain position on the page, regardless of any changes you make to the page or document, choose the Put Box on Current Page (Page Anchor) option in the Box Position dialog box.

- If you want the box to stay with the paragraph preceding it, choose Put Box in Current Paragraph (Paragraph Option). Then, if you add/delete material from the document or move the paragraph, the graphics box will move, too.

- If you want the graphics box treated as a character, choose the Treat Box as Character (Character Anchor) option. Then, the box will move as text and wrap, if necessary, as new text is added before the box.

In this exercise, you will create a letterhead using two figure boxes and one text box. You will rotate, size and position the text box. You will size, position and copy the figure box.

EXERCISE DIRECTIONS:

1. Start with a clear screen.
2. Set the left, right, top and bottom margins to .5"
3. Create a text box and type The Perennial Potter, as shown.
4. Set the text to serif 48 point; set the first letter in each word to 56 point bold.
5. Size and position the text box as follows:
   - Size To Content.
   - Set the anchor type as *Page*.
   - Set the horizontal position to 0" From Left Edge of Page.
   - Set the vertical position 0" from Center of Margins.
   - Rotate it 90 degrees.
6. Create a figure box and import the graphic ROSE.WPG.
7. Size and position the first figure box as follows:
   - Size the width to 1" and the height to 1.96"
   - Set the anchor type as *Page*.
   - Set the horizontal position to 0" from Left Edge of Page.
   - Set the vertical position to 0" from Top Margin.
8. Copy the rose graphic. Use the Advance feature to bring the insertion point to Ln 8", and paste the graphic.
9. Position the second figure box as follows:
   - Set the anchor type as *Page*.
   - Set the horizontal position to 0" from Left Edge of Page.
   - Set the vertical position to 7.93" from Top Margin.
10. Type the address and phone number text next to the top graphic in serif 10 point italic.
11. Print one copy.
12. Save the file; name it **FLOWLET**.
13. Close the document window.

14 Highway 37
Middletown, NJ 07740
908-555-5555

The Perennial Potter

Lesson 5 ▪ Graphics Boxes

EXERCISE 33
BORDERS AND FILLS

CONCEPTS:

- Although each graphics box type has its own default border style, you may change the style. You may also add fills (shading) to a graphics box. The default border for a figure box is a single line. The default border for a text box is a thick top and bottom line:

Figure Box

Text Box

Note the thick top and bottom border lines.

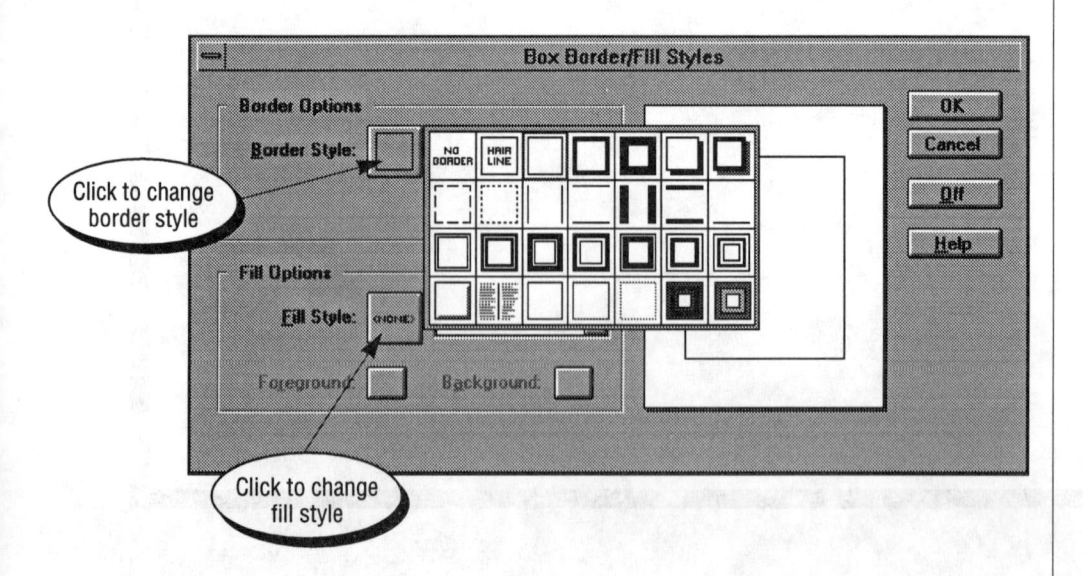

To change the border/fill:

- Select the graphics box.
  If feature bar is not displayed:
- Click **Graphics**, **Edit Box**
- Click **Border/Fill** on the Feature Bar.
- Choose a border/fill style from the palette.

- Your printer determines how the printed copy will look. For example, some printers cannot produce the fine points needed for gradients (*like the samples shown on page 126*).

- You may select a border and/or fill while creating or editing the graphic by selecting **Border/Fill** on the Graphics Feature Bar. You may select from 28 border styles and 30 fill styles or create a custom style.

Click to change border style

Click to change fill style

124

- In the Customize Border dialog box, you may edit individual sides, change the line style, change the spacing inside and outside the border, change the corners from square to round, and add a drop shadow effect.

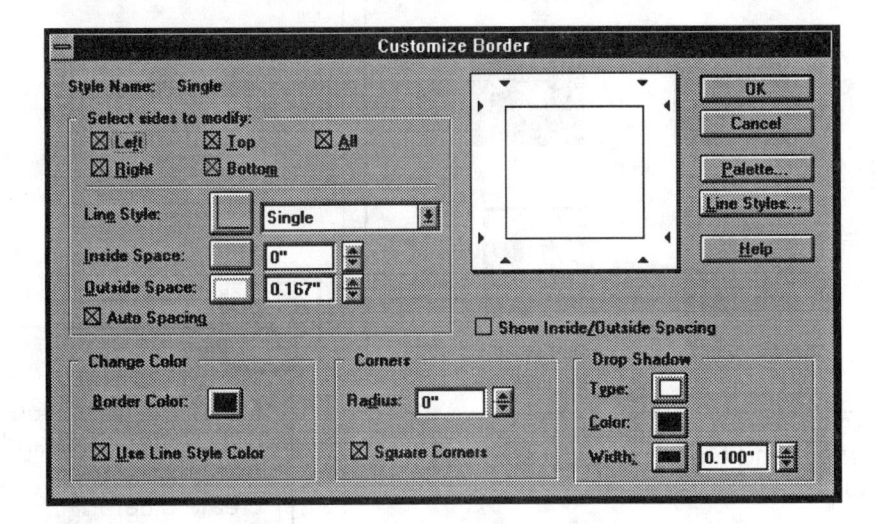

- The following samples illustrate some border possibilities:

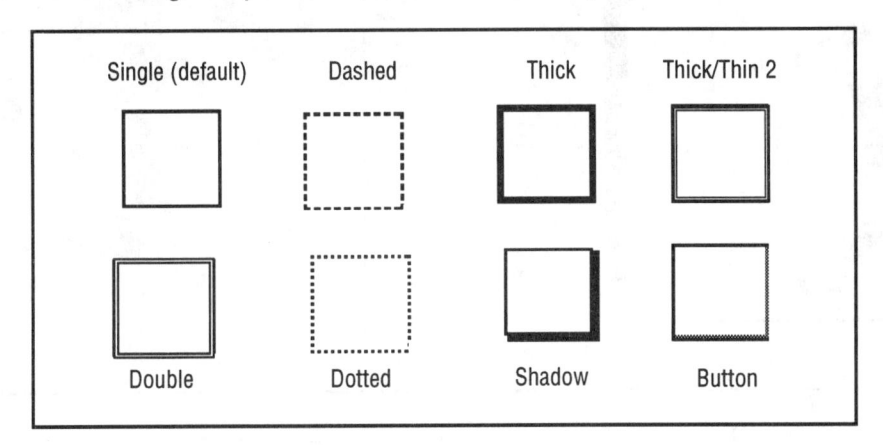

  Single (default)   Dashed   Thick   Thick/Thin 2
  Double   Dotted   Shadow   Button

- In the Box Border/Fill Styles dialog box, you may fill the box with shading ranging in 10 percent increments from none to 100%, with patterns, or with gradients displayed in the drop-down palette. If you have a color printer or if you are creating a graphic for presentation on a monitor, you may want to change the foreground and/or background colors.

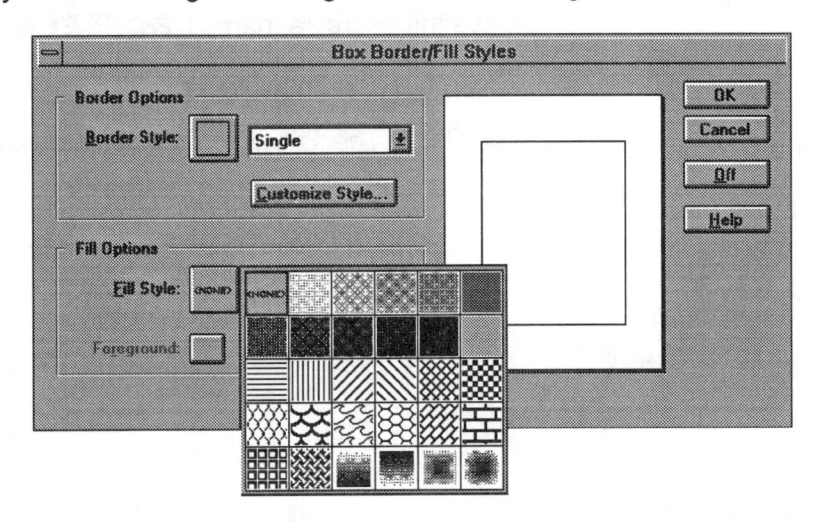

Lesson 5 ■ Exercise 33

- The following samples illustrate some fill patterns.

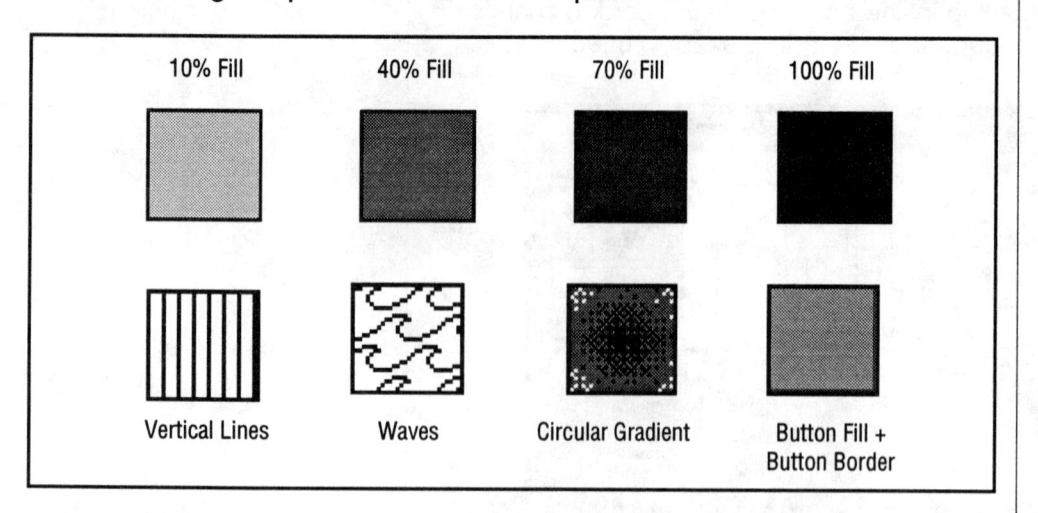

10% Fill	40% Fill	70% Fill	100% Fill
Vertical Lines	Waves	Circular Gradient	Button Fill + Button Border

- The sample below uses rounded corners and a drop shadow selected from the Customize Border dialog box.

In this exercise, you will create figure and text boxes, and create different borders and fill styles for each.

EXERCISE DIRECTIONS:

1. Start with a clear screen.

2. Begin the exercise on Ln 1".

3. Create the figure and text boxes as shown in the exercise. Use POINTER.WPG and HORSE.WPG as the graphic images.

4. Use the sizes and positions indicated in the exercise.

5. Change the borders and fills as directed in each caption or text box.

6. Preview your exercise.

7. Print one copy.

8. Save the exercise; name it **BORDERS**.

9. Close the document window.

   - NOTE: The following directions assume the Graphic Feature Bar is displayed. If not, select the graphic, click the right mouse button and select Feature Bar from the QuickMenu.

Begin: Ln 1"
Size: Default
Position: Default
Border: None

Begin: 4.15"
Size: Default
Position: 0" from center of paragraph
Border: Thick Shadow

The border style on this text box has been changed to **thick shadow**. No fill has been added.

Begin: Ln 5.33"
Size: Default
Position: Default
Border: Extra Thick
Fill: Button

The border style on this text box has been changed to **extra thick** with a **button fill**.

Begin: Ln 6.51"
Size: 2" by 2"
Position: 0" from Left Margin
Border: Shadow
Fill: Rectangular Gradient

CHANGE BORDER STYLE

1. Click the graphic box........... `Shift` + `F11` to select it.
2. Click **B**order/Fill....... `Alt` + `Shift` + `B`
3. Click **B**order Style button.................. `B`

   OR

   Drop-down Border Style list.
4. Click desired style.
5. Click **OK** to return to document.

CHANGE FILL STYLE

1. Click the graphic box........... `Shift` + `F11` to select it.
2. Click **B**order/Fill....... `Alt` + `Shift` + `B`
3. Click **F**ill Style button .... `F`

   OR

   Drop-down Fill Style list.
4. Click desired style.
5. Click **OK** to return to document.

CUSTOMIZE BORDER STYLE

1. Click the graphic box........... `Shift` + `F11` to select it.
2. Click **B**order/Fill....... `Alt` + `Shift` + `B`
3. Click **C**ustomize Style. .... `C`
4. Make changes to desired elements.

To create round corners, in Corners panel:

Note: This procedure works only with box with 4 identical side line styles.

a. Deselect **S**quare Corners .... `Q`
b. In Ra**d**ius box, enter....................... `D` desired radius.

To create custom drop shadow, in Drop Shadow panel:

a. Click T**y**pe button. .... `Y`
b. Click desired placement for shadow (default is No-shadow).
c. Click **W**idth: button, click desired width.

   OR

   Enter measurement for desired width.
5. Click **OK** to return to previous dialog box.
6. Click **OK** to return to document.

Lesson 5 ■ Exercise 33

Lesson 5 ▪ Graphics Boxes

EXERCISE 34

▪ TEXT WRAP OPTIONS ▪ CAPTIONS

CONCEPTS:

Text Wrap

■ WordPerfect provides you with several options for wrapping text around the graphics box (figure or text box). You can control the type and the position of the text wrap. Note the text wrap options illustrated below and on the next page.

To wrap text:
- Select graphic to be wrapped.
- Click **Graphic**
- Click **Edit Box**
- Click **Wrap** on Graphics Feature Bar.
- Choose a text wrap option.

```
This text is designed to show you how text flows
around a graphic.  Wrapping Type options determine
the shape of the wrapped text, and Wrap Text Around
options determine its location. You choose the
Contour option to remove the figure border and have
text fill in any extra white space within the box.
Each option creates its own effect, as well as each
combination of options. Be sure to check the effects
of text wrap. You may need to reposition the graphic to avoid awkward line breaks.
```

SQUARE - LARGEST SIDE

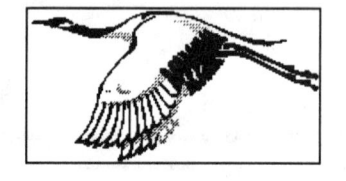

```
This text is designed to show
you how text flows around a
graphic.  Wrapping Type
options determine the shape
of the wrapped text, and Wrap
Text Around options determine
its location. You choose the
Contour option to remove the figure border and have text fill in any extra white space
within the box. Each option creates its own effect, as well as each combination of
options. Be sure to check the effects of text wrap. You may need to reposition the
graphic to avoid awkward line breaks.
```

SQUARE - LEFT SIDE - CENTERED IMAGE

```
This text is designed to show you how text flows around a graphic. Wrapping Type
                                     options determine the
                                     shape of the wrapped
                                     text, and Wrap Text
                                     Around options determine
                                     its location. You choose
                                     the  Contour option to
                                     remove the figure border
                                     and have text fill in
                                     any extra white space
within the box. Each option creates its own effect, as well as each combination of
options. Be sure to check the effects of text wrap. You may need to reposition the
graphic to avoid awkward line breaks.
```

SQUARE - RIGHT SIDE - CENTERED IMAGE; VERTICAL POSITION LOWERED

This text is designed to show graphic. Wrapping Type the wrapped text, and Wrap its location. You choose the figure border and have space within the box. effect, as well as each to check the effects of text reposition the graphic to avoid awkward line breaks.
you how text flows around a options determine the shape of Text Around options determine the Contour option to remove text fill in any extra white Each option creates its own combination of options. Be sure wrap. You may need to

SQUARE - BOTH SIDES - CENTERED IMAGE

This text is designed to show you how text flows around a graphic. Wrapping Type options determine the shape of the wrapped text, and Wrap Text Around options determine its location. You choose the Contour option to remove the figure border and have text fill in any extra white space within the box. Each option creates its own effect, as well as each combination of options. Be sure to check the effects of text wrap. You may need to reposition the graphic to avoid awkward line breaks.

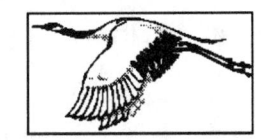

SQUARE - ON NEITHER SIDE OF CENTERED IMAGE

This text is designed to show you how text flows around a graphic. Wrapping Type options determine the shape of the wrapped text, and Wrap Text Around options determine its location. You   choose the Contour option to remove the figure border and have   text fill in any extra white space within the box. Each option   creates its own effect, as well as each combination of options.   Be sure to check the effects of text wrap. You may need to reposition the graphic to avoid awkward line breaks.

CONTOUR - BOTH SIDES OF CENTERED IMAGE

This text is designed to show you how text flows around a graphic. Wrapping Type options determine the shape of the wrapped text, and Wrap Text Around options determine its location. You choose the Contour option to remove the figure border and have text fill in any extra white space within the box. Each option creates its own effect, as well as each combination of options. Be sure to check the effects of text wrap. You may need to reposition the graphic to avoid awkward line breaks.

NO WRAP - BORDER REMOVED

Lesson 5 ▪ Exercise 34

- To select text flow options, select the graphic and click Wrap on the Graphics Feature Bar or click the right mouse button and choose Wrap.

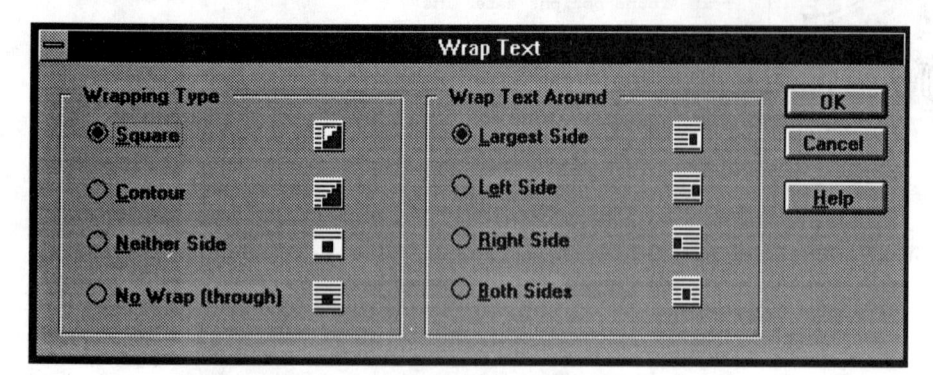

- Choose one Wrapping Type option. If you choose Square or Contour, you also choose one Wrap Text Around option. You may wrap text around the largest side, left side, right side or both sides of the graphic box.

- The Contour wrapping type removes any border from the graphic figure and flows text in a silhouette pattern up to/around the image. You may manually remove the border from any other text wrap option.

Captions

- A **caption** is text that you write to appear below a graphic, usually a label or explanation.

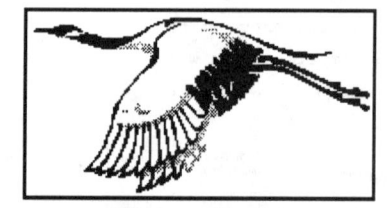

The Crane

- To create a caption, click Caption on the Graphics Feature Bar. The Box Caption dialog box enables you to position the caption on any side of the box, inside, outside or on the border, and at the top, bottom, or center. By default, the caption width matches the graphic width, but you may set your own width. You may rotate the caption to appear along any side of the figure box. You may also control the automatic caption numbering feature.

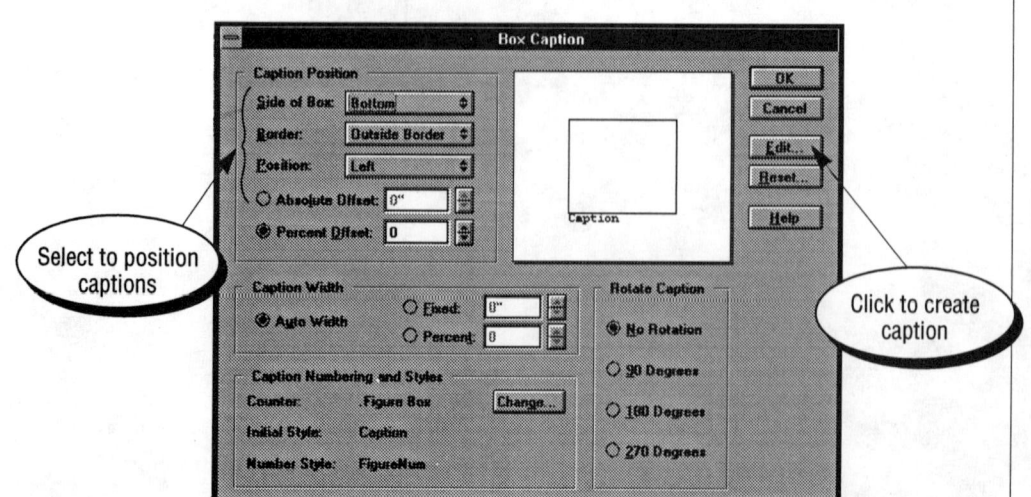

Select to position captions

Click to create caption

When using text wrap, carefully proofread the text that flows around the graphics box. You may need to adjust the graphic position to avoid awkward word breaks.

To add a caption:
- Select graphic to receive caption.
- Click **Graphic**
- Click **Edit Box**
- Click **Caption** on Graphics Feature Bar.
- Choose a Caption Position option.
- Click **Edit**
- Type caption.
- Click **OK**

To remove a caption:
- Select graphic to receive caption.
- Click **Graphic**
- Click **Edit Box**
- Click **Caption** on the Graphics Feature Bar
- Click **Reset**

In this exercise, you will open a file, import a graphic and use a text wrap option. You will also include a caption.

- To create the caption, click Edit. The Caption Editor appears with the box or figure number already entered and the insertion point in place for you to type the caption. Normal editing and formatting features apply here. For instance, to delete the provided figure number, press Backspace.

EXERCISE DIRECTIONS:

1. Start with a clear screen.
2. Use the default margins.
3. Begin the exercise on Ln 2".
4. Keyboard the heading in sans serif 24 point bold. Return three times.
5. Create two newspaper columns.
6. Prepare the report illustrated on the right. Use sans serif 14 point bold for subheadings and serif 11 point for paragraph text.
7. Import MARSH.WPG in the first column where shown.
   - Center and size the graphic to .5" wide by .5" high.
   - Include a caption in sans serif 8-point bold italics that reads, *The Flamingo*.
   - Wrap text on both sides (of centered image).
8. Import HUMBIRD.WPG in the second column where shown.
   - Center and size the graphic to .5" wide by .5" high.
   - Include a centered caption in sans serif 8-point bold italics that reads, *The Hummingbird*.
   - Wrap text on neither side (of centered image).
9. Import CRANE_J.WPG
   - Size the graphic to 2" wide by 2" high.
   - Include a centered caption in sans serif 10-point bold italics that reads *The Crane*.
   - Use a Contour Text Wrap.
   - Using the mouse, position the graphic between the columns as shown. Adjust the graphic as necessary to avoid awkward work breaks.
10. Preview your document.
11. Print one copy.
12. Save the file; name it **BIRDS**.
13. Close the document window.

WRAP TEXT

1. Select graphic.
2. Click **Wrap** on .... `Alt` + `Shift` + `W`
   Graphics Feature Bar
3. Click a **Wrapping Type** option:

   Square .... `S`

   Contour .... `C`

   Neither Side .... `N`

   No Wrap (through) .... `O`

4. For Square or Contour, click a Wrap Text Around option:

   Largest Side .... `L`

   Left Side .... `E`

   Right Side .... `I`

   Both Sides .... `B`

5. Click **OK** .... `Enter`

ADD A CAPTION

1. Select graphic.
2. Click **Caption** on .... `Alt` + `Shift` + `A`
   Graphics Feature Bar
3. Click **Edit** .... `Alt` + `E`
4. Type and format caption text.
5. Click **Close**. .... `Alt` + `Shift` + `C`
6. Click **OK** .... `Enter`

REMOVE A CAPTION

1. Select graphic.
2. Click **Caption** on .... `Alt` + `Shift` + `A`
   Graphics Feature Bar
3. Click **Reset**. .... `Alt` + `R`
4. At warning box, click **OK** .... `Enter`
5. Click **OK** .... `Enter`

EXOTIC BIRDS

The Flamingo

The flamingo is a bird known for its long, stiltlike legs and curved bill and neck. Flamingos live in many parts of the world and spend their entire life near lakes, marshes and seas. Most flamingos are from 3 to 5 feet tall. The color of a flamingo's feathers varies from bright red to pale pink.

Flamingos live in colonies, some of which have thousands of members. They feed on small animals and plants that they find in marshy areas. They live from 15 to 20 years in their natural surroundings and can live even longer in captivity.

Different species of flamingo live in different parts of the world. The greater flamingo lives in Africa, Europe, southern Asia, southern South America and the West Indies. The lesser flamingo lives in Africa. Wild flamingos once lived in southern Florida, but people killed them for their beautiful feathers.

The Hummingbird

The hummingbird is one of the smallest birds in the world. They live in the western hemisphere. They get their name from the sound that is made by the rapid flapping of their wings. Their wings can move 60-70 times per second.

The smallest hummingbird is no larger than a bumblebee and is brightly colored. They have long bills which enable them to suck the flower nectar with ease. Hummingbirds eat insects inside flowers and on spider webs. The next time you hear a humming sound, look quick; it might be a hummingbird! Hopefully, it's not a large bumble bee.

The Crane

The crane, which resembles the flamingo, has long legs and a long neck. Cranes also live in marshy areas in many parts of the world. South America and Antarctica are the only continents that have no cranes.

Cranes stand about 5 feet high. The wingspan of a crane can measure up to 7.5 feet. The male and female look alike. They range in color from white to dark gray and brown.

There are 15 species of crane. Only two species are native to North America -- the whooping crane and the sandhill crane. Whooping cranes remain one of the rarest birds in North America. Sandhill cranes nest in northern Russia, Canada and the northern United States. Only the sandhill cranes that nest in the north migrate south for the winter.

Lesson 5 ▪ Graphics Boxes

EXERCISE 35

TEXT WRAP OPTIONS

CONCEPTS:

- In Exercise 34, you used three different text wrap options. Each one wrapped text around the graphic in a different style.

- In this exercise, you will experiment with no wrap, in which the text overlays the graphic:

> This is an example of no text wrap in which the text overlays the graphic. It can create an interesting effect. However, if the graphic image is too dark, you will not be able to see the text. When you are using border graphics, you must use this wrap option if you want the text to appear inside the border. Otherwise, the text will print outside the border.

- When working with border graphics, you must use this wrap type if you want the text to appear inside the border:

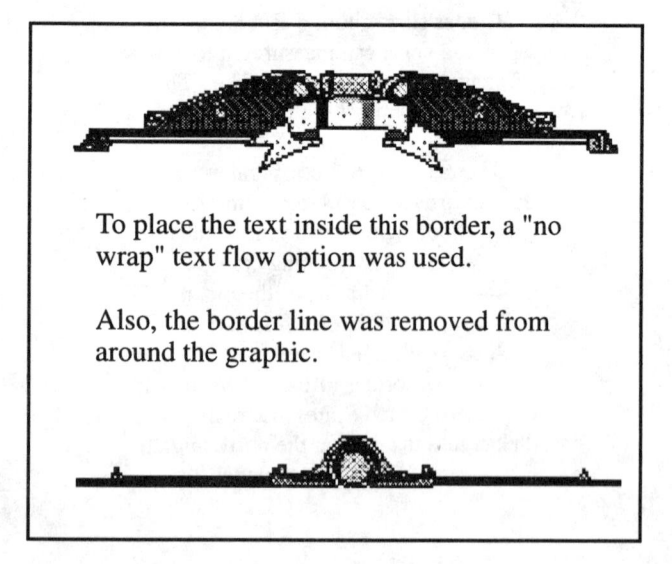

> To place the text inside this border, a "no wrap" text flow option was used.
>
> Also, the border line was removed from around the graphic.

In this exercise, you will use a figure box and insert a border graphic. You will choose a no wrap option and insert (import) a previously saved file. The document will overlay the graphic, allowing the text to appear inside the border.

134

EXERCISE DIRECTIONS:

1. Start with a clear screen.
2. Use the default margins.
3. Import BORD17.WPG. Size the border width and height to *Full*.
4. Remove the border line from around the graphic.
5. Select a "no wrap" text wrap option.
6. Insert (Insert, File) CONGRATS (a previously saved file).
7. Enter several times to vertically center the document between the top and bottom of the border.
8. Preview the exercise.
9. Print one copy.
10. Save the file AS **CONGRAT1**.

MORITZ & CHASE
1603 East 7th Street
Astoria, OR 94101

Is Pleased to Announce that the following Associates will become members of the firm on

January 1, 1995

DENVER	Steven M. Jones
NEW YORK	Arthur J. Williams
SAN FRANCISCO	Roberta W. Asher
	Donna Newman
WASHINGTON, D.C.	Pamela T. Blanco

and that the following Of Counsel will become members of the firm on

January 1, 1995

LONDON	Raymond T. Sedgewick
LOS ANGELES	Angela Tsacoumis
	Roberto Vasquez

Lesson 5 ▪ Graphics Boxes

EXERCISE 36

SCALE, ROTATE AND FLIP A GRAPHIC IMAGE

CONCEPTS:

- In addition to moving and resizing a graphics box, you can also edit the image inside the box. You can scale, rotate, and mirror ("flip") images with the Image Tools palette. These actions affect the image within the box, but not the box itself. Note the examples on the next pages of an image that has been scaled, rotated, moved within the box, and flipped.

- When the Tools palette is displayed, the Status bar reports the selected graphics X (horizontal) and Y (vertical) axis position, scale percent and degree of rotation.

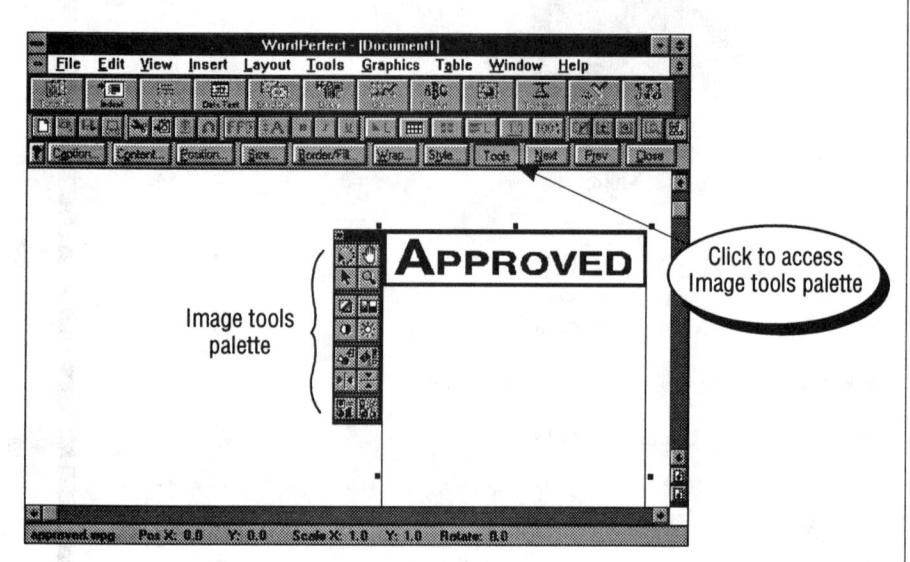

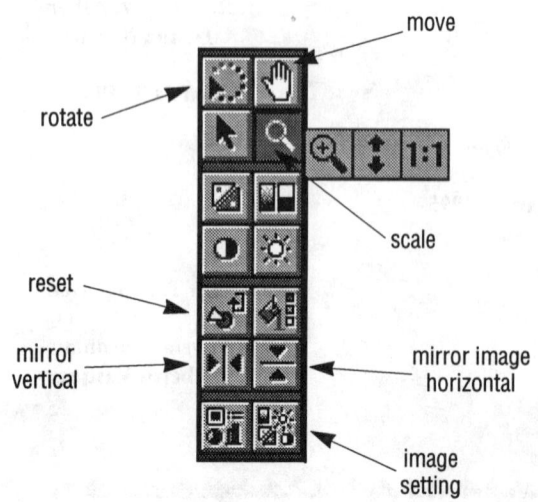

To access Image Tools Palette:

- Select the graphic.
- Click **Graphic**
- Click **Edit Box**
- Click **Tools** on Feature Bar

OR

- Click *right* mouse button or graphic
- Choose **Image Tools**

- Point to any tool icon to see its name and description on the WordPerfect title bar.

Scale an Image

- The scaling option lets you enlarge or reduce the graphic image horizontally, vertically, or proportionally. You may scale the image with the mouse or mathematically. The default scaling ratio is X:1.0, Y:1.0.

SCALE WIDTH: (X): 1.0
SCALE HEIGHT: (Y): 1.0
(The Default)

SCALE WIDTH (X): .6
SCALE HEIGHT: (Y): 1.2

- **To scale the image with the mouse,** click the Scale tool, then click the About Image Center (up/down arrow) tool. When a scroll bar appears, you slide the scroll box *up* to *reduce* the image or *down* to *enlarge* it.

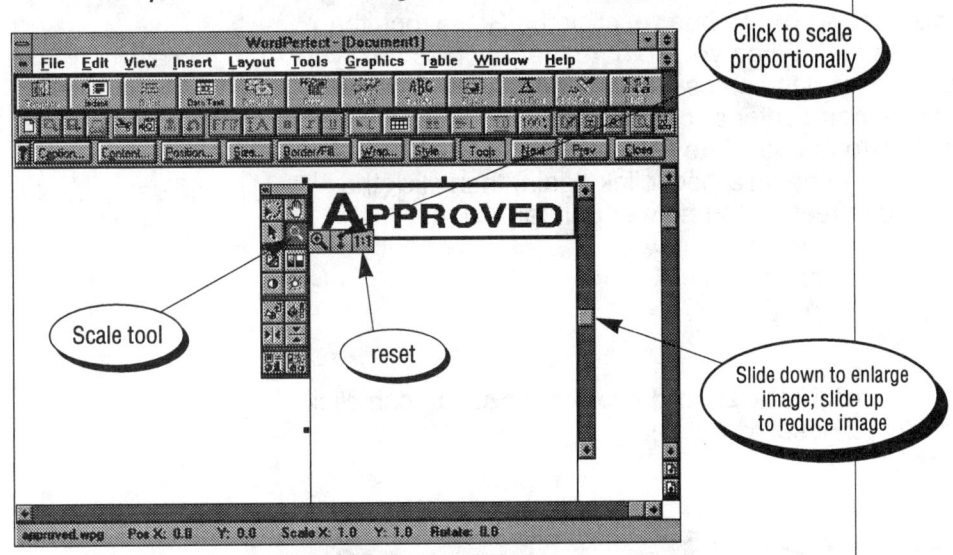

- **To scale an image mathematically**, click the Image Settings tool. At the Image Settings box, select the Scale Image option, then enter the desired scaling ratios.

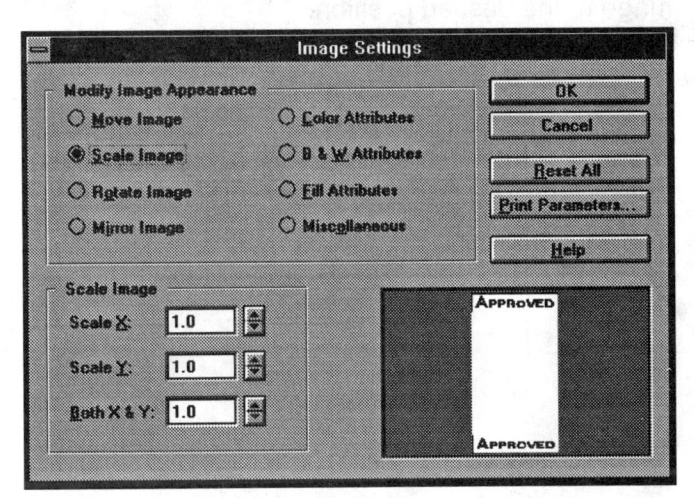

Lesson 5 ■ Exercise 36   137

Lesson 5 ■ Exercise 36

- **To scale the image but retain its original proportions**, either enter equal numbers in the Scale X and Scale Y boxes or enter the desired number in the Both X & Y box. You may increase the value up to 1000% (10.0) or reduce it as far as 1/1000 (.01). The graphics box on the top left of the previous page illustrates a proportional image.

- **To "stretch" or distort the image**, enter unequal values in the X and Y boxes. A larger X value makes the image "tall and skinny"; a larger Y value makes the image "short and fat."

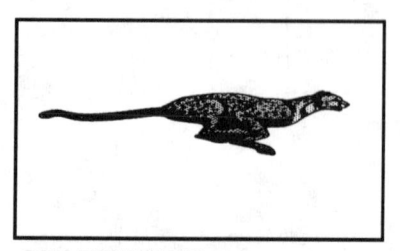

SCALE WIDTH: (X): 1.0
SCALE HEIGHT: (Y): 0.5

- **To enlarge a selected portion of the image,** click the Scale tool, then click the Magnifying Glass tool. When you point to the graphics box, you see dotted lines extending from the cross-hairs of the magnifying-glass pointer. Position the cross-hair center at one corner of the area you want to enlarge, click then drag to the opposite corner of the area. When the dotted box defines the area to be enlarged, click again, then click the Pointer tool on the palette to restore the normal pointer action.

- **To reset the image to its original size and proportions**, you can click the Scale tool, then click the Reset tool (1:1).

Move an Image Within the Border

- **To move an image within the border or frame** with the mouse, click the Move tool. When you point to the selected graphic, the pointer becomes an open hand which you use to drag the image to the desired position. This is often referred to as "panning" the image. It allows you to display any desired part of the image.

SCALE WIDTH: (X): 2.5
SCALE HEIGHT: (Y): 2.5
Moved within the border using Move tool

- **To move an image within the border mathematically** (by a specific amount), click the Image Settings tool to display the Image Settings dialog box. There you select the Move Image option, then enter the horizontal and vertical distance you want the image to move.

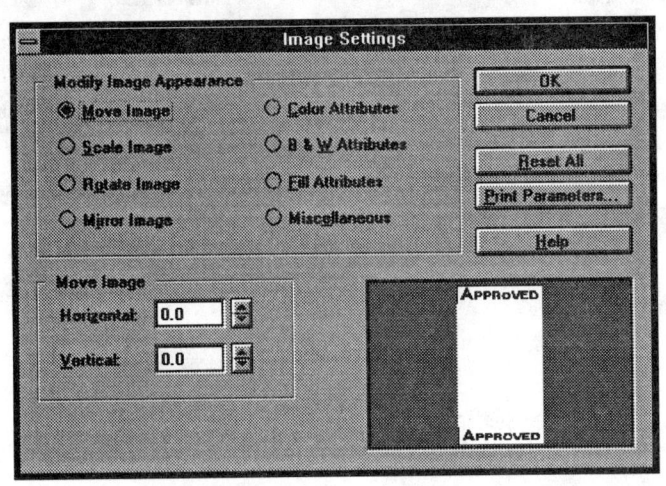

Rotate and Flip an Image

- **To "flip" an image**, you can click the Mirror Vertical (switch right-to-left) icon or the Mirror Horizontal (switch up-to-down) icon. Or you can select Mirror Image at the Image Settings dialog box, then select Flip Horizontal or Flip Vertical.

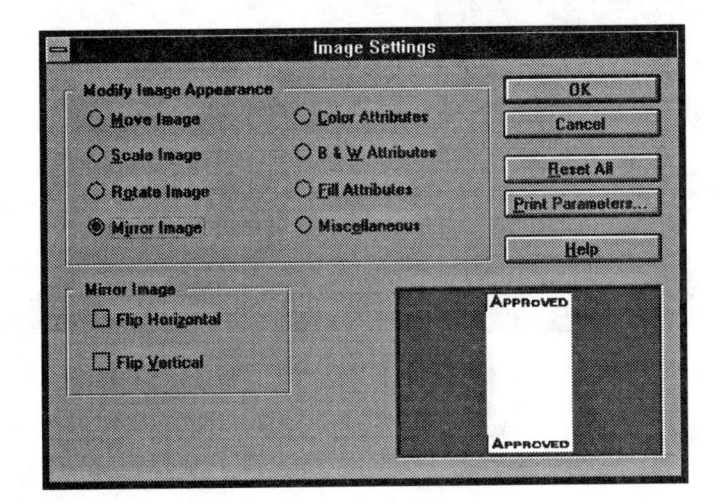

FLIP VERTICALLY

FLIP HORIZONTALLY

Lesson 5 ▪ Exercise 36

- **To rotate an image with the mouse**, you click the Rotate tool 🔲 to activate the point-of-rotation and the corner rotation handles. By default, the point-of-rotation is in the center or the image. You can move it to a new position within the graphics box. Then drag a corner rotation handle until the figure is at the desired angle. The Status bar reports the exact rotation angle.

ROTATED -30.0 DEGREES

- **To rotate an image mathematically**, click the Image Settings tool 🔲, then click Rotate Image and enter the desired degree of rotation (0 to +/-360 degrees).

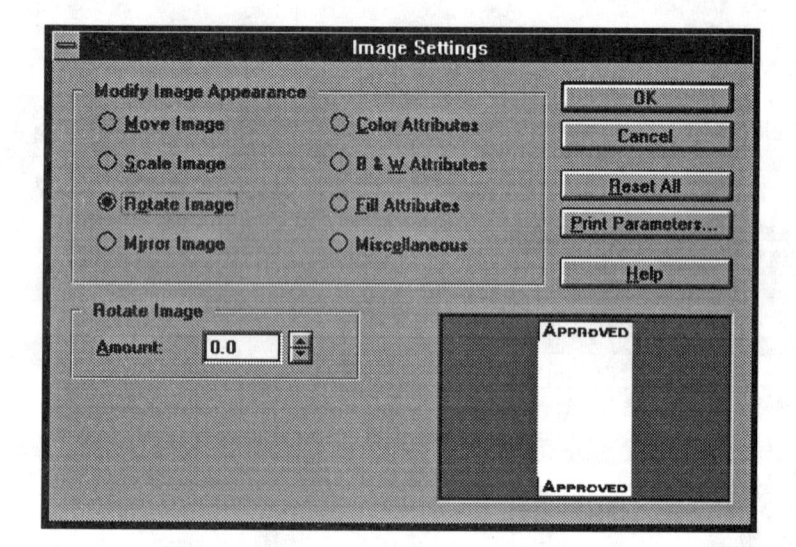

> It is easier to rotate the image within the Image Settings Dialog box than by using the mouse.

> In this exercise, you will create a letterhead using scaled, rotated flipped, and moved graphic images.

140

EXERCISE DIRECTIONS:

1. Start with a clear screen.
2. Use the default margins.
3. Import POINTER.WPG. and position it on the right (the default).
4. Copy the graphic and position it 0" from the left margin.
5. Edit the *left* graphic as follows:
   - Select the graphic.
   - Select Tools from the Graphics Feature Bar.
   - Enlarge the dog's head to fill the box (scale the height (Y) to 3 and the width (X) to 3).
   - Move the image within the box so the head is visible.
   - Size the box to 1" wide by 1" tall.
   - Create a shadow border.
   - Move the graphic to the top left corner of the page.
7. Edit the *right* graphic as follows:
   - Select the graphic.
   - Select Tools from the Graphic Feature Bar.
   - Flip (mirror) the graphic vertically.
   - Enlarge the dog's head to fill the box (scale the height (Y) to 3 and the width (X) to 3).
   - Move the image within the box so the head is visible.
   - Size the box to 1" wide by 1" tall.
   - Create a shadow border.
   - Move the graphic to the bottom right corner of the page.
8. Center and right-align letterhead text using sans serif 14 point bold for the title and sans serif 10 point for the address and phone number as shown.
9. Preview your document.
10. Print one copy.
11. Save the letterhead file; name it **PETS**.
12. Close the document window.

Lesson 5 ■ Exercise 36

Lesson 5 ▪ Exercise 36

SCALE AN IMAGE

1. Select graphic to be scaled.
2. Click **Tools** on .... `Alt` + `Shift` + `L`
   Graphics Feature bar.
3. Click **Scale** tool .... 🔍
4. Click **Up/Down Arrow** tool.
5. Drag scroll box up to reduce, down to enlarge image.

OR

1. Click **Image Settings** tool ....
2. Click **S**cale Image .... `S`
3. Type desired scale values.

   In **Scale X** box, type.............. `Alt` + `X`
   scale height.

   In **Scale Y** box, type.............. `Alt` + `Y`
   scale width.

   OR

   In **B**oth X & Y box, type .... `Alt` + `B`
   common scale value.
4. Click **OK** .... `Enter`

ENLARGE PORTION OF IMAGE

1. Select graphic to be enlarged.
2. Click **Tools** on .... `Alt` + `Shift` + `L`
   Graphics Feature bar.
3. Click **Scale** tool .... 🔍
4. Click **magnifying glass** icon...............
5. Click in one corner of area to be enlarged, drag to diagonally opposite corner, click when outline box encloses desired area.
6. Click **Pointer** tool ....
   to restore normal pointer action.

MOVE IMAGE WITHIN THE BOX

1. Select graphic to be moved.
2. Click **Tools** on .... `Alt` + `Shift` + `L`
   Graphics Feature bar.
3. Click **Move** tool .... ✋
4. With open hand pointer, drag image to desired position within the box.

OR

1. Click **Image Settings** tool.
2. Click **M**ove Image....................... `M`
3. Type measurement .... `Alt` + `Z`
   for desired **horizontal** distance.
4. Type measurement .... `Alt` + `V`
   for desired **vertical** distance.
5. Click **OK** .... `Enter`

FLIP AN IMAGE

1. Select graphic to be flipped.
2. Click **Tools** on .... `Alt` + `Shift` + `L`
   Graphics Feature bar.

   Click **Mirror Vertical** tool ....
   flip right-to-left.

   Click **Mirror Horizontal** tool ....
   to flip upside down.

OR

1. Click **Image Settings** tool..................
2. Click **Mi**rror Image....................... `I`
3. Click Flip Hori**z**ontal................ `Alt` + `Z`
   and/or

   Click Flip **V**ertical.................. `Alt` + `V`
4. Click **OK**............................... `Enter`

ROTATE AN IMAGE

1. Select graphic to be flipped.
2. Click **Tools** on .... `Alt` + `Shift` + `L`
   Graphics Feature bar.
3. Click Rotate tool ....
4. Drag corner rotation handle to desired rotation angle.
5. Click **Pointer** tool ....
   to restore normal pointer action.

OR

1. Click **Image Settings** tool..................
2. Click R**o**tate Image .... `O`
3. In **A**mount box, type............... `Alt` + `A`
   desired rotation angle.
4. Click **OK** .... `Enter`

RESTORE ORIGINAL SETTINGS

1. Select graphic.
   to be restored.
2. Click **Tools** on .... `Alt` + `Shift` + `L`
   Graphics Feature bar.
3. Click Reset tool ....

OR

1. Click **Image Settings** tool..................
2. Click **R**eset All .... `Alt` + `R`

BOW WOW CHOW
Pet Supplies and Grooming

354 Northern Boulevard
Baldwin, NY 11755
Phone: 566-876-5555
Fax: 566-555-5555

Lesson 5 ▪ Graphics Boxes

EXERCISE 37
WATERMARKS

CONCEPTS:

- A **watermark** is a lightened graphic image or text that prints in the background, behind the printed text. A watermark can appear on every page of your document or on selected pages. Also, you may have two separate watermarks on a page.

- When you access the Watermark feature, the Watermark Feature Bar appears.

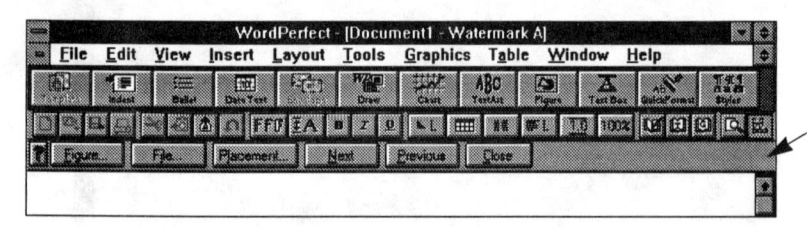

Watermark feature bar

- When the watermark screen appears (it is blank), you can insert a graphic (figure), a file, or type text. You can edit text content, apply font changes, and use most figure editing features at the Watermark window.

- Among the graphics provided in WordPerfect's GRAPHICS directory are graphics designed for use as page borders.

To create a watermark:
- Click **L**ayout
- Click **W**atermark

While you can create watermarks in any view, they do not display in Draft view.

In this exercise, you will create an invitation using a page border and a watermark.

EXERCISE DIRECTIONS:

1. Start with a clear screen.
2. Use the default margins.
3. Import BORD16.WPG as a watermark.
4. Create the invitation shown on the right. Use script 16 point for the invitation text and 24-point bold for Pamela Davis.
5. Center the text top to bottom.
6. Preview your document.
7. Print one copy.
8. Save the exercise; name it **WISH**.
9. Close the document window.

*You are cordially invited
to attend a birthday party
in honor
of*

Pamela Davis

*who will be celebrating her
21st Birthday
on
September 9, 1994*

*8:00 p.m.
234 Maple Drive
South Hampton, New York*

R.S.V.P. 515-999-9999

CREATE A WATERMARK

1. If in Draft view, ... **Alt** + **F5**
   click **V**iew. then **P**age.

   OR

   Click **V**iew, ... **Alt** + **V**, **T**
   then **T**wo Page

2. Click **L**ayout .... **Alt** + **L**

3. Click **W**atermark. .... **W**

4. Click Watermark **A** .... **A**

   OR

   Click Watermark **B** .... **B**

5. Click **C**reate .... **C**

   (Watermark Feature Bar and window appears.)

To enter text in this screen:

Type text.

OR

Click F**i**le, insert file as usual .... **I**

To enter graphics in this screen:

- Click **F**igure.
- Select graphic .... **Alt** + **Shift** + **F**
  to be inserted.
- Click **OK**.
- Click **C**lose .... **Alt** + **Shift** + **C**
  to return to watermark window.

6. Click **C**lose .... **Alt** + **Shift** + **C**
   to return to document.

7. Type document text as desired.

Lesson 5 ▪ Graphics Boxes

EXERCISE 38

WATERMARKS

CONCEPTS:

▪ In the last exercise, you used a graphic image as your watermark. Text may also be used as a watermark.

▪ When the watermark screen appears, you may type the text you desire as your watermark. If you want the watermark to appear across or down the page, you will need to use a large type size.

You can create interesting effects using large size Wingdings and Special Characters (see exercises 17 and 45) as watermarks.

In this exercise, you will create an advertisement containing two watermarks.

EXERCISE DIRECTIONS:

1. Start with a clear screen.
2. Use the default margins.
3. Center the page top to bottom.
4. Center the heading in 14 point italic bold. Press Enter twice.
5. Set a first line indent of 2" for the paragraphs.
   (Layout, Paragraph, Format).
6. Type the text as shown using serif 12 point. Use the ? (question mark) and a Wingding font to create the hand symbol before each centered word.
7. Import ROSE.WPG four times. After each graphic is imported, size it to 1" by 1" and place each below the text side by side, as shown.
8. Flip the second and fourth images horizontally.

▪ *NOTE: Select the image first before you click Tools on the Graphics Feature Bar.*

9. Create Watermark A at the top of the page by typing two lines of the word ROSEWATER in sans serif 30 point bold. Use the the letter O and the Wingding font to create the flag between each word. Size the flag to 36 point.
10. Return to the document screen.
11. Create Watermark B at the bottom of the page (at approximately Ln 8.77") in sans serif 30 point bold. Use the the letter O and the Wingding font to create the flag between each word. Size the flag to 36 point.
12. Return to the document screen.
13. Preview your document.
14. Print one copy.
15. Save the file; name it **PAPER**.
16. Close the document screen.

ROSEWATER ROSEWATER
ROSEWATER ROSEWATER

ROSEWATER PAPER

Papers that perform. Consistently. Time after time. That's what you can always expect when you specify ROSEWATER'S premium text, cover and writing finishes. And now you can see how brilliantly our papers perform with a variety of inks thanks to our new *Think Ink Guide*.

This invaluable tool features more than 400 visual references to help you make accurate color choices. And get the results you expect. You'll find printed examples of black, metallic and solid colors in halftones, line art and screen tints on every one of our four leading lines of paper:

- **ENVIRONMENT**
- **CLASSIC LINEN**
- **CREST LINEN**
- **RAIN DROP**

Discover for yourself how ***ROSEWATER PAPER*** can be combined with a myriad of inks to expand your creativity.

For your copy of our new *Think Ink Guide*, just call the representatives listed on the enclosed brochure and ask for your guide.

ROSEWATER ROSEWATER
ROSEWATER ROSEWATER

LESSON 5
SUMMARY EXERCISE A

EXERCISE DIRECTIONS:

1. Start with a clear screen.

2. Use the default left and right margins. Set .5" top and bottom margins.

3. Center the page top to bottom.

4. Import CRANE_J.WPG graphic. Remove the border from around the graphic.

5. Size the graphic to approximately 2.15" wide by 1.35" tall.

6. Copy the graphic 5 times. Size and position each to approximately the same as those shown in the exercise.

7. Use the Advance feature to bring the insertion point to Ln. 3.99" on the page.

8. Create two balanced newspaper columns.

9. Type the exercise as shown.

10. Turn off the column feature.

11. Copy each of the graphics and position them below the text as shown. Flip each horizontally and rotate each -15.0 degrees.

12. Enter enough times to bring the insertion point to approximately 9.99" on the page.

13. Type the bottom text in serif 10 point. Use the letter S and the Wingding font to create the symbols between words. Set the justification to *All*.

14. Preview the exercise.

15. Print one copy.

16. Save the file; name it **CONDOR**.

17. Close the document window.

In this exercise, you will create an advertisement using two column, balanced newspaper columns and graphics.

The **CALIFORNIA CONDOR**, a vulture, is the largest flying land bird in North America and makes its home in Southern California. Black Feathers cover most of the bird's body, except for the white area on the underside of the condor's wings. The neck and head have no feathers and are red-orange color. The condor is a unique bird because it does not build a nest but lays its eggs in caves, holes or among rocks. It is also a particularly strong flier. It can soar and glide in the air for long distances.

By the end of the 1980s, only 30 condors remained in the United States. The diminished number of condors is the result of hunting. The growth of urban areas in Southern California also poses a threat to the natural habitat of the bird. Help us to **SAVE THE SPECIES**. Write to your Congressperson and local government officials to inform them of your support of more land for sanctuaries to help keep the condor alive.

SAVE THE SPECIES ♦ 1356 Pacific Road ♦ San Francisco ♦ California ♦ 90456

LESSON 5
SUMMARY EXERCISE B

EXERCISE DIRECTIONS:

1. Start with a clear screen.

2. Set .5" left and right margins.

3. Import TIGER_J.WPG graphic. Remove the border from around the graphic.

4. Size the graphic to 3.5" wide by 3.5" high. Position it 0" from Center of Paragraph.

5. Enlarge the head to fill the box as shown (scale the height (Y) to 2.56 and the width (X) to 2.56). Move the head in the box so the face is centered.

6. Use the Advance feature to bring the insertion point to Ln 4.93" on the page.

7. Type and center the first three lines in sans serif 24 point bold. Press Enter twice.

8. Create two parallel columns. Use the default column margins and space between columns. Add a vertical line between columns.

9. Type the exercise as shown in serif 15 point. Use a script 24 point font for the first letter in each paragraph.

10. After typing the first column of text, press Ctrl + Enter.

11. Type SAVE THE SPECIES as shown (each word on a separate line) in sans serif 50 point bold.

12. Change the font size to 8 point and unbold. Press Enter four times.

13. Type the organization address. Set the justification to *All*.

14. Preview the exercise.

15. Print one copy.

16. Using the + (plus) and a Wingding font, insert the envelope symbol before the second paragraph. Set the character to 24 points.

17. Center the page top to bottom.

18. Save the file; name it **ROAR.**

19. Close the document window.

In this exercise, you will create an advertisement using the same subject matter as the previous exercise. You will use two parallel columns for the text. In addition, you will insert, size and scale a graphic image. Using a different layout and different design elements, a completely different look will develop.

WHILE TIGERS BORN IN ZOOS ARE NUMEROUS, WILD TIGERS ARE AN *ENDANGERED SPECIES*

*W*ild tigers are found only in Asia. Until the 1800's, many lived throughout most of the southern half of the continent. Tigers still live in some of this area, but only a few are left. Because so many die before they reach adulthood, and because people have hunted tigers for years and cleared the forests in which they live, the tiger is an endangered species.

*H*elp us to SAVE THE SPECIES. Write to your Congressperson and local government officials to inform them of your support to keep the Tiger alive.

SAVE THE SPECIES

1356 Pacific Road, San Francisco, CA 90456

LESSON 5
SUMMARY EXERCISE C

EXERCISE DIRECTIONS:

1. Start with a clear screen.
2. Set .5" left and right margins.
3. Center the page top to bottom.
4. Import TIGER_J.WPG graphic as a watermark.
5. Create two parallel columns.
   - Set the first column to 3".
   - Set the second column to 2.5".
   - Set the space between the columns to .75".
6. Create a text box in the first column; type and center the text in sans serif 18 point bold. Change the text border to *thin top and bottom*.
7. Press Ctrl + Enter to begin the second column text.
8. Type SAVE THE SPECIES as shown (each word on a separate line) in sans serif 50 point bold. Change the line height to 1.09".
   - NOTE: The text box on the top left and the title on the top right of the page should end at approximately the same point on the page. Therefore, since fonts vary, you may need to use a different line height than the one specified in the directions. Experiment with different line heights until you achieve the desired result.
9. Turn off the column feature.
10. Press Enter twice.
11. Set line spacing to 1.5.
12. Type the exercise as shown in serif 14 point.
13. Type and right align the organization name and address in single space. Set the name to sans serif 12 point bold; set the address to 10 point.
14. Create a text box.
    - Using the + (plus) and a Wingding font, insert the envelope symbol.
    - Set it to 36 point.
    - Remove the border from around the text box.
    - Size it to 1" by 1".
    - Position it as shown using a paragraph anchor.
15. Preview the exercise.
16. Print one copy.
17. Save the file name it **ROAR1.**
18. Close the document window.

In this exercise, you will create an advertisement using the same subject matter as the previous two exercises. You will use parallel columns for the text box and text. In addition, you will insert a watermark as the background image. While the message is the same, the effect is different.

TIGER CUBS HAVE A VERY HAZARDOUS LIFE AND ABOUT HALF DIE BEFORE THEY REACH ADULTHOOD.

WHILE TIGERS BORN IN ZOOS ARE NUMEROUS, WILD TIGERS ARE AN ENDANGERED SPECIES.

SAVE THE SPECIES

The tiger is the largest member of the cat family. Since tigers can live in almost any climate, they may be found in the hot rain forests of Malaya, or the dry thorn woods of India, or the snowy spruce forests of Manchuria. Wild tigers are found only in Asia. Until the 1800's, many lived throughout most of the southern half of the continent. Tigers still live in some of this area, but only a few are left. Because so many die before they reach adulthood, and because people have hunted tigers for years and cleared the forests in which they live, the tiger is an endangered species.

Help us to SAVE THE SPECIES. Write to your Congressperson and local government officials to inform them of your support to keep the Tiger alive.

Save the Species
1356 Pacific Road
San Francisco, California 90456

LESSON 5
SUMMARY EXERCISE D

EXERCISE DIRECTIONS:

1. Start with a clear screen.
2. Set left, right, top and bottom margins to .5"
3. Change paper size to landscape (Layout, Page, Paper Size, Create, click Wide).
   - ■ NOTE: See Exercise 5 for information on changing paper size.
4. Create a text box and type CHOCOLATE in san serif 48 point bold within it. Remove the border from around the box. Size to content.
5. View the document at *Full Page*. (View, Zoom, 50%).
6. Position the text box vertically at approximately 2" down from the top of the page and horizontally so it appears centered on the first half of the page.
7. Use the Advance feature to bring the insertion point to 4.93".
8. Create 6 newspaper columns.
   - Use the default column margins.
   - Set the spacing between columns to 0.3"; set the spacing between columns 3 and 4 to 0.5".
9. Make the following text changes:
   - Type the text as shown in serif 12 point.
   - Set justification to *Full*.
   - Set line spacing to 1.3.
10. Create a text box and type THE CHOCOLATE FACTORY information as shown in 12 point bold.
    - Use a sans serif face for THE CHOCOLATE FACTORY and HOURS: 9-7 DAILY.
    - Size the box width to 1.55" and the box height to 3.45". Change the border to *shadow* and the fill to *button*.
    - Center the text within the box.
    - Position (drag) the box in the second column of the left page. (The text should adjust into the other columns).
    - ■ NOTE: If the text runs onto another page, adjust the line spacing amount to 1.2.
11. Import the ENDER04.WPG graphic image.
    - Size the box width to 4.85" and the box height to 3.65".
    - Change the fill to *100%*.
    - Position the graphic at the top right of the page as shown.
12. Change view to 100%.
13. Spell check.
14. Print one copy.
15. Save the exercise; name it **COCOA1**.
16. Close the document window.

Create this document in full-page view since placement of text boxes and graphics will be easier to see. While typing text in this view is difficult to read, you can change back to 100% view after formatting the page to spell check and proofread the text.

In this exercise you will create a brochure using 6 newspaper columns and graphic boxes. You will also use landscape orientation to position your page sideways, creating a document that can be folded in half as a brochure.

CHOCOLATE

Chocolate is probably the world's favorite food. You can drink it hot or cold, or eat it as a snack or as part of a meal. It is made into pies, cakes, cookies, candy, ice cream and even breakfast cereal.

Chocolate comes in lacy Valentine boxes and in survial kits. It is nourishing, energy-giving and satisfying.

Chocolate came to us from Mexico, by way of Europe. When the Spanish explorer Cortez arrived at the court of Montezuma, the Aztec Emperor, he found him drinking a cold, bitter drink called Chocolatl. It was made from seeds of the cacao tree, ground in water and mixed with spices. Montezuma gave Cortez the recipe and some cacao and vanilla beans. Cortez took them back to Spain, where the Spanish king and queen quickly improved the drink by adding sugar and serving it hot. For about 100 years, chocolate was exclusively a royal Spanish treat.

The Dutch settlers brought chocolate to the American colonies, and in 1765 a man named Baker started a chocolate mill near Boston. A hundred years later a man in Switzerland found a way to make solid sweet milk chocolate, and a great candy business was born.

THE CHOCOLATE FACTORY has been specializing in the finest chocolate products for over 50 years. Stop in and sample some of our outstanding chocolate delights.

THE CHOCOLATE FACTORY

754 Riverbend Drive
San Francisco
CA 94107

415-555-5555
HOURS: 9-7
DAILY

Lesson 6 ▪ Graphics Lines, Paragraph and Page Borders

EXERCISE 39

CREATING AND EDITING HORIZONTAL GRAPHICS LINES

CONCEPTS:

- You can use the Graphics Lines feature to insert horizontal and vertical lines in your document, in headers, or in footers. In desktop publishing, lines are sometimes referred to as *rules*. Lines are used to create designs, to separate parts of a document, or to draw attention to a particular place.

- You may adjust the position, length, and thickness of the lines. You may select decorative line styles such as triple, thick-thin, and dashed. Sample line styles appear below:

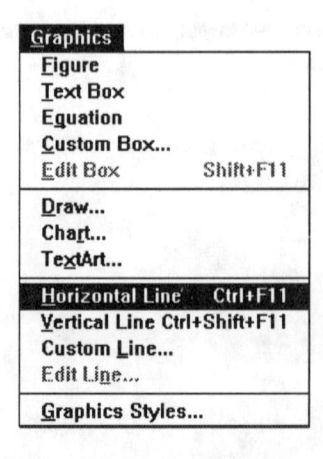

To create a horizontal line:
- Click **Graphics**
- Click **Horizontal Line**

To create a custom horizontal line:
- Click **Graphics**
- Click **Custom Line**

To select a line:
- Point to line. When insertion point turns to arrow, click and handles will appear.

- After choosing Horizontal Line from the Graphics main menu, WordPerfect automatically inserts a *full* line (a single line that extends from the left to the right margin) at the insertion point position.

Custom Line/Edit Line

Using the Dialog Box

- To create a line of a particular thickness, size or style other than the default, you may create a custom line.

- Or, you may select an existing horizontal line, then select Edit Line from the Graphics main menu. The Edit Graphics Lines dialog box appears when you create a custom line or you are editing an existing line:

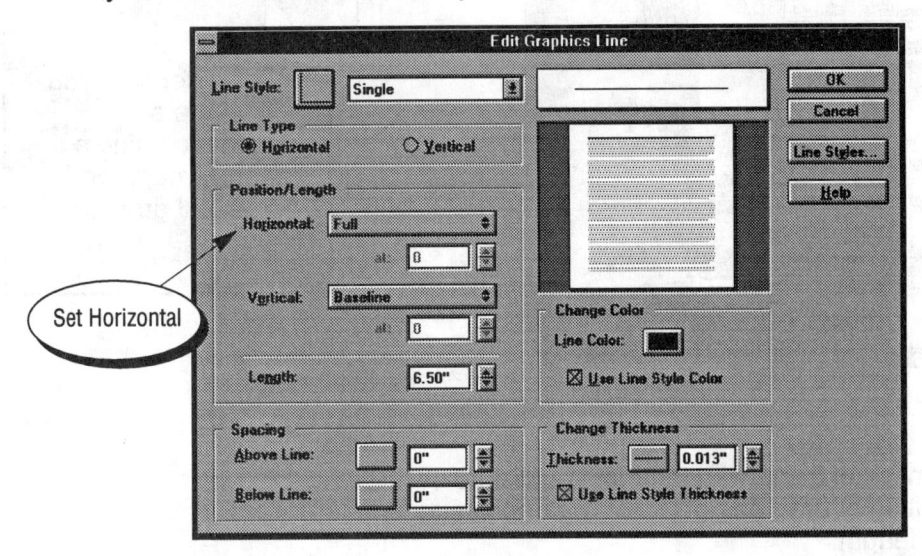

- You may specify the horizontal position and length of the line. If you select Full, the length automatically extends from the left to the right margin of the page or column. The remaining options (Left, Right, Centered, and Set) allow you to specify the line length.

- You may determine the amount of spacing to leave blank above and/or below the horizontal line.

- You may also specify the thickness of the line at the Change Thickness panel by either clicking the Thickness button and visually selecting a line or by entering the measurement in the text box. The default thickness is 0.013" -- about 1 point.

Lesson 6 ■ Exercise 39

- You may select a line style by sight or by name. When you click the Line Style button, a palette of defined styles pops up. When you select a style, it appears on the Line Style button, its name is listed in the drop-down list box, and its appearance displays in both preview windows.

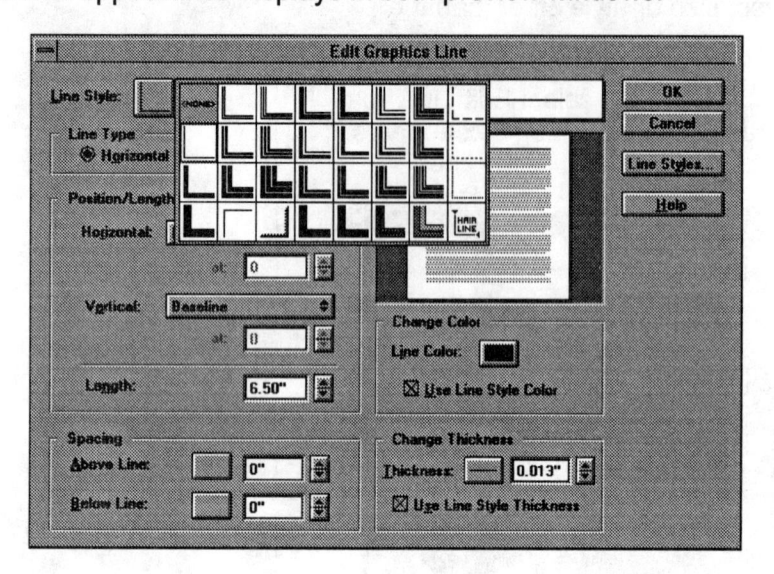

In this exercise, you will create a letterhead using a graphic image and horizontal graphic lines.

Using the Mouse

- To move, size or change the thickness of a line with the mouse, click to select it, then drag it to a new position or drag one of the sizing handles to enlarge or reduce its width and/or length.

EXERCISE DIRECTIONS:

1. Start with a clear screen.
2. Set the top and bottom margins to .5".
3. Create a horizontal line between the margins (full). Use the default thickness (.013).
4. Press Enter twice.
5. Create a **left** horizontal line 1" in length, using the default width (.013").
6. Center text "The DownHill Inn" in serif 18 point bold. Using the letter P and a Wingding font, create a flag between each word.
7. Create a *right* horizontal line 1" in length, using the default width (.013").
8. Press Enter once.
9. Create a *left* horizontal line 1" in length, setting the width to 0.03". Create a right horizontal line using the same measurements.
10. Press Enter twice.
11. Create a *left* horizontal line 1" in length, setting the width to .1".
12. Import and center INKSKIER.WPG. Size the graphic to 3" wide by .5" high. Remove the border from around the graphic.
13. Create a *right* horizontal line 1" in length, setting the width to .1".
14. Press Enter as many times as necessary to bring the insertion point to Ln 10".
15. Create a **left** horizontal line .5" in length, using the default width; center the footer text in sans serif 8 point. Use the same Wingding symbol (the flag) as above between each word. Create a **right** horizontal line using the same measurements.
16. Preview your document.
17. Print one copy.
18. Save the exercise; name it **INN**.
19. Close the document window.

[Letterhead sample:]

The ⚑ DownHill ⚑ Inn

123 Wheel Avenue ⚑ Ann Arbor ⚑ Michigan ⚑ 48187 ⚑ 313 ⚑ 555-5555

CREATE DEFAULT HORIZONTAL LINE

Ctrl+F11

1. Place insertion point at desired horizontal position for line.
2. Click **G**raphics .... `Alt`+`G`
3. Click **H**orizontal Line .... `H`

CREATE CUSTOM HORIZONTAL LINE

1. Follow steps 1-2 above.
2. Click Custom **L**ine .... `L`
3. In Line Type panel, click **H**orizontal ... `H`
4. Select one or more of the following options:

   a. Click Ho**r**izontal .... `Alt`+`R`
      pop-up list, Select one:
      - **S**et .... `S`

      Type position where line is to begin
      - **L**eft .... `L`
      - **R**ight .... `R`
      - **C**entered .... `C`
      - **F**ull .... `F`

   b. Click V**e**rtical .... `Alt`+`E`
      pop-up list, Select one:
      - **S**et .... `S`

      Type distance from top of page.
      - **B**aseline .... `B`

   c. Click Le**n**gth text box .... `Alt`+`N`

      Type length.

   d. Click Spacing **A**bove Line .... `Alt`+`A`

      Type amount.

   e. Click Spacing **B**elow Line .... `Alt`+`B`

      Type amount.

   f. Click **T**hickness .... `Alt`+`T`
      button, select thickness from list.

      OR

      Type desired thickness.

   g. Click **L**ine Style .... `Alt`+`L`
      button, select style from palette

      OR

      Click **L**ine Style .... `Alt`+`L`
      drop-down list.

      double click desired style.

5. Click **OK** .... `Enter`

Lesson 6 ▪ Exercise 39

Lesson 6 ▪ Graphics Lines, Paragraph and Page Borders

EXERCISE 40

CREATE AND EDIT VERTICAL GRAPHICS LINES

CONCEPTS:

- Vertical lines may be created using similar methods as horizontal lines.

- After choosing <u>V</u>ertical Line from the <u>G</u>raphics main menu, WordPerfect automatically inserts a full length vertical line at the left margin position.

Custom Line/Edit Line

Using the Dialog Box

- You may create a custom vertical line by selecting **Custom <u>L</u>ine** from the <u>G</u>raphics main menu. Or, you may select an existing vertical line (position mouse pointer on line and click), then select **Edit Li<u>n</u>e** from the <u>G</u>raphics main menu. The Edit Graphics Lines dialog box appears when you create a custom line or you are editing an existing line:

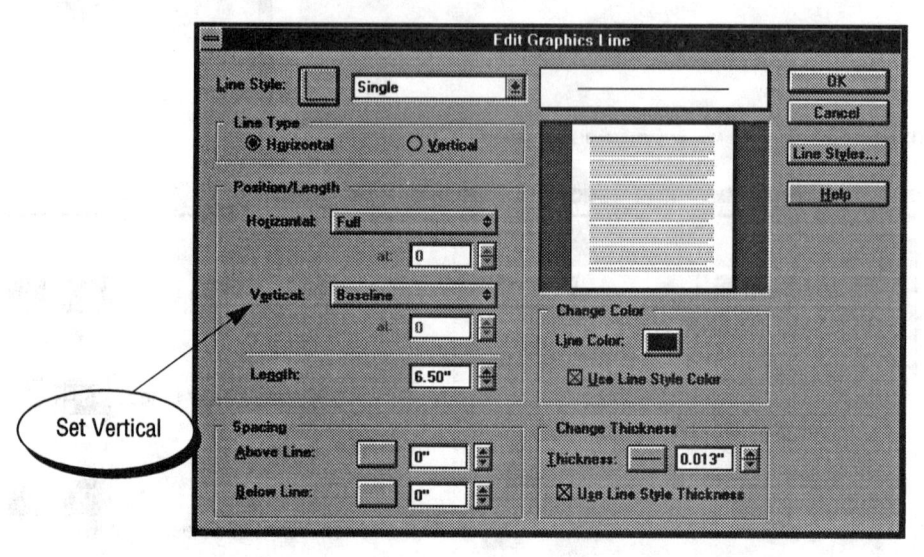

(Edit Graphics Line dialog box, with "Set Vertical" labeled pointing to the Vertical position setting)

- You may specify the vertical position and length of the line. If you select Full, the length automatically extends from the top to the bottom margin. The remaining options (Top, Bottom, Centered, and Set) allow you to specify the line length.

- The default Baseline vertical position places the line at the base of the current line of text. Or, you can manually set the vertical position by choosing Set and entering the distance you want the line drawn from the top of the page.

Using the Mouse

- You may move, size or change the thickness of a vertical line with the mouse as you did with the horizontal line.

✓

To create a vertical line:
- Click <u>G</u>raphics
- Click <u>V</u>ertical Line

✓

To create a custom vertical line:
- Click <u>G</u>raphics
- Click **Custom <u>L</u>ine**

☞ In this exercise, you will enhance a menu you created earlier by adding vertical and horizontal lines.

160

CREATE DEFAULT VERTICAL LINE

Ctrl+F11

1. Place insertion point at desired vertical line position.
2. Click **G**raphics .... Alt + G
3. Click **V**ertical Line V

CREATE CUSTOM VERTICAL LINE

1. Follow steps 1-2 above.
2. Click Custom **L**ine. L
3. In Line Type panel,

   Click **V**ertical. V
4. Select one or more of the following options:

   a. Click Ho**r**izontal .... Alt + R
   pop-up list, select one:
   - **S**et .... S

   Type position
   - **L**eft L
   - **R**ight .... R
   - **C**entered C
   - Column **A**ligned .... A

   Type column number.

   b. Click **V**ertical .... Alt + E
   pop-up list, select one:
   - **S**et .... S

   Type distance from left margin
   - **T**op .... T
   - **B**ottom .... B
   - **C**entered C
   - **F**ull .... F

   c. Click Le**n**gth text box .... Alt + N

   Type length.

   d. Click Spacing **B**order .... Alt + B
   Offset

   Type amount.

   e. Click **T**hickness .... Alt + T
   button, Select thickness.

   OR

   Type desired thickness

   f. Click **L**ine Style .... Alt + L
   button, Select style.

   OR

   Click **L**ine Style drop-down list

   Select style.

5. Click OK .... Enter

Lesson 6 ▪ Exercise 40

EXERCISE DIRECTIONS:

1. Start with a clear screen.

2. Open **FOOD.**

3. Set the top and bottom margins to .5"

4. With your insertion point at the top of the screen, create a **left** vertical line extending the full length of the page, setting a .3" thickness.

5. Create a *right* vertical line extending the full length of the page, setting a .3" thickness.

6. Change the typeface, type style and type sizes of the text as follows:

   - "The Sherwood Forest Inn" to serif 36-point.

   - Address and phone number text to serif 10 point.

   - Food item headings to serif 14 point.

   - Food items to serif 12 point.

7. Press Enter 6 times after the phone number.

8. Create a centered horizontal line below "BREAKFAST MENU." Set the length to 5" and the thickness to .02"

9. Import BUCK.WPG.

   - Set the size to 1" by 1".

   - Scale the height to 1.2" and the width to 1.7".

   - Center the graphic.

10. Delete two hard returns before David Zeiss, Proprietor so that his name remains on the page.

11. Preview your document.

12. Print one copy.

13. Close the file; save the changes.

The Sherwood Forest Inn

125 Pine Hill Road
Arlington, VA 22207
703-987-4443

BREAKFAST MENU

BEVERAGES

Herbal Tea...$1.00
Coffee...$2.00
Cappuccino...$2.50

◆❖◆❖◆

FRUITS

Berry Refresher...$3.00
Sparkling Citrus Blend...$3.00
Baked Apples...$3.50

◆❖◆❖◆

GRAINS

Fruity Oatmeal...$3.50
Bran Muffins...$3.00
Whole Wheat Zucchini Bread...$3.00
Four-Grain Pancakes...$5.00

◆❖◆❖◆

EGGS

Baked Eggs with Creamed Spinach...$6.50
Poached Eggs with Hollandaise Sauce...$6.00
Scrambled Eggs...$2.50
Sweet Pepper and Onion Frittata...$6.50

David Zeiss, Proprietor

Lesson 6 ▪ Graphics Lines, Paragraph and Page Borders

EXERCISE 41

COPY, DELETE AND SHADE GRAPHICS LINES

CONCEPTS:

- Lines, like graphics images and boxes, may be copied and deleted.

- When the graphics line is selected, handles appear and the line is in an edit mode. Once in an edit mode, the line may be copied, deleted, sized or moved.

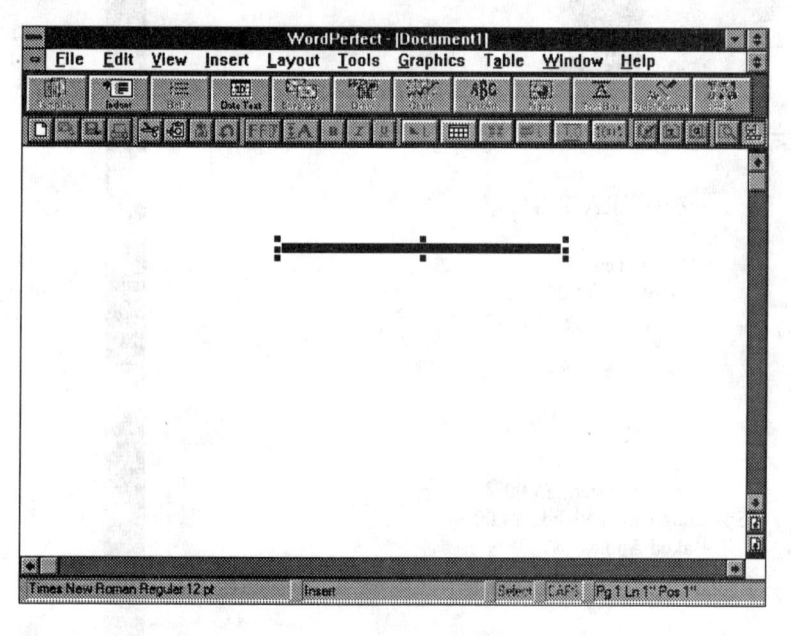

- Like fonts, lines may be tinted in shades of gray or in color. This can add interesting effects to your document. However, you must have a printer that supports color to get color output.

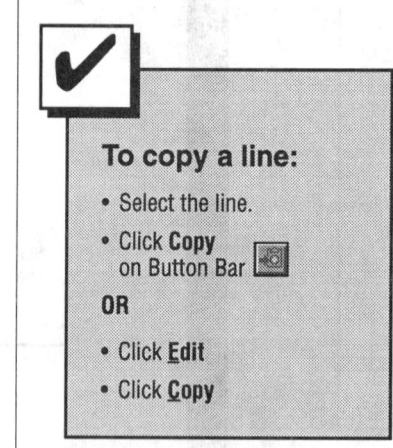

✓ To copy a line:
- Select the line.
- Click **Copy** on Button Bar

OR

- Click **Edit**
- Click **Copy**

✓ To paste a line:
- Click where line is to be inserted.
- Click **Paste** on Button Bar

OR

- Click **Edit**
- Click **Paste**

✓ To delete a line:
- Select the line.
- Press **Delete**

✓ To shade a line:
- Select the line.
- Click **Edit Line**
- Click **Line Color**

EXERCISE DIRECTIONS:

1. Start with a clear screen.
2. Use the default margins.
3. Begin the exercise at the top margin.
4. - Create a *full horizontal* black line.
   - Size the thickness to 0.238".
5. - Copy the line once.
   - Using your mouse, position one copy of the line approximately .25" down from the first black line.
   - Color the line dark gray.
   - Using your mouse, size the line thickness to be slightly narrower.
6. - Copy the line once.
   - Using your mouse, position it approximately .25" below the dark gray line.
   - Color the line light gray.
   - Using your mouse, size the line thickness to be slightly narrower than the dark gray line.
7. Type the address as shown between lines in sans serif 10 point.
8. Enter enough times to bring the insertion point to approximately 2.89".
9. Type SARAH GRAY, placing each letter on a separate line as shown. Set the text to serif 36 point bold.
10. - Create a *full vertical* line. Set the thickness to .088"
    - Position it to the left of the name.
    - Color the line dark gray.
    - ■ NOTE: You may need to adjust the horizontal lines so they don't overlap the vertical line.
11. Copy the black horizontal line and position it at the bottom of the page as shown.
12. Preview the exercise.
13. Delete the bottom black horizontal line.
14. Print one copy.
15. Save the file; name it **GRAYLET.**
16. Close the document window.

> In this exercise, you will create a letterhead using various line thicknesses and different shades of gray

Lesson 6 ■ Exercise 41

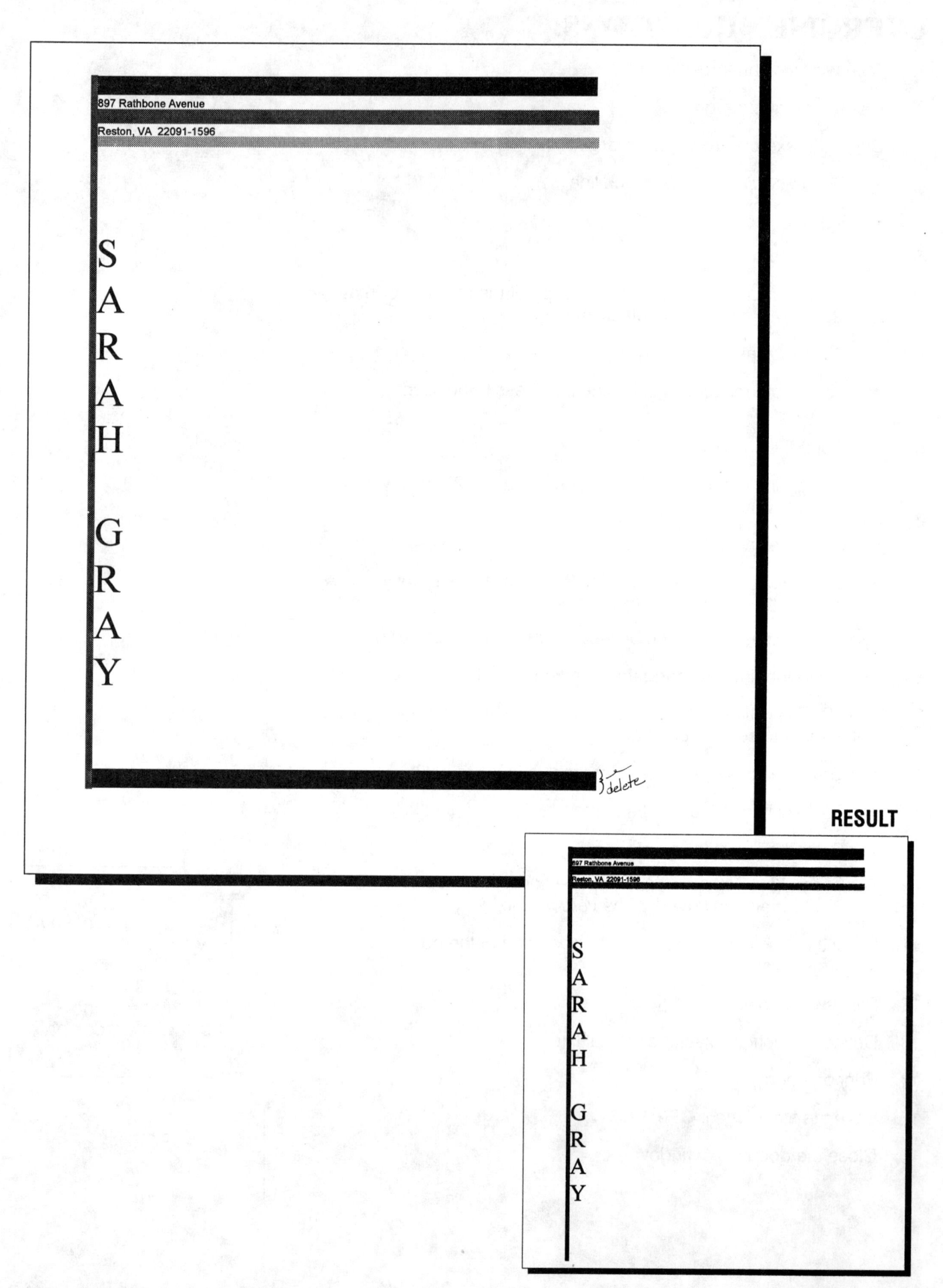

897 Rathbone Avenue

Reston, VA 22091-1596

S
A
R
A
H

G
R
A
Y

delete

RESULT

897 Rathbone Avenue

Reston, VA 22091-1596

S
A
R
A
H

G
R
A
Y

NEXT EXERCISE!!

Lesson 6 ▪ Graphics Lines, Paragraph and Page Borders

EXERCISE 42

PARAGRAPH, PAGE BORDERS AND FILLS

CONCEPTS:

- WordPerfect's Border/Fill feature allows you to place a border around, and add shading to, a paragraph, page, or column. This feature is similar to the Border/Fill option for graphics boxes.

- The Paragraph, Page, and Column options on the Layout main menu each offer the Border/Fill option. In each case, you may select from a list of border styles or create a custom style. You may also select or create a fill style. You may limit the border to the current page, paragraph, or column group, or have it apply to the entire document.

- To place a border around a paragraph or page, position the insertion point in the desired paragraph or page, and follow the keystrokes outlined below. By default, the border applies to just that particular paragraph or page, but you may have the border appear around not only that paragraph/page, but all paragraph/pages following. Or, you may select, for example, several paragraphs, then apply the border to that selection.

- To place a border around columns, position the insertion point anywhere in a column. The border will enclose all columns in the document.

In this exercise, you will gain practice applying various paragraph border and fill styles, as well as a page border to a document you created earlier.

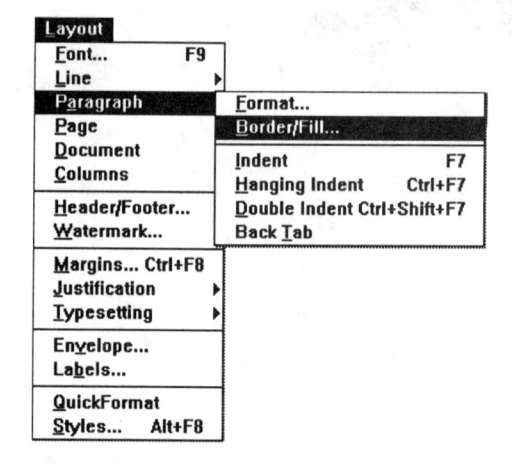

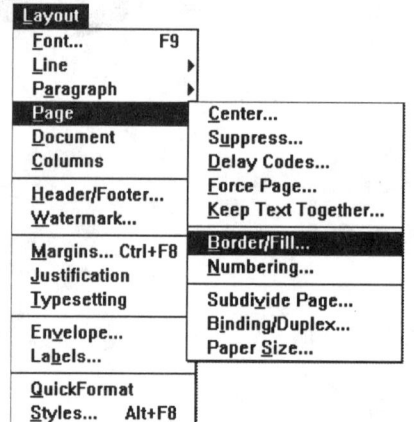

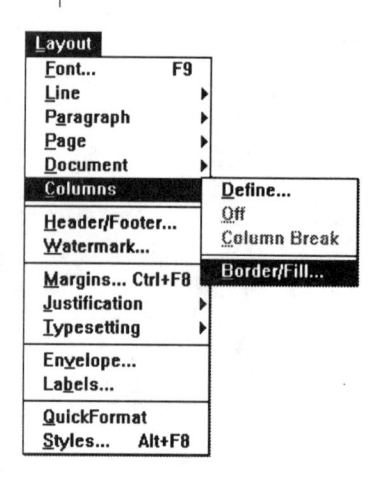

EXERCISE DIRECTIONS:

1. Start with a clear screen.
2. Open **COMPANY**.
3. Create a single line paragraph border and no fill for the first text paragraph as shown.
4. Select the block of ACCOUNTING companies and create a dashed paragraph border and a 10% fill for the second section as indicated.
5. Select the block of BUSINESS AND PRESENTATION SOFTWARE companies.

- Create an extra thick border and a button fill for the third section as indicated.
6. Create a gray mat border and no fill for the fourth section as indicated.
7. Create a thick shadow page border as shown.
8. Preview your document.
9. Print one copy.
10. Close the file; save the changes.

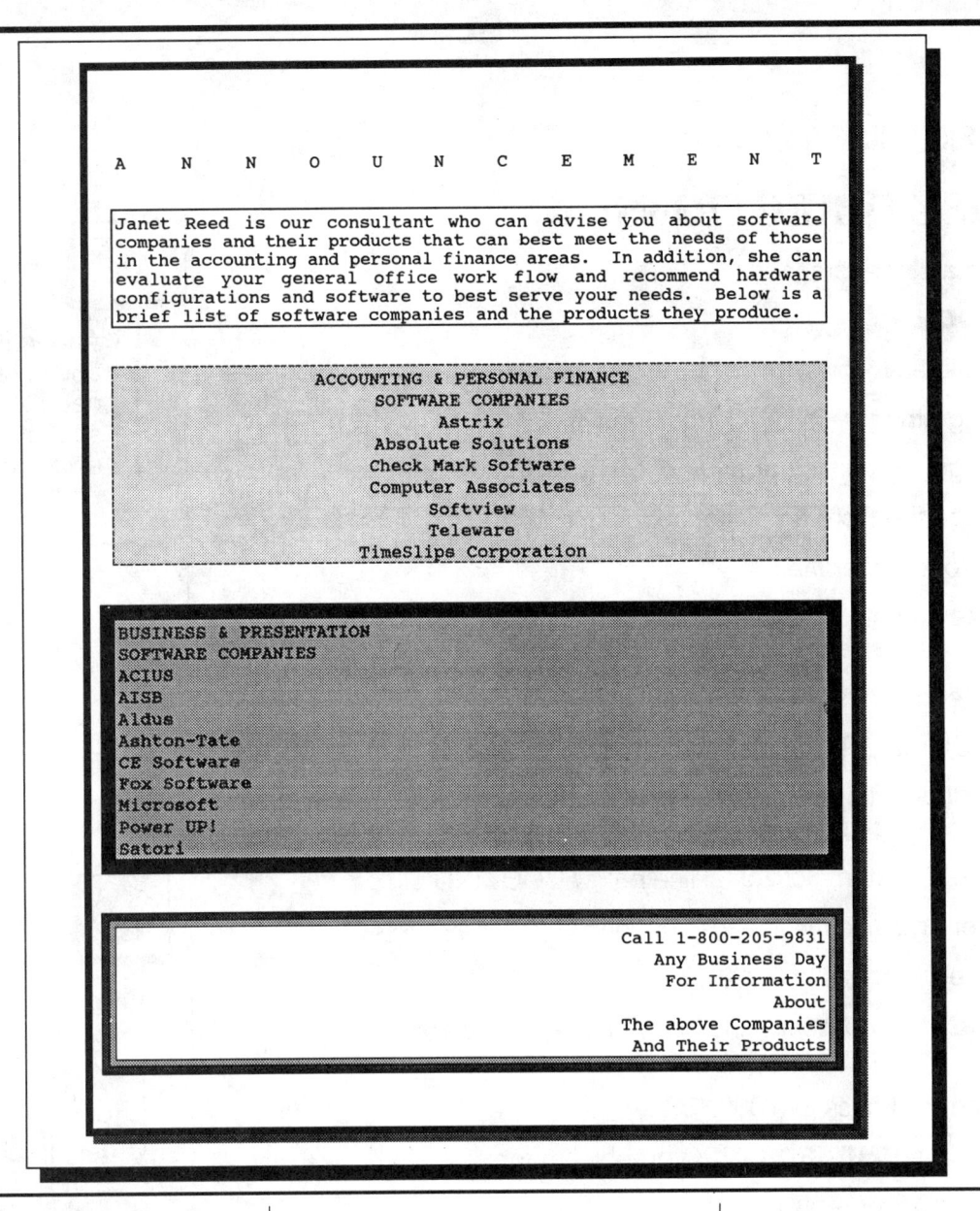

```
                A N N O U N C E M E N T

    ┌─────────────────────────────────────────────────┐
    │ Janet Reed is our consultant who can advise you about software │
    │ companies and their products that can best meet the needs of those │
    │ in the accounting and personal finance areas.  In addition, she can │
    │ evaluate your general office work flow and recommend hardware │
    │ configurations and software to best serve your needs.  Below is a │
    │ brief list of software companies and the products they produce. │
    └─────────────────────────────────────────────────┘
```

```
              ACCOUNTING & PERSONAL FINANCE
                    SOFTWARE COMPANIES
                          Astrix
                      Absolute Solutions
                     Check Mark Software
                     Computer Associates
                          Softview
                          Teleware
                     TimeSlips Corporation
```

```
BUSINESS & PRESENTATION
SOFTWARE COMPANIES
ACIUS
AISB
Aldus
Ashton-Tate
CE Software
Fox Software
Microsoft
Power UP!
Satori
```

```
                            Call 1-800-205-9831
                               Any Business Day
                               For Information
                                         About
                            The above Companies
                            And Their Products
```

ADD PAGE OR PARAGRAPH BORDER/FILL

1. Place insertion point on desired page or paragraph.

    OR

    Select desired pages or paragraphs.

2. Click **L**ayout .... **Alt** + **L**

3. Click **P**age .... **P**

    OR

    Click **P**aragraph .... **A**

4. Click **B**order/Fill .... **B**

5. Select desired Border Style from palette or drop-down list.

6. Select desired Fill Style from palette or drop-down list.

7. To apply border to all paragraphs/pages from insertion point on:

    Deselect Apply border .... **P**
    to current page only

    OR

    Deselect Apply border .... **P**
    to current paragraph only

8. Click **OK** .... **Enter**

ADD COLUMN BORDER/FILL

1. Set insertion point anywhere in a column.

2. Click **L**ayout .... **Alt** + **L**

3. Click **C**olumns .... **C**

4. Click **B**order/Fill .... **B**

5. Select desired Border Style from palette or drop-down list.

    To add only a vertical separator between columns, select Column Between.

    To add a vertical separator between columns and a border on the outside edge as well, select Column All.

6. Select desired Fill Style from palette or drop-down list.

NOTE: The following option applies only if you have more than one column group defined in the document.

7. To apply border to just the currently selected column group, select Apply border to current column group only.

8. Click **OK** .... **Enter**

Lesson 6 ▪ Exercise 42

LESSON 6
SUMMARY EXERCISE A

EXERCISE DIRECTIONS:

1. Start with a clear screen.
2. Open **COOK**.
3. Edit the title as follows:
   - Change the title font to script 48 point bold.
   - Change the text to upper- and lowercase.
   - Change the word and letter spacing to 100% of optimal.
   - Enter once after the title.
4. - Create a custom horizontal line below the heading as shown. Center and size the line to 3.5" long.
   - Set the thickness to 0.038.
5. Center COOKING TIPS and enter once.
6. Create a double line paragraph border around the COOKING TIPS section and use a 10% fill.
7. - Create a custom horizontal line below COOKING TIPS.
   - Center and size the line to 1.75" long.
   - Set the thickness to 0.038.
8. - Create a *full horizontal* line below the second column as shown.
   - Set the thickness to 0.038.
9. - Import the **ENDER05.WPG** graphic image.
   - Size it to 1" wide by 1" long.
   - Center it below the second column as shown.
   - Remove the border from around the graphic.
10. - Enter five times after *Are you getting hungry?*
11. - Copy the graphic.
    - Size it to .5" wide by .5" long.
    - Use a 10% fill.
    - Center it below *Are you getting hungry?*
12. Create a single line page border.
13. Preview the exercise.
14. Print one copy.
15. Close the file; save the changes.

After enhancing this document, you may need to adjust text so that you avoid awkward paragraph breaks.

In this exercise, you will enhance a document created earlier using lines, a paragraph border and fill, and a page border.

The Art of Cooking

Preparing a meal requires skill and patience. The results may mean the difference between eating just to exist and the satisfaction that comes from one of the major pleasures of life.

Cooking is an art. Every recipe should be prepared with tender, loving care and it should be one of the primary ingredients. A cook must develop a feeling for what each ingredient will do in a recipe.

QUALITY RAW MATERIALS

An outstanding meal must be prepared with high-quality raw materials, cooked simply but perfectly to enhance their natural flavor. It is important to plan your meal carefully. The menu should contain a contrast in textures, flavor and color. Salad should be served as a separate course. Use the best natural foods of the season and plan menus around them. Try not to use packaged frozen items if you can get them fresh. If you have a garden, use the fresh garden vegetables and fruit whenever you can. It's a challenge to try to fit all the fruit--strawberries, raspberries, cantaloupes, watermelons, blueberries, blackberries, peaches, nectarines, cherries, and plums into the menu. You might want to use fresh herbs like dill, parsley, basil, or tarragon.

Or, you might want to try a variety of garden lettuces and home-grown tomatoes like beefsteaks, plum and cherry-size.

COOKING TIPS

❖ Never serve a dish which you have not prepared at least once before.

❖ Do not serve too much on a plate.

❖ The menu should contain a contrast in textures, flavor and color.

Are you getting hungry?

LESSON 6
SUMMARY EXERCISE B

EXERCISE DIRECTIONS:

1. Start with a clear screen.

2. Open **CONDOR.**

3. Create a new paragraph beginning with "Write to your Congress person...".

4. Set the new paragraph text to 11 point bold.

5. Create a shadow paragraph border around the new paragraph as shown. Use a button fill.

6. Full justify all text except the new paragraph.

7. Create a full horizontal line above and below the name and address information. Use the default line thickness.

8. Create a thick/thin2 page border.

9. Preview the exercise.

10. Print one copy.

11. Close the file; save the changes.

> In this exercise, you will enhance a document created earlier using lines, a paragraph border and fill, and a page border.

The **CALIFORNIA CONDOR**, a vulture, is the largest flying land bird in North America and makes its home in Southern California. Black Feathers cover most of the bird's body, except for the white area on the underside of the condor's wings. The neck and head have no feathers and are red-orange color. The condor is a unique bird because it does not build a nest but lays its eggs in caves, holes or among rocks. It is also a particularly strong flier. It can soar and glide in the air for long distances.

By the end of the 1980s, only 30 condors remained in the United States. The diminished number of condors is the result of hunting. The growth of urban areas in Southern California also poses a threat to the natural habitat of the bird. Help us to **SAVE THE SPECIES**.

Write to your Congressperson and local government officials to inform them of your support of more land for sanctuaries to help keep the condor alive.

SAVE THE SPECIES ♦ 1356 Pacific Road ♦ San Francisco ♦ California ♦ 90456

Lesson 6 ■ Exercise B

LESSON 6
SUMMARY EXERCISE C

EXERCISE DIRECTIONS:

1. Start with a clear screen.
2. Set left, right, and top margins to .5"; set bottom margin to .3".
3. Center the heading in script 48 point bold.
4. Enter twice.
5. Change the font to sans serif 10-point bold italic.
6. Create a full horizontal line (between the margins) using a hairline thickness.
7. Enter once.
8. Enter dateline information as shown (left align Volume 1, center Quarterly Newsletter of the Wildlife Society and right align Summer 1994).
9. Create a full horizontal line using the default thickness.
10. Enter three times.
11. Create three newspaper columns.
12. Open **SPECIES** from the data disk; save as **SPECIES1**.
    or
    Type the newsletter as shown.
    - NOTE: To insure that the text flows into the columns, place your insertion point within the column mode before you insert the file.

    Note the following:
    - Center the headlines; set them to sans serif 14-point bold.
    - Set all paragraph text to serif 12 point.
    - Full justify all paragraph text.
    - Create a dashed box around "Save the Species...." and center each line within the column as shown.
    - Import **CRANE.WPG**. Use the mouse to size it to approximately 1.5" wide by 1" high; use a contour text wrap and place it as shown. Create a centered caption in sans serif 10-point bold that reads, KEEP ME FLYING.
    - Set "*In the next issue:*" information to 14-point.
    - Create a gray mat border around "*In the next issue*" text.
13. To create the pull quote:
    - Type the following text into a text box:
      "*If we continue to ignore the need for wildlife conservation, today's endangered species will soon become extinct.*"
    - Use a thick top and bottom border and a button fill.
    - Size the box to approximately 2.5" wide by 1.75" high
    - Position it as shown.
    - Use a square text wrap on both sides.

To draw the reader's attention to emphasize a major point in an article, a *pull quote* may be used. A pull quote is set off in larger point size and a different type style than the body text. In this exercise, the pull quote has been placed in a text box.

In this exercise, you will create a newsletter using the design elements you have learned.

...continued

14. Spell check.
15. Preview your document.
16. Print one copy.
17. 💾 Close the file; save the changes.
    or
    ⌨ Save the file; name it **SPECIES1**.
18. Close the document window.

Save the Species

Volume 1   Quarterly Newsletter of the Wildlife Society   Summer 1994

What is Wildlife Conservation?

Wildlife Conservation includes all human efforts to preserve wild animals and plants and save them from extinction. Our organization supports the protection and wise management of wild species and their environment. The greatest danger to wildlife results from human activities; your contributions aid us in funding demonstrations and activities which help educate others about the dangers of these activities and help preserve the existence of disappearing species. Send contributions to:

Save the Species
1356 Pacific Road
San Francisco, CA 90456

If we continue to ignore the need for wildlife conservation, today's endangered species will soon become extinct. Extinction is particularly dangerous due to the economic, scientific and survival value of wildlife. Wild species of animals and plants provide many substances which are valuable to the economies of different countries, both as food products and as products for trade. The study of wildlife provides important knowledge about life processes which has lead to the discovery of medical and scientific products. Additionally, the existence of many species of wildlife maintains the balance of living systems on the earth. The loss of certain species will affect the existence of others that depend on it perhaps for food. Volunteer for Save the Species and help us convince Washington that it is vital to protect the existence of endangered species through legislation!

Endangered Species of the Season:
The California Condor

The California condor, a vulture, is the largest flying land bird in North America and makes its home in Southern California. Black feathers cover most of the bird's body except for the white area on the underside of the condor's wings. The neck and head have no feathers and are a red-orange color. The condor is a unique bird because it does not build a nest, but lays its eggs in caves, holes, or among rocks. It is also a particularly strong flier; it can soar and glide in the air for long distances, flapping its wings an average of only once an hour. It is a carnivore and eats the remains of dead animals.

"If we continue to ignore the need for wildlife conservation, today's endangered species will soon become extinct."

KEEP ME FLYING

By the end of the 1980s, only 30 condors remained in the United States. The diminished number of condors is a result of hunting. The growth of urban areas in Southern California also poses a threat to the natural habitat of the bird. Save the Species urges you to write to your Congressperson and local government officials to inform them of your support of more land for sanctuaries to help keep the condor alive.

In the next issue: What is happening to the Killer Whale and its cousin, The Dolphin.

Lesson 6 ■ Exercise C   175

LESSON 6
SUMMARY EXERCISE D

EXERCISE DIRECTIONS:

1. Start with a clear screen.
2. 💾 Open **JACKET** from the data disk; save file as **JACKET2**.

   or

   ⌨ Type the exercise as shown in illustration A
3. Delete the first two words, NOW AVAILABLE and the fifth word, TEAM, from the first paragraph.
4. Create a table with one column and one row.
5. Move the text into the table.
6. Size the table to 4.5" wide and center it.
7. Create a thick double line border around the table.
8. Format the flyer as shown in illustration B.
   - Center all text within the table.
   - Insert hard returns in the text as indicated in the exercise.
   - Set font faces and sizes as indicated in the exercise.
   - Create a 3" custom line below the headline. Set the thickness to .060".
9.
   - Create a text box. Type NOW AVAILABLE in sans serif 24 point bold.
   - Create an extra thick border around the text box.
   - Size the text box width to 4.5"; size the height to contents.
   - Place the text box just above the table box.
10. Create a single line page border.
11. Create six 9.48" custom vertical lines using the default thickness.

    Position the lines as shown.

    HINT: *Create one line; then select the line, press Ctrl + C to copy the line, then press Ctrl + V to paste the line. To create additional lines, repeatedly press Ctrl + V, then move each line into position.*
12.
    - Create nine 1.08" custom vertical lines using the default thickness. *NOTE: Adjust your vertical line lengths as necessary to achieve the desired results.*
    - Position the lines below the table box as shown.
13. Preview your document.
14. 💾 Close the file; save the changes.

    or

    ⌨ Save the file; name it **JACKET2**.
15. Close the document window.

> In this exercise, you will create a flyer from previously created text.

176

ILLUSTRATION A

NOW AVAILABLE: Authentic baseball team jackets personalized with your own name. Harold's Sportswear Store now carries the genuine article. Our jackets are exactly the same as the ones worn by every baseball team.

The jackets are personalized for you absolutely free. Choose your favorite team and have your name on the jacket. You can look like a professional baseball player in your authentic jacket!

And the price is right. Just $149.99 plus $5.50 for shipping and handling. Remember, there is no charge for personalizing the jacket with your name.

Each jacket is made by the same company that makes the jackets for the professional baseball team members. They fit the same. They have the same logo. They even have the same label inside as the professional team jacket.

WHAT ARE YOU WAITING FOR? Be the first in your neighborhood to own the official baseball team jacket. To order your authentic jacket, call Harold's Sportswear Store today. Dial 1-800-555-BALL. You can charge the jacket and receive it within one week.

Lesson 6 ■ Exercise D

ILLUSTRATION B

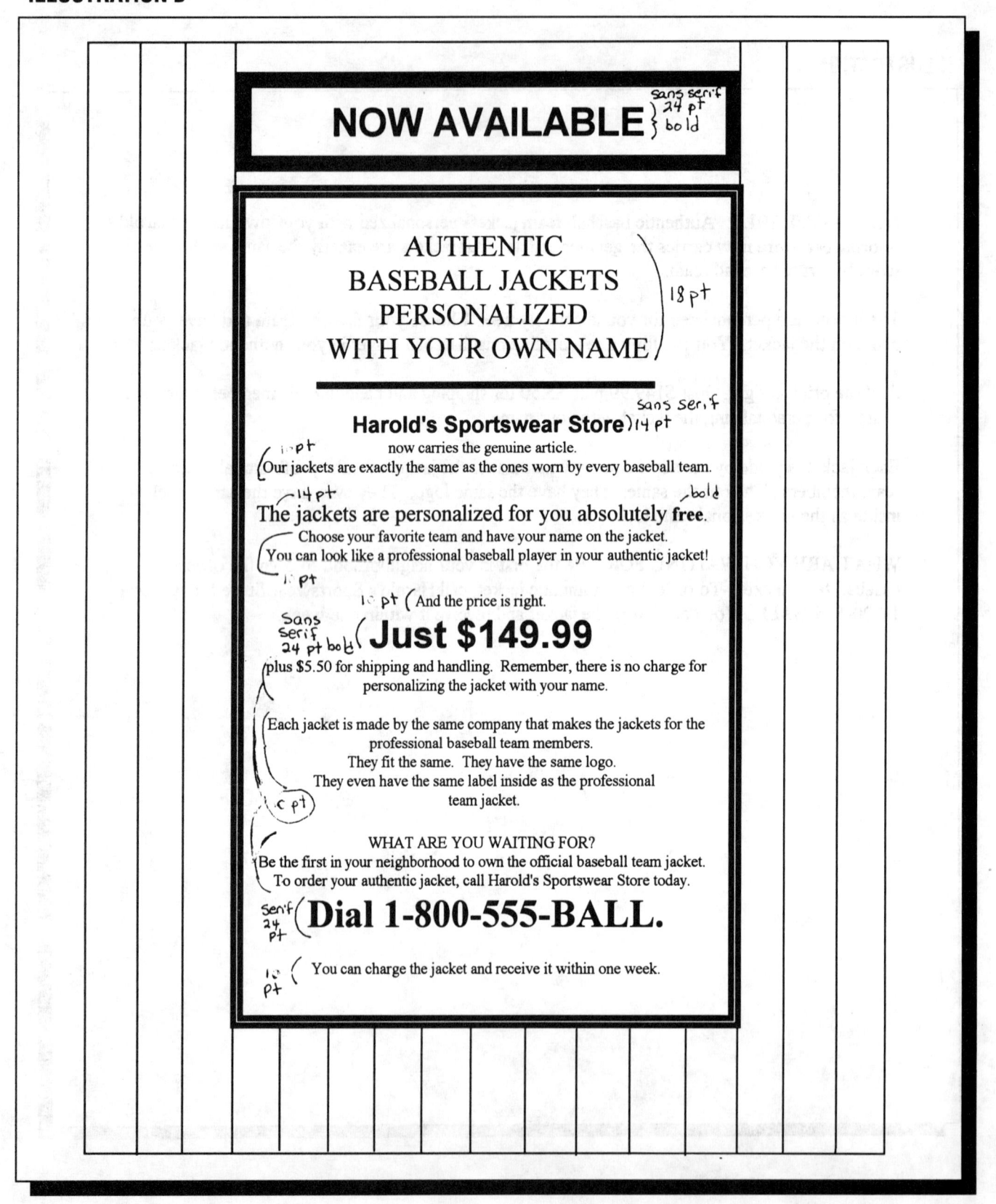

NOW AVAILABLE   {sans serif 24 pt bold}

AUTHENTIC
BASEBALL JACKETS
PERSONALIZED
WITH YOUR OWN NAME   } 18 pt

Harold's Sportswear Store) 14 pt sans serif

(10 pt) now carries the genuine article.
Our jackets are exactly the same as the ones worn by every baseball team.

(14 pt) The jackets are personalized for you absolutely **free**. ← bold

Choose your favorite team and have your name on the jacket.
You can look like a professional baseball player in your authentic jacket!

12 pt

10 pt (And the price is right.

Sans serif 24 pt bold (**Just $149.99**

plus $5.50 for shipping and handling. Remember, there is no charge for
personalizing the jacket with your name.

Each jacket is made by the same company that makes the jackets for the
professional baseball team members.
They fit the same. They have the same logo.
They even have the same label inside as the professional
team jacket.

(c pt)

WHAT ARE YOU WAITING FOR?
Be the first in your neighborhood to own the official baseball team jacket.
To order your authentic jacket, call Harold's Sportswear Store today.

Serif 24 pt (**Dial 1-800-555-BALL.**

10 pt (You can charge the jacket and receive it within one week.

NEXT LESSON!!

Lesson 7 • Special Enhancements

EXERCISE 43
REVERSE TEXT

CONCEPTS:

- **Reverse text** is text that appears white against a dark background. Black letters on a white background are converted to white (or colored) letters on a black background.

Reverse Text

- Using reverse text adds interest to the type. Reversing a small amount of text is an attention-getting technique. Avoid reversing a large amount of text because it is difficult to read and will, therefore, probably be ignored.

- Text is reversed by selecting a graphics box, paragraph border or page border with a 100% (black) Fill Style and a Font Color of white.

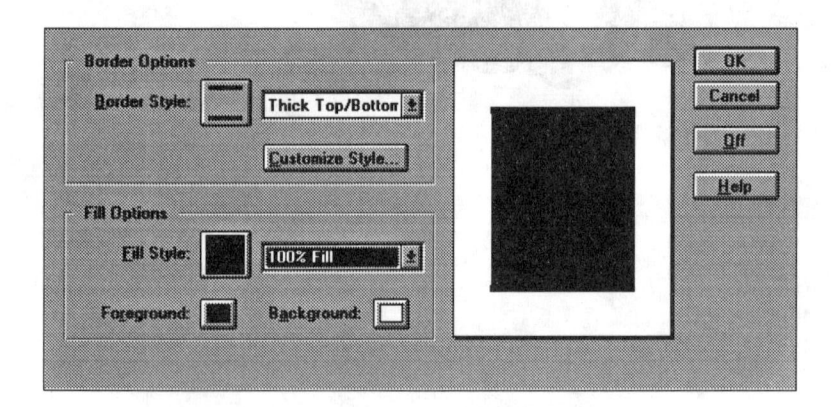

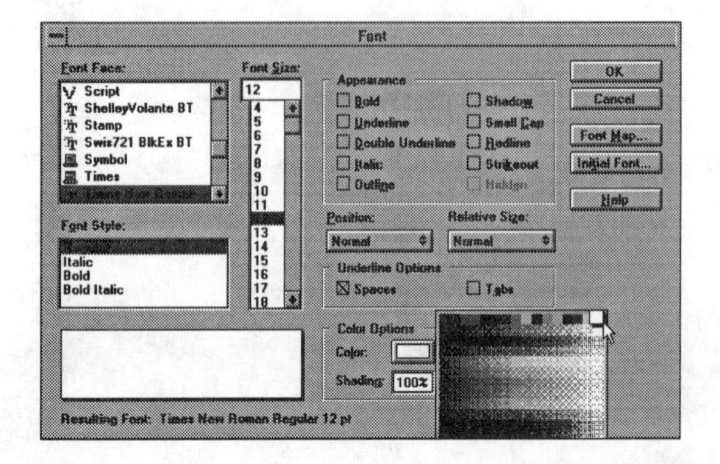

To reverse text:
- Click **T**ools
- Click **M**acros
- Click **P**lay
- Type *REVERSE.WCM*.
- Click **P**lay

OR
- Click **G**raphics
- Click **T**ext Box
- Click **B**order/Fill
- Click **F**ill Style
- Select Black or 100% Fill.
- Click **L**ayout
- Click **F**ont
- Click **C**olor
- Select White.
- Type text.

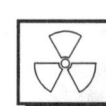

When the box fill is changed to black, the text will not show up since it is black text in a black box. When selecting/highlighting the text, the highlighting will show up as white.

180

- WordPerfect has a macro named REVERSE.WCM that automates the process of reversing text in a graphics box. After text is typed, the macro is played and stops for you to choose a Text Color and a Fill Style/Color. The default is White Text Color with a 100% Black Fill Style/Color.

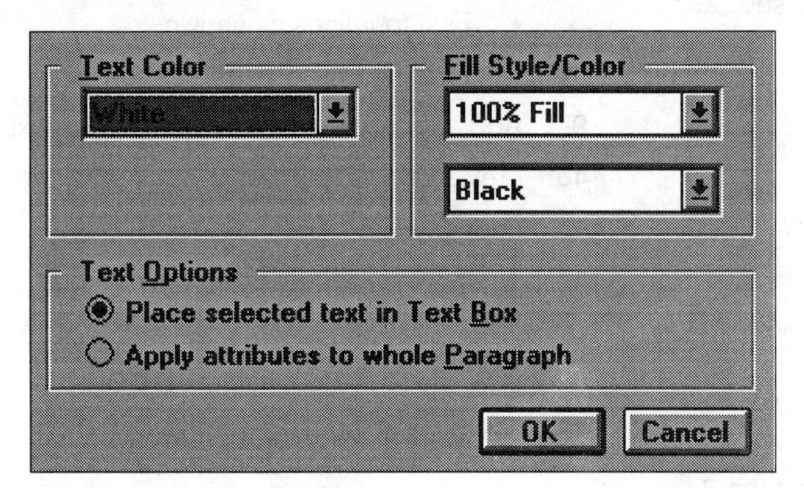

> Use a large point size in a sans serif font face to improve type clarity. If a small point size is used, bold the font face.

> When reversing text, the color of the text can be any light color or light shade of gray.

- A **border** can be placed around a graphics box containing the reversed text. When the REVERSE.WCM macro is used, the border style for the graphics box is added by editing the box (see Exercise 33).

> In this exercise, you will create a flyer using reverse text and shaded text.

REVERSE TEXT WITH GRAPHICS BOX BORDER

Lesson 7 ■ Exercise 43

EXERCISE DIRECTIONS:

1. Start with a clear screen.
2. 📀 Open **BOOK** from data disk; save as **BOOK2**.

   or

   ⌨ Type the exercise as shown.
3. Center the text vertically and horizontally.
4. Set 1" left and right margins and 1.25" top and bottom margins.
5. Use a serif font face and the point sizes indicated on the right.
6. Manually kern the double o's in BOOK and NOOK so the o's overlap as shown.
7. Use the Wingding font, 24 point, and the **&**, to insert:
   - Seven centered Wingdings below BOOK NOOK.
   - Two centered Wingdings two lines below the last line.
8. Use the REVERSE.WCM macro to reverse the text for the:
   - First four lines as shown.
   - Final two Wingdings as shown.
9. Add a thick page border around the text.
10. Preview your document.
11. Print one copy.
12. 📀 Close the file; save the changes.

    or

    ⌨ Save the file; name it **BOOK2**.
13. Close the document window.

REVERSE TEXT

Reverse Text Macro

1. Type text to reverse, using desired font

   OR

   Select/highlight text to reverse.
2. Click Tools .... Alt + T
3. Click Macros .... M
4. Click Play .... P
5. Type *REVERSE.WCM.*
6. Click Play .... Alt + P
7. Select desired color.
8. Click OK .... Enter

CREATE REVERSE TEXT

1. Click Graphics .... Alt + G
2. Click Text Box .... T
3. Click Border/Fill .... Shift + Alt + B
4. Click Border Style .... B
5. Select desired border style.
6. Click Fill Style .... F
7. Select 100% Fill (black).
8. Click OK .... Enter
9. Click Layout .... Alt + L
10. Click Font .... F
11. Click Color L
12. Select White.
13. Click OK .... Enter
14. Type Text .... *text*
15. Close Graphics .... Shift + Alt + B
    Feature Bar.

Grand Opening
of the
BOOK NOOK

— 48pt
— 24pt
— 72pt
— 24pt

Come in and take a good look.
We specialize in books on the
following topics:

} 24pt

36pt 30pt

RELIGION

EDUCATION

ART

DO-IT-YOURSELF

} 24pt

Lesson 7 ▪ Special Enhancements

EXERCISE 44
DROP CAP

CONCEPTS:

■ A **drop cap** is an enlarged capital letter that drops below the first line of body text. It is usually the first letter of a paragraph. It is often used to draw the reader's attention to chapter beginnings, section headings and main body text.

Drop Cap

> Drop caps are large, decorative letters often used to mark the beginning of a document, section or chapter. Drop caps are set to a much larger font than the text, and often span the height of three or four lines.

■ WordPerfect provides a macro which automatically creates the drop cap for you. After selecting the letter you wish to enlarge, select **Macro** from the **T**ools main menu, and play the macro DROPCAP.WCM. The macro stops midway and offers you a chance to change the font face and/or size of the drop cap. The default size is 48 pt.

EXERCISE DIRECTIONS:

1. Start with a clear screen.
2. Open **SPECIES1**.
3. Change the nameplate (*Save the Species*) to a sans serif font face.
4. Use the **DROPCAP.WCM** macro to create drop initial capitals for the paragraphs shown.
5. Lower the graphic between columns 1 and 2 to the bottom of the columns.
6. Change the format of the pull quote as follows:
   - Graphics Box Border: No Border
   - Graphics Box Fill Style: 100% Fill
   - Font Color: White
7. Preview your document.
8. Print one copy.
9. Close the file; save the changes.

To create a drop cap:
- Select/highlight letter to enlarge.
- Click **T**ools
- Click **M**acro
- Click **P**lay
- Type *DROPCAP.WCM*.

A drop cap will not work with a paragraph that begins with a tab stop.

To edit a drop cap that has been created, you must edit the text box contents. It is easier to delete the text box, retype the letter, and replay the DROPCAP.WCM macro.

In this exercise, you will add drop caps and reverse text in a newsletter created earlier.

Save the Species

Volume 1   Quarterly Newsletter of the Wildlife Society   Summer 1994

What is Wildlife Conservation?

Wildlife Conservation includes all human efforts to preserve wild animals and plants and save them from extinction. Our organization supports the protection and wise management of wild species and their environment. The greatest danger to wildlife results from human activities; your contributions aid us in funding demonstrations and activities which help educate others about the dangers of these activities and help preserve the existence of disappearing species. Send contributions to:

Save the Species
1356 Pacific Road
San Francisco, CA 90456

If we continue to ignore the need for wildlife conservation, today's endangered species will soon become extinct. Extinction is particularly dangerous due to the economic, scientific and survival value of wildlife. Wild species of animals and plants provide many substances which are valuable to the economies of different countries, both as food products and as products for trade. The study of wildlife provides important knowledge about life processes which has lead to the discovery of medical and scientific products. Additionally, the existence of many species of wildlife maintains the balance of living systems on the earth. The loss of certain species will affect the existence of others that depend on it perhaps for food. Volunteer for Save the Species and help us convince Washington that it is vital to protect the existence of endangered species through legislation!

"If we continue to ignore the need for wildlife conservation, today's endangered species will soon become extinct."

Endangered Species of the Season: The California Condor

The California condor, a vulture, is the largest flying land bird in North America and makes its home in Southern California. Black feathers cover most of the bird's body except for the white area on the underside of the condor's wings. The neck and head have no feathers and are a red-orange color. The condor is a unique bird because it does not build a nest, but lays its eggs in caves, holes, or among rocks. It is also a particularly strong flier; it can soar and glide in the air for long distances, flapping its wings an average of only once an hour. It is a carnivore and eats the remains of dead animals.

KEEP ME FLYING

By the end of the 1980s, only 30 condors remained in the United States. The diminished number of condors is a result of hunting. The growth of urban areas in Southern California also poses a threat to the natural habitat of the bird. Save the Species urges you to write to your Congressperson and local government officials to inform them of your support of more land for sanctuaries to help keep the condor alive.

In the next issue: What is happening to the Killer Whale and its cousin, The Dolphin.

CREATE DROP CAP

Alt + F10, then step 5

1. Select letter to drop cap.
2. Click **T**ools .... Alt + T
3. Click **M**acro .... M
4. Click **P**lay .... P
5. Type *DROPCAP.WCM* .... Alt + N
   in **N**ame text box.
6. Click **P**lay .... P

If you wish to make change to font or size:

Click **Y**es .... Y

Make desired changes.

Click **O**K .... Enter

OR

Click **N**o .... N

Lesson 7 ■ Exercise 44   185

Lesson 7 ▪ Special Enhancements

EXERCISE 45
SPECIAL CHARACTERS

CONCEPTS:

■ WordPerfect provides **special characters** that may be used for special purposes or to enhance your document. If your printer supports graphics, you can print most of the characters in the character sets. There are 15 different symbol/character sets available:

- ASCII (the default character set)
- Multinational
- Phonetic
- Box Drawing
- Typographic Symbols
- Iconic Symbols
- Math/Scientific
- Math/Scientific Extended
- Greek
- Hebrew
- Cyrillic
- Japanese
- User-Defined
- Arabic
- Arabic Script

To add special characters:

Ctrl + W

OR

- Click **Insert**
- Click **Character**

The symbols used most frequently in business and publishing are those in the Typographic and Iconic character sets.

- Special characters may be accessed by selecting **Character** on the Insert menu, or by pressing Ctrl+W. The following dialog box appears, with the most recently used character set selected:

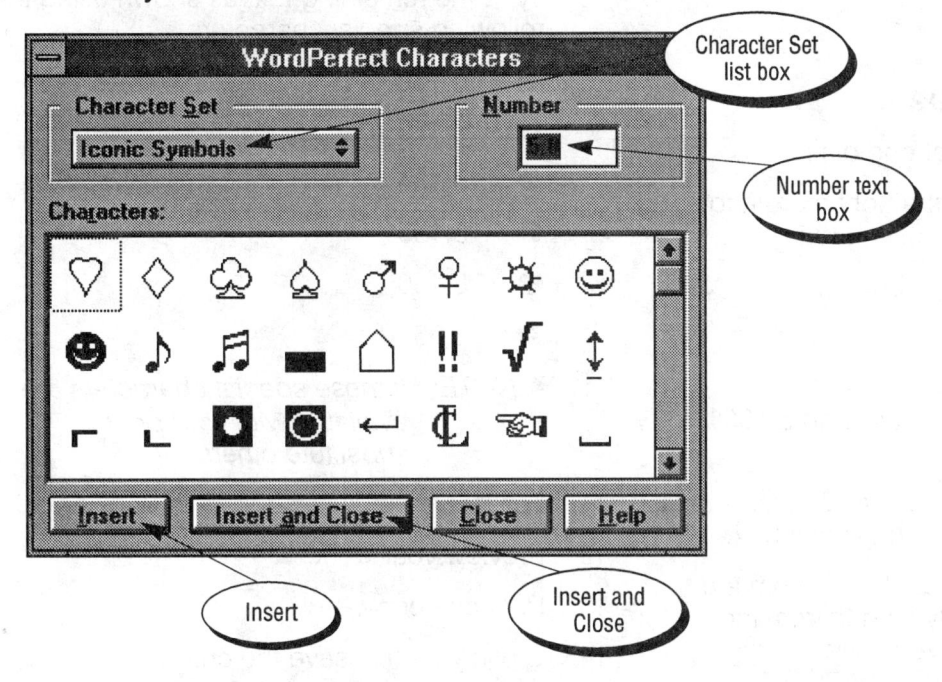

[WordPerfect Characters dialog box showing Character Set list box (Iconic Symbols), Number text box, Characters grid, and Insert, Insert and Close, Close, and Help buttons]

- To select a symbol, select the desired character set and then click the symbol, or enter the character code (Set#,Character#) in the Number text box.

- To insert the selected symbol, click Insert if you plan to insert more than one symbol; otherwise click Insert and Close. You may move back and forth between the Characters dialog box and your document.

- You may change the size of a symbol as you would any other character, by changing the point size.

There are two files in the WPC20 directory that provide information about special characters. CHARACTR.DOC contains a list of every special character and includes:
- The set and character number
- The character itself
- The character's name

CHARMAP.WPD contains a list of all the character sets. You can print this file using a particular font to see how the characters appear when printed from your printer.

In WordPerfect 6.0a and later versions, the special character sets are also found as fonts. They can be accessed through the Font menu and all begin with *WP*.

In this exercise, you will type a flyer on a previously saved letterhead using special characters and reverse text.

Lesson 7 ■ Exercise 45

Lesson 7 ■ Exercise 45

EXERCISE DIRECTIONS:

1. Start with a clear screen.
2. Open **FLOWLET**.
3. Save the file as **FLOWER2**.
4. Place the insertion point at end of file.
5. Set left margin to 2", and the right margin to .75"
6. Use the Advance feature to bring the insertion point to line 1.5".
7. Create a text box:
    - Choose a triple border style and a 100% fill.
    - Use a serif font, 24 point, white color and bold to center the titles in the text box.
    - Choose a paragraph anchor, 0" from the left margin horizontally, and 0" from the top of the paragraph vertically.
    - Size the width at full and the height to contents.
8. Press the Enter key twice.
9. Change the line height for the remaining text to .250".
10. Type the remaining text as shown using the following special characters.
    - ❶ 5,182
    - ❷ 5,183
    - ❸ 5,184
    - ❹ 5,185
    - ❺ 5,186
    - ✿ 5,95
    - ■ *NOTE: If these special characters are not available with your printer, substitute others.*
11. Full justify the text.
12. Preview your work.
13. Print one copy.
14. Close your file; save the changes.

INSERT SPECIAL CHARACTERS

Ctrl + W

1. Place your insertion point to the left of where you wish to insert character.
2. Press .... `Ctrl` + `W`

    OR

    Click **I**nsert .... `Alt` + `I`

    Click **C**haracter .... `C`

3. Click **C**haracter **S**et.. `Alt` + `S`, `Space` list box to display character set list.
4. Click desired character set .... `Enter`
5. Click desired symbol.

    OR

    Click in Number text box.......... `Alt` + `N`

    Type number of desired symbol..........*#,#*

6. Click **I**nsert .... `Alt` + `I`

    Click **C**lose............................. `Alt` + `C`

    OR

    Click **I**nsert **a**nd Close .... `Alt` + `A`

14 Highway 37
Middletown, NJ 07740
908-555-5555

THIRD ANNUAL
GARDEN DESIGN CONTEST

The Perennial Potter

❶ ***HOW TO ENTER:*** Complete the official entry form and return it to our store with photographs of your garden. Entries must be received by September 1, 1995. All entry materials become the property of **The Perennial Potter** and none will be returned.

❀❀

❷ ***JUDGING:*** All members of our staff will judge. Three finalists will be selected.

❀❀

❸ ***PRIZES:*** Each finalist will receive a $500 gift certificate to **The Perennial Potter**.

❀❀

❹ ***NOTIFICATION:*** Finalists will be notified by both telephone and certified mail on or about September 10, 1995.

❀❀

❺ ***FINALIST LIST:*** The names of the finalists and photographs of their prize-winning gardens will be posted near the register in the store on September 11, 1995.

❀❀

Lesson 7 ▪ Special Enhancements

EXERCISE 46

BULLETS AND NUMBERS

CONCEPTS:

- A **bullet** is a dot or symbol used to highlight points of information or itemize a list that does not need to be in any particular order.

  Bulleted text:

▶ red	● apple
▶ blue	● pear
▶ green	● orange

- Using the Bullets and Numbers feature, you can insert bullets automatically to create a bulleted list for each paragraph or item you type.

- You can also select from a variety of bullet symbols. Symbol bullets enable you to create interesting bullets, something other than the typical round dot.

- The Bullets and Numbers feature also allows you to create numbered paragraphs for items that need to be in a particular order. The numbers you insert increment automatically.

- The Bullets and Numbers feature is accessed by selecting Bullets & Numbers from the Insert main menu or by clicking the Bullet Button on the Button Bar.

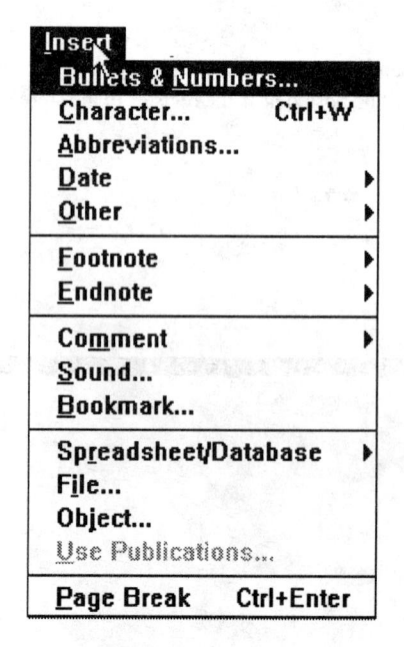

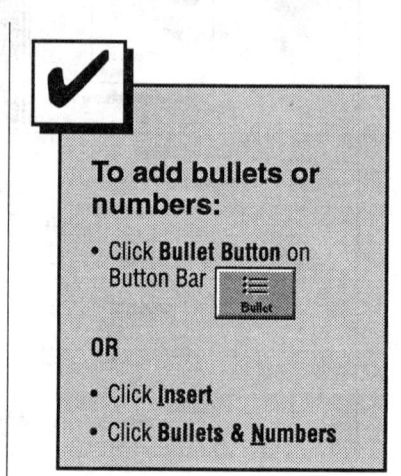

To add bullets or numbers:

- Click **Bullet Button** on Button Bar

OR

- Click **Insert**
- Click **Bullets & Numbers**

When using the Bullets and Numbers feature for numbered paragraphs, adding or deleting paragraphs will result in all paragraphs being automatically renumbered.

- After selecting a bullet or number style, the text is typed or you can add bullets and numbers to existing text by selecting/highlighting the text and then choosing Bullets & Numbers from the Insert main menu. By selecting New Bullet or Number on ENTER the bullet or number will automatically be inserted each time the Enter key is pressed.

In this exercise, you will create a flyer using bullets to emphasize text.

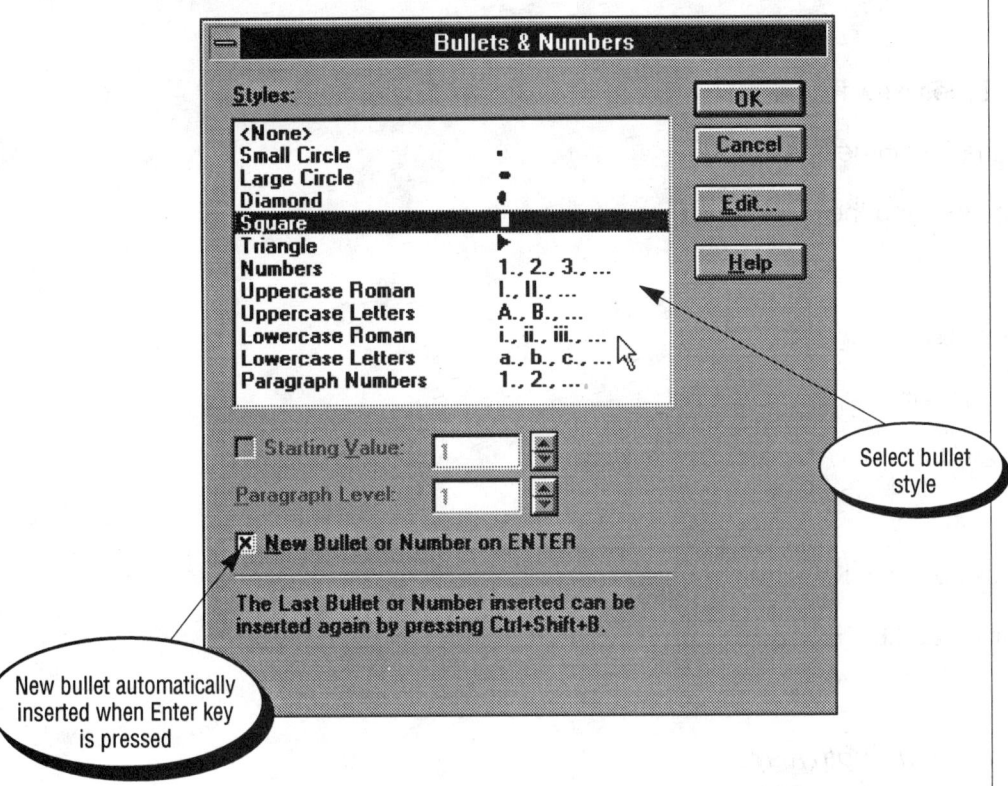

- Bullet and number styles may be changed in the Bullets & Numbers dialog box.

- Special characters can also be used as bullets but will not provide for the automatic insertion of bullets.

Lesson 7 ▪ Exercise 46

EXERCISE DIRECTIONS:

1. Start with a clear screen.
2. Center the page from top to bottom.
3. Set all margins to .5".
4. Select a serif font face (Times New Roman).
5. Use a 1" line height for the first three lines.
6. Use the Advance feature to bring the insertion point to line 4.5".
7. Change the left margin to 3.5".
8. Use a diamond bullet as shown.
   - Add a custom vertical line:
   - Use a double line.
   - Set the horizontal position at 3.1".
   - Set the vertical position at 4.6"
   - Set the length to 5.5"
   - ▪ NOTE: The line position and length may vary depending on the font face chosen. Adjust it with the mouse.
9. Preview your work.
10. Print one copy.
11. Save the exercise; name it **FLOWER3**.
12. Close the document window.

CREATE A BULLETED OR NUMBERED LIST

Place insertion point where bulleted or numbered list is to begin.

Click Insert .... Alt + I

Click Bullets & Numbers .... N

OR

Click Bullet Button .... Bullet

To insert automatic bullet when Enter is pressed:

a. Click in New Bullet or number on ENTER check box.
b. Click desired bullet or number style.
c. Click OK .... Enter

THE PERENNIAL POTTER

} 1" line height
} 72 pt bold

New Plants in Stock: } 36 pt bold

- Royal Fern
- Gloriosa Daisy
- Pixie Carnation
- Hardy Amaryllis
- Zenith Zinnias
- Heavenly Hibiscus
- Orangeade Impatiens
- English Ivy
- Ruffled Petunia

} 24 pt

Located in Aisle 2. } 36 pt bold

Lesson 7 ▪ Special Enhancements

EXERCISE 47
TEXTART

CONCEPTS:

- WordPerfect's **TextArt** feature can create striking text effects for special uses such as flyer headings or logos. Waves, pennants, circles and crescents are among the effects included.

- To access the TextArt program, select TextArt from the Graphics main menu or click TextArt on the Button Bar. The TextArt program enables you to create an image which will then be imported into the current document.

- At the TextArt screen, you enter up to 58 characters on one, two or three lines of text. You can select a font, font style, justification and/or capitalization style. You can select a textart shape from a palette of shapes. You may also change the text color, define an outlined character format, fills, shadow direction and width. For the image itself, you may set a rotation degree, as well as, width and height.

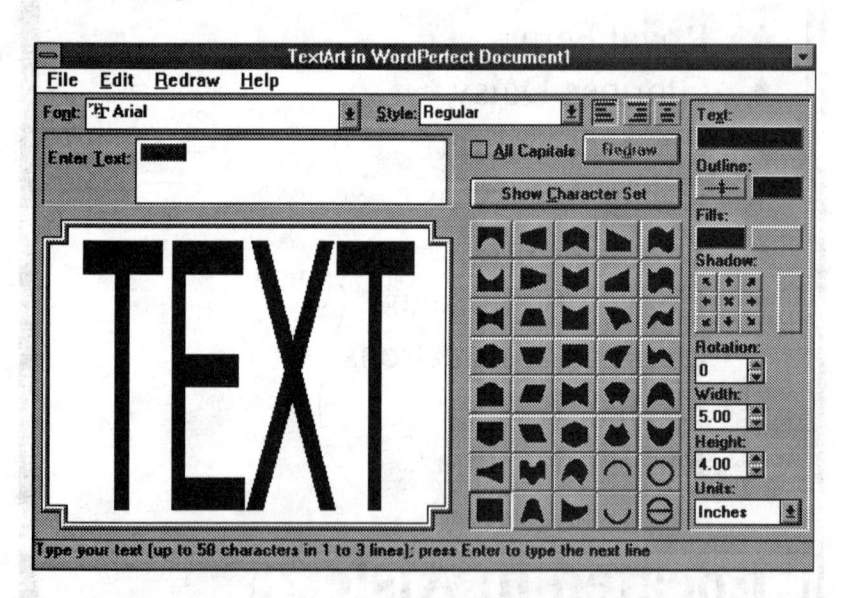

- At the TextArt screen, the Status Bar gives instructions on using whatever feature the pointer is on.

To add textart:
- Click **Graphics**
- Click **TextArt**

The textart image is placed in a graphics box which can then be positioned and sized like any other graphics box on the page.

In this exercise, you will create a flyer enhanced with textart.

CREATE A TEXTART IMAGE

1. Place insertion point where you want to insert the image.
2. Click **G**raphics..................... `Alt` + `G`
3. Click Te**x**tArt............................ `X`

   OR

   Click TextArt on Button Bar............ [ABC TextArt]

4. Click **R**eDraw................ `Alt` + `R`, `A` on menu bar; set to **A**uto.
5. Enter text in text box.
6. From Fo**n**t list, select font......... `Alt` + `N`
7. From **S**tyle list, select.............. `Alt` + `S` font style if applicable.
8. Click appropriate icon................ [icons] to select left, right or center justification.
9. Click desired shape on shape palette.
10. To make optional changes:

    Select/deselect **A**ll Capitals...... `Alt` + `A`

    Click Te**x**t Button.................. `Alt` + `X` to select text color

    Click Outline Button to select outline thickness and color.

    Click Fills Button to select fill pattern and color.

    Click Shadow arrow to select shadow direction; click repeatedly to increase/decrease shadow width. Click second Shadow Button; select shadow color.

    In Rotation text box, enter desired angle of rotation.

    In Width text box, enter desired width of finished image.

    In Height text box, enter desired height of finished image.

11. Click **F**ile on menu bar............. `Alt` + `F`
12. Click E**x**it & Return to WordPerfect...... `X`
13. At prompt box, click **Y**es..................... `Y` to embed object in document

    OR

    Click **N**o... `N` to return without inserting the TextArt image.

EXERCISE DIRECTIONS:

1. Start with a clear screen.
2. With your insertion point at the top of screen, select TextArt.
3. Using a sans serif font, type HIGH NOTE on the first line and MUSIC ASSOCIATION on the second line of the Enter Text box.
4. Select the design in the lower right corner of the palette.
5. Adjust the height and width to 6".
6. Exit & Return to Word Perfect, embedding the object.
7. Edit the Position of the graphic box to the Center of Paragraph.
8. Import **PIANO.WPG** graphic; set the size to approximately 1.5" by 1.5" and remove the border.
9. Insert the graphic in the middle of the heading text as shown.
10. Type the remaining text beginning below the textart graphics box (approximately 7.3"). Set "Presents..." to serif 30 point bold; set remaining text to serif 14 point bold.
11. Include a button paragraph border around the last sentence.
12. Add a Thick/Thin1 page border to the entire flyer.
13. Preview your document.
14. Print one copy.
15. Save the exercise; name it **MUSIC**.
16. Close the document window.

HIGH NOTE MUSIC ASSOCIATION

Presents...
its annual *spring music festival*
on
Friday, May 12, 1995
at
Bridgewater Auditorium
8:00 p.m.

Tickets are on sale at the box office

Lesson 7 ▪ Special Enhancements

EXERCISE 48

USING SHAPE TOOLS, GRIDS, RULERS AND ALIGNMENT GUIDES

CONCEPTS:

Creating a Shape

- WordPerfect's Draw feature allows you to create your own graphics or edit the graphics that come with WordPerfect.

- After Draw is accessed, a blank WP Draw window appears. This screen overlays your document screen.

- The **tool palette** to the left of the Draw screen allows you to access a variety of shapes and special effects to create your graphic. The menus at the top of the window provide options for you to further enhance your creation.

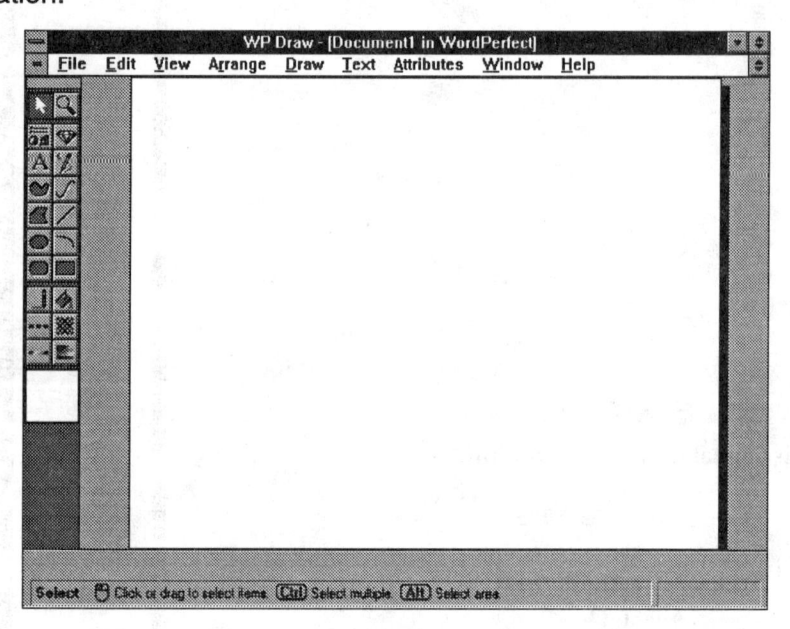

> **To access draw:**
> - Click Draw Button on Button Bar
>
> **OR**
>
> - Click **Graphics**
> - Click **Draw**

- To create **shapes** and **fills**, you must use the appropriate icons on the tool palette:

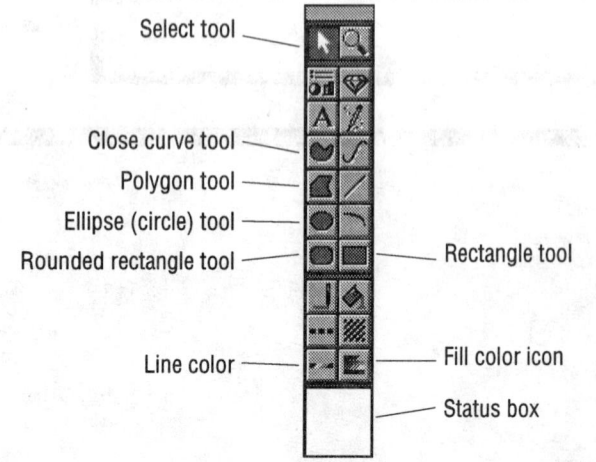

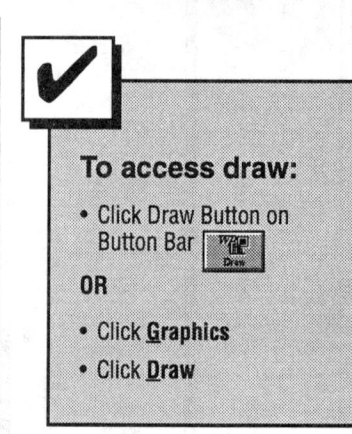

  - Select tool
  - Close curve tool
  - Polygon tool
  - Ellipse (circle) tool
  - Rounded rectangle tool
  - Rectangle tool
  - Fill color icon
  - Line color
  - Status box

- To draw a **circle** or **oval**, click on the **ellipse (circle) tool**. The mouse pointer turns to a crossbar. (The mouse pointer turns into different shapes depending on the tool selected.) Click and hold the mouse as you drag diagonally. To draw a perfect circle, hold down the Shift key as you drag the mouse. When you release the mouse, a circle or oval shape appears. To draw a circle from the center outward, hold Alt + Shift as you drag.

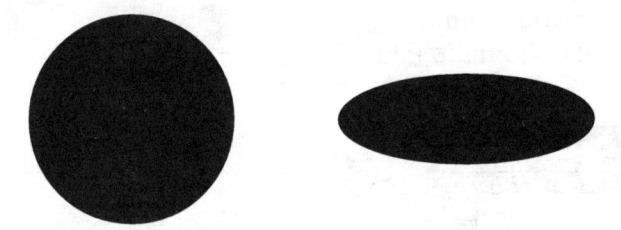

- Similarly, if you wish to draw a **square** or **rectangle**, click on the **square tool** and drag diagonally. To draw a perfect square, hold down the Shift key as you drag the mouse. To draw a rectangle with rounded corners, click the square with rounded corner tool.

- The **polygon tool** is used to draw closed shapes with straight lines. Typically, you would use this tool to draw **triangles**. To draw a shape with straight lines, select the polygon tool from the tool palette. Click once in the drawing window to begin the shape. Then, drag to each point in the shape and click once. Double click to complete the shape. You must completely close the shape in order for it to be filled with the default fill pattern.

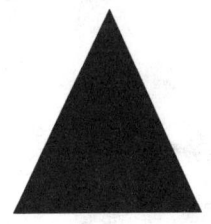

- The **closed curve tool** is used like the polygon tool. Click the Drawing window to begin the shape. Click again to create a curve. Double-click to finish drawing the object. Your image will fill with the default fill pattern.

Clearing the Draw Window

- If you decide you don't like your creation, select Clear from the File menu and a new blank window appears.

Insert Image in Document

- After creating the desired image, you can insert it into your current document without exiting WP Draw by selecting Update from the File menu.

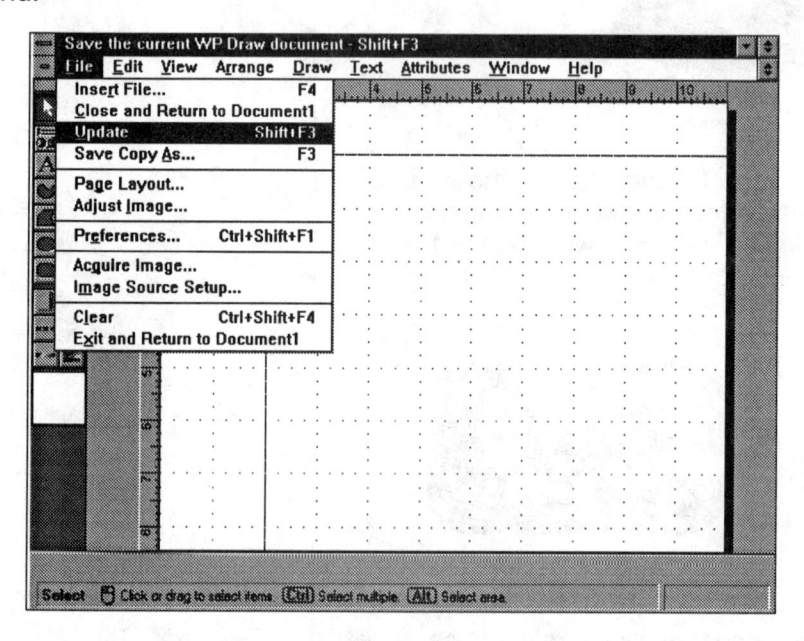

- When you are ready to return to your document and exit WP Draw, select Exit and Return to Document from the File menu. You will be prompted to update your document with the image which appears in the draw window.

Saving the Image

- If you wish to save your image so that you can use it in other documents, select Save Copy As from the File menu. Your image will be saved along with the other WordPerfect graphics in the WPWIN60\GRAPHICS subdirectory.

Grids, Rulers and Alignment Guides

- **Grids** allow you to measure and align your drawings, while **rulers** allow you to size your art as you create. Rulers are indicated in inches (the default), but the unit of measurement may be changed (to points, for example) by selecting Preferences from the File menu.

- Hidden behind the horizontal and vertical rulers are **alignment guides**. Alignment guides enable you to align your graphics. To access an alignment guide, position your insertion point on a ruler and drag a guide into the window screen. To move a guide, click the Select Tool, point to the guide and drag it to a new position.

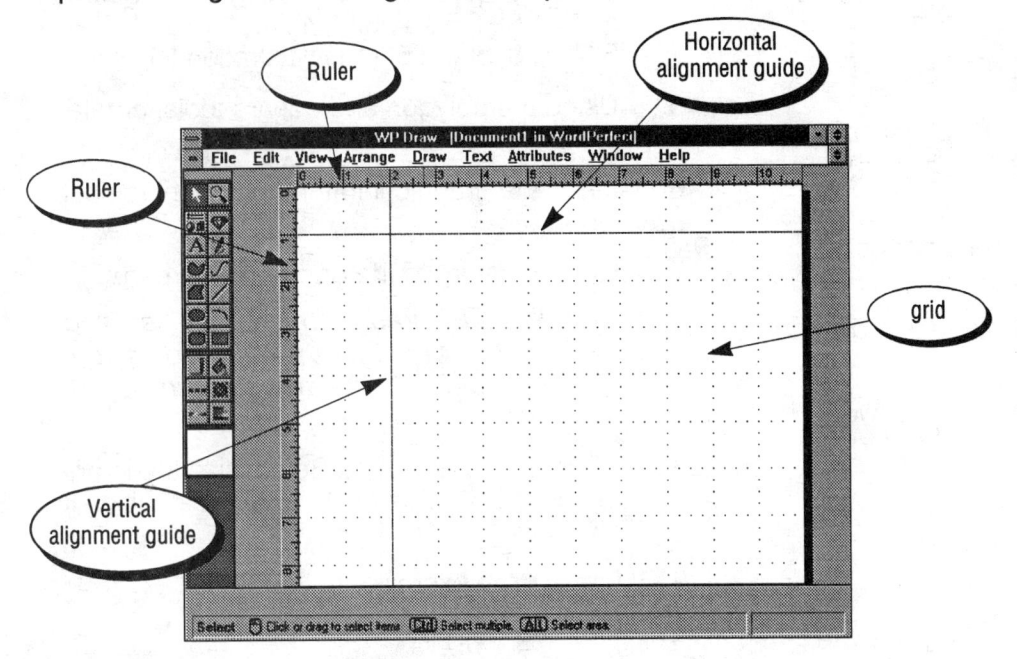

- Rulers and grids do not automatically display. (You may change the default by selecting File, Preferences, Display). To display them, select Ruler and/or Grid from the View menu.

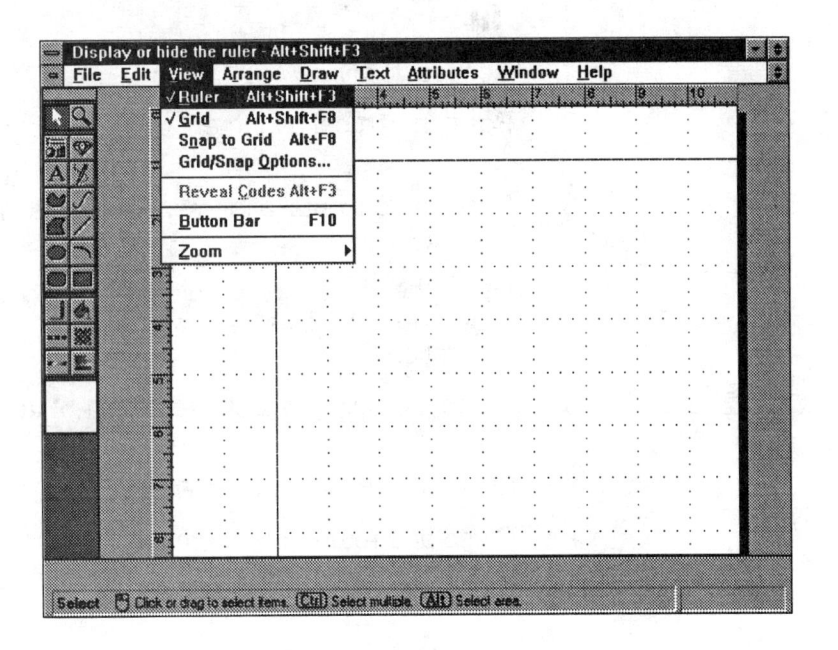

In this exercise, you will practice creating shapes. You will then create a letterhead and use the drawing tools to create a graphic for the document.

Lesson 7 ■ Exercise 48

Lesson 7 ▪ Exercise 48

EXERCISE DIRECTIONS:

Part I

1. Start with a clear screen.
2. Access WPDraw.
3. Display the rulers and grid.
4. Using the circle tool, create a perfect circle (hold down the Shift key while drawing) and an oval.
5. Using the square tool, create a perfect square and a rectangle.
6. Using the polygon tool, create a triangle and any other desired shape.
7. Using the closed curve tool, create two shapes.
8. Clear the draw window.
9. Create a 1" circle and a 2" square.
10. Clear the draw window.
11. Exit and return to document screen.

Part II

1. Create the letterhead shown in illustration A:
   - Type the company name in serif 14 point bold.
   - Set justification to *All*.
   - Press Enter once.
   - Create a full horizontal line below the company name. Use the default thickness.
   - Press Enter five times.
   - Create another full horizontal line using the default thickness.
   - Press Enter once.
   - Type the name, address and phone information in same font (as company name) in 12 point.
   - Set justification to *All*.
2. Access WP Draw.
3. Display the rulers and grid.
4. Position horizontal alignment guides at 2", 3", 5", 5.5" 6"; position vertical alignment guides at 1", 1.5", 2.5", 3", 3.5", 4", 4.5" 5", 5.5", 6" 6.5" 7", 8" and 8.5" (see illustration B).
5. Using the polygon and square tools, create the image as shown in illustration B.
6. Insert the graphic into the document (select Update).
7. Exit and return to the document screen.
   - *NOTE: The graphic image may be sized, moved, rotated or scaled as you did with other graphics in Lesson 5.*
8. Click on Graphics/Edit Box to size the image to about 1.8" wide by 1" high and position it as shown.
9. Preview the exercise.
10. Print one copy.
11. Save the file; name it **TRONICS**.
12. Close the document window.

Part III

1. Access WP Draw.
2. Position vertical alignment guides at 5.5" and 7".
3. Position horizontal alignment guides at 1" and 1.5".
4. Using the circle tool, create a 5.5" long by .5" wide body of the fish as shown in illustration C.
5. Using the polygon tool, create a 1.5" tail as shown.
6. Save the image; name it **FISHY**.
7. Close and return to document.
8. Close the document window.

ILLUSTRATION A

ATHENS   ELECTRONIC   SUPPLY   COMPANY

987 Chip Lane, Megaboard, IL 60577 Phone 708 555-2045 Fax 708 555-5556

ILLUSTRATION B

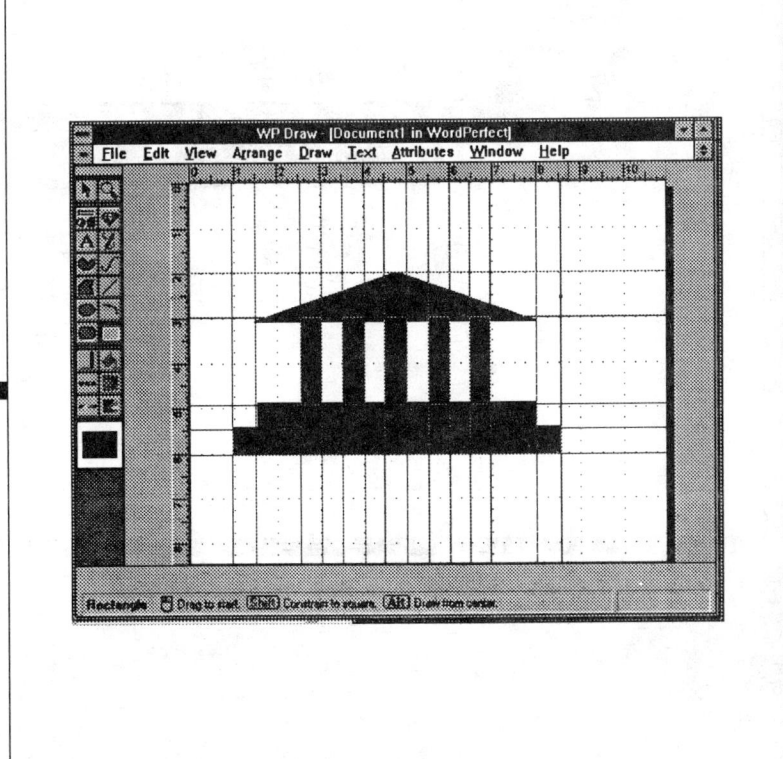

ILLUSTRATION C

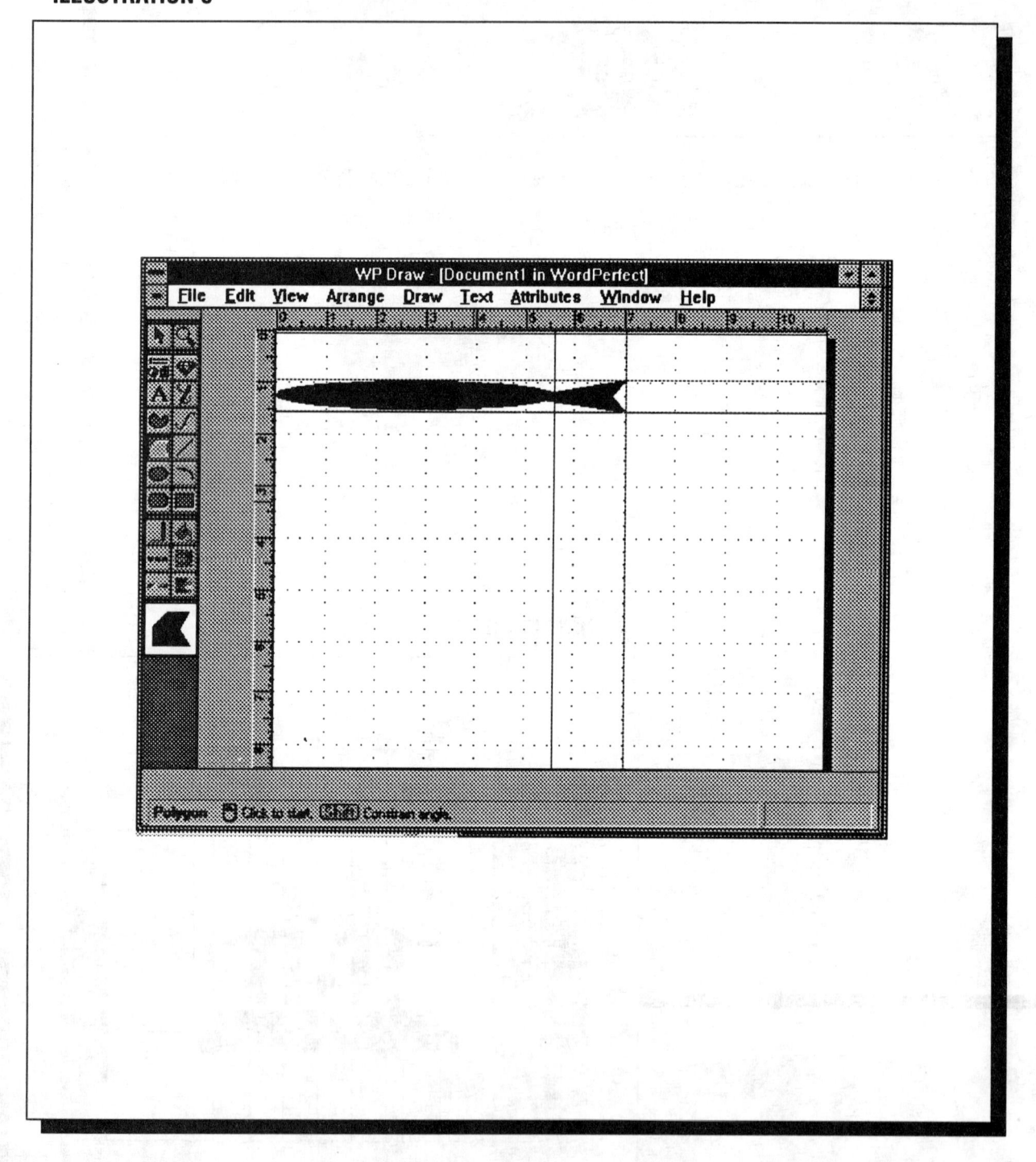

ACCESS DRAW

While in document, click Draw Button on Button Bar.

OR

1. Click **G**raphics .... `Alt` + `G`
2. Click **D**raw .... `D`

DRAW SHAPES

While in Draw Program:

1. Select desired tool.
2. Position crosshair within drawing area.
3. Click and drag mouse to position where object will end.

   OR

   Click to begin multiple sided figures.

   Drag to end of line or side and click.

4. Release mouse button.
5. Double click to end drawing.

CLEAR DRAW WINDOW

1. Click **F**ile .... `Alt` + `F`
2. Click C**l**ear .... `L`

SAVE GRAPHICS IMAGE

F3

1. Click **F**ile .... `Alt` + `F`
2. Click **S**ave Copy **A**s .... `A`
3. Type filename.
4. Click **S**ave .... `Alt` + `S`

INSERT IMAGE IN DOCUMENT

1. Click **F**ile .... `Alt` + `F`
2. Click **U**pdate Document .... `U`

   OR

   Click **C**lose and Return to Document Window .... `C`

   When prompted to update,

   Click Yes .... `Y`

   OR

   Click E**x**it and Return to Document Window .... `X`

   When prompted to update,

   Click Yes .... `Y`

Lesson 7 ■ Exercise 48   205

Lesson 7 ▪ Special Enhancements

EXERCISE 49

▪ USING LINE TOOLS, SHADING AND FILLS ▪ SELECTING GRAPHICS

CONCEPTS:

Creating Lines

- WordPerfect's **line tools** allow you to create several line types: a straight line, a curved line, an elliptical arc or a freehand design.

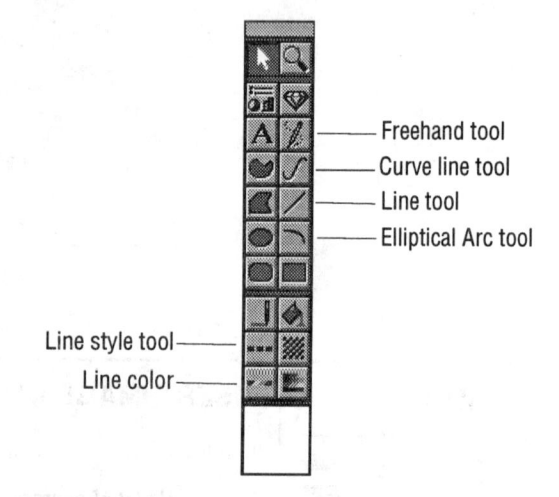

Freehand tool
Curve line tool
Line tool
Elliptical Arc tool

Line style tool
Line color

To create a line:
- Click the line tool on the tools palette.

OR

- Click **Draw**
- Click **Line**

OR

Elliptical Arc

OR

Curve

OR

Freehand.

- To draw a **straight line**, select the **line tool** from the Tool palette. Click to start the line. Move the mouse to the desired length. If you desire the line to contain a joint, click the mouse again and move the mouse in another direction. Double-click to end the line.

- If you wish to move the line while you are drawing it, hold down the *right* mouse button and drag the line to a new position.

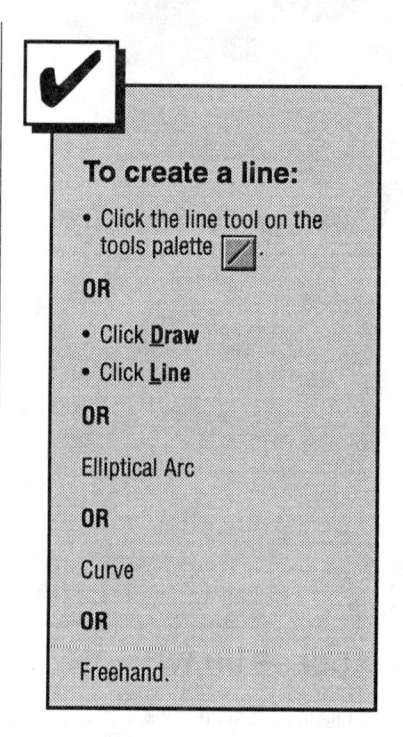

To select a line or object:
- Select the pointer tool.
- Point to the line or object and click once until the handles appear.

- Use the **elliptical arc tool** to draw part of an **ellipse**. Click to begin the line, drag the mouse in an upward or downward direction (depending on the desired curve). Double-click to end the line.

- The **curve tool** is used to draw **curved** lines. Click once to begin the line. Move the mouse until you get to where you desire a curve. To draw a curve, click the mouse button again to indicate the curve point. Double-click to end your line.

- The **Freehand** tool allows you to draw as if you were using a pen or pencil. Click to begin the drawing and drag the mouse as though it were a pencil. When you release the mouse, the line ends.

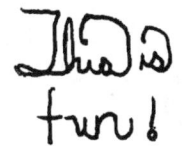

Arrowheads

- If you need to have your line point to something, you can create an arrowhead where the line begins, where the lines ends or at both the beginning and end of the line.

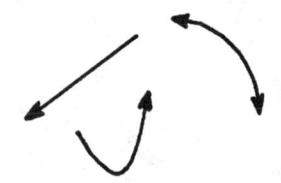

- To create an arrowhead, select Attributes, Line.

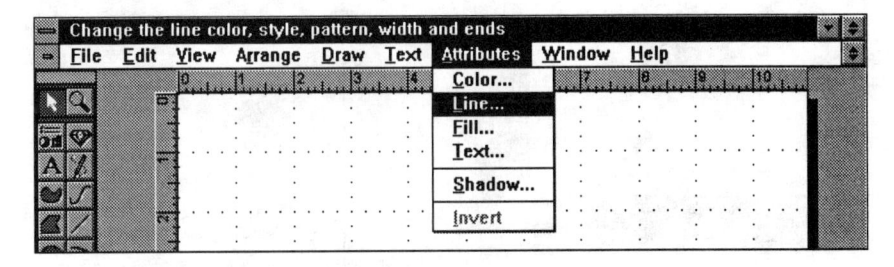

- In the Line Attributes dialog box which follows, click the Arrowhead list box and select desired arrowhead style.

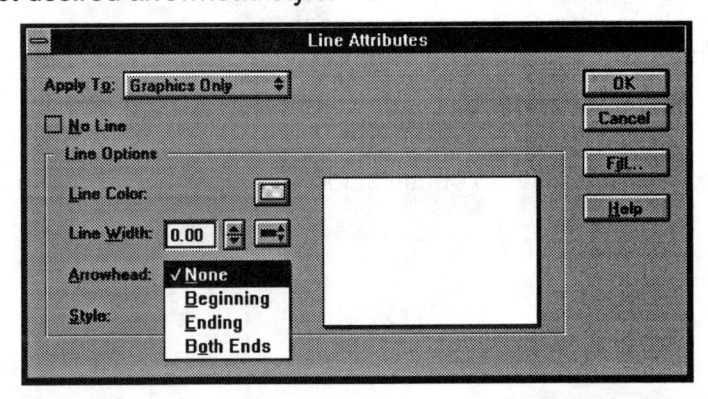

Lesson 7 ▪ Exercise 49

Line Styles, Fill Patterns and Colors

- You may change the **line style** or the **line color** of a line before or after creating it. To change the line style or color *before* creating the line, select the line style or line color tool on the tool palette and choose from the palette of choices.

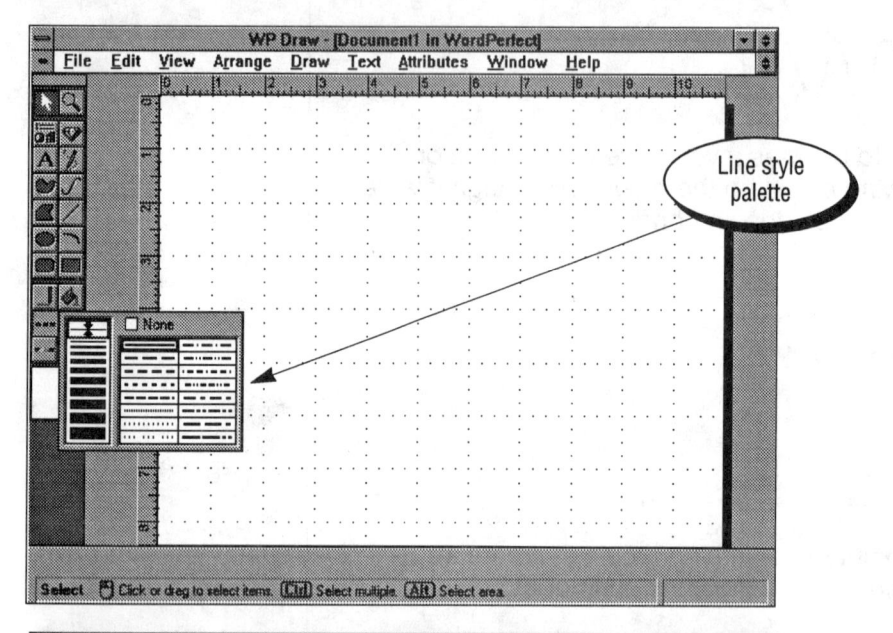

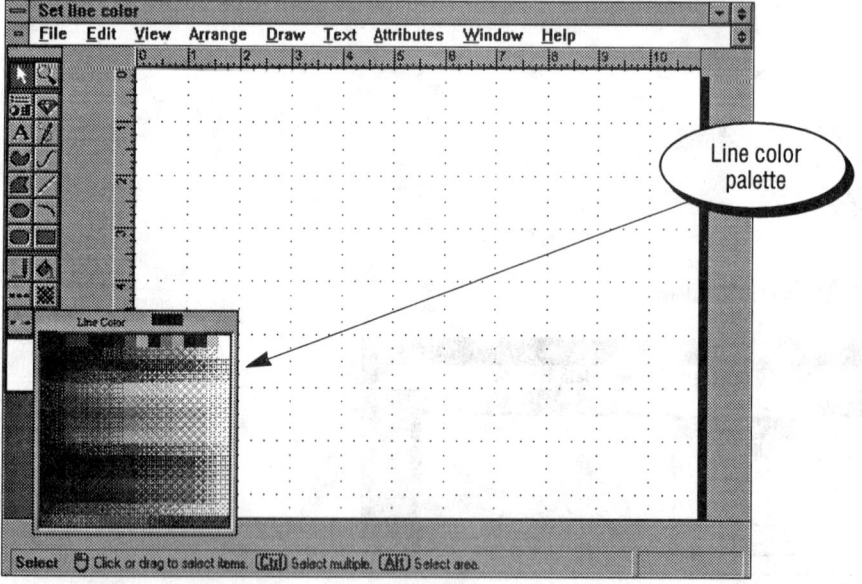

To change the line style *after* creating the line, select the line (select the pointer tool, point to the line and click once), then choose the line style or color from the line style and color palettes. As you learned in Lesson 6, a selected line displays handles. When handles appear, the line is in an *Edit* mode.

- Closed objects (circles, squares, rectangles) can be filled with various patterns and colors. Of course, you need a color printer to obtain color output.

- Objects, like lines, must first be selected to change the fill pattern or color. When sizing handles appear, click the pattern or color tool and choose a fill option.

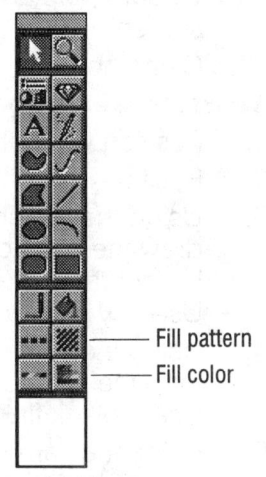

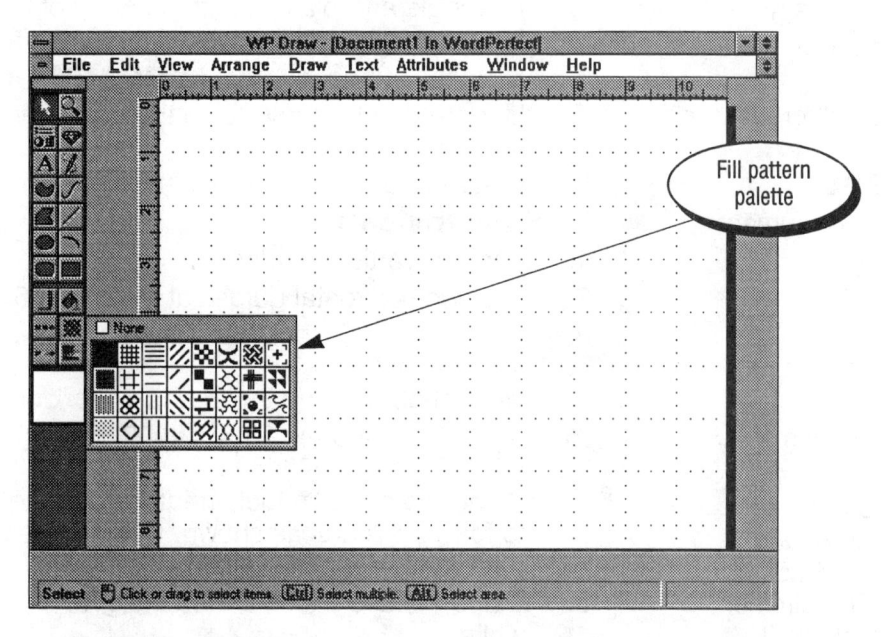

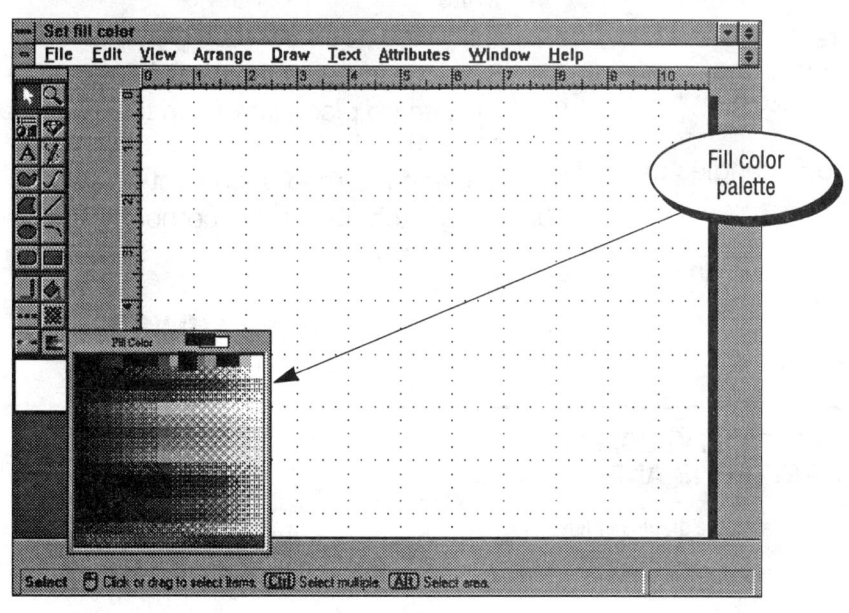

Fill pattern
Fill color

Fill pattern palette

Fill color palette

In this exercise, you will create shapes to form objects and save each as a graphic image. After each is created, you will place them in the same document. In later exercises, you will retrieve each image.

Lesson 7 ■ Exercise 49   209

Lesson 7 ■ Exercise 49

EXERCISE DIRECTIONS:

To draw the glass:
1. Start with a clear screen.
2. Access WP Draw.
3. Position vertical alignment guides at 3", 4.5" 5", 5.5" and 7".
4. Position horizontal alignment guides at 2", 4" and 7".
5. Using the polygon tool, draw the top part of the glass between the 3" and 7" vertical guides and the 2" and 4" horizontal guides as shown. Use a black fill.
6. Draw a straight line on the 5" vertical ruler guide to form the stem of the glass. Use any desired thickness.
7. Using the polygon tool, draw the bottom part of the glass between the 4.5" and 5.5" vertical ruler guides as shown. Use a black fill.
8. Using the circle tool and white fill, create the *olive* in the glass.
9. Save the image; name it **GLASS**.
10. Update (to place image on the document screen).
11. Clear the draw window.

To draw the camera:
1. Position vertical alignment guides at 3", 3.25," 3.75" 4" 6", 7.75".
4. Position horizontal alignment guides at 2.5", 3", 4.25", 5" and 7.5".
5. Using the circle tool, draw two circles to represent the *reels* between the 4" and 7" vertical guides and the 2.5" and 4.25 horizontal guides as shown. The circles should slightly overlap. Use a black fill.
6. Using the square tool, draw a rectangle over the circles to form the bottom part of the camera between the 3" and 5" horizontal guides as shown.
7. Using the square tool, draw two rectangles to form the lens of the camera in the approximate sizes shown.
8. Using the line tool, create three lines in any desired thickness to form the tripod (the camera stand).
9. Save the image; name it **CAMERA**.

10. Update (to place image on the document screen).
11. Clear the draw window.

To draw the luggage:
1. Position vertical guides at 2" and 7".
2. Position horizontal guides at 3" and 6.25".
3. Using the rectangle with rounded corner tool, draw the base of the luggage between the horizontal and vertical ruler guides as shown. Use any desired pattern fill.
4. Using the same tool, draw a rectangle to form the first part of the luggage handle. Use a black fill.
5. Using the same tool, draw a smaller rectangle and place it in the middle of the black rectangle. Fill it white.
6. Save the image; name it **LUGGAGE**.
7. Update (to place image on the document screen).
8. Clear the draw window.

To draw the cat:
1. Position vertical guides at 2" and 7".
2. Position horizontal guides at 1", 2" and 6".
3. Using the circle tool, draw the face between the 3" and 7" vertical guides and the 2" and 6" horizontal guides. Fill it gray. Change the line style to a thicker one, as desired.
4. Using the polygon tool, create two triangles to form the "ears" as shown. Use any desired pattern fill.
5. Using the circle tool, create the eye. Fill it white.
6. Using the freehand tool, create the mouth.
7. Save the image; name it **CAT**.
8. Update (to place image on the document screen).
9. Exit and return to document screen.
10. Drag each object to a corner on the page (see Result).
11. Print one copy.
12. Save the file; name it **THINGS**.
13. Close the document window.

SELECT A GRAPHIC or LINE
1. Click the pointer tool.
2. Point to the graphic or line and click once.
   NOTE: Handles appear.
3. Click off the graphic or line to deselect the image.

LINES STYLES, FILL PATTERNS AND COLORS
1. Select the graphic or line.
2. Click the desired tool:
   - Line Style
   - Line Color
3. Select a desired line style, fill pattern or color.

- Fill Style
- Fill Color

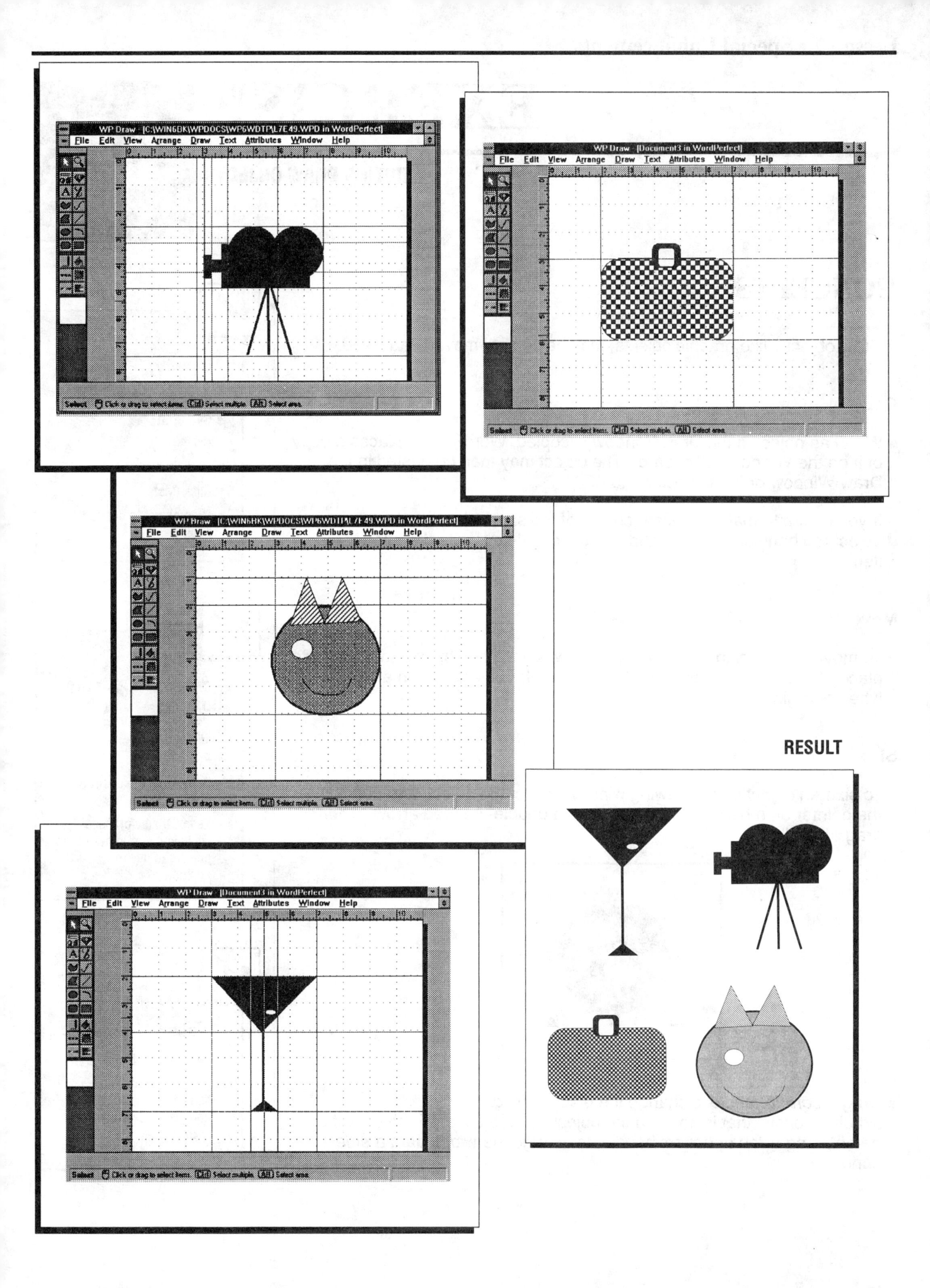

RESULT

Lesson 7 ▪ Exercise 49

Lesson 7 ▪ Special Enhancements

EXERCISE 50

EDITING DRAW OBJECTS

CONCEPTS:

- Draw objects, like graphic objects, may be copied, moved and sized.

Copy

- When an object in the Draw Window is copied, WordPerfect places a copy of it on the Windows Clipboard. The object may then be pasted in the Draw Window or in the document.

- If you desire to make duplicate copies of the same object, select the object (so handles appear), and press the Ctrl key while dragging the item.

Move

- To move an object in the drawing window, select the object and drag it into place. Position your pointer on the edge of the object, not on a handle, when dragging.

Size

- To size an object in the drawing window, select the object, and position the pointer on a handle until it becomes a double-headed arrow. Then, drag a handle.

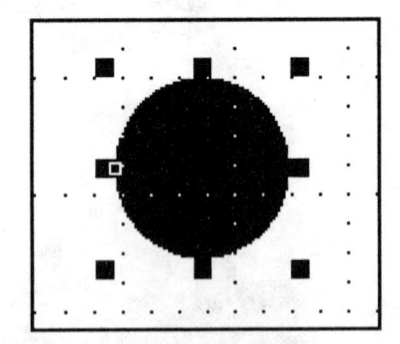

- Drag a *corner handle* to change the object's *height and width* simultaneously; that is, to keep the object's proportions. To change the *height,* drag a *top or bottom* handle; to change the *width,* drag a *side* handle.

To copy:
- Select the object.
- Click **Edit**
- Click **Copy**
- Click **Edit**
- Click **Paste**
- Drag object to desired position.

To make duplicate copies:
- Select the object.
- Press **Ctrl** key.
- **Drag object** to desired position.
- Keep Ctrl key pressed while you continue to drag objects to desired position.

To size:
- Select the object.
- Position pointer on a handle until it becomes a double-headed arrow.
- Drag handle.

- **To size an object by a specific amount**, select the object and position the pointer on a handle until it becomes a double-headed arrow. Then, click the right mouse button. A pop-up dialog box appears, allowing you to specify the amount you wish the object sized or stretched. The Around Center option allows you to size the object outward from its center while the object is anchored in place.

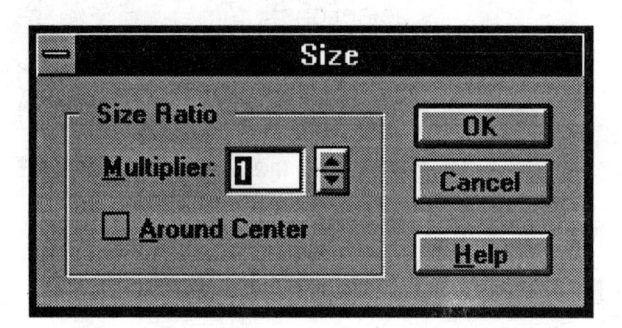

> In this exercise, you will copy and move objects to create a flower pot graphic. This graphic will be used in a later exercise to create a flyer.

- The numbers indicate how much to increase or decrease the object size in relation to the original object size. For example, to double the size of the object, enter the number 2 in the Multiplier text box.

Lesson 7 ■ Exercise 50

EXERCISE DIRECTIONS:

1. Start with a clear screen.
2. Access WPDraw.
3. Display rulers and grid.
4. Position vertical alignment guides at 2", 3", 7" and 8" and horizontal alignment guides at 4" and 8".
5. Using the polygon tool, create the flower pot between the 2" and 8" vertical guides and the 4" and 8" horizontal guides as shown in the illustration. Fill it black.
6. Using the line tool, create a .5" vertical line to represent the flower's stem. Use a medium thickness.
7. Using the ellipse tool (circle), draw a circle to sit on the stem. Size it similar to the illustration. Fill it white. (The circle will serve as a guide to overlay the small circles).
8. Create one small circle and place it just above the base of the stem. Fill it black.
9. Using the method to make duplicate copies, duplicate the small circle and position each next to another and one in the middle of the circle to form the flower.
10. Save the graphic as **FLOWPOT**. (The graphic becomes one of your graphic selections).
11. Update your document. (The graphic becomes part of your document.)
12. Save the file; name it **REPEAT**.
13. Print one copy.
14. Close the document window.

COPY

1. Select object.
2. Click **Edit** .... `Alt` + `E`
3. Click **Copy** .... `C`
4. Click **Edit** .... `E`
5. Click **Paste** .... `P`
6. Position pointer on the edge of the graphic, (not a handle).
7. Drag object into desired position.

MOVE

1. Select object.
2. Position pointer on the edge of the graphic, (not a handle).
3. Drag object to desired position.

SIZE

1. Select object.
2. Position pointer on a handle until it becomes a double-headed arrow.
3. *To size height and width proportionally:*
   - Drag a corner handle.

To size the height:
- Drag a top or bottom handle.

To size the width:
- Drag a side handle.

To size by a specific amount:
- Click *right* mouse button.
- Click **Multiples** text box .... `M`
- Enter a number.
- Click **OK** .... `Enter`

Lesson 7 ▪ Exercise 50

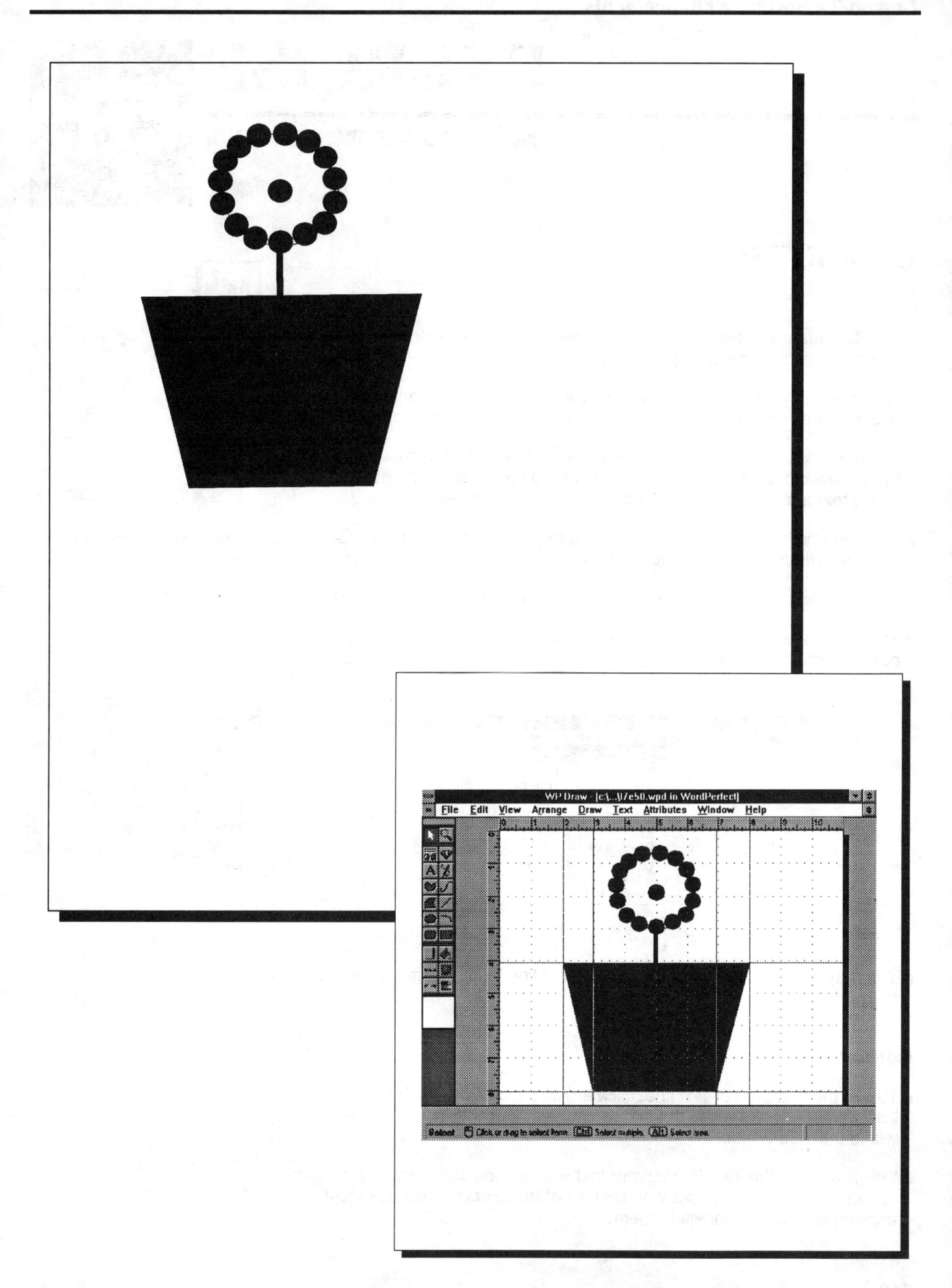

Lesson 7 ▪ Special Enhancements

EXERCISE 51
USING TEXT IN THE DRAWING WINDOW

CONCEPTS:

Create Text

- The Text feature within Draw lets you create and manipulate text. The text may stand alone or be part of your drawing.

- Text may be typed in a *text area* or in a *text line*. A text area is used for multiple lines of text, while a text line is used for a single line of text.

- To enter text in a text area, select the text tool from the tool palette [A]. In the draw window, drag the pointer (it is now a crossbar) to the desired size of the text area. You are, in effect, creating your own text box.

- To enter text in a text line, select the text tool from the tool palette [A]. In the draw window, click once to start a text line.

- Once the text area or text line is created, you can type or retrieve text in it.

- Text may be entered in any desired font, style, or size by selecting the desired option from the Text menu.

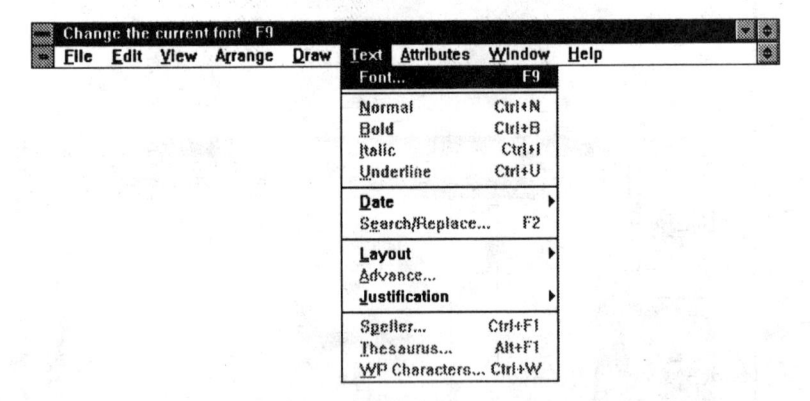

- You may change the size of the text area or line by dragging on a handle to the desired size.

Exit Text Area

- To exit the text area or text line, click anywhere outside the area or line box. When you are within the text area or text line box, you are working within the Text Editor.

- When you exit the Text Editor, your text is now considered an object. Text objects, like graphics or draw objects, must be selected (handles must appear) to edit or manipulate them.

To create text:
- Click text tool on the tool palette.
- Drag crossbar to define text area.

OR

- Click once to create text line.

In this exercise, you will create a logo using rotated, colored and shadowed text.

Align Text

- Text may be aligned (left, right, center) within the text area or text line by selecting Justification from the Text menu.

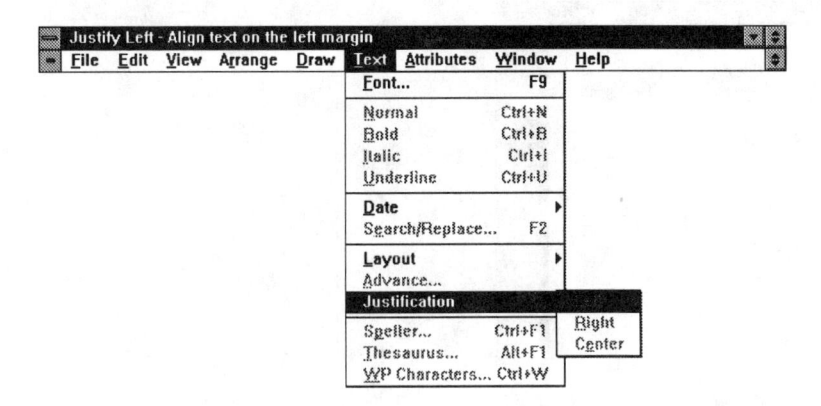

Edit Text

- To edit text, your insertion point must be within the text area or line.

- You can quickly re-enter the text area or line if you exited it by placing the pointer on the text, clicking the *right* mouse button, and selecting Edit Text from the QuickMenu.

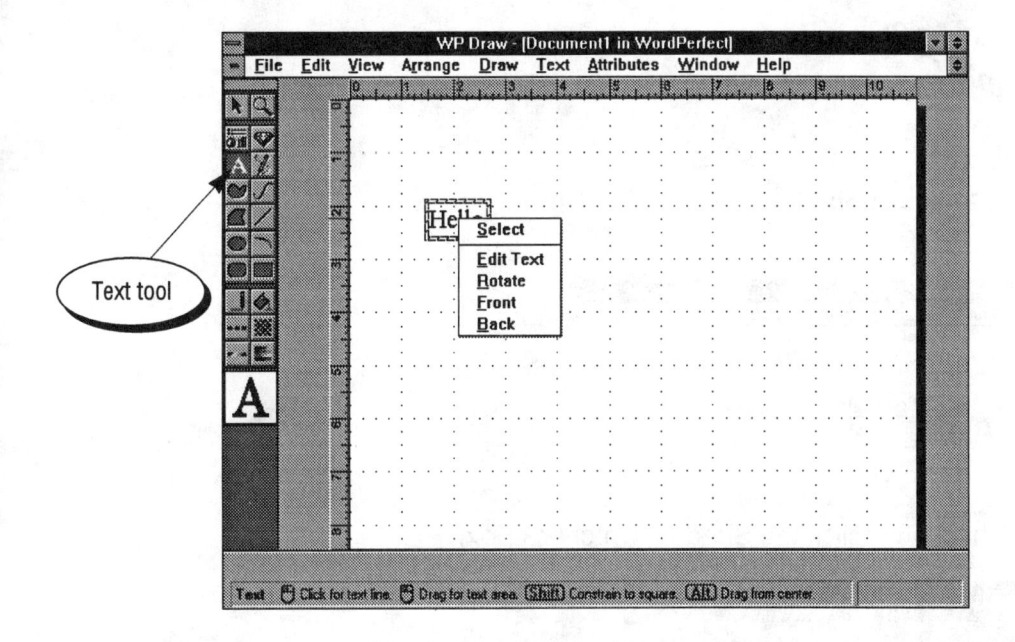

Rotate, Color and Shadow Text

- Interesting effects may be created by rotating, and/or coloring and/or shadowing text. To create the example below left, text was rotated, colored white and overlayed on a black rectangle. To create the example below right, text was rotated and shadowed.

Lesson 7 ▪ Exercise 51   217

Lesson 7 ■ Exercise 51

- To rotate text, place the pointer on the text, click the *right* mouse button and select Rotate.

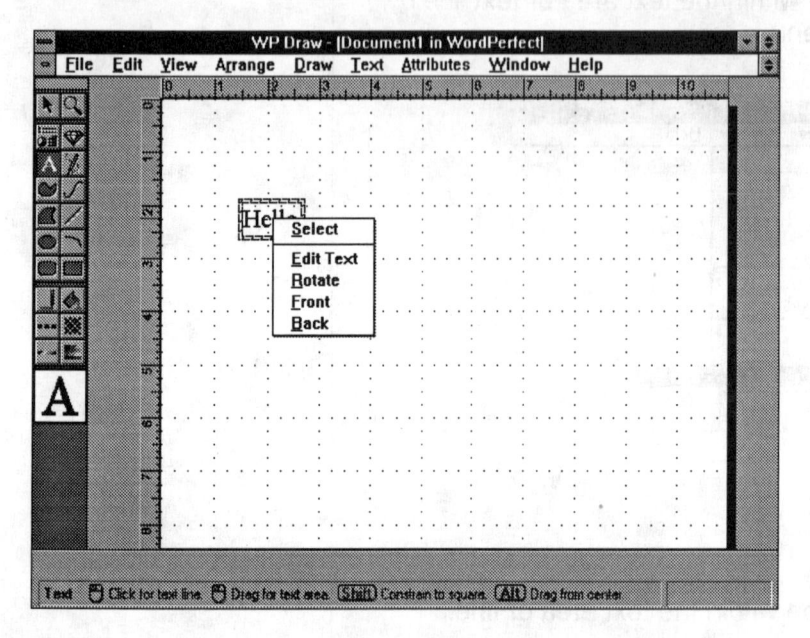

Then, drag on a corner handle to rotate the text in the desired direction. Dragging on a middle handle will stretch the text as shown in the illustration below.

Stephanie Roberts

- To shadow text, select the text and select Shadow from the Attributes menu.

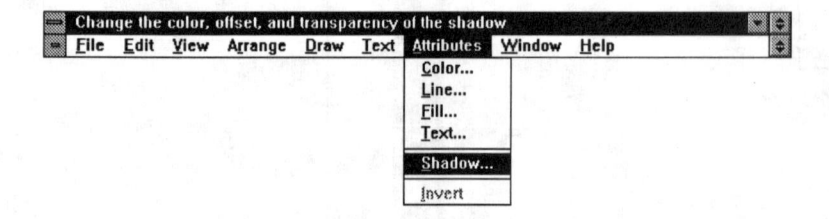

- In the Attributes dialog box which follows, click the Shadow On check box.

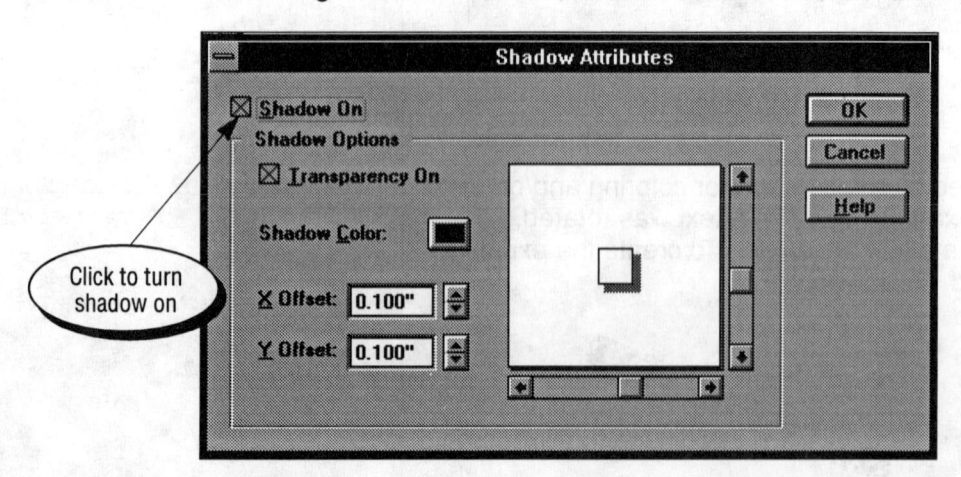

Click to turn shadow on

CREATE TEXT

1. Click **Text Tool** .... `A`
   in tools palette.
2. Drag pointer to desired size of text area.

   OR

   Click once to create text line.
3. Type text.

EXIT TEXT AREA

Click anywhere outside area or line box.

ALIGN TEXT

1. Select text to be aligned.
2. Click **Text** .... `Alt`+`T`
3. Click **Justification** .... `J`
4. Select a justification option

   Left .... `L`

   Right .... `R`

   Center .... `C`

EDIT TEXT

1. Position insertion point within text area or line.
2. Click *right* mouse button.
3. Select **Edit Text** .... `E`
   from QuickMenu.

ROTATE TEXT

1. Position insertion point within text area or line.
2. Click *right* mouse button.
3. Select **Rotate** .... `R`
4. Drag the right or left handles up or down to the desired rotation angle.

COLOR TEXT

1. Edit text area or line.
2. Highlight text to color.
3. Click **Attributes**. .... `Alt`+`A`
4. Click **Color** .... `C`
5. Click **Text Color** button.
6. Click desired color from palette.
7. Click **OK** .... `Enter`

SHADOW TEXT

1. Select text object to shadow (handles should appear).
2. Click **Attributes** .... `Alt`+`A`
3. Click **Shadow** .... `S`
4. Click **Shadow On** check box. .... `S`
5. Click **OK** .... `Enter`

Lesson 7 ■ Exercise 51

Lesson 7 ■ Exercise 51

EXERCISE DIRECTIONS:

1. Start with a clear screen.
2. Access WPDraw.
3. Display the rulers and grid.
4. Position vertical alignment guides at 1" and 6" and horizontal alignment guides at 1", 4", 5" and 6".
5. Using the rectangle with rounded corner tool, draw a rectangle between the 1" and 6" vertical alignment guide and the 1" and 4" horizontal alignment guide, and fill it black.
6. Create a text line between the 5" and 6" horizontal alignment guides.
7. • Type SUNSPORT within the text line in sans serif 36 point (use Swis721 Blk ExBT, if available).
   • Color SUN to grey; color SPORT to white.
   • Insert the special character 5,6 before the word SUNSPORT.
8. Rotate the text diagonally as shown.
9. Drag the text and position it over the black rectangle as shown.
10. Create another text line between the 5" and 6" horizontal alignment guides.
11. • Type Golf Supplies in serif 14 point.
    • Color the text white.
    • Position it as shown.
12. Save the image (Save Copy As); name it **WORDS**.
    ■ *NOTE: In a later exercise, you will create a letterhead using this logo.*
13. Exit and return to document screen.
14. Close the document window.

Lesson 7 ■ Exercise 51

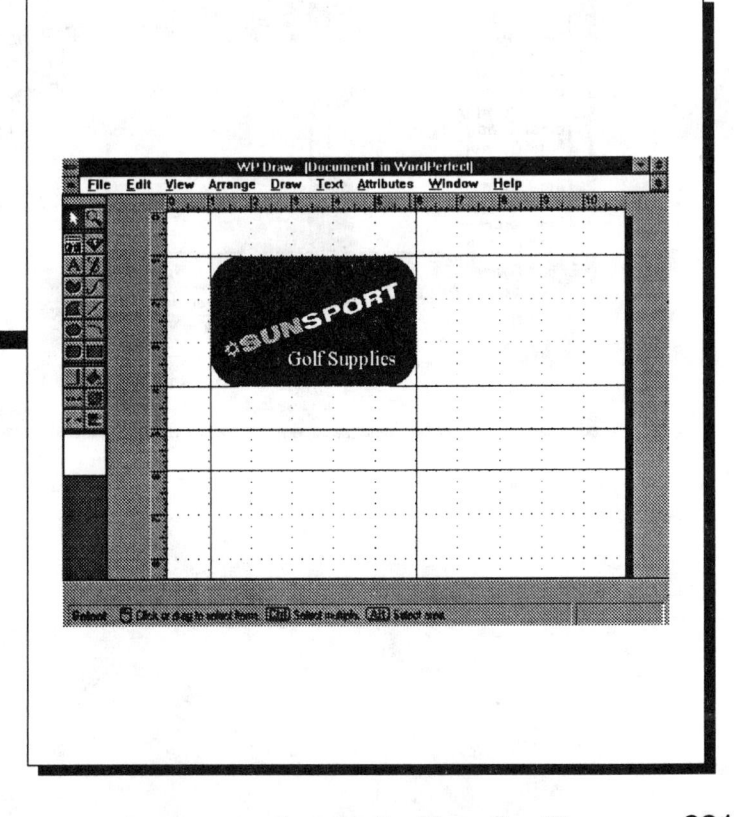

Lesson 7 ▪ Special Enhancements

EXERCISE 52

▪ RETRIEVING AND EDITING GRAPHIC PARTS ▪ CONTOURING TEXT

CONCEPTS:

Retrieve Graphic into Draw Window

- As you learned in a previous lesson, you can retrieve a graphic into a WordPerfect document and manipulate it (size, stretch, move, copy). You can also retrieve a graphic into the WPDraw window if you want to alter it or add text around it.

- To retrieve a graphic into the Draw Window, you must first define the area in the window where the graphic is to be inserted. To do this, click the diamond icon on the tools palette and position the pointer in the Draw window. Note that the insertion point changes to a hand attached to a square. Drag to define the area in which you wish the graphic to be inserted. Or, you may click once in the drawing window to define the entire window to receive the graphic.

- From the Retrieve Figure dialog box which follows, select the graphic you desire and click Retrieve.

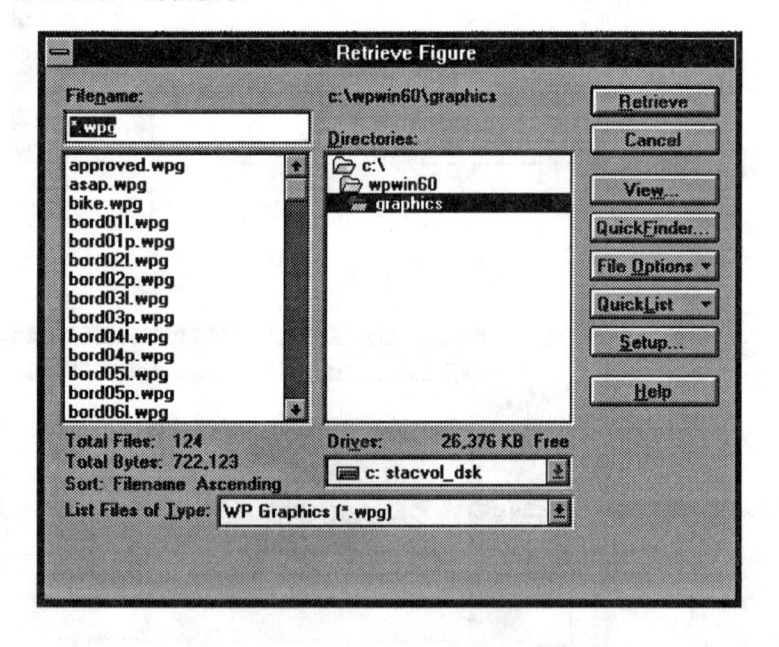

To retrieve a graphic:

- Click diamond on tool palette.

OR

- Click **Draw**
- Click **Figure**
- Drag to define graphic area.
- Select graphic from dialog box.
- Click **Retrieve**

To change fill, color or size of part of graphic:

- Click select tool on tool palette.
- Click figure to select it.
- Click **Edit**
- Click **Edit Figure**
- Click individual graphic part.
- Select color or fill pattern from appropriate palette.

OR

- Drag on a handle to size the part.

Edit Graphic Parts

- if you wish to alter the graphic, you can do so by changing the fill, color or shape of the individual parts that comprise the graphic. You might also want to delete one of the parts.

For example, in the *jockey.wpg* graphic illustrated below, you can change the fill color of the rider's helmet or change the size of the rider's hand or the shape of the saddle blanket to create an interesting effect. You can also use the freehand tool to add more grass, or a flying tail above the horse (instead of below it).

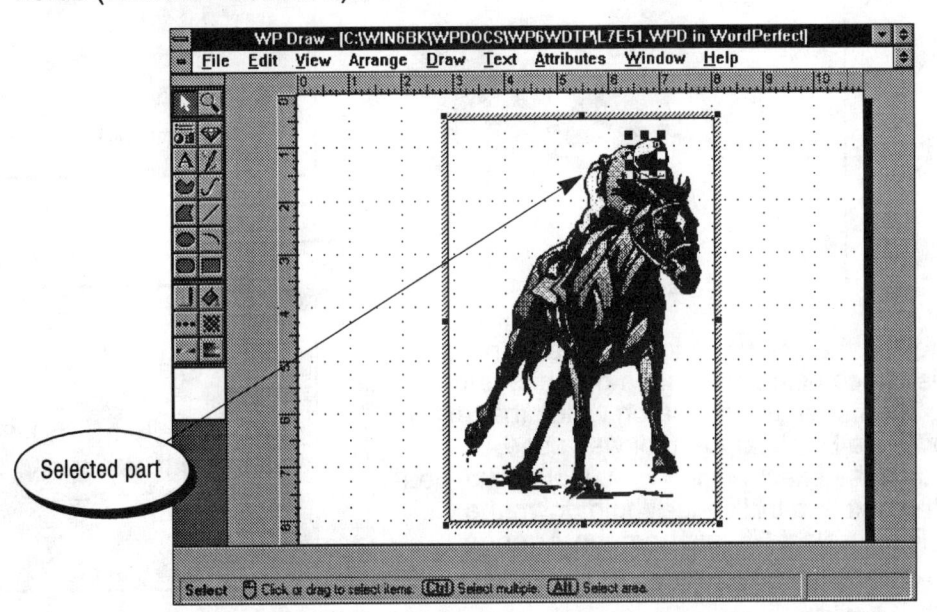

To change shape of part of graphic:
- Click select tool on tool palette.
- Click figure to select it.
- Click **E**dit
- Click **E**dit **Figure**
- Click individual graphic part.
- Click **E**dit
- Click **E**dit **Points**
- Drag a point to desired shape.

Selected part

- **To change fill color** of an individual graphic part, select the graphic in the Draw window and select **E**dit Figure from the **E**dit menu. Then, click the individual graphic part and select a new color or fill from the color/fill palette.

- **To change shape of an individual graphic part**, select the graphic in the draw window and select **E**dit Figure from the **E**dit menu. Then, click the part of the graphic and select **E**dit Points from the **E**dit menu. Drag on one of the points (editing handle) to the desired shape. The illustration below left is the original graphic. In the illustration below right, note the helmet is filled with a pattern and the blanket's shape is changed.

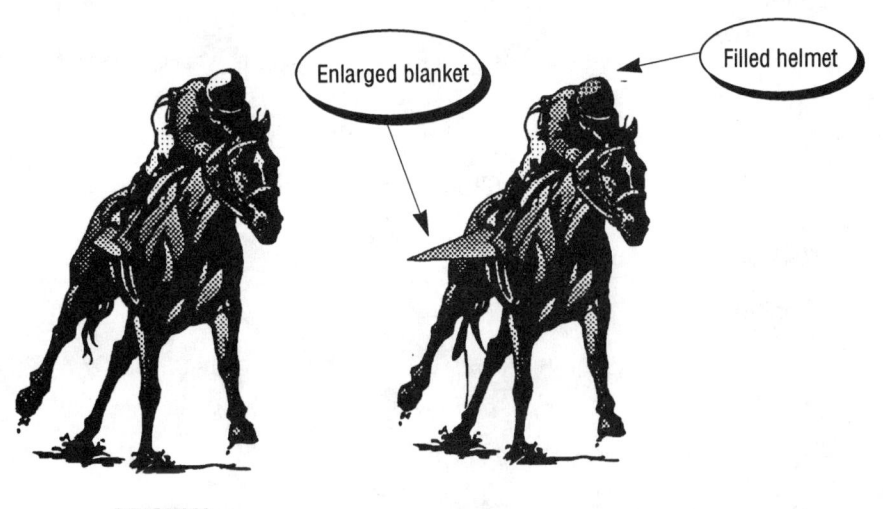

Enlarged blanket

Filled helmet

ORIGINAL

Lesson 7 ▪ Exercise 52

Contour Text

- The Contour text feature lets you create a line of text, then wrap it around a shape. The shape can be combined with the graphic to create an interesting effect:

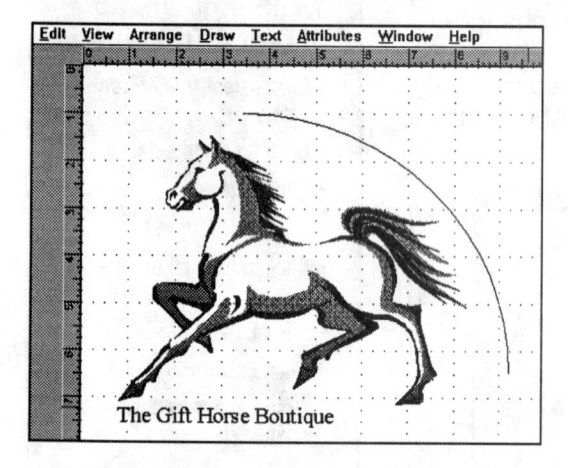

To contour text:
- Create the text.
- Create the shape
- Select the text.
- Hold down the Ctrl and select the shape.
- Click **A**rrange
- Click **E**ffects
- Click Co**n**tour Text

In this exercise, you will contour text around a shape and combine it with a graphic to create a logo.

- To contour text, first create the text in the Draw window as you learned in the previous exercise. If you wish to combine text with a graphic, retrieve a graphic into the draw window. Then, create a shape on which the text will wrap. In the illustration above, the Elliptical Arc tool was used. If, after you draw the shape, it is not in the exact position you would like, you can move it later. Select both the text and the shape (hold down the Ctrl key to select multiple objects). Then, select Effects from the Arrange menu, and choose Contour Text.

EXERCISE DIRECTIONS:

1. Start with a clear screen.
2. Access WPDraw.
3. Retrieve CRANE_J.WPG graphic into the draw window. Define the entire window to receive the graphic.
4. Create a text line and type "Fly with the BEST!" as shown.
5. Using the Elliptical Arc tool, draw a curve around the crane's head as shown.
6. Contour the text on the shape. Position it Top Center.
7. Save the graphic as FLY. (The graphic becomes one of your graphic selections).
8. Update your document. (The graphic becomes part of your document).
9. Save the file; name it **ANNOTATE**.
10. Print one copy.
11. Close the document window.

RETRIEVE A GRAPHIC

Click diamond tool .... 🔶

OR

1. Click **Draw** .... Alt + D
2. Click **Figure** .... F
3. Drag to define graphic area.

   OR

   Click once in window to define entire window as graphic area.

4. Select desired graphic.
5. Click **Retrieve** .... R

EDIT GRAPHIC PART

Change Fill, Color or Size

1. Click **Select tool** .... ▶
2. Click figure to select it.
3. Click **Edit** .... Alt + E
4. Click **Edit Figure** .... E
5. Click individual graphic part.
6. Click **Color or Fill** tool .... ▣ or ◆
   - Select desired color or fill.

   OR

   - Drag on a handle to desired size.
7. Click anywhere off the graphic to deselect.

Change shape

1. Follow steps 1-5.
2. Click **Edit** .... Alt + E
3. Click **Edit Points** .... E
4. Drag a point to desired shape.
5. Click anywhere off the graphic to deselect it.

CONTOUR TEXT

1. Create a text line:
   - Click **text tool**. .... A
   - Click in draw window.
   - Type text.
2. Create a shape:
   - Click desired line shape tool.
   - Draw shape.
3. Click to select the text.
4. Hold **Ctrl** while you click the shape.
5. Click **Arrange** .... Alt + R
6. Click **Effects** .... E
7. Click **Contour Text** .... N
8. Define desired position.
   - Select position.
   - Select/deselect **Display Text Only** ... Y
9. Click OK .... Enter

Lesson 7 ■ Exercise 52   225

Lesson 7 ▪ Special Enhancements

EXERCISE 53

▪ ARRANGING OBJECTS ▪ GROUPING/UNGROUPING

CONCEPTS:

Front and Back

- When you draw multiple objects in the Draw window, WordPerfect stacks one on top of the other. It is like using a new transparency page for each object you draw and overlaying it on the previous object.

- You can change the layering of the objects that overlap by selecting the object and then either Front or Back from the Arrange menu. Using this feature has no effect if objects do not overlap.

- **Front** moves an item to the front of all other items in the stack; **Back** moves an item to the bottom of all other items in the stack.

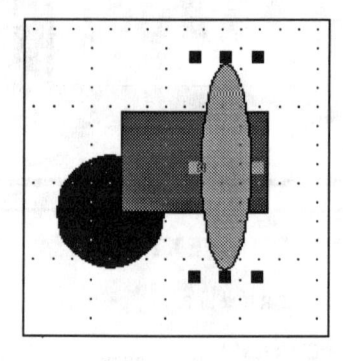

Selected object

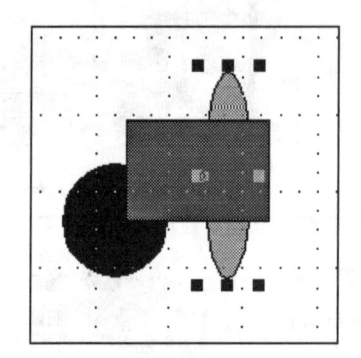

Selected object moved back

- To change the layering of an object, select the object and select Front or Back from the Arrange menu.

To arrange an object (front to back or back to front):
- Select the object to move.
- Click **Arrange**
- Click **Front** or **Back**

Group and Ungroup

- **Grouping** creates one object out of the individual parts. Note the individual parts of the flower pot created in the previous exercise. The illustration left is ungrouped (note editing points); the illustration right is grouped.

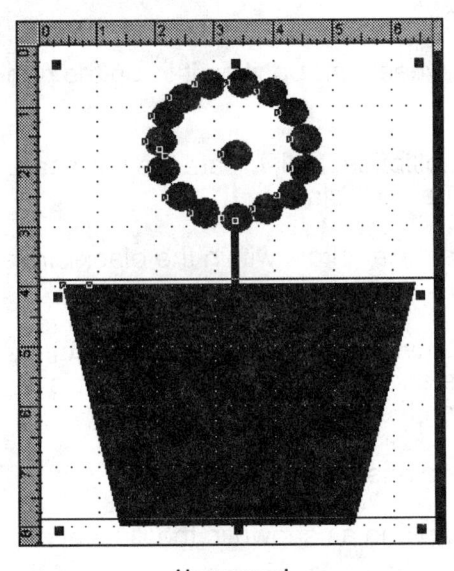

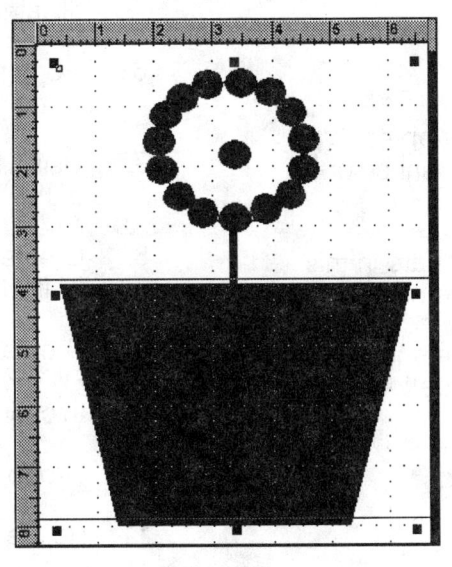

Ungrouped   Grouped

- To move, size, or copy the whole object and not each part while you are in the Draw window, you must first group the objects.

- If after you group a drawing, you then wish to edit one part of the drawing, you must **ungroup** the drawing.

To group an object:
- Click **E**dit
- Click **S**elect
- Click **A**ll
- Click **A**rrange
- Click **G**roup

In part I of this exercise, you will create several shapes and change the layering order. In Part II of this exercise, you will create a logo, group the parts, then rotate it. The graphic will then be used in a later exercise.

Lesson 7 ■ Exercise 53

EXERCISE DIRECTIONS:

Part I

1. Start with a clear screen.
2. Access WPDraw.
3. Display rulers and grid.
4. Draw three shapes and overlap each as shown. Fill each one a different color or pattern as desired.
5. Select the top shape (the square in this illustration) and send it to the back.
6. Select the bottom shape (the square with rounded corners in this illustration) and send it to the front.
7. Clear the draw window.

Part II

1. Position vertical alignment guides at 2" and 8" and horizontal alignment guides at 2" and 6".
2. Draw a circle in the middle of alignment guides as shown. Fill it black.
3. Using the elliptical tool (circle), draw the top wing of the plane between the 2" and 8" vertical alignment guides.
4. Copy the wing and position it at the bottom of the circle.
5. Using the elliptical tool, create the left wheel; fill it black.
6. Copy the wheel and position it to be the right wheel.
7. Using the elliptical tool, create the top head of the plane; fill it black.
8. Create a smaller circle within the black circle; fill it white.
9. Create a smaller circle within the white circle. Fill it white and change the border so it is thicker than the default.
10. Group the plane.
11. Rotate the plane as shown in the illustration.
12. Save the graphic as **AIRPLANE**.
13. Update your document.
14. Save the file; name it **GROUP**.
15. Print one copy.
16. Close the document window.

ARRANGE OBJECTS (FRONT/BACK)

1. Select the object to be moved.
2. Click **A**rrange .... Alt + R
3. Click **F**ront .... F
   or
   Click **B**ack .... B

GROUP/UNGROUP

Group

1. Select all parts of the object:
   - Click **E**dit .... Alt + E
   - Click **S**elect .... S
   - Click **A**ll .... A
2. Click **A**rrange .... Alt + R
3. Click **G**roup .... G

Ungroup

1. Select grouped object.
2. Click **A**rrange .... Alt + R
3. Click **U**ngroup .... U

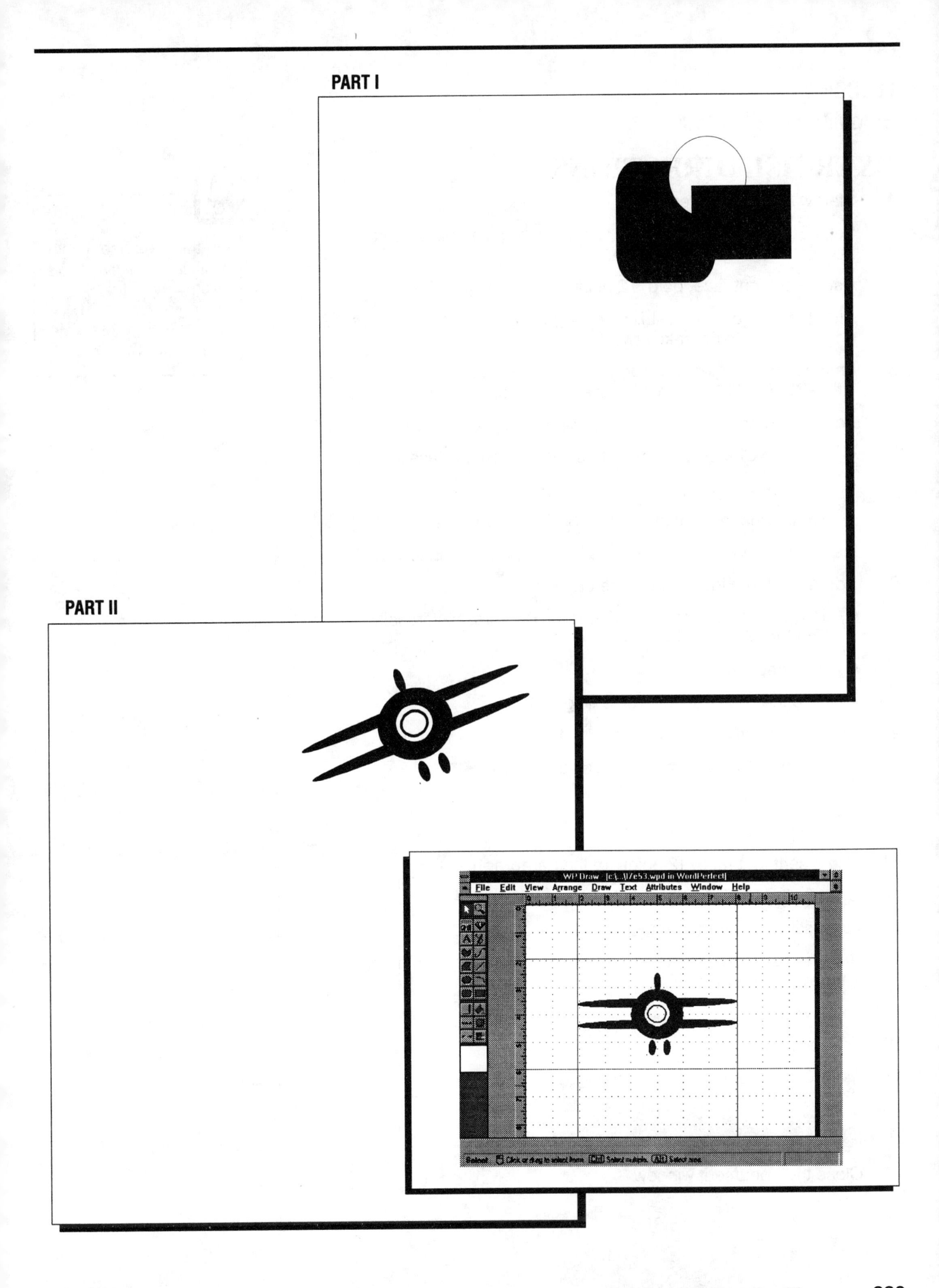

PART I

PART II

Lesson 7 ▪ Exercise 53

LESSON 7
SUMMARY EXERCISE A

EXERCISE DIRECTIONS:

1. Start with a clear screen.
2. Set 1.5" left and right margins, a 1" top margin and a .5" bottom margin.
3. Use a serif font face, bold, 72 point, for the first four lines.
4. After typing the *Y* in HEALTHY, change to a sans serif font face, 12 point. Press the Enter key two times.
5. Enhance the first letter of each of the four words by playing the **REVERSE.WCM** macro to place the first letter in reverse text.
6. Edit each graphic box containing the reverse text as follows:
   - Choose Character Anchor, Position Content at Baseline.
   - Size the box 1" by 1".
   - Center the text within the box (*Shift + F7 before each letter*).
7. Place the insertion point two lines below the word HEALTHY.
8. Add a Custom Figure Box to the page:
   - Page Anchor, horizontally Center of Paragraph; vertically 0" from Top Margin.
   - No Wrap
   - Size the width, 5.2", and the height, 9.45".
9. Change the left and right margins to 2.25".
10. Import **FISH** from data disk; save as **FISH2**.

    or

    Type the exercise as shown.
11. Use a serif font face, 12 point, for the paragraph text.
12. Change the line leading to .05".
13. Full justify the paragraph text.
14. Add the special character, *5,110,* to the right margin in the blank line after each paragraph.
15. Preview your document.
16. Print one copy.
17. Close the file; save the changes.

    or

    Save the file; name it **FISH2**.
18. Close the document window.

> In this exercise, you will create a flyer from saved text using reverse text, special characters, and a figure box.

FISH IS SUPER HEALTHY

If you are health-conscious or diet-conscious, fish is the way to go. You can never get bored with fish since there are so many varieties you can prepare in so many different ways.

Whether you poach, steam, broil, pan fry, deep fry, stir fry, barbecue, saute, bake or smoke fish, it is still the food to eat.

You can have salmon, sole, shark, snapper, halibut, haddock, smelts, swordfish, tuna, bluefish, carp, catfish, sardines, monkfish, mackerel, scrod, pompano, herring, trout, shad or turbot.

You can serve fish as an hors d'oeurvre, appetizer or main dish.

LESSON 7
SUMMARY EXERCISE B

EXERCISE DIRECTIONS:

1. Start with a clear screen.

2. Open **RSVP**.

3. Set left and right margins at 1.75" a top margin at 1.5" and bottom margin at 2".

4. Change all text to a serif font face.

5. Make indicated changes in the announcement.

   - Insert a 2" single horizontally centered horizontal line.

   - Use 1.5 line spacing where indicated.

   - Center the lines as indicated.

   ■ NOTE: Do not use Center Justification. The lines must be individually centered (Shift + F7) in order to add special characters to the lines.

   - Insert the following special characters using varied sizes from 14 points to 24 points.

     ★   5,72
     ●   5,108
     ■   5,110
     ▲   5,115
     ◆   5,117

   ■ NOTE: Use the spacebar and tab key to place the special characters. To cluster the special characters close together after the last line of text, change the line height to Fixed at .1".

6. Add a Double Page Border.

7. Preview your document.

8. Print one copy.

9. Close the file; save the changes.

10. Close the document window.

> In this exercise, you will use special characters to enhance an announcement that was previously created.

CELEBRATE {50 pt bold}

ON THE HUDSON {18 pt} ★

───────────────

{2" single line centered}

{1.5 line spacing}

This New Year's Eve,
there is no more elegant, more beautiful spot
than the Hudson River Cafe.

★

Dance with the Statue of Liberty in view
to the sounds of our live band and DJ.

★

Enjoy a six-course Hudson Valley feast
and a spectacular dessert
to be remembered as the last memory of the year.

{10 pt}

★

NEW YEAR'S EVE DINNER DANCE {18 pt}

★

{1.5 line spacing}

★Call for reservations 212-876-9888.
Our courteous staff will be glad to assist you at any time.
◆We are located at Four World Financial Center.▲★

{10 pt}

HUDSON RIVER CLUB● {18 pt}

★▲   ▲   ●
▲◆ ★ ● ◆ ★ ●

Lesson 7 ■ Exercise B   233

LESSON 7
SUMMARY EXERCISE C

EXERCISE DIRECTIONS:

1. Create the magazine cover as shown.
2. Set top and bottom margins to .5"
3. Use desired TextArt design to create the heading in a bold sans serif font.
4. Add an extra thick line below the heading.
5. Import **WORLD.WPG** as the top graphic and remove the border.
6. Import **INKSKIER.WPG** as the bottom graphic, add a button border around it and place the caption centered on the bottom, outside the border.
7. Use a sans serif font in 14 point for the centered text and a large circle for the bullet.
8. Place the centered text in a reverse text box:
   - paragraph anchored in the center horizontally.
   - sized approximately 3.5" in width and sized to content in height.
   - ■ NOTE: It may not be possible to make your magazine cover appear exactly as illustrated since available fonts and printers vary.
9. Preview your document.
10. Print one copy.
11. Save the exercise; name it **MAGAZINE**.
12. Close the document window.

> In this exercise, you will create a magazine cover using textart, bullets, reverse type and graphics.

VACATIONING

june 1995   volume 16 number 3

In This Issue:

- Skiing in the Alps
- Dining in the Bahamas
- Fishing Vacations
- Safaris Anyone?
- Shopping in Florence

Skiing in the Alps

LESSON 7
SUMMARY EXERCISE D

EXERCISE DIRECTIONS:

Part I

1. Start with a clear screen.
2. Set .5" left, right and top margins.
3. - Import the **WORDS.WPG** graphic (created in Exercise 51).
   - Position it right; size the width to 2.5" and the height to 1.75".
4. Type and right align the address and phone information in sans serif 10 point (use Swis721 Blk ExBT, if available).
5. Create a full horizontal line below each line as shown. Use the default thickness.
6. Print one copy.
7. Save the file; name it **SUNLET**.
8. Close the document window.

Part II

1. Start with a clear screen.
2. Open **FLOWER1**.
3. Set .5" top and bottom margins.
4. Delete One-Day Sale--July 21, 1995.
5. Left align paragraphs 2, 3 and 4 (remove the indents).
6. - Import the **FLOWPOT.WPG** graphic (created in Exercise 53).
   - Position it center and use a Contour text wrap as shown.
   - Size the width to 2.35" and the height to 3.5".
7. Set the last line of text to Initial Capitals in a 18 point italic.
8. - Create a text box.
   - Type and center One-Day Sale--July 21, 1995 in serif 36 point bold.
   - Size width to 4.96" and the height to .700".
   - Position it at the bottom of the page as shown.
   - Use a black fill to shade the box.
   - Color the text white.
9. Preview the file.
10. Print one copy.
11. Save the file; name it **PLANTER**.
12. Close the document window.

> In Part I of this exercise, you will create a letterhead, using a graphic you created in a previous exercise. In Part II, you will create a flyer, using a graphic you created earlier.

PART I

7777 Swing Lane

Line Drive, IL 60177

708-555-5555

SunSPORT
Golf Supplies

PART II

The Perennial Potter

14 Highway 37
Middletown, NJ
908-671-5555

It is another new year and by now you are ready to add to your existing garden. This year we have over 75 perennial plants to choose from. There are all sizes and types to suit your needs.

We have perennials that can be grown in full sun or on partial shade. We even have some that require full shade and some that require full sun.

We have perennials that will survive temperatures below 50 degrees and perennials that need at least 40 degrees to survive.

We have perennials that bloom in early spring and perennials that bloom in the late fall.

Below is a sampling of some of our favorites:

DELPHINIUM: One of the tallest of our perennials, the delphinium comes in brilliant colors such as blue, purple, white, pink and lavender. The plants grow as tall as 72" in full sun.

✽✽

PLATYCODON: The "Balloon Flower" is a medium sized perennial that comes in violet, white, and pink. The plants grow as tall as 36" in full sun to partial shade.

✽✽

COREOPSIS: These daisy-like perennials come in yellow and pink. The plants grow as tall as 24" in full sun to partial shade.

✽✽

SEDUM: This ground cover comes in pink, red, yellow, and white. The plants grow up to 6" tall and spread quickly in full sun.

From High to Low, We Have the Perennial for You!

One-Day Sale -- July 21, 1995

Lesson 7 ■ Exercise D

LESSON 7
SUMMARY EXERCISE E

EXERCISE DIRECTIONS:

1. Start with a clear screen.
2. Set the top margin to .2".
3. - Create a text box.
   - Type and center the text shown within the gray box in serif 12 point bold. Set the line spacing to 1.5".
   - Size the box to 1.5" wide by 4.5" tall.
   - Remove the border.
   - Use a button fill to shade the box.
   - Position the box 2" from the top of the page and center it horizontally. (You will adjust the horizontal centering later).
4. - Retrieve **AIRPLANE**.WPG (the graphic you created in Exercise 53).
   - Size it to 3.25" wide by 1.75" tall.
   - Position it above the gray text box as shown.
5. Advance to Ln 3.5" on the page.
6. Create 2 newspaper columns using the default widths and gutter space.
7. - Type the column text as shown.
   - Full justify column text.
8. - Retrieve **LUGGAGE**.WPG (the graphic you created in Exercise 49).
   - Size it to .5" and position it as shown.
9. - Position your insertion point to the left of the word Smoking.
   - Access WPDraw.
   - Create the no-smoking symbol.
   - Update the document (to insert the graphic into the paragraph).
   - Close and return to the document.
   - Size the graphic to .5" and position it as shown.
10. - Retrieve **GLASS**.WPG (the graphic you created in Exercise 49).
    - Size it to .5" and position it as shown.
11. - Create a text box and type the letter Q within it.
    - Set the Q to a Wingding font in 36 point to create the small airplane graphic.
    - Remove the border from the text box.
    - Size it to .5" and position it as shown.
12. - Position your insertion point to the left of the word Electronic equipment.
    - Access WPDraw.
    - Create the Electronic equipment graphic.
    - Update the document (to insert the graphic into the paragraph).
    - Exit and return to the document.
    - Size the graphic to .5" and position it as shown.
13. - Create a text box and type the minus sign (-) within it.

> In this exercise, you will create new graphics and use graphics you created in previous exercises to create a flyer.

Continued...

- Set the minus sign to a Wingding font in 36 point to create the mailbox.
- Remove the border from the text box.
- Size it to .5" and position it as shown.

14. Insert a vertical line between columns (Layout, Columns, Border/Fill, Border Style).
15. Adjust the gray text box to center it between the columns (use the vertical line as your guide).
16. Create a Gray Mat page border (Layout, Page, Border/Fill).
17. Preview the exercise.
18. Save the exercise; name it **WELCOME.**
19. Print one copy.
20. Close the document window.

Thank you for choosing Glide Airlines today. Here is some important information that will help make your trip safe and comfortable.

All of us at Glide Airlines wish you a pleasant journey. If there is anything we can do to make your flight more enjoyable, please press the flight-attendant button at your seat.

Luggage--Please attach your name to each piece of checked baggage. Free bag-identification tags are available at Glide Airlines check-in counters. Pack identification inside your bags, too, and carry all valuables, medicines, and keys with you onto the plane.

Smoking-- is not permitted on any Glide flights or on Glide's domestic U.S. flights of less than six hours, including those to and from Hawaii, San Juan, St. Thomas, St. Croix and Canada. On flights where smoking is permitted, cigar and pipe smoking are prohibited, as is smoking in the aisles or lavatories.

Beverage service--is available on most American flights. Only liquor served by your flight attendant may be consumed on board, however, and only customers twenty-one or older will be served alcoholic beverages.

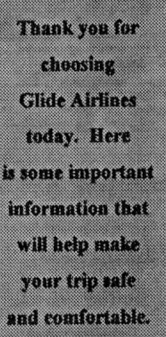

Cockpit visits are available while the aircraft is parked at the airport gate. Please ask one of your flight attendants if you're interested in seeing it. While the aircraft is in motion, however, the cockpit door must remain closed.

Electronic equipment-- Portable electronic devices are not allowed to be used during taxi, takeoff, and landing. Following takeoff and the flight crew's approval announcement, all portable electronic devices may be used, except the following: cellular telephones, radios, TV cameras, TV sets, electronic games and toys with remote control.

We welcome your comments! If you would like to write to us about our service, please send your letters to James Pilot, Glide Airlines Managing Director of Consumer Relations, P. O. Box 4564, DFW Airport, TX 72555-5555.

Lesson 8 ▪ Multiple-Page Documents

EXERCISE 54

▪ CREATE HEADERS AND FOOTERS ▪ ADD PAGE NUMBERS

CONCEPTS:

- A **header** is text printed at the top of every page or every other page, just below the top margin; a **footer** is text which prints at the bottom of every page or every other page, just above the bottom margin. Examples of header and footer text are publication names, chapter names or numbers, section titles, dates, or a company name.

```
2                    HEADER

In this example, a page
number is placed in the
upper left corner of the
page. The right margin
has the section title.
```

```
In books and magazines, a
separate footer is often created
for odd pages and even pages.
This is an odd page footer.

FOOTER                      3
```

- After the desired header or footer text is typed, the header/footer feature automatically inserts it on every page, or on specified pages of your document.

- You can create two different headers (specified as either A or B) and two different footers (specified as either A or B) at any place in the document. You can have only two headers and two footers active on any given page.

- Headers/Footers may be accessed by selecting **Header/Footer** from the Layout main menu; then, select *Create* on the Header/Footer dialog box:

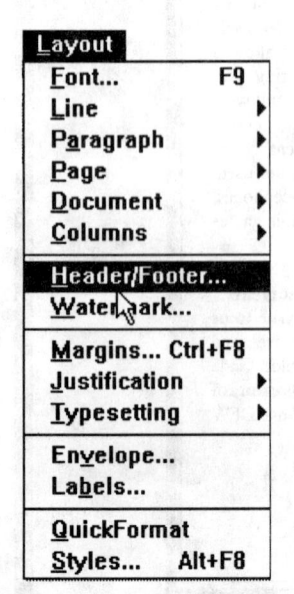

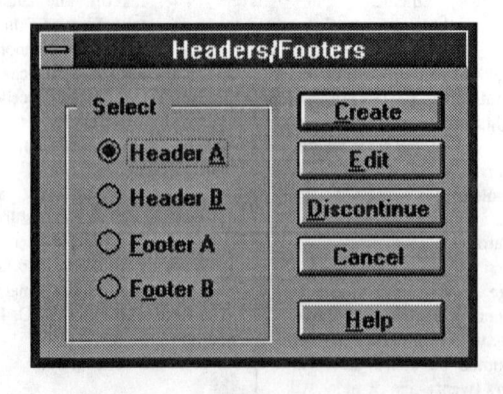

```
Layout
  Font...           F9
  Line               ▶
  Paragraph          ▶
  Page               ▶
  Document           ▶
  Columns            ▶
  Header/Footer...
  Watermark...
  Margins... Ctrl+F8
  Justification      ▶
  Typesetting        ▶
  Envelope...
  Labels...
  QuickFormat
  Styles...    Alt+F8
```

```
Headers/Footers

Select              Create
  ● Header A        Edit
  ○ Header B        Discontinue
  ○ Footer A        Cancel
  ○ Footer B        Help
```

✔ **To add a header or footer:**
- Click **L**ayout
- Click **H**eader/Footer
- Click **C**reate

✔ **To return to document window after creating a header/footer:**

Click anywhere outside the header or footer.

OR

Press **Ctrl + F4**

✔ **To edit a header or footer:**
- Click **L**ayout
- Click **H**eader/Footer
- Click **E**dit

- When you create a header or footer, the Header/Footer Feature Bar automatically displays. The Feature Bar provides options for creating and editing headers/footers. When you click outside the header/footer area, the Feature Bar is deactivated.

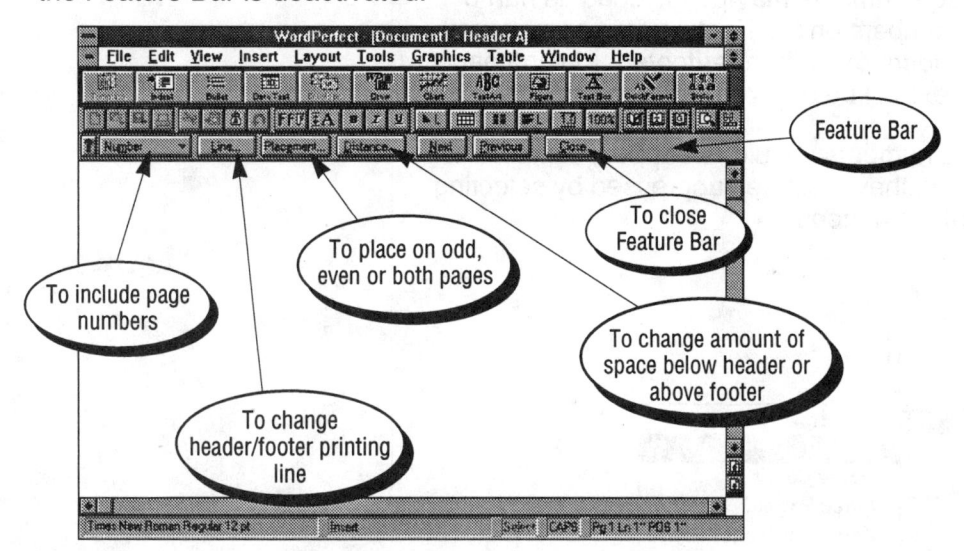

Screenshot of WordPerfect - [Document1 - Header A] window with callouts:
- Feature Bar
- To close Feature Bar
- To place on odd, even or both pages
- To include page numbers
- To change amount of space below header or above footer
- To change header/footer printing line

> Headers and footers will not display in draft view.

> If your header/footer and document margins do not match and should, change the Document Initial Code Style to correct this situation.

- To add a line to separate the header or footer from the body text, select Line on the Feature Bar and make the desired adjustments the same way you would using the Custom Line feature in the document window.

- The amount of space beneath a header or above a footer may be changed. To do so, select Distance on the Feature Bar and make the desired adjustments.

- Headers and footers display in Page or Two Page view.

- If you plan to insert a header on the left side of your pages, insert page numbers on the top right side or bottom of your pages. Be sure that your header/footer text does not overlap or appear too close to the page number.

- Headers, footers and page numbers may be inserted after the document is typed.

- If you want headers and footers to align with the body text, you must set margins for the document, not for the page.

- You can do any of the following procedures in a header or footer the same way you would in the document window:
  - Add graphics boxes with images or text.
  - Change the font shading, font style, and point size.
  - Cut, copy and paste text.

> If your header/footer text has different margins than the rest of your document, a margin change can be made inside the header/footer.

Editing Headers/Footers

- To **edit** a header or footer, click inside the header or footer or select **Header/Footer**, Edit from the Layout main menu. To display the Feature Bar, you may click the *right* mouse button while inside the header or footer, then select Feature Bar.

> In this exercise, you will add a header and footer to previously saved text.

Lesson 8 ■ Exercise 54   241

Lesson 8 ■ Exercise 54

Page Numbers

■ **Page numbers** should be included on the second and succeeding pages of multiple page documents. Page numbers may be included as part of header/footer text by selecting Numbers on the Feature Bar, or they may be placed in a document independent of the header/footer. Placing page numbers outside header/footer text will be covered in Exercise 55.

■ Since headers, footers and page numbers should *not* appear on the first page of a multiple page document, they must be suppressed by selecting **Page**, Suppress from the Layout main menu.

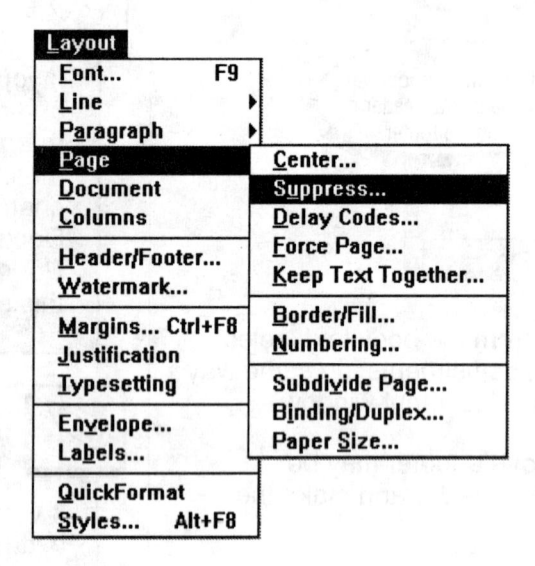

```
Layout
 Font...           F9
 Line               ▶
 Paragraph          ▶
 Page               ▶   Center...
 Document               Suppress...
 Columns                Delay Codes...
                        Force Page...
 Header/Footer...       Keep Text Together...
 Watermark...
                        Border/Fill...
 Margins... Ctrl+F8     Numbering...
 Justification
 Typesetting            Subdivide Page...
                        Binding/Duplex...
 Envelope...            Paper Size...
 Labels...

 QuickFormat
 Styles...   Alt+F8
```

CHANGE DOCUMENT MARGINS

1. Click **L**ayout .... `Alt` + `L`
2. Click **D**ocument .... `D`
3. Click Initial Codes **S**tyle .... `S`
4. Click **L**ayout in Styles .... `L`
   Editor dialog box
5. Click **M**argins .... `M`
6. Change left, right, top and bottom margins.
7. Click OK .... `Enter`
8. Click OK .... `Enter`

CREATE HEADER/FOOTER

1. Place insertion point on first page where you want new header/footer to appear.
2. Click **L**ayout .... `Alt` + `L`
3. Click **H**eader/Footer .... `H`
4. Select Header **A** or Header **B** .. `A` or `B`
   and/or
   Select **F**ooter A or F**o**oter B .... `F` or `O`
5. Click **C**reate .... `Alt` + `C`
6. Type .... *header/footer text*
   header/footer text.

To add page number:

Position cursor where number will appear.

Click Nu**m**ber .... `Alt` + `Shift` + `M`
on Feature Bar.

Click **P**age Number .... `P`

Click **C**lose .... `Alt` + `Shift` + `C`

To adjust space between header/footer and document text:

Click **D**istance .... `Alt` + `Shift` + `D`
on Feature Bar.

Type amount of space .... *number*
in text box.

OR

Click increment arrows

7. Click **C**lose .... `Alt` + `Shift` + `C`
   on Feature Bar.

To add line to header/footer:

Click **L**ine .... `Alt` + `Shift` + `L`

Select desired options:

Line Style .... `L` , `Space`
to choose line styles.

Line Type:

   H**o**rizontal .... `Alt` + `O`

   OR

   Vertical .... `Alt` + `V`

Ho**r**izontal Position .... `Alt` + `R`
to set horizontal position.

V**e**rtical Position .... `Alt` + `E`
to set vertical position.

Le**n**gth to set length of line ...... `Alt` + `N`

Spacing to specify spacing:

   Above .... `Alt` + `A`

   and **B**elow line .... `Alt` + `B`

Change Color .... `Alt` + `I`
to change L**i**ne color.

Change **T**hickness .... `Alt` + `T`
to change line thickness.

Click OK .... `Enter`

RETURN TO DOCUMENT WINDOW AFTER CREATING HEADER/FOOTER

Ctrl + F4

Click anywhere outside header/footer.

SUPPRESS HEADER/FOOTER/PAGE NUMBER ON FIRST PAGE

1. Place insertion point on page where text is to be suppressed.
2. Click **L**ayout .... `Alt` + `L`
3. Click **P**age .... `P`
4. Click S**u**ppress .... `U`
5. Click appropriate check box to suppress desired item.
6. Click OK .... `Enter`

EDIT HEADER/FOOTER

1. Place insertion point on first page where you want change to occur.
2. Click **L**ayout .... `Alt` + `L`
3. Click **H**eader/Footer .... `H`
4. Click **E**dit .... `Alt` + `E`
   OR
   Click anywhere inside header or footer.

   NOTE: To display Feature Bar, click right mouse button inside header/footer, then select Feature Bar.

5. Edit header/footer text.
6. Click **C**lose .... `Alt` + `Shift` + `C`
   on Feature Bar.

Lesson 8 ▪ Exercise 54

Lesson 8 ▪ Exercise 54

EXERCISE DIRECTIONS:

1. Start with a clear screen.

2. Open **COMPLND** from data disk; save as **COMPLND1**.

    or

    Type the exercise text.

    NOTE: *While the exercise is shown in single space, you are to use 1.5 space. Your printed document will result in four pages.*

3. Set the document left and right margins to 2.5" and the top and bottom margins to 3".

4. Change the justification to full.

5. Change the line spacing to 1.5.

6. Add bold and italics to the title ***ComputerLand***.

7. Create Header A for every page:

    - Type "ComputerLand" in bold and italics at left margin.
    - Press the Enter key.
    - Type "Chapter 1" right aligned in bold and italics.
    - Add a single full horizontal line and set the vertical position at the baseline.
    - Set the distance between the header and text to .25"

8. Create Footer A for every page:

    - Add a single horizontal line.
    - Create a user box and import a graphic image, **FATHRTME.WPG:**
    - Set the graphic height to .5" and the width sized to content.
    - Change the horizontal position to center of paragraph.
    - Set the vertical position to .1" from top of paragraph.

9. Edit the header you created and change the following:

    - Delete "Chapter 1".
    - Add a right-aligned page number in bold and italics.

10. Suppress the header and footer on the first page.

11. Exit to the document window.

12. Preview your document.

13. Print one copy.

14. Close the file; save the changes.

    or

    Save the file; name it **COMPLND1**.

15. Close the document window.

ComputerLand

Once upon a time, in ComputerLand, there lived a king named Header and a queen named Footer. King Header loved to create extravagant headers and Queen Footer loved to create extraordinary footers.

The king was clever. "Look at what I did," he said to the queen one day. "I put a page number on the right side of my header. After typing *Chapter One* on the left side. I just used flush right and added the automatic page numbering command." And the next day the king came running into the room and showed Queen Footer another project. This time, the header had three lines of text in addition to the page number on the right side. Well, the queen was impressed, but she was not to be outdone.

Two days went by and on Wednesday at 4:35 p.m., the queen came out of the Computer Tower and casually dropped a sheet of paper in front of the king. King Header was flabbergasted. "I didn't know you could use graphics in headers and footers," he said in amazement. "Look at that line! Look at that graphic image! This is wonderful," he shouted, and off he went to the Computer Tower.

King Header started having his meals served in the Computer Tower, and he even had a small bed brought in so he could sleep there. Two weeks later he emerged, bleary-eyed and weak from lack of exercise. He showed Queen Footer his masterpiece.

Queen Footer cried, "This is spectacular! This is magnificent! But however in the world did you get the header to move to the middle of the page?"

"It took me a long time," he confessed, "but I finally discovered that I could use Advance to accomplish that little trick!"

Well, Queen Footer was jealous and a little angry that King Header had uncovered such secrets. She almost went into a rage, but she soon calmed down and realized that by working together and sharing their knowledge, she and King Header could remain the true "computer Queen and King of ComputerLand."

On occasion, in the wee hours of the night, you can spot a light shining from the window of the Computer Tower, but now you can rest assured that Queen Footer and King Header are sharing the room and creating wondrous headers and footers together.

Lesson 8 ▪ Exercise 54

Lesson 8 ▪ Multiple-Page Documents

EXERCISE 55

▪ MULTIPLE HEADERS/FOOTERS ▪ PAGE NUMBER PLACEMENT AND STYLE

CONCEPTS:

Multiple Headers and Footers

- The header/footer for a two sided document such as a book, newsletter or magazine is usually different on the left and right pages.

EXAMPLE OF LEFT AND RIGHT PAGE HEADER/FOOTER:

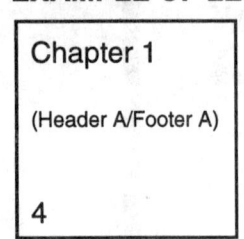

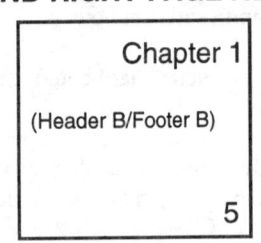

```
Chapter 1                    Chapter 1

(Header A/Footer A)          (Header B/Footer B)



4                                         5
```

- When using multiple headers and footers, the placement must be specified.

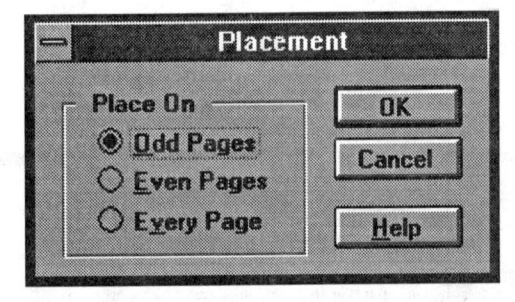

Page Numbering Placement

- As indicated in the previous exercise, page numbers may be included independent of the header/footer text by selecting **P**age, **N**umbering from the **L**ayout main menu.

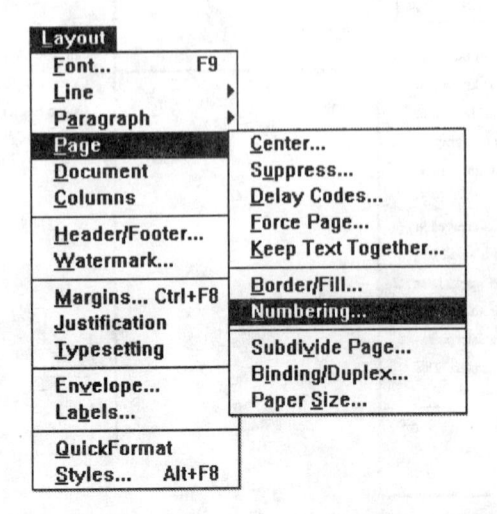

✔

To add multiple headers/footers:

AFTER SELECTING HEADER/FOOTER A OR B

- Click **Placement**
- Click **O**dd, **E**ven or E**v**ery Page

☢

Make sure your Header/Footer A text does not run into your Header/Footer B text.

✔

To add page numbering with styles:

- Click **L**ayout
- Click **P**age
- Click **N**umbering
- Click **O**ptions

246

- WordPerfect provides numerous page numbering position options. Numbers may be inserted at the top or bottom left, center or right. The Page Numbering dialog box (which appears after Page, Numbering is selected) displays the page numbering position you select on the sample facing pages.

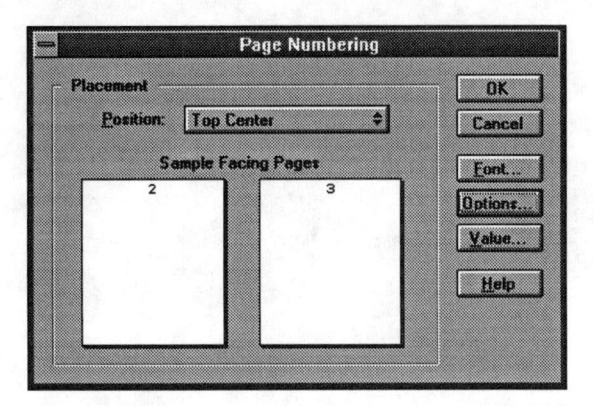

Page Numbering Styles

- WordPerfect provides five different numbering styles. Numbering styles may be selected by clicking Options on the dialog box shown above.

    - Numbers: 1, 2, 3, 4, 5, etc.
    - Lowercase Letter: a, b, c, d, e, f, etc.
    - Uppercase Letter: A, B, C, D, E, F, etc.
    - Lowercase Roman: i, ii, iii, iv, v, etc.
    - Uppercase Roman: I, II, III, IV, V, etc.

- Once selected, the numbering style displays in the Page Numbering Options dialog box on the sample facing pages.

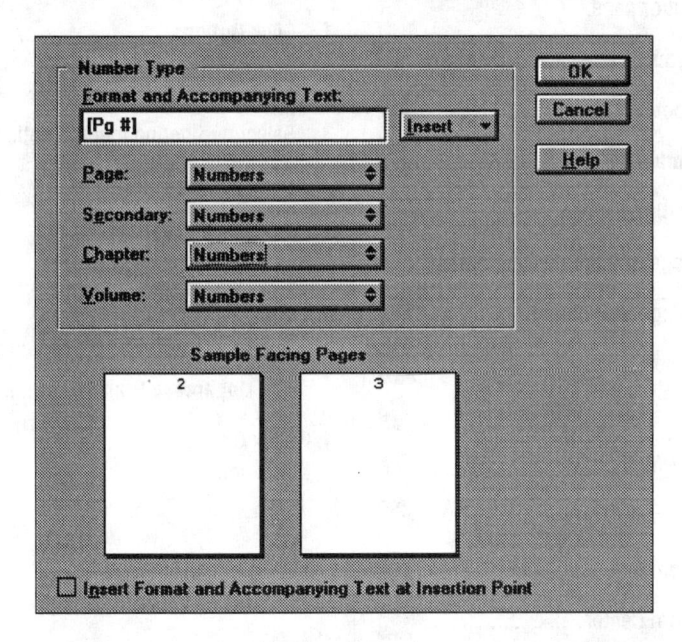

In this exercise you will create a portion of a report using multiple headers and page numbers.

MULTIPLE PAGE HEADERS AND FOOTERS

1. Place insertion point on first page where you want new header/footer to appear.
2. Click **L**ayout .... Alt + L
3. Click **H**eader/Footer .... H
4. Select Header **A** or Header **B** .... A or B

    and/or

    Select **F**ooter A or F**o**oter B .... F or O
5. Click **C**reate C
6. Type .... *header/footer text*
   header/footer text
7. Repeat as necessary.

INSERT PAGE NUMBERS

1. Place insertion point at beginning of document or page.
2. Click **L**ayout .... Alt + L
3. Click **P**age .... P
4. Click **N**umbering .... N
5. Click **P**osition list box .... P
6. Click a page number position option:
   - **N**o Page Numbering .... N
   - Top **L**eft L
   - Top **C**enter C
   - Top **R**ight .... R
   - **A**lternating Top .... A
   - B**o**ttom Left .... O
   - B**o**ttom Center .... O
   - Bot**t**om Right .... T
   - Alt**e**rnating Bottom .... E

To change numbering style:

1. Click **O**ptions .... O
2. Click **P**age list box .... Alt + P
3. Select numbering method option:
   - **N**umbers .... N
   - **L**owercase Letter L
   - **U**ppercase Letter .... U
   - L**o**wercase Roman .... O
   - U**p**percase Roman .... P
4. Click OK .... Enter

   until you return to document.

EXERCISE DIRECTIONS:

1. Start with a clear screen.
2. 💾 Open **SAVE** from data disk; save as **SAVE1**.

   or

   ⌨ Type the exercise as shown.
3. Use 1" left, right, top and bottom margins.
4. Double space the body of the report.
5. Use a serif font.
6. Create a multiple header:
   - Header A is on odd pages. The text, "Save the Species," is 24 point bold and italics, right aligned. Use three special characters (5,115) after the text. Press Enter after the Wingdings and add a thick single line.
   - Header B is on even pages. The text "Save the Species," is 24 point bold and italics, left aligned. Use three special characters (5,115) before the text.
   Press Enter and add a thick single line.
7. Set the space below the header to 0.25".
8. Include alternating page numbers at the bottom of the page and change the font to 24 point bold.
9. Type the paragraph titles in 30 point bold.
10. Add a paragraph border, single line, around the paragraph titles.
11. Type the paragraph text in 14 point.
12. Include the following graphic images in graphic user boxes:
    - **TIGER_J.WPG** under the first paragraph title at the right margin, 3.25" in width, the height sized to content.
    - **CRANE_J.WPG** under the second paragraph title at the right margin, 3.25" in width, the height sized to content.
13. Preview your document.
14. Print one copy.
15. 💾 Close the file; save the changes.

    or

    ⌨ Save the file; name it **SAVE1**.
16. Close the document window.
    - NOTE: *It must be assumed that this report would be printed on both sides of the page and bound.*

The Comeback of an Endangered Species: The Cougar

The large cats can be categorized two ways. There are the *roaring* cats such as lions, tigers, and leopards, and there are the *purring* cats such as the cougar, puma, panther and mountain lion. Many of these large cats face extinction whether it be from the human hunter or loss of land, which is needed to roam and forage.

While the tiger and cheetah population in the wild keeps diminishing, the cougar has come back from extinction in North America.

The cougar, tawny in color, with a black mustache and long tail was so worshiped through the centuries that Indian tribes revered it as a god, and even today many teams are named after this animal. The cougar once roamed the largest territory of any land mammal in the Western Hemisphere. By the 1950s, bounty hunting nearly drove the species to the vanishing point in North America. Restrictions were placed on hunting the cougar and this has succeeded in bringing the population back.

The cougar's comeback is also important because of its ecological role at the top of the food pyramid, and because countless other species will automatically be protected as well.

Because of its solitary and elusive nature (traits which have helped the cougar survive the hunter), it is not known how many cougars there are today but estimates place the numbers at 9,000 to 12,000 just in California, Colorado and Idaho.

Endangered Species of the Season: The California Condor

The California condor, a vulture, is the largest flying land bird in North America and makes its home in Southern California. Black feathers cover most of the bird's body except for the white area on the underside of the condor's wings. The neck and head have no feathers and are a red-orange color. The condor is a unique bird because it does not build a nest, but lays its eggs in caves, holes, or among rocks. It is also a particularly strong flier; it can soar and glide in the air for long distances, flapping its wings an average of only once an hour. It is a carnivore and eats the remains of dead animals.

By the end of the 1980s, only 30 condors remained in the United States. The diminished number of condors is a result of hunting. The growth of urban areas in Southern California also poses a threat to the natural habitat of the bird.

What is Wildlife Conservation?

Wildlife conservation includes all human efforts to preserve wild animals and plants and save them from extinction.

If we continue to ignore the need for wildlife conservation, today's endangered species will soon become extinct. Extinction is particularly dangerous due to the economic, scientific and survival value of wildlife. Wild species of animals and plants provide many substances which are valuable to the economies of different countries, both as food products and as products for trade. The study of wildlife provides important knowledge about life processes which has led to the discovery of medical and scientific products. Additionally, the existence of many species of wildlife maintains the balance of living systems on the earth. The loss of certain species will affect the existence of others that depend on it perhaps for food. Volunteer for Save the Species and help us convince Washington that it is vital to protect the existence of endangered species through legislation! Write to your representatives in Congress and your local government officials to inform them of your support for saving endangered species. We need more success stories like that of the North American cougar!

Save the Species ▲▲▲

The Comeback of an Endangered Species: The Cougar

The large cats can be categorized two ways. There are the *roaring* cats such as lions, tigers and leopards, and there are the *purring* cats such as the cougar, puma, panther and mountain lion. Many of these large cats face extinction whether it be from the human hunter or loss of land, which is needed to roam and forage.

While the tiger and cheetah population in the wild keeps diminishing, the cougar has come back from extinction in North America.

The cougar, tawny in color, with a black mustache and long tail was so worshiped through the centuries that Indian tribes revered it as a god, and even

1

▲▲▲*Save the Species*

today many teams are named after this animal. The cougar once roamed the largest territory of any land mammal in the Western Hemisphere. By the 1950s, bounty hunting nearly drove the species to the vanishing point in North America. Restrictions were placed on hunting the cougar and this has succeeded in bringing the population back.

The cougar's comeback is also important because of its ecological role at the top of the food pyramid, and because countless other species will automatically be protected as well.

Because of its solitary and elusive nature (traits which have helped the cougar survive the hunter), it is not known how many cougars there are today but estimates place the numbers at 9,000 to 12,000 just in California, Colorado and Idaho.

Endangered Species of the Season: The California Condor

The California condor, a vulture, is the largest flying land bird in North America and makes its home in Southern California. Black feathers cover most of

2

Save the Species ▲▲▲

the bird's body except for the white area on the underside of the condor's wings. The neck and head have no feathers and are a red-orange color. The condor is a unique bird because it does not build a nest, but lays its eggs in caves, holes, or among rocks. It is also a particularly strong flier; it can soar and glide in the air for long distances, flapping its wings an average of only once an hour. It is a carnivore and eats the remains of dead animals.

By the end of the 1980s, only 30 condors remained in the United States. The diminished number of condors is a result of hunting. The growth of urban areas in Southern California also poses a threat to the natural habitat of the bird.

What is Wildlife Conservation?

Wildlife conservation includes all human efforts to preserve wild animals and plants and save them from extinction.

If we continue to ignore the need for wildlife conservation, today's

3

▲▲▲*Save the Species*

endangered species will soon become extinct. Extinction is particularly dangerous due to the economic, scientific and survival value of wildlife. Wild species of animals and plants provide many substances which are valuable to the economies of different countries, both as food products and as products for trade. The study of wildlife provides important knowledge about life processes which has led to the discovery of medical and scientific products. Additionally, the existence of many species of wildlife maintains the balance of living systems on the earth. The loss of certain species will affect the existence of others that depend on it perhaps for food. Volunteer for Save the Species and help us convince Washington that it is vital to protect the existence of endangered species through legislation! Write to your representatives in Congress and your local government officials to inform them of your support for saving endangered species. We need more success stories like that of the North American cougar!

4

Lesson 8 ▪ Multiple-Page Documents

EXERCISE 56

▪ WIDOW AND ORPHAN PROTECTION ▪ HYPHENATION

CONCEPTS:

Widow and Orphan Protection

- A **widow** line occurs when the last line of a paragraph is printed by itself at the top of a page. An **orphan** line occurs when the first line of a paragraph appears by itself on the last line of the page. These isolated lines look awkward and should be avoided.

- The Widow/Orphan Protect feature eliminates widows and orphans in a document and may be accessed by selecting **Page** from the Layout main menu.

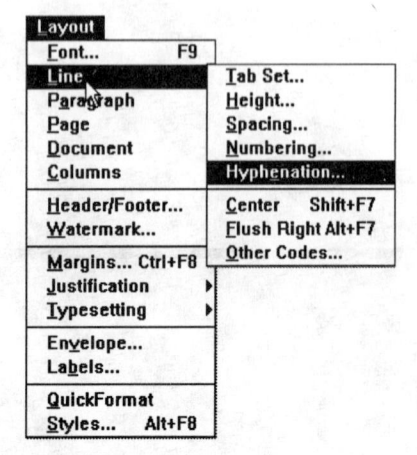

✓ **To add widow/orphan protection:**
- Click **Layout**
- Click **Page**
- Click **Keep Text Together**
- Click **Prevent the first and last lines of paragraphs from being separated across the page.**

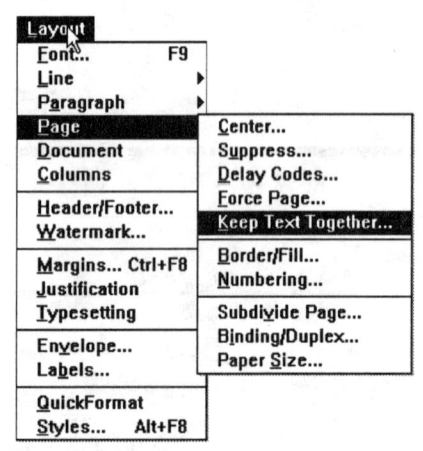

Hyphenation

- **Hyphenation** produces a tighter right margin by dividing words that extend beyond the right margin rather than wrapping them to the next line. If text is full-justified and hyphenated, there will be smaller gaps between words.

- Hyphenation may be accessed by selecting **Line** from the Layout main menu.

✓ **To access hyphenation feature:**
- Click **Layout**
- Click **Line**
- Click **Hyphenation**
- Click **Hyphenation On** check box.

✏️ If Hyphenation was turned on before the hyphenation zone was changed, you may be prompted to re-hyphenate some of the words.

252

- By default, WordPerfect's hyphenation feature is set to Off. In the Off position, WordPerfect will wrap any word that extends beyond the right margin. When hyphenation is On, a word that starts before the left edge of the hyphenation zone and extends beyond the right edge of the zone will be hyphenated. To change the width of the space a word must span before hyphenation divides it, change the hyphenation zone. *Increase* the percentage of the zone to hyphenate *fewer* words; *decrease* to hyphenate *more* words.

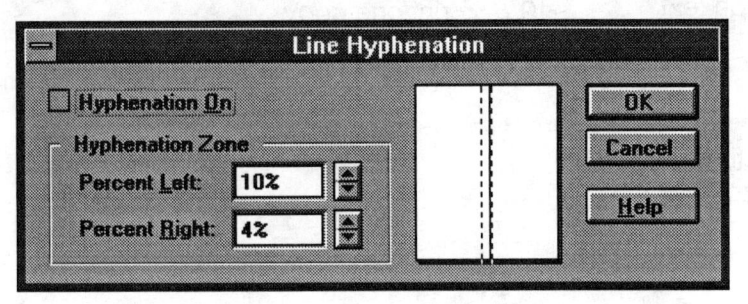

> In this exercise, you will hyphenate and protect against widows and orphans in a previously saved report.

- With hyphenation on, you are prompted to hyphenate words that extend beyond the right margin. In the Position Hyphen dialog box indicate whether or how you want to hyphenate the word.

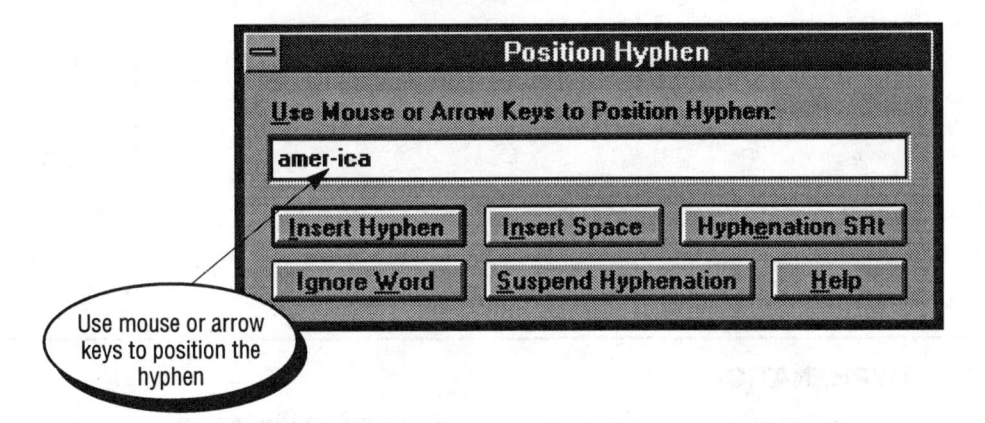

Use mouse or arrow keys to position the hyphen

- To keep words such as sister-in-law or self-control together on a line, even if they span the hyphenation zone, type a **hard hyphen** (Ctrl + -) between the words.

Lesson 8 ▪ Exercise 56

Lesson 8 ■ Exercise 56

EXERCISE DIRECTIONS:

1. Start with a clear screen.
2. Open **SAVE1**.
3. Use widow and orphan protection.
4. Change the font size for the paragraph text to 12 point.
5. Full justify the report.
6. Select Hyphenation On and change the Percentage Left in the hyphenation zone to 8%.
7. Scroll through the text to see if any hyphenation decisions must be made.
8. Change the page numbering position to Bottom Center and the page numbering font size to 14 point.
9. Preview your document.
10. Print one copy.
11. Close the file; save the changes.

SET WIDOW/ORPHAN PROTECTION

1. Place insertion point on page where you want protection to begin.
2. Click Layout .... Alt + L
3. Click Page .... P
4. Click Keep Text Together .... K
5. Click Prevent .... P
   the first and last lines of paragraphs from being separated across pages check box.
6. Click OK .... Enter

HYPHENATION

1. Position insertion point where hyphenation is to begin.
2. Click Layout .... Alt + L
3. Click Line L
4. Click Hyphenation .... E
4. Click Hyphenation On check box .... O
5. Click OK .... Enter

To change hyphenation zone:

a. Click in Percentage Left text box L
b. Type a new left percentage.
c. Click in Percentage Right text box .... R
d. Type a new right percentage.
e. Click OK .... Enter

To position the hyphen:

a. Select desired hyphen position in word (tab leader) → ← .
b. Select desired option:
   - Insert Hyphen I
     to divide word using soft hyphen.
   - Insert Space .... N
     to divide word using a space.
   - Hyphenation Srt .... E
     to divide word using a hyphenation soft return instead of a hyphen.
   - Ignore Word .... W
     to bring the entire word to the next line.
   - Suspend Hyphenation .... S
     to turn off hyphenation temporarily until command is completed.

Save the Species ▲▲▲

The Comeback of an Endangered Species: The Cougar

The large cats can be categorized two ways. There are the *roaring* cats such as lions, tigers and leopards, and there are the *purring* cats such as the cougar, puma, panther and mountain lion. Many of these large cats face extinction whether it be from the human hunter or loss of land, which is needed to roam and forage.

While the tiger and cheetah population in the wild keeps diminishing, the cougar has come back from extinction in North America.

The cougar, tawny in color, with a black mustache and long tail was so worshiped through the centuries that Indian tribes revered it as a god, and even today many teams are named after this animal. The cougar once roamed the largest territory of any land mammal in the Western Hemisphere. By the 1950s, bounty hunting nearly drove the species to the vanishing point in North America. Restrictions were placed on hunting the cougar and this has succeeded in bringing the population back.

1

▲▲▲*Save the Species*

The cougar's comeback is also important because of its ecological role at the top of the food pyramid, and because countless other species will automatically be protected as well.

Because of its solitary and elusive nature (traits which have helped the cougar survive the hunter), it is not known how many cougars there are today but estimates place the numbers at 9,000 to 12,000 just in California, Colorado and Idaho.

Endangered Species of the Season: The California Condor

The California condor, a vulture, is the largest flying land bird in North America and makes its home in Southern California. Black feathers cover most of the bird's body except for the white area on the underside of the condor's wings. The neck and head have no feathers and are a red-orange color. The condor is a unique bird because it does not build a nest, but lays its eggs in caves, holes, or among rocks. It is also a particularly strong flier; it can soar and glide in the air for long distances, flapping its wings an average of only once an hour. It is a carnivore and eats the remains of dead animals.

2

Save the Species ▲▲▲

By the end of the 1980s, only 30 condors remained in the United States. The diminished number of condors is a result of hunting. The growth of urban areas in Southern California also poses a threat to the natural habitat of the bird.

What is Wildlife Conservation?

Wildlife conservation includes all human efforts to preserve wild animals and plants and save them from extinction.

If we continue to ignore the need for wildlife conservation, today's endangered species will soon become extinct. Extinction is particularly dangerous due to the economic, scientific and survival value of wildlife. Wild species of animals and plants provide many substances which are valuable to the economies of different countries, both as food products and as products for trade. The study of wildlife provides important knowledge about life processes which has led to the discovery of medical and scientific products. Additionally, the existence of many species of wildlife maintains the balance of living systems on the earth. The loss of certain species will affect the existence of others that depend on it perhaps for food. Volunteer for Save the Species and help us convince Washington that it is vital to protect the existence of endangered species through legislation! Write to your representatives in Congress and your local government officials to inform them of your support for saving endangered species. We need more success stories like that of the North American cougar!

3

LESSON 8
SUMMARY EXERCISE A

EXERCISE DIRECTIONS:

1. Start with a clear screen.
2. Use the default margins.
3. Create a text box and center MARSH COLLEGE using a 48 point bold serif font.
4. Edit the text box as follows:
   - Set the anchor type as Page.
   - Size the Width to content, and the Height to full.
   - Set the horizontal position to 0" From Left Margin.
   - Set vertical position to 0" from Center of Margins.
5. Edit the text in the text box by changing the color to white.
6. Edit the Border/Fill of the text box to no border, 100% fill.
7. Rotate the content of the box 90° and resize if necessary (Width sized to content; Height to full).
8. Create a graphic custom user box and import the graphic **MARSH.WPG**.
9. Size and position the user box as follows:
   - Size the width to 4" and the height to contents.
   - Set the anchor type as Paragraph.
   - Set the horizontal position to .275" from the right margin.
   - Set the vertical position to 1.5" from top of paragraph.
10. Beginning approximately 9" from the top of the page, center and bold "Fall Registration" on one line and "Information" on the next line using a serif font, 24 point bold.
11. Begin a new page.
12. Open **MARSH** from data disk; save as **MARSH1**.
    or
    Type the exercise text.
13. Single space the body text.
14. Use a 14 point serif font.
15. Use widow and orphan protection.
16. Create the centered header, Fall Registration Information, using 18 point bold. Use three Special Characters (5,110) before and after the text. Press Enter and add a thick double horizontal line.
17. Set the distance between the header and text to 0.25".

> In this exercise, you will create a brochure using a header, footer, widow/orphan protection and hyphenation.

256

18. Create a footer beginning with a thick double horizontal line. Press the Enter key and center Page Number, using 12 point bold. Use three Special Characters (5,110) before and after the page number. Set the distance between the text and footer to 0.167".

19. Create a two-column regular newspaper-style format.

20. Type the paragraph titles in 14 point bold and italic at the left margin and press the Enter key twice after each paragraph title.

21. Double space between each paragraph.

22. Between each section add a graphic custom user box and import the **MARSH.WPG** graphic.

23. Size and position the user box as follows:
    - Size the height to .5" and the width to contents.
    - Set the anchor type as Character, Centered.

24. Center the graphic horizontally.

25. After the last paragraph graphic, center the following in a text box:

> 📖📖
> 10% student discount
> on textbooks
> at the
> Campus Bookstore
> when purchased
> between
> April 16 and April 25
> 📖📖

26. Use a thick border and a 30% fill for the text box.

27. Type the text in 18 point and use the Wingding font and the **&** for the book Wingdings in 24 point.

28. Place insertion point at the beginning of the column text and select hyphenation on. Scroll through the text for hyphenation decisions, if any.

29. Print one copy.

30. ▫ Close the file; save the changes.

    or

    ▫ Save the file; name it **MARSH1**.

31. Close the document window.

    ■ NOTE: It must be assumed that this report would be printed on 17 x 11 paper and folded in half to form a booklet. See illustration on Page 259.

About Marsh College

The main campus of Marsh College is located on Farm College Road in Princeton, New Jersey. Marsh College grants four types of degrees: Associate of Arts, Associate of Science, Bachelor of Arts, and Bachelor of Science.

About Admission to Marsh College

Anyone with a high school diploma is eligible to attend. Degree students are those enrolled in a program of study leading to a degree. As a degree student, you may attend part time or full time during the day, evening, or a combination of both.

Upon receipt of your application, the Admissions Office will schedule you for a basic reading, language arts, and arithmetic skills placement test. If, however, you attended another college and have at least 15 credits, the placement test is waived. Bring proof of college credits (student transcript) with you on the date of your skills placement test appointment. At the time of waiver, or after the test, you will be given the name of a counselor who will evaluate results and/or assist in course selection. After meeting with a counselor, you are eligible to register.

About Tuition, Fees and Payment

The application fee is $25 and is non-refundable. Tuition is $125 per credit. You may choose to pay in full upon registration or defer payment. All payments must be made no later than August 8. Payment is only accepted in the form of cash or check.

About Financial Aid

If you wish to apply for financial aid, you can obtain the necessary forms by calling 609-555-1366 or by coming to the Admissions Building.

About Registration

Open registration for the Fall Term begins April 16. The hours are Monday through Thursday from 9 a.m. to 9 p.m. To register, you must present a registration form endorsed by your counselor. Do not attempt to register for any courses for which you do not have the proper prerequisites.

About Senior Citizens

Senior citizens (65 or older) who enroll at Marsh College on a seat-available basis are eligible for a waiver of tuition. New students may obtain a Waiver of Tuition Form from the Admissions Office. Returning senior citizens will be mailed their waiver to present at their time of registration. While there is no charge for tuition, students are required to pay the appropriate general services fees and lab fees.

Senior citizens who wish to register for courses on a seat-available basis for the Fall Term will be allowed to register in person starting on September 8. For further information, please contact the Admissions Office at 555-3720.

About Dropping, Adding or Changing Courses and Refunds

All changes on your registration schedule must be made in person in the Records and Registration Office by submitting the change on a Drop/Add Form. If you are adding a course, the form must be presented to a counselor in order to receive approval to register for the new course. You may drop/add for Fall Term courses through September 10. A 100% refund will be granted *only* for courses officially dropped before the first day of the term. After the first day of the term, the refunds decrease as follows: 80% refund from September 11 through September 18 and a 60% refund from September 19 through September 26. After these final dates, no refunds will be granted. A 100% refund of tuition will be automatically mailed to you if Marsh College cancels your course and you do not register for another course in its place.

Fall Term Schedule of Courses

The schedule for the Fall Term will be available beginning February 18. You must come to the Registration and Records Office to pick up your schedule. We will not mail a copy to you. Any changes in scheduling will be posted in the lobby of the Conference Hall.

About Using the Fall Term Schedule of Courses

Course Code: The course code identifies the course. It consists of three capital letters followed by three numbers (i.e., ACC101 is Principles of Accounting 1).

Section Code: The section code designates the particular class section of the course and is followed in the schedule by the times and days that particular class section meets. When you register for a section, you may not attend or switch to any other section unless you file a Drop/Add form in the Registration and Records Office. The section code consists of a letter and a number (i.e., T1).

Day Code: The day code designates the day of the week the course meets: M=Monday, T=Tuesday, W=Wednesday, R=Thursday, F=Friday, S=Saturday and N=Sunday.

Room Code: The room code refers to the building in which a class is being held: AHI = Applied Humanities, BUS = Business, CFH = Conference Hall, CRA = Creative Arts Center, GYM = Gymnasium, NAS = Natural and Applied Sciences, PAC = Performing Arts, SOS = Social Sciences and TEC = Technology.

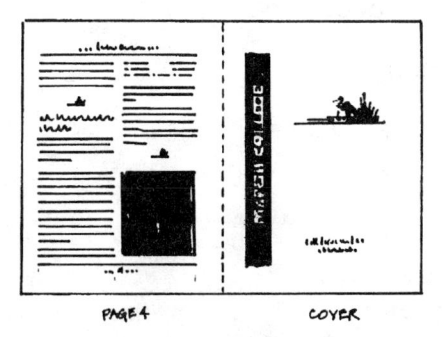

▰▰▰ Fall Registration Information ▰▰▰

through Thursday from 9 a.m. to 9 p.m. To register, you must present a registration form endorsed by your counselor. Do not attempt to register for any courses for which you do not have the proper prerequisites.

About Senior Citizens

Senior citizens (65 or older) who enroll at Marsh College on a seat-available basis are eligible for a waiver of tuition. New students may obtain a Waiver of Tuition Form from the Admissions Office. Returning senior citizens will be mailed their waiver to present at their time of registration. While there is no charge for tuition, students are required to pay the appropriate general services fees and lab fees.

Senior citizens who wish to register for courses on a seat-available basis for the Fall Term will be allowed to register in person starting on September 8. For further information, please contact the Admissions Office at 555-3720 between 9 a.m. and 5 p.m., Monday through Friday.

About Dropping, Adding or Changing Courses and Refunds

All changes on your registration schedule must be made in person in the Records and Registration Office by submitting the change on a Drop/Add Form. If you are adding a course, the form must be presented to a counselor in order to receive approval to register for the new course. You may drop/add for Fall Term courses through September 10. A 100% refund will be granted *only* for courses officially dropped before the first day of the term. After the first day of the term, the refunds decrease as follows: 80% refund from September 11 through September 18 and a 60% refund from September 19 through September 26. After these final dates, no refunds will be granted. A 100% refund of tuition will be automatically mailed to you if Marsh College cancels your course and you do not register for another course in its place.

Fall Term Schedule

The schedule for the Fall Term will be available beginning February 18. You

▰▰▰ 3 ▰▰▰

▰▰▰ Fall Registration Information ▰▰▰

must come to the Registration and Records Office to pick up your schedule. We will not mail a copy to you. Any changes in scheduling will be posted in the lobby of the Conference Hall.

About Using the Fall Term Schedule of Courses

Course Code: The course code identifies the course. It consists of three capital letters followed by three numbers (i.e., ACC101 is Principles of Accounting 1).

Section Code: The section code designates the particular class section of the course and is followed in the schedule by the times and days that particular class section meets. When you register for a section, you may not attend or switch to any other section unless you file a Drop/Add form in the Registration and Records Office. The section code consists of a letter and a number (i.e., T1).

Day Code: The day code designates the day of the week the course meets: M=Monday, T=Tuesday,

W=Wednesday, R=Thursday, F=Friday, S=Saturday and N=Sunday.

Room Code: The room code refers to the building in which a class is being held:
AHI = Applied Humanities, BUS = Business, CFH = Conference Hall, CRA = Creative Arts Center, GYM = Gymnasium, NAS = Natural and Applied Sciences, PAC = Performing Arts, SOS = Social Sciences and TEC = Technology.

10% student discount
on textbooks
at the
Campus Bookstore
when purchased
between
April 16 and April 25

▰▰▰ 4 ▰▰▰

▰▰▰ Fall Registration Information ▰▰▰

About Marsh College

The main campus of Marsh College is located on Farm College Road in Princeton, New Jersey. Marsh College grants four types of degrees: Associate of Arts, Associate of Science, Bachelor of Arts, and Bachelor of Science.

About Admission to Marsh College

Anyone with a high school diploma is eligible to attend. Degree students are those enrolled in a program of study leading to a degree. As a degree student, you may attend part time or full time during the day, evening, or a combination of both.

Upon receipt of your application, the Admissions Office will schedule you for a basic reading, language arts, and arithmetic skills placement test. If, however, you attended another college and have at least 15 credits, the placement test is waived. Bring proof of college credits (student transcript) with you on the date of your skills placement test appointment. At the time of waiver, or after the test, you will be given the name of a counselor who will evaluate results and/or assist in course selection. After meeting with a counselor, you are eligible to register.

About Tuition, Fees and Payment

The application fee is $25 and is non-refundable. Tuition is $125 per credit. You may choose to pay in full upon registration or defer payment. All payments must be made no later than August 8. Payment is only accepted in the form of cash or check.

About Financial Aid

If you wish to apply for financial aid, you can obtain the necessary forms by calling 609-555-1366 or by coming to the Admissions Building.

About Registration

Open registration for the Fall Term begins April 16. The hours are Monday

▰▰▰ 2 ▰▰▰

MARSH COLLEGE

Fall Registration Information

LAYOUT ILLUSTRATION

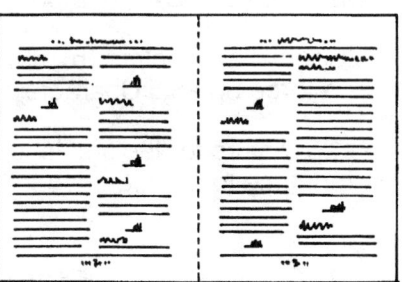

COVER

PAGE 2   PAGE 3

PAGE 4   COVER

Lesson 8 ▪ Exercise A   259

LESSON 8
SUMMARY EXERCISE B

EXERCISE DIRECTIONS:

1. Start with a clear screen.

2. Open **COMPLND1**.

3. Select hyphenation on.

6. Use widow and orphan protection.

7. Change the font face for the title on page 1 to a decorative font (i.e., Blackletter 686BT), 24 point.

8. Edit Header A:

    - Delete the page number.

    - Horizontally center the header text, using a decorative serif font (i.e. Blackletter686BT), 24 point.

    - Use five Special Characters (5,165) before *ComputerLand* and five Special Characters (5,159) after.

    - Change the horizontal line to dotted.

9. Edit Footer A:

    - Change the horizontal line to dotted.

    - Delete the graphic.

    - Insert a centered automatic page number using a decorative serif font (i.e. Blackletter686BT) in 12 point..

    - Use three Special Characters (5,165) before the automatic page number and three Special Characters (5,159) after.

10. Use the drop cap feature for the first letter of each paragraph changing the font face to a decorative font and the font size to 48 point.

11. Set the spacing between paragraphs to 1.25".

12. Preview your document.

13. Print one copy.

14. Close the file; save the changes.

> In this exercise, you will edit a header and footer, add widow/orphan protection and hyphenation to a previously saved report.

Computer Land

Once upon a time, in ComputerLand, there lived a king named Header and a queen named Footer. King Header loved to create extravagant headers and Queen Footer loved to create extraordinary footers.

The king was clever. "Look at what I did," he said to the queen one day. "I put a page number on the right side of my header. After typing *Chapter One* on the left side, I just used flush right and added the automatic page numbering command." And the next day the king came running into the room and showed Queen Footer another project. This time, the header had three lines of text in addition to the page number on the right side. Well, the queen was impressed, but she was not to be outdone.

❧❧❧❧❧ Computer Land ❧❧❧❧❧

Two days went by and, at a minute before midnight on Thursday, the queen came out of the Computer Tower and casually dropped a sheet of paper in front of the king. King Header was flabbergasted. "I didn't know you could use graphics in headers and footers," he said in amazement. "Look at that line! Look at that graphic image! This is wonderful," he shouted, and off he went to the Computer Tower.

King Header started having his meals served in the Computer Tower, and he even had a small bed brought in so he could sleep there. Two weeks

❧❧❧ 2 ❧❧❧

❧❧❧❧❧ Computer Land ❧❧❧❧❧

later he emerged, bleary-eyed and weak from lack of exercise. He showed Queen Footer his masterpiece.

Queen Footer cried, "This is spectacular! This is magnificent! But however in the world did you get the header to move to the middle of the page?"

The king confessed, "It took me a long time, but I finally discovered that I could use Advance to accomplish that little trick!"

Well, Queen Footer was jealous and a little angry that King Header had uncovered such secrets. She almost went into a rage, but she soon calmed down and realized that by working together and

❧❧❧ 3 ❧❧❧

❧❧❧❧❧ Computer Land ❧❧❧❧❧

sharing their knowledge, she and King Header could remain the true "computer Queen and King of ComputerLand."

On occasion, in the wee hours of the night, you can spot a light shining from the window of the Computer Tower, but now you can rest assured that Queen Footer and King Header are sharing the room and creating wondrous headers and footers together.

❧❧❧ 4 ❧❧❧

Lesson 9 ▪ Tables

EXERCISE 57

■ CREATE A TABLE ■ MOVE WITHIN A TABLE ■ ENTER TEXT

CONCEPTS:

- The **Table** feature allows you to organize information into columns and rows without using tabs or tab settings.

- A table consists of **rows**, which run horizontally and are identified by number (1, 2, 3, etc.), and **columns**, which run vertically and are identified by letter (A, B, C, etc.). The rows and columns intersect to form empty boxes, called **cells**.

  Note the example below of a table with three rows and three columns:

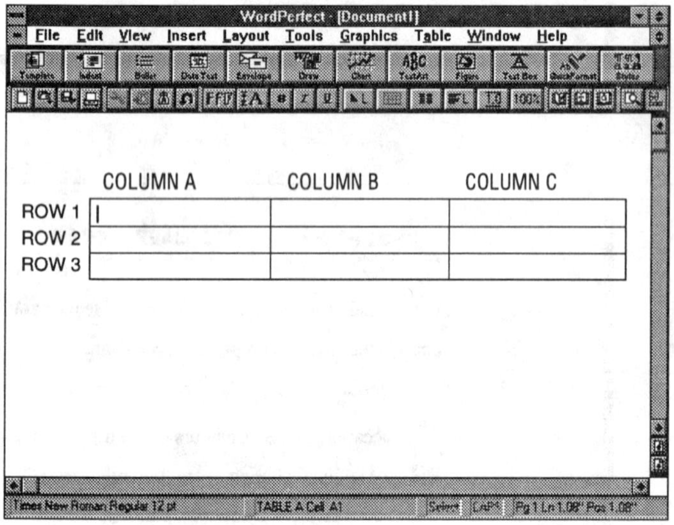

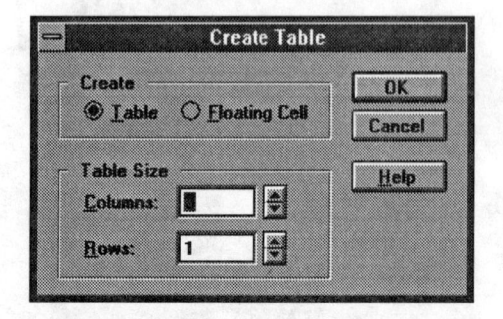

> **To create a table structure:**
> - Click on the 🔲 Power Button.
>
> **OR**
>
> - Click T**a**ble
> - Click **C**reate

- Text, graphics, numbers or formulas are entered into cells after you have defined the structure of your table—that is, how many columns and rows you require for your table.

Create the Table Structure

- Select **Create** from the **T**able main menu. In the Create Table dialog box, indicate the desired number of columns and rows.

- You can also create tables quickly by clicking the Table Quick Create Button on the Power Bar ▦ , and dragging the mouse pointer to select the desired number of rows and columns.

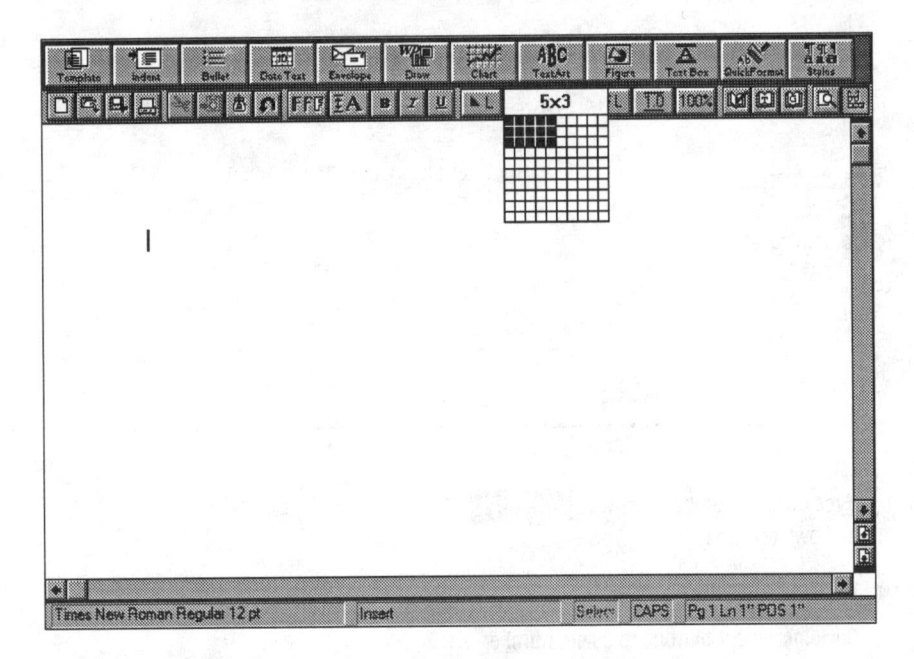

- The columns adjust automatically to fit between the left and right margins.

- You can create a table with up to 64 columns and 32,765 rows.

Move Within a Table

- The insertion point moves in a table the same way it moves in a document. You may use the mouse to click in the desired cell or you may use keystrokes to move around the cells (*see keystrokes on following page*).

- If there is no text in a cell, the directional arrow keys move the insertion point from cell to cell; otherwise, they move the insertion point through text in the cell.

- When the insertion point is in a table cell, the Status Bar indicates the cell location by displaying the cell's column letter and row number.

    EXAMPLE: *Cell* A1

Enter Text in a Table

- As you enter text in a table cell, the cell expands downward to accommodate the text.

- Use the Tab key to advance the insertion point from one cell to the next, even at the end of the row.

> Pressing Enter in a cell extends the cell vertically. It will not advance you to the next cell. The tab key must be used to move from cell to cell.

> In this exercise, you will create a table with 2 columns and 9 rows.

Lesson 9 ■ Exercise 57

Lesson 9 ■ Exercise 57

EXERCISE DIRECTIONS:

1. Start with a clear screen.
2. Use the default margins.
3. Center the page from top to bottom.
4. Center the title; press the Enter key 3 times.
5. Create the table shown on the right using 2 columns and 9 rows.
6. Enter the table text as shown.
7. Preview your document.
8. Print one copy.
9. Save the exercise; name it **REVIEW**.
10. Close the document window.

CREATE A TABLE STRUCTURE:

1. Position insertion point at left margin where you want table to appear.
2. Click Table Button .... 📇 on Power Bar.

   Drag to select desired number of columns and rows.

   Release mouse.

   OR

   Click T**a**ble .... Alt + A

   Click **C**reate C

   Type desired number .... Alt + C
   of columns in **C**olumns text box.

   OR

   Click increment buttons to select number of columns.

   Type desired number of rows .. Alt + R
   in **R**ows text box

   OR

   Click increment buttons to select number of rows.

   Click OK .... Enter

ENTER TEXT IN TABLES:

1. Click cell to receive text.
2. Type text .... *text*
3. Press Tab to advance to next cell .... Tab

   OR

   Use the following insertion point movements:

TO MOVE	PRESS
One cell right	Tab or Alt +
One cell left	Shift + Tab or Alt +
One cell down	Alt +
One cell up	Alt +
First cell in row	Home, Home
Last cell in row	End, End
Top line of multi-line cell	Alt + Home
Bottom line of multi-line cell	Alt + End

SMILEY'S RESTAURANT REVIEW

RESTAURANT	RATING
Big Bad Wolfs	☺☺☺
Cathy's Cafe	☺☺☺☺
Fish Stories	☺☺☺
Mama's Chicken Soupery	☺☺☺
The Crabby Crab	☺☺
The Extra Rib	☺☺
Villa Venison	☺

Lesson 9 ▪ Tables

EXERCISE 58

▪ CREATE A TABLE ▪ ENTER TEXT

CONCEPTS:

- If a cell is not wide enough for the text, extra text will automatically drop to the next line within the cell.

> In this exercise, you will create a table with 5 columns and 18 rows.

EXERCISE DIRECTIONS:

1. Start with a clear screen.
2. Use the default margins.
3. Center the page from top to bottom.
4. Center the titles; press the Enter key 3 times.
5. Create the table, as shown on the right, using 5 columns and 18 rows.
6. Enter the table text as shown.
7. Preview your document.
8. Print one copy.
9. Save the exercise; name it **ATBAT**.
10. Close the document window.

THE WORLD SERIES

WINNERS/LOSERS
1955-1970

YEAR	WINNER	LEAGUE	LOSER	W:L
1955	Brooklyn	National	New York	4:3
1956	New York	American	Brooklyn	4:3
1957	Milwaukee	National	New York	4:3
1958	New York	American	Milwaukee	4:3
1959	Los Angeles	National	Chicago	4:2
1960	Pittsburgh	National	New York	4:3
1961	New York	American	Cincinnati	4:1
1962	New York	American	San Francisco	4:3
1963	Los Angeles	National	New York	4:0
1964	St. Louis	National	New York	4:3
1965	Los Angeles	National	Minnesota	4:3
1966	Baltimore	American	Los Angeles	4:0
1967	St. Louis	National	Boston	4:3
1968	Detroit	American	St. Louis	4:3
1969	New York	National	Baltimore	4:1
1970	Baltimore	American	Cincinnati	4:1

Lesson 9 ▪ Tables

EXERCISE 59

▪ LEFT AND RIGHT TEXT JUSTIFICATION ▪ VERTICAL ALIGNMENT

CONCEPTS:

- WordPerfect allows you to change the justification and vertical alignment of text for a cell, a column or the entire table.
- You may left, center, right, full, all, or decimal align text either during the table creation process or afterward.

JUSTIFICATION EXAMPLES:

Left	Decimal Align: .1
	10.0
	1000.00
Center	Full justify needs more than one line to show its effect.
Right	All justify also needs more than one line to show its effect.

- You may align text at the top, center or bottom of a table cell either during the table creation process or after it.

VERTICAL ALIGNMENT EXAMPLES:

To the right is an example of a cell containing text with top vertical alignment.	**Top vertical alignment.**
To the right is an example of a cell containing text with center vertical alignment.	**Center vertical alignment.**
To the right is an example of a cell containing text with bottom vertical alignment.	**Bottom vertical alignment.**

To align text in tables:
- Click **T**able
- Click **F**ormat
- Click C**e**ll
- Click **V**ertical Alignment and/or **J**ustification
- Click Co**l**umn
- Click **J**ustification

It is easier to align text after it has been entered in the table.

In this exercise, you will center column headings, right-align column C text and vertically center align columns A and C.

268

- To align text in a table, place the insertion point in any cell or select several cells or columns in which you wish to align text. In the Format dialog box:

  - click the Justification list box and select the desired justification option.

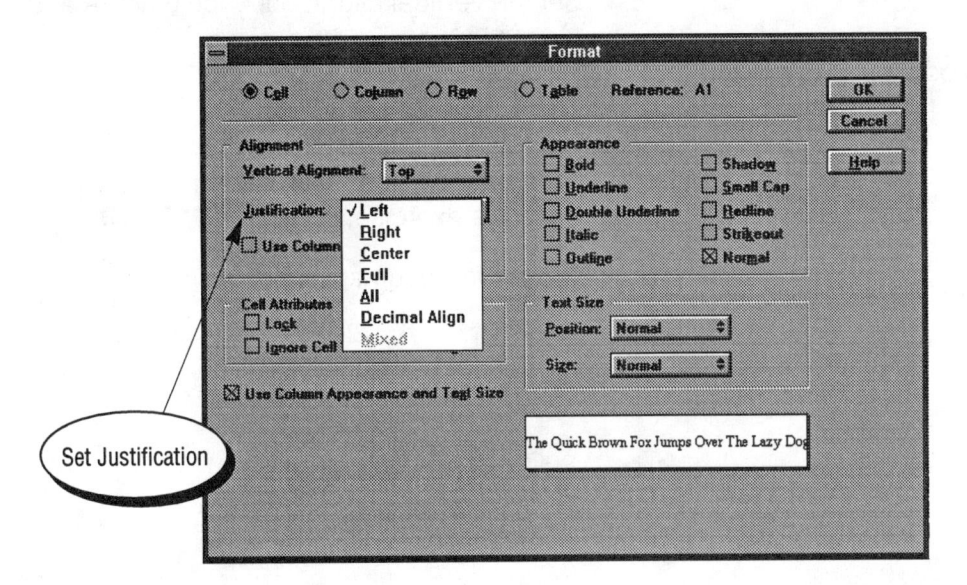

  Set Justification

  - click the Vertical Alignment list box and select the desired vertical alignment option.

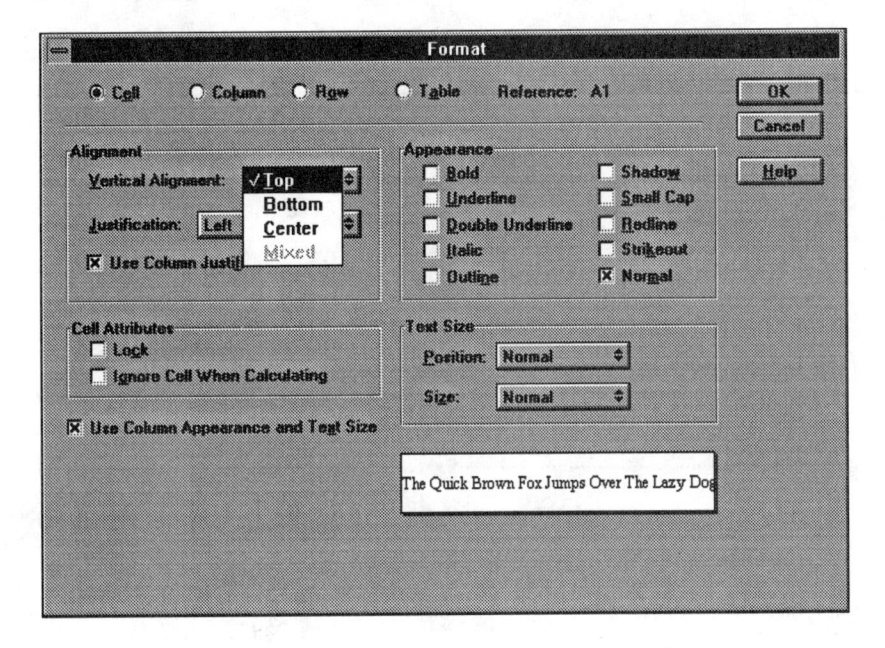

Lesson 9 ■ Exercise 59

Lesson 9 ■ Exercise 59

EXERCISE DIRECTIONS:

1. Start with a clear screen.
2. Use the default margins.
3. Center the page from top to bottom.
4. Center the title; press the Enter key 3 times.
5. Create the table as shown on the right using 3 columns and 10 rows.
6. Center align the column headings.
7. Right align column C text.
8. Set the vertical alignment of columns A and C to center.
9. Preview your document.
10. Print one copy.
11. Save the exercise; name it **NUMBER**.
12. Close the document window.

ALIGN TEXT WITHIN CELLS, COLUMNS OR TABLE

1. Place insertion point in table.

    OR

    Select a cell, several cells or columns to receive alignment change.

2. Click *right* mouse button and select **Format**.

    OR

    Click **Table** .... `Alt` + `A`
3. Click **Format** .... `O`
4. Click desired option:

    C**e**ll .... `E`
    Co**l**umn .... `L`
    T**a**ble .... `T`

5. Click Justification list box .... `Alt` + `J`
6. Click desired justification (alignment) option:

    Left .... `L`
    Right .... `R`
    Center .... `C`
    Full .... `F`
    All .... `A`
    Decimal align .... `D`

7. Click **OK** .... `Enter`

VERTICALLY ALIGN TEXT WITHIN CELLS

1. Place insertion point in table.

    OR

    Select a cell, several cells or columns to receive alignment change.

2. Click *right* mouse button and select **Format**.

    OR

    Click **Table** .... `Alt` + `A`
3. Click **Format** .... `O`
4. Click C**e**ll .... `Alt` + `E`
5. Click **V**ertical .... `Alt` + `V`, `F4`
   Alignment
6. Choose desired alignment options:

    Top .... `T`
    Bottom .... `B`
    Center .... `C`

7. Click **OK** .... `Enter`

270

NEW EMPLOYEES
(January, February, March)

EMPLOYEE NAME	ADDRESS	DEPARTMENT
Braxton, Sally	600 Woodrow Lane Staten Island, NY 718-555-1126	962
Carlson, Kimberly	1267 East 18 Street Brooklyn, NY 718-555-3720	8751
Holmes, Jamal	11 Forest Hills Road Queens, NY 718-555-2821	87602
Johanna, Marly	987 Tremont Avenue Bronx, NY 212-555-2909	8761
Jones, Bobby	1565 Park Avenue New York, NY 212-555-9686	883
Sanchez, Roberto	86 Eighth Avenue New York, NY 212-555-6745	821
Yanny, Istrait	79 Stratford Road Brooklyn, NY 718-555-9876	999
Zapa, Frank	218 Arthur Avenue Bronx, NY 212-555-6120	800
Zaslow, Sam	14 East End Avenue New York, NY 212-555-8050	8013

Lesson 9 ▪ Tables

EXERCISE 60

DECIMAL ALIGNMENT OF TEXT IN TABLES

CONCEPTS:

- Text containing numbers with decimal points may be aligned at the decimal point by choosing Decimal Alignment.

- To decimal align text in a table place the insertion point in a column or highlight several columns. In the Format dialog box select <u>D</u>ecimal Align from the <u>J</u>ustification drop-down list.

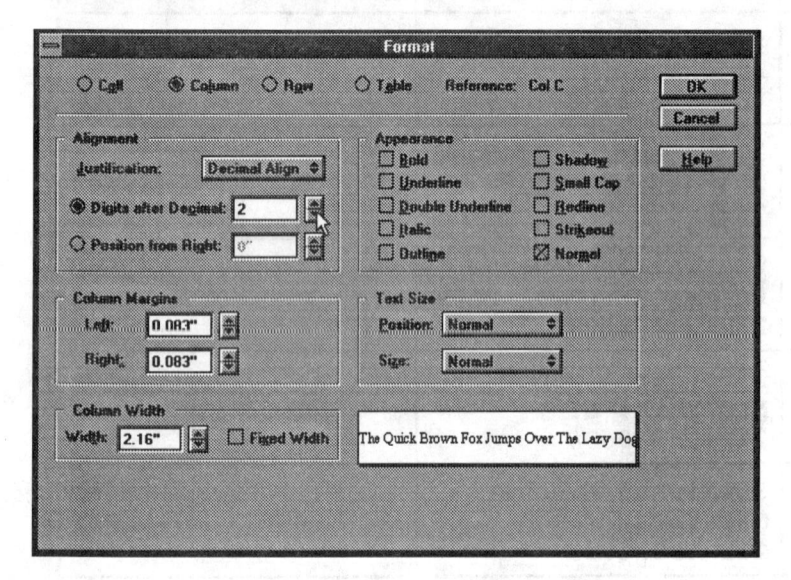

✔ **To decimal align text in a table:**
- Click T<u>a</u>ble
- Click F<u>o</u>rmat
- Click <u>J</u>ustification
- Select <u>D</u>ecimal Align

✔ It is easier to align text after it has been entered in the table.

☞ In this exercise, you will decimal-align text in column B and right-align text in column C after completing the table.

EXERCISE DIRECTIONS:

1. Start with a clear screen.
2. Use the default margins.
3. Center the page from top to bottom.
4. Center the title; press the Enter key 3 times.
5. Create the table shown on the right using 3 columns and 5 rows.
6. Decimal-align column B text and right-align column C text.
7. Print one copy.
8. Save the exercise; name it **RMS**.
9. Close the document window.

```
                RAPID MESSENGER SERVICE
          EMPLOYEE HOURLY WAGES AND TOTAL EARNINGS
                         FOR 1994
```

Charles Palenlogis	$10.50	$115
Gina Abrams	7.85	76
Robin M. Rahmin	9.25	26
George Torres	8.55	122
Hudson Giles	7.75	9

DECIMAL ALIGN

1. Place insertion point in a column or table (before entering text).

   OR

   Select/highlight columns to receive decimal alignment (after entering text).

2. Click *right* mouse button and select **Format**.

   OR

   Click T**a**ble .... Alt + A

3. Click F**o**rmat .... O

4. Click desired option:

   Co**l**umn L

   T**a**ble .... A

5. Click **J**ustification list box .... Alt + J

6. Click **Decimal Align** ....

7. Click **Digits after De**c**imal** C

   OR

   Click **Position from Ri**g**ht** .... G

8. Specify the number of digits .... *number*

   OR

   Specify the Position from Right .... *number*

9. Click **OK** .... Enter

Lesson 9 ▪ Tables

EXERCISE 61
CENTER ALIGNMENT OF TEXT IN TABLES

CONCEPTS:

▪ Since the columns in this exercise contain a small amount of text, it would be visually more attractive to center the text in those columns.

In this exercise, you will create a table with center-aligned columns.

EXERCISE DIRECTIONS:

1. Start with a clear screen.
2. Use the default margins.
3. Center the page from top to bottom.
4. Center the title; press the Enter key 3 times.
5. Create the table as shown on the right. Determine the columns and rows needed.
6. Center-align the columns.
7. Preview your document.
8. Save the exercise; name it **WINGDING**.
9. Print one copy.
10. Close your file; save the changes.

MY FAVORITE WINGDINGS

Character on Keyboard	Wingding Symbol
"	✂
R	☼
J	☺
=	💾
!	✎
+	✉
Q	✈
(	☎

Lesson 9 ▪ Tables

EXERCISE 62

▪ INSERT AND DELETE COLUMNS AND ROWS ▪ DELETE TABLE

CONCEPTS:

- One or more rows and/or columns may be inserted or deleted before or after the insertion point position.

- In the Insert Columns/Rows dialog box, you must indicate if you wish to insert a column or a row, and if you wish to insert the column or row before or after the insertion point position.

(Insert Columns/Rows dialog box shown with Table Size: Columns: 6, Rows: 3; Insert options for Columns/Rows; Placement options Before/After. Callouts: "Insert column or row" and "Insert before or after insertion point".)

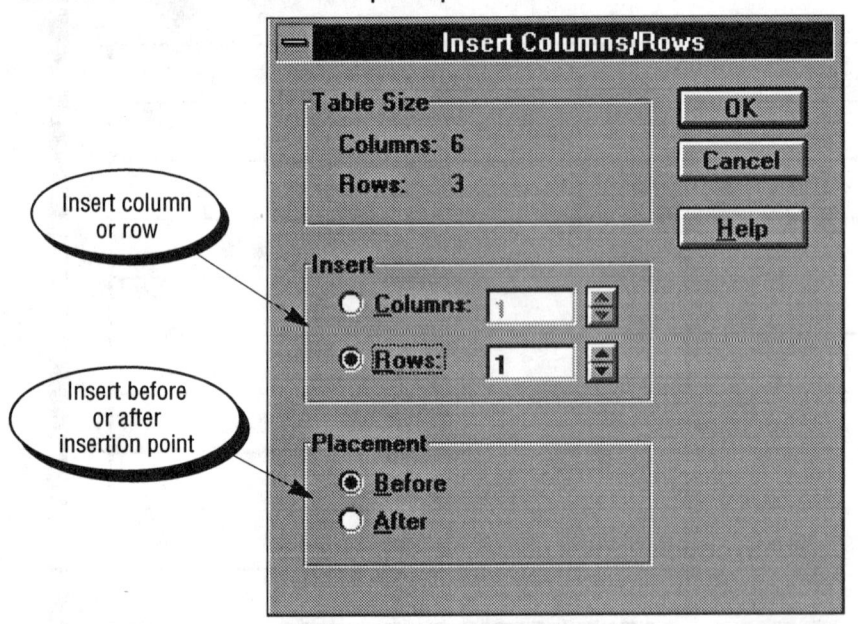

- In the Delete dialog box, you must indicate whether you wish to delete a column or row and the number of columns or rows to delete (if you did not select them first).

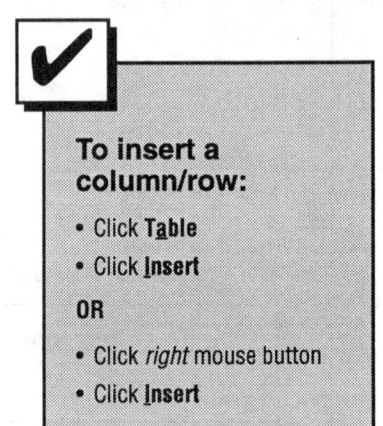

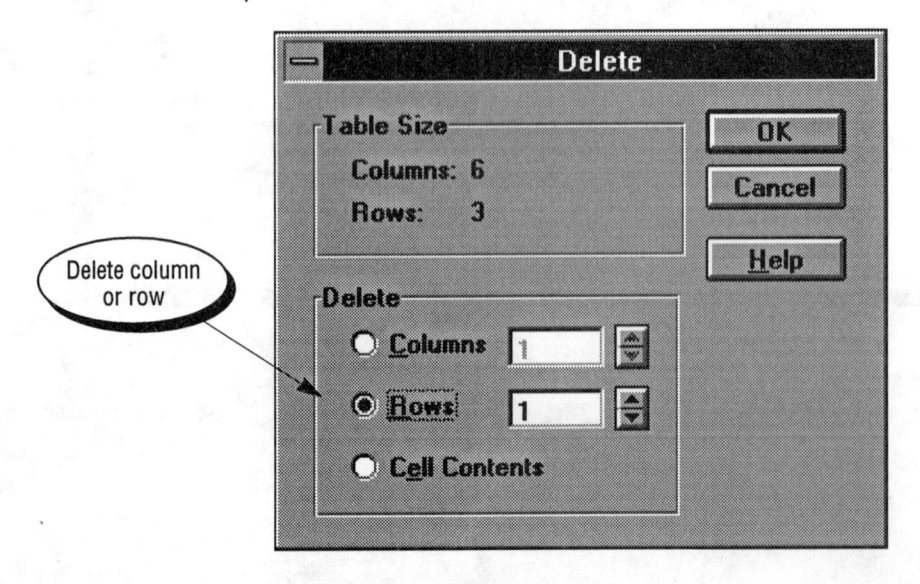

(Delete dialog box shown with Table Size: Columns: 6, Rows: 3; Delete options for Columns, Rows, Cell Contents. Callout: "Delete column or row".)

✓ **To insert a column/row:**
- Click **T**able
- Click **I**nsert

OR

- Click *right* mouse button
- Click **I**nsert

✎ To insert a new row at the end of a table, press the Tab key in the last cell.

✓ **To delete a column/row:**
- Click **T**able
- Click **D**elete

OR

- Click *right* mouse button
- Click **D**elete

276

- The entire table may be deleted

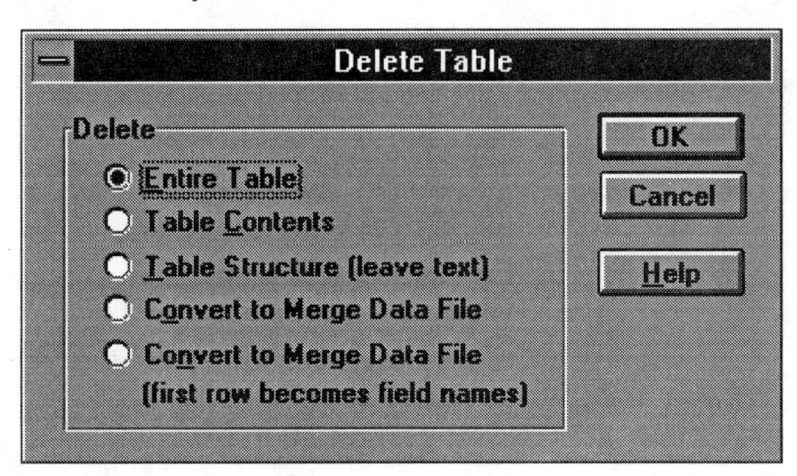

Delete Table

Delete:
- ◉ Entire Table
- ○ Table Contents
- ○ Table Structure (leave text)
- ○ Convert to Merge Data File
- ○ Convert to Merge Data File (first row becomes field names)

[OK] [Cancel] [Help]

To delete the entire table:
- Select the entire table.
- Click **Table**
- Click **Delete**

When a column or row is deleted, the contents of that column or row are also deleted.

In this exercise, you will insert one column and insert and delete one row in a previously created table.

Lesson 9 ■ Exercise 62   277

Lesson 9 ▪ Exercise 62

EXERCISE DIRECTIONS:

1. Open **REVIEW**.
2. Delete the first row (Big Bad ...).
3. Insert one row as shown.
4. Insert one column as shown by placing cursor in last column.
5. Enter the new column/row text.
6. Print one copy.
7. Close your file; save the changes.

INSERT ROWS/COLUMNS

1. Place insertion point inside table, before or after where desired insertion is to occur.
2. Click **T**able .... `Alt` + `A`
3. Click **I**nsert .... `I`

   OR

   Click *right* mouse button and select **I**nsert.
4. Click button of item to insert:

   Columns .... `Alt` + `C`

   Rows .... `Alt` + `R`
5. Type number of columns or rows to be inserted.

   OR

   Click increment arrows to desired number.
6. Click Placement radio button (before or after insertion point location)

   Before .... `Alt` + `B`

   After .... `Alt` + `A`
7. Click OK .... `Enter`

DELETE ROWS/COLUMNS

1. Place insertion point in column or row to delete.

   OR

   Select/highlight columns or rows to delete.
2. Click **T**able .... `Alt` + `A`
3. Click **D**elete .... `D`

   OR

   Click *right* mouse and select Delete.
4. Click button of item to be deleted

   Columns .... `Alt` + `C`

   Rows .... `Alt` + `R`
5. Type number of columns or rows to delete.
6. Click OK .... `Enter`

DELETE TABLE OR CELL CONTENTS

1. Select entire table.
2. Click **T**able .... `Alt` + `A`
3. Click **D**elete .... `D`
4. Click a delete option:

   Entire Table .... `Alt` + `E`

   Table **C**ontents .... `Alt` + `C`

   Table Structure (leave text) ..... `Alt` + `T`
5. Click OK .... `Enter`

SMILEY'S RESTAURANT REVIEW

RESTAURANT	TYPE	RATING
~~Big Bad Wolfs~~ (delete row)	~~Diner~~	☺☺☺
Cathy's Cafe	Continental	☺☺
Cynthia's Seafood Shanty (insert row)	Seafood	☺☺☺
Fish Stories	Seafood	☺☺☺
Mama's Chicken Soupery	Bistro	☺☺☺
The Crabby Crab	Seafood	☺☺
The Extra Rib	Steak House	☺☺
Villa Venison	Steak House	☺

insert column

Lesson 9 ▪ Tables

EXERCISE 63
CHANGE COLUMN WIDTHS

CONCEPTS:

- Column widths may be changed by dragging the vertical lines between columns to the desired width. The table margins can be changed by dragging the outside borders of the table to the desired position. When the insertion point is on the margins or the vertical lines between the margins, the insertion point changes to a double sided arrow:

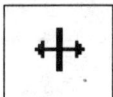

- Dragging lines between columns allows you to see the immediate effect of the change on the table as it is being made.

- You may also adjust column widths and margins by dragging the column margin markers or the table sizing markers on the ruler line.

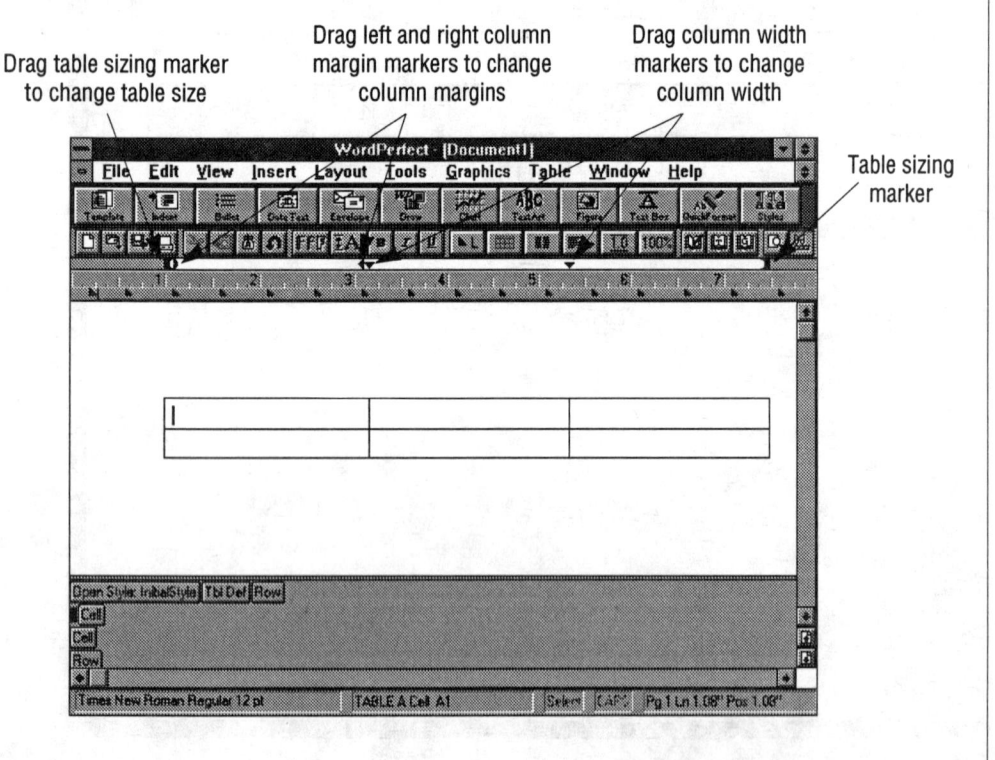

Drag table sizing marker to change table size

Drag left and right column margin markers to change column margins

Drag column width markers to change column width

Table sizing marker

✔ To adjust column width:

- Click *right* mouse button.

OR

- Click T**a**ble
- Click F**o**rmat
- Click Co**l**umn
- Click Wid**t**h

OR

- Drag lines between columns.

✔ To display the Ruler Bar:

- Click **V**iew
- Click **R**uler Bar

- You may also adjust column widths and margins using a specific measurement in the Format dialog box.

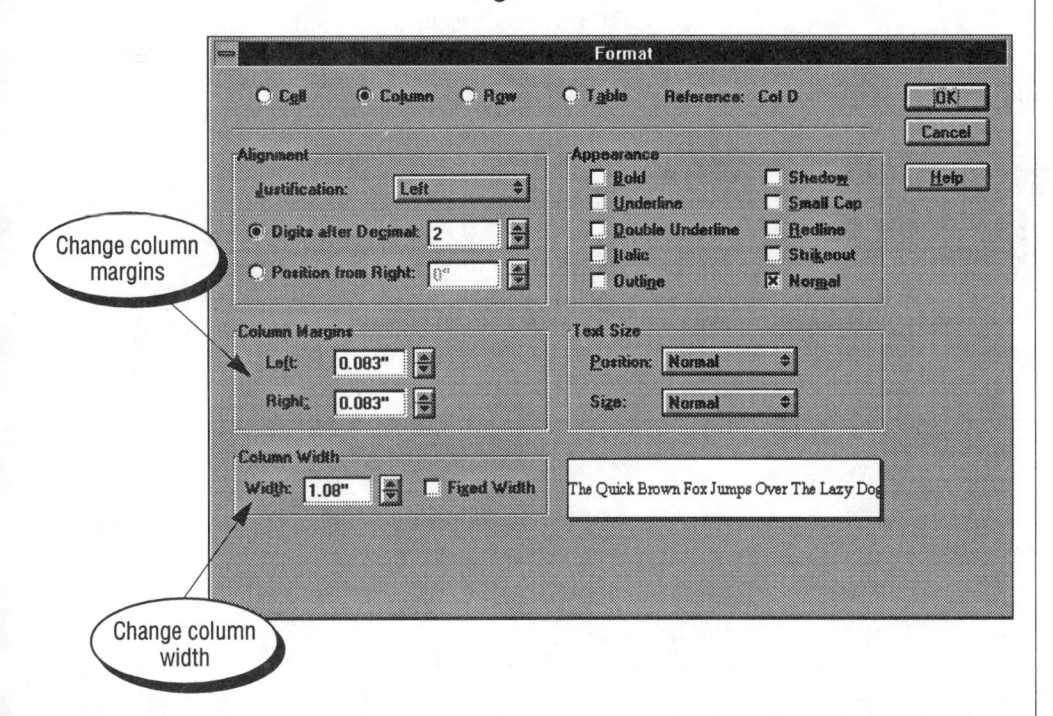

Change column margins → (Column Margins area)

Change column width → (Column Width area)

[Format dialog box showing options: Cell, Column, Row, Table; Reference: Col D; Alignment with Justification: Left, Digits after Decimal: 2, Position from Right: 0"; Column Margins Left: 0.083", Right: 0.083"; Column Width: 1.08", Fixed Width checkbox; Appearance checkboxes: Bold, Underline, Double Underline, Italic, Outline, Shadow, Small Cap, Redline, Strikeout, Normal (checked); Text Size: Position: Normal, Size: Normal; Sample text: "The Quick Brown Fox Jumps Over The Lazy Dog"; Buttons: OK, Cancel, Help]

- For ease of reading, leave at least .5" after longest column entry and the next column. You can leave more space, however, if you desire.

> Note Illustration A on Page 283. Once the new column is inserted (for the date), column A becomes shorter and truncates the names. You can, however, adjust column widths so that column A has more space and columns C and D have less space.

> In this exercise, you will insert two rows and one column, and delete one row. You will then adjust the column widths to make the table more visually attractive.

Lesson 9 ■ Exercise 63

EXERCISE DIRECTIONS:

1. Open **RMS**.
2. Insert two rows and one column as shown in Illustration A.
3. Enter the new column/row text.
4. Delete the second row (Gina Abram's information).
5. Adjust column widths in all columns as shown; leave approximately .5" between column text.
6. Preview the exercise.
7. Print one copy.
8. Close the file; save the changes.

CHANGE COLUMN WIDTH/MARGINS

—USING MOUSE (TO SEE IMMEDIATE CHANGE)—

1. Place mouse pointer on a vertical line separating the column until it changes to a table sizing arrow ↔.
2. Drag sizing arrow left or right to desired width.

OR

1. Place insertion point in the table.
2. Display Ruler Bar ..... [Alt]+[Shift]+[F3]
3. Drag markers and guides to change the table:

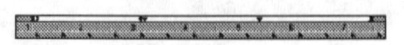

—USING DIALOG BOX FOR SPECIFIC SETTINGS—

1. Place insertion point in column to format.

OR

Select several columns to format.

2. Click T**a**ble .... [Alt]+[A]
3. Click F**o**rmat .... [O]
4. Click button of item to be formatted:
   - Co**l**umn .... [Alt]+[L]
   - T**a**ble .... [Alt]+[A]

To set column margins:

a. Click in Column .... [Alt]+[F]
   Margins Le**f**t text box.
b. Type a left column ....*number*
   margin amount.

c. Click in Column .... [Alt]+[T]
   Margins Righ**t** text box.
d. Type a right column.................*number*
   margin amount.

To set column widths:

a. Click in Wid**t**h text box .... [Alt]+[T]
b. Type a column width amount ...*number*

To keep width of current column same regardless of changes to other columns:

Click Fi**x**ed Width .... [Alt]+[X]

5. Click OK .... [Enter]

ILLUSTRATION A

RAPID MESSENGER SERVICE
EMPLOYEE HOURLY WAGES AND TOTAL EARNINGS
FOR 1994

Charles Palenlogis	June 17, 1989	$10.50		$115
Gina Abrams *(delete row)*	March 4, 1990	7.85		76
Robin M. Rahmin	April 6, 1993	9.25		26
George Torres	September 6, 1989	8.55		122
Hudson Giles	November 4, 1993	7.75		9
Julie Marciano *(insert rows)*	February 1, 1994	9.15		5
Calvin Verioski	April 9, 1994	8.75		1

ILLUSTRATION B

RAPID MESSENGER SERVICE
EMPLOYEE HOURLY WAGES AND TOTAL EARNINGS
FOR 1994

Charles Palenlogis	June 17, 1989	$10.50	$115
Robin M. Rahmin	April 6, 1993	9.25	26
George Torres	September 6, 1989	8.55	122
Hudson Giles	November 4, 1993	7.75	9
Julie Marciano	February 1, 1994	9.15	5
Calvin Verioski	April 9, 1994	8.75	1

Lesson 9 ▪ Tables

EXERCISE 64

▪ CHANGE COLUMN WIDTH ▪ JOIN CELLS ▪ HORIZONTAL POSITION OF A TABLE

CONCEPTS:

Join Cells

■ **Joining cells** lets you remove the dividing lines between cells to create a single, larger cell, which may be used for a heading.

ORIGINAL TABLE:

TABLE WITH JOINED CELLS:

4 cells are joined here		
2 cells are joined here		4 cells are joined here

■ **Splitting cells** lets you divide cells.

ORIGINAL TABLE:

TABLE WITH SPLIT CELLS:

| The cell below is split into 4 columns. | The 2 cells below are split into 3 columns. | The cell on the right is split into 2 rows. | |

To join cells:
- Select cells to join.
- Click **T**able
- Click **J**oin
- Click **C**ell

To Split cells:
- Select cells to join.
- Click **T**able
- Click **S**plit
- Click **C**ell

To reposition the table:
- Click **T**able
- Click **F**ormat
- Click **T**able
- Select position.

284

Horizontal Position of a Table

- Column widths are automatically spread out evenly between the margins whether your table contains two or ten columns. When you change column width in the Table Format dialog box, the left margin remains the same. This means the table is no longer centered across the page and must be repositioned.

- You may position the table to the left or right of the page, centered, or a specific amount from the left edge of the page.

> In this exercise you will adjust the column widths of a previously created table, insert a new row, move the title to a new row, and reposition the table horizontally.

LEFT:

RIGHT:

CENTERED:

FULL:

SET POSITION .5" FROM LEFT EDGE OF PAPER:

Lesson 9 ■ Exercise 64   285

Lesson 9 ▪ Exercise 64

- To change the horizontal position you must select T**a**ble in the Table Format dialog box.

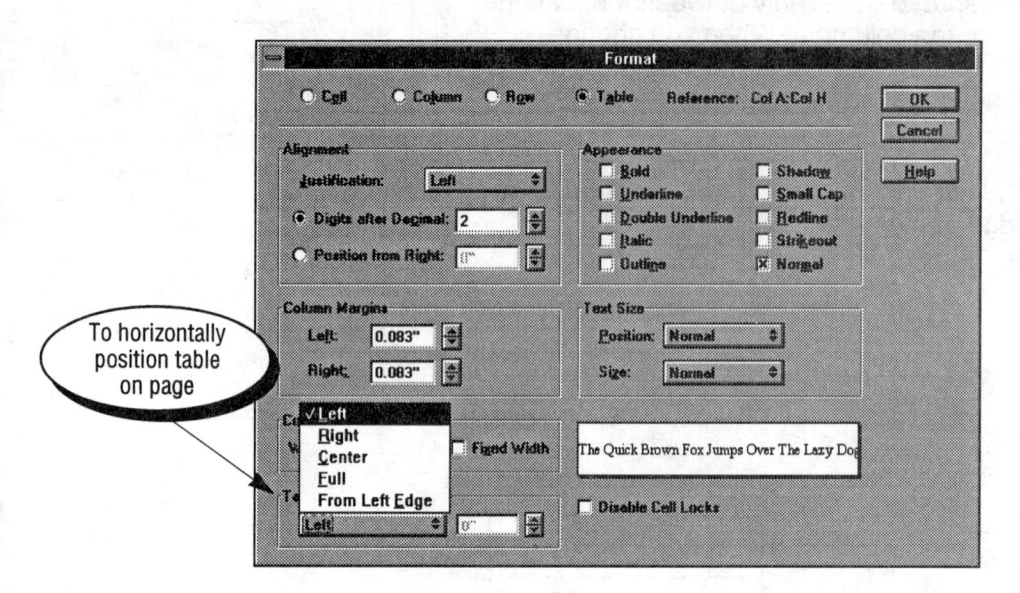

To horizontally position table on page

EXERCISE DIRECTIONS:

1. Start with a clear screen.
2. Open **ATBAT**.
3. Center-align columns A, C and E.
4. Adjust column widths in all columns; leave approximately .5" between columns.
5. Insert one row above the current first row and join the cells.
6. Move the title into the new row.
7. Reposition the table so it is centered horizontally.
8. Preview the exercise.
9. Print one copy.
10. Close the file; save the changes.

JOIN CELLS

1. Select cells to be joined.
2. Click **Table** .... `Alt` + `A`
3. Click **Join** .... `J`
4. Click **Cell** .... `C`

HORIZONTALLY POSITION TABLE ON PAGE

1. Place insertion point in table.
2. Click **Table** .... `Alt` + `A`
3. Click **Format** .... `O`
4. Click **Table** button .... `Alt` + `A`
5. Click **Table Position** list box and select desired position:
   - **L**eft .... `L`
   - **R**ight .... `R`
   - **C**enter .... `C`
   - **F**ull .... `F`
   - From Left **E**dge .... `E`

   Type amount from left edge.
6. Click **OK** .... `Enter`

THE WORLD SERIES

WINNERS/LOSERS
1955-1970

YEAR	WINNER	LEAGUE	LOSER	W:L
1955	Brooklyn	National	New York	4:3
1956	New York	American	Brooklyn	4:3
1957	Milwaukee	National	New York	4:3
1958	New York	American	Milwaukee	4:3
1959	Los Angeles	National	Chicago	4:2
1960	Pittsburgh	National	New York	4:3
1961	New York	American	Cincinnati	4:1
1962	New York	American	San Francisco	4:3
1963	Los Angeles	National	New York	4:0
1964	St. Louis	National	New York	4:3
1965	Los Angeles	National	Minnesota	4:3
1966	Baltimore	American	Los Angeles	4:0
1967	St. Louis	National	Boston	4:3
1968	Detroit	American	St. Louis	4:3
1969	New York	National	Baltimore	4:1
1970	Baltimore	American	Cincinnati	4:1

RESULT

Lesson 9 ▪ Tables

EXERCISE 65

■ LINES (INSIDE, OUTSIDE, INDIVIDUAL) ■ BORDERS ■ FILLS (SHADING/PATTERN)

CONCEPTS:

Table Lines and Borders

- A **table border** is a line (or lines) that surrounds a table. A **table line** divides the columns and rows to form the cells. By default, tables print with a single line around the outer edge (table border) and with single lines that divide columns and rows (table lines). Note the example below:

- WordPerfect lets you change the table border and table line style, and provides you with numerous line types:

THICK BORDER AND DASHED TABLE LINES

- To change table lines and borders, place insertion point in the table, and select **Lines/Fill** from the T_able main menu, or click the *right* mouse button and select **Lines/Fill**. Then, in the Table Lines/Fill dialog box, click the Table button.

- To select a table line style, click the T_able and _Line Style buttons in the Table Line/Fill dialog box and choose a style from the drop-down palette or list.

- To select a border line style, click the T_able and _Border buttons in the Table Line/Fill dialog box and choose a style from the drop-down palette or list

> ✓ **To change table lines, borders and fills:**
> • Click T**a**ble
> • Click **L**ines/Fill

288

- For each line and border type you select, you will see a sample in the preview window.

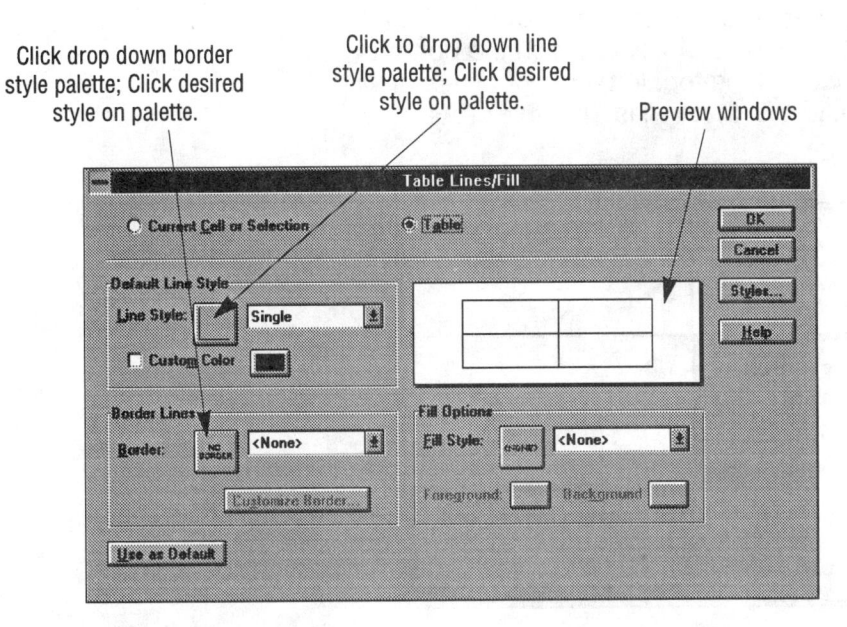

Click drop down border style palette; Click desired style on palette.

Click to drop down line style palette; Click desired style on palette.

Preview windows

Inside and Outside Lines

- You may also change the line type of inside and outside lines. Lines that surround the selection are **outside lines**; lines within the selection are **inside lines**.

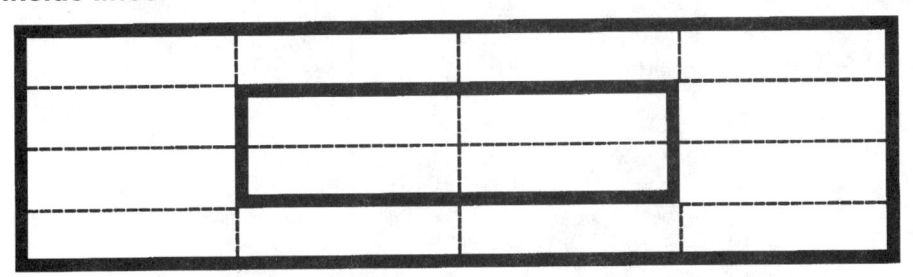

- Inside and outside line styles may be changed by selecting the cells to affect, then selecting **Lines/Fill** from the T**a**ble main menu. In the Table Lines/Fill dialog box, select the Outside and/or Inside button and choose a line style from the drop-down palette or list.

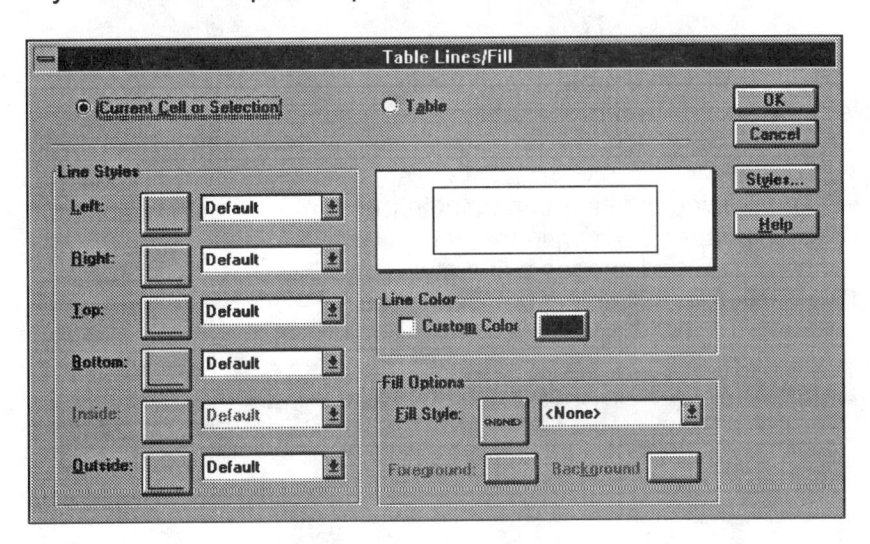

Lesson 9 ■ Exercise 65   289

Lesson 9 ■ Exercise 65

Individual Lines

■ Changing the line type of individual lines is an effective way of emphasizing data within a cell. Note the table below in which the bottom and right lines of the cell A1 are Thick and the top, left and right lines of cell B2 are Double, while the bottom line of that cell is Thin/thick. All lines around cell C3 are Thick.

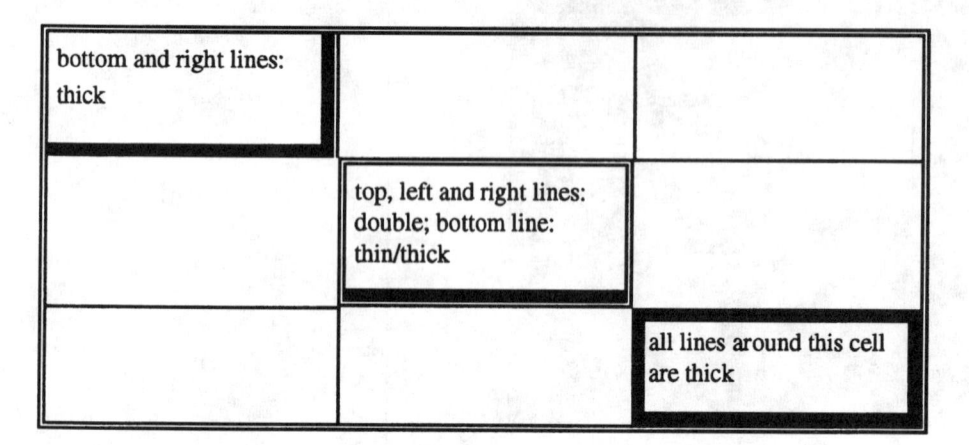

bottom and right lines: thick		
	top, left and right lines: double; bottom line: thin/thick	
		all lines around this cell are thick

■ There are many variations you can experiment with to emphasize data or make your table visually appealing.

■ Or, you may choose to eliminate all the lines, making the table look like a tabular column:

```
NAME OF STOCK        PURCHASE PRICE      NO. SHARES

R & L                     $ 60.00             100

TECH LABS                   45.35              80

ASTEC IND.                  14.85             250

X-MATION                     2.50             800

IDM                         50.00               8

NORDAK INDUSTRIES          101.44           1,000
```

■ When you remove all lines, the table appears to be double spaced; it is not. While table lines are not visible, they are still part of the table structure.

■ Individual lines styles may be changed by placing the insertion point in the individual cell, or selecting a group of cells to affect. Then, in the Table Line/Fill dialog box, click the specific line button and choose a line style from the drop-down palette or list (See Table Line/Fill dialog box illustrated on previous page.).

■ While color shading options are available for lines and borders, you need a color printer to output color.

Fills (Shading/Patterns)

- The **Fill** feature lets you emphasize a cell, row, column, or group of cells by adding a pattern or shade. The shading options are indicated as percents of black. Note the samples below:

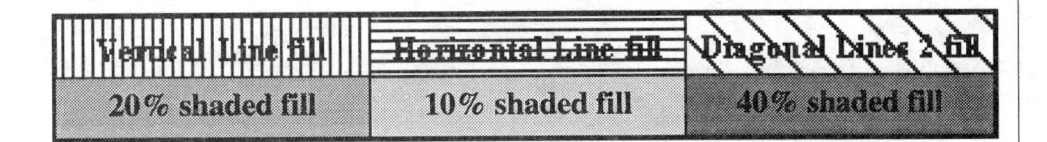

Vertical Line fill	Horizontal Line fill	Diagonal Lines 2 fill
20% shaded fill	10% shaded fill	40% shaded fill

- Fills may be changed in the Table Lines/Fill dialog box by clicking the Fill Style Button and choosing a fill option from the drop-down palette or list.

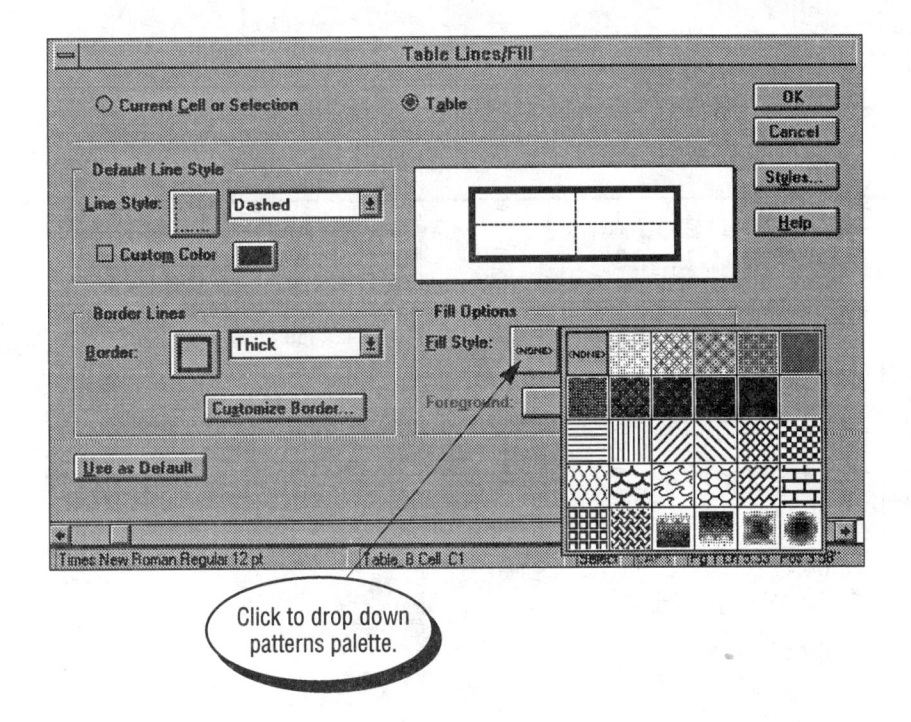

Click to drop down patterns palette.

> In this exercise, you will change lines and borders and add fill to a previously created table.

Lesson 9 ■ Exercise 65

Lesson 9 ■ Exercise 65

EXERCISE DIRECTIONS:

1. Start with a clear screen.
2. Open **ATBAT**.
3. Edit the table as follows:
   - Use Button Bottom /Right line outside line style for column heading row.
   - Use Diagonal Lines 1 pattern as shown.
   - Use a 10% Fill to shade the "National League" rows as shown.
   - Use a Thick Single Line on the bottom and right of cells indicated.
   - Change the table border to a Double line.
4. Preview the exercise.
5. Print one copy.
6. Close your file; save the changes.

TABLE LINES AND BORDERS

1. Place insertion point in table.
2. Click **T**able .... `Alt`+`A`
3. Click **L**ines/Fill .... `L`
4. Click **T**able button .... `Alt`+`A`
5. Click **L**ine style button .... `Alt`+`L`
6. Click desired line style from drop-down palette or list.
7. Click Border style button .... `Alt`+`B`
8. Click desired border style from drop-down palette or list.
9. Click **OK** .... `Enter`

INSIDE/OUTSIDE AND INDIVIDUAL LINES

1. Select/highlight cells to affect.
   OR
   Place insertion point in cell to affect.
2. Click **T**able .... `Alt`+`A`
3. Click **L**ines/Fill .... `L`
4. Click .... `Alt`+`C`
   Current **C**ell or Selection.
5. Click line to affect
   - **L**eft .... `L`
   - **R**ight .... `R`
   - **T**op .... `T`
   - **B**ottom .... `B`
   - **I**nside .... `I`
   - **O**utside .... `O`

   NOTE: When changing all sides of a single cell, the Inside option will have no effect.

6. Click desired line style from drop-down palette or list.
7. Click **OK** .... `Enter`

FILLS AND PATTERNS

1. Follow previous steps 1-4.
2. Click **F**ill Style .... `F`
3. Click desired fill style from drop-down palette.
4. Click **OK** .... `Enter`

THE WORLD SERIES

WINNERS/LOSERS
1955-1970

YEAR	WINNER	LEAGUE	LOSER	W:L
1955	Brooklyn	National	New York	4:3
1956	New York	American	Brooklyn	4:3
1957	Milwaukee	National	New York	4:3
1958	New York	American	Milwaukee	4:3
1959	Los Angeles	National	Chicago	4:2
1960	Pittsburgh	National	New York	4:3
1961	New York	American	Cincinnati	4:1
1962	New York	American	San Francisco	4:3
1963	Los Angeles	National	New York	4:0
1964	St. Louis	National	New York	4:3
1965	Los Angeles	National	Minnesota	4:3
1966	Baltimore	American	Los Angeles	4:0
1967	St. Louis	National	Boston	4:3
1968	Detroit	American	St. Louis	4:3
1969	New York	National	Baltimore	4:1
1970	Baltimore	American	Cincinnati	4:1

Lesson 9 ■ Tables

EXERCISE 66

■ TABS IN TABLE CELLS ■ TABLE LINES, BORDERS, FILLS ■ JOIN CELLS

CONCEPTS:

- To include a left tab in a table, you must use a hard tab.
- After you change column width, reposition the table so it is horizontally centered.

To tab in a table cell:
- Press **CTRL + TAB** for a left tab.

EXERCISE DIRECTIONS:

1. Start with a clear screen.
2. Center the page from top to bottom.
3. Set .5" left and right margins.
4. Create the table shown on the right using 3 columns and 22 rows.
5. Join cells in the first row and center all title lines.
6. Change column A width to 4.5".
   - NOTE: You will adjust columns B and C widths later.
7. Right-align text in columns B and C.
8. Type column text.
9. Edit the table as follows:
   - Change width of columns B and C to 1.5".
   - Reposition the table so it is centered horizontally.
   - Create a dotted border around the table; remove the table lines.
   - Use a 10% fill to shade the rows as shown.
   - Use a double line on all sides of the cell for the Net Income amount as shown.
10. Preview the exercise.
11. Print one copy.
12. Save the exercise; name it **IS**.
13. Close the document window.

In this exercise, you will create a table with 3 columns and 22 rows for an income statement. (An **income statement** shows the net income or loss earned by a business during a particular period.) You will modify column widths and use the Lines/Fill feature to emphasize data.

PAUL B'S CARD SHOPPE
INCOME STATEMENT
For the Month Ended April 30, 199-

Revenue:

Sales	25700	
Less Sales Returns and Allowances	700	
Net Sales		25000

Cost of Merchandise Sold:

Merchandise Inventory, April 1	50250	
Purchases	9250	
Merchandise Available for Sales	59500	
Less Merchandise Inventory, April 30	40000	
Cost of Merchandise Sold		19500
Gross Profit on Sales		5500

Operating Expenses:

Salaries	4000	
Rent	1666	
Taxes	400	
Utilities	345	
Advertising	500	
Depreciation on Equipment	210	
Insurance	65	
Total Operating Expenses		7186
Net Income:		-1686

Lesson 9 ▪ Tables

EXERCISE 67

CREATE TABLES WITHIN A DOCUMENT

CONCEPTS:

- When a table is placed within a document, the table should appear indented on both sides of the paragraph margins. This gives the table more emphasis.

- After creating the table, you will need to make it smaller so it is indented approximately .5" from the left and right margins.

In this exercise, you will create a flyer with an inserted table.

EXERCISE DIRECTIONS:

1. Start with a clear screen.
2. Use the default margins.
3. Center the page from top to bottom.
4. Create the flyer on the right using a serif font face and the point sizes shown.
5. Create a table using 4 columns and 6 rows.
6. Shorten the table size approximately .5" on the left and right.
7. Center each column heading within its cell; enter remaining table text.
8. Edit the table as follows:
   - Adjust column widths so titles of columns C and D fit on one line.
   - Remove all table lines.
   - Add 10% shading to the table.
   - Reposition the table so it is horizontally centered.
9. Preview the exercise.
10. Print one copy.
11. Save the file; name it **BUY**.
12. Close the document window.

While the table text appears double spaced in this exercise, it is not. Remember, table lines are still part of the table structure even though they have been removed. Since the table accommodates the lines, the text appears double spaced.

BUY LATER—NOT NOW! {36p bold}

We are happy to once again bring you our annual BUY LATER—NOT NOW sale. If you place your order by the third week of this month, you will receive our special BUY LATER prices. You will receive delivery next month on anything you order and will be billed upon delivery. {14pt}

Below are our specials:

ITEM	DESCRIPTION	REGULAR PRICE	BUY LATER PRICE
R16	RazerJet 5 Printer	$750.00	$600.00
C111	Carson Disk Case	8.00	5.75
R300	RazerJet 5 Toner	75.00	62.00
M2	Medom Modem	250.00	225.00
C35	Craze Clip Art	79.00	65.50

{12pt}

Place your order by phone immediately. Call our special BUY LATER number: {14pt}

800-555-SAVE {24pt bold}

Lesson 9 ▪ Tables

EXERCISE 68

▪ TABLE LINES, BORDERS ▪ ROW AND COLUMN MARGINS ▪ FILLS

CONCEPTS:

- When using a thick border, row and/or column margins have to be changed so the text is not blocked by the thick border.

> THIS TEXT IS TOO CLOSE TO THE LEFT, TOP AND BOTTOM BORDERS

- To create the effect shown above without hiding text, in the Table Format dialog box click the Row button and increase the Top and Bottom Row Margin.

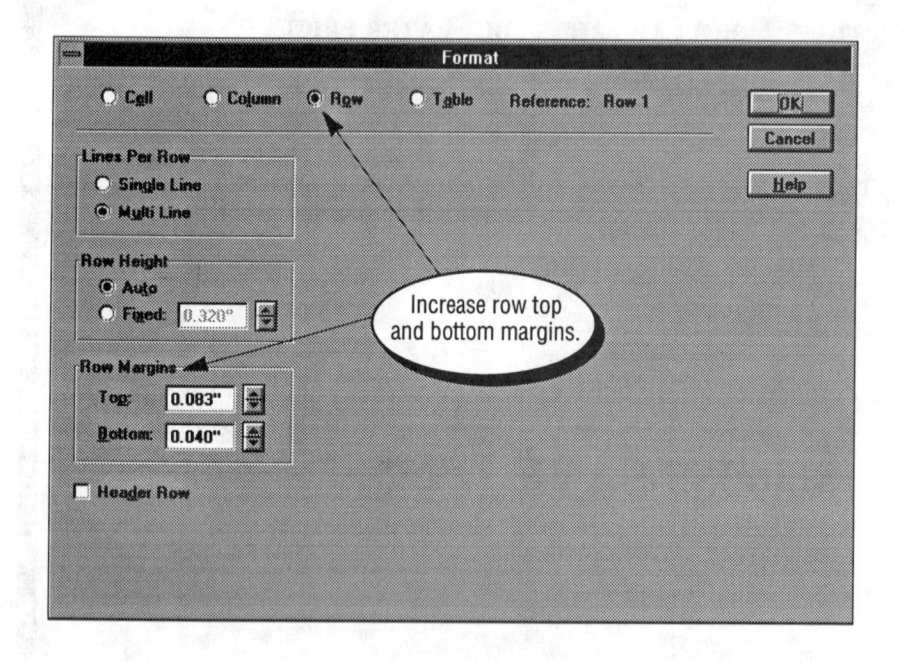

Increase row top and bottom margins.

To change column/row margins:
- Click **Table**
- Click **Format**
- Click **Row** or **Column**

In this exercise, you will create a table changing the table border, table lines, shading, joining a row, and changing row and column margins.

298

- Click the Column button and increase the Left: and Right: Column Margins.

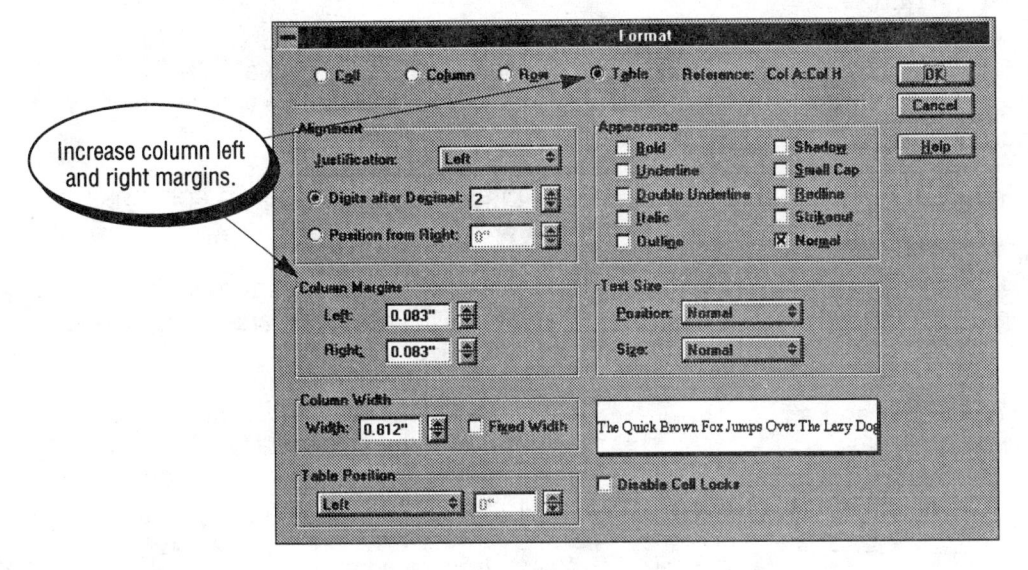

Increase column left and right margins.

- The increase in margins allows the text to be seen inside the thick border:

> THIS TEXT IS NOT TOO CLOSE TO THE LEFT, TOP AND BOTTOM BORDERS

- The row margins are changed by selecting Row in the Table Format dialog box.
- The column margins are changed by selecting Column in the Table Format dialog box.

EXERCISE DIRECTIONS:

1. Start with a clear screen.
2. Center the page from top to bottom.
3. Set 1" left and right margins.
4. Create the table on the right using 4 columns and 11 rows.
5. Join cells in the first row.
6. Use an 18 point serif font for the title and a 14 point serif font for the two subtitles.
7. Type the table text using a 12 point serif font.
8. Edit the table as follows:

   - Change column width of column A to 2".
   - Change the left column margin in column A to .125".
   - Change the bottom row margin in row 11 to .125".
   - Reposition the table so it is centered horizontally.
   - Change to a Thick Shadow table border around the table.
   - Cells B2, C2, D2: Use a 10% fill to shade and change the top and bottom lines to double.
   - Center the two-line titles in columns B, C, and D.
   - Change the column alignment in columns B and C to Center Justification.
   - Change the column alignment justification in column D to Decimal Align. Set the Position from Right to approximately .65" in order to center the numbers in the column.

9. Preview the exercise.
10. Print one copy.
11. Save the exercise; name it **SUN**.
12. Close the document window.

Sunlight Industries
SALES COMPARISON
Third and Fourth Quarters

	Third Quarter	Fourth Quarter	Percent of Change
Wanda Enrico	293,982	356,545	21.3
Jamaal Moon	314,432	309,129	-1.7
Rochelle Pollack	342,565	389,302	13.6
Tina Wong	543,987	456,893	-16.0
Ilene Fewer	165,432	217,592	31.5
Tony Nakamura	256,854	321,834	25.3
Kishna Patel	387,532	507,425	30.9
Kathleen O'Hara	198,884	278,481	40.0
Ida Nathan	407,323	492,823	20.8

ROW MARGINS

1. Click T<u>a</u>ble .... Alt + T
2. Click F<u>o</u>rmat .... O
3. Click R<u>o</u>w .... O
4. Click To<u>p</u> .... P
   Type new margin number .... *number*
5. Click <u>B</u>ottom .... B
   Type new margin number .... *number*
6. Click OK .... Enter

COLUMN MARGINS

1. Click T<u>a</u>ble .... Alt + T
2. Click F<u>o</u>rmat .... O
3. Click Co<u>l</u>umn L
4. Click Le<u>f</u>t .... F
   Type new margin number .... *number*
5. Click Right: .... :
   Type new margin number .... *number*
6. Click OK .... Enter

Lesson 9 ■ Exercise 68

Lesson 9 ▪ Tables

EXERCISE 69
TABLES WITH GRAPHICS

CONCEPTS:

- When adding a graphic to a table, a user box should be used. This allows the graphic to be placed in a cell with no border around it.

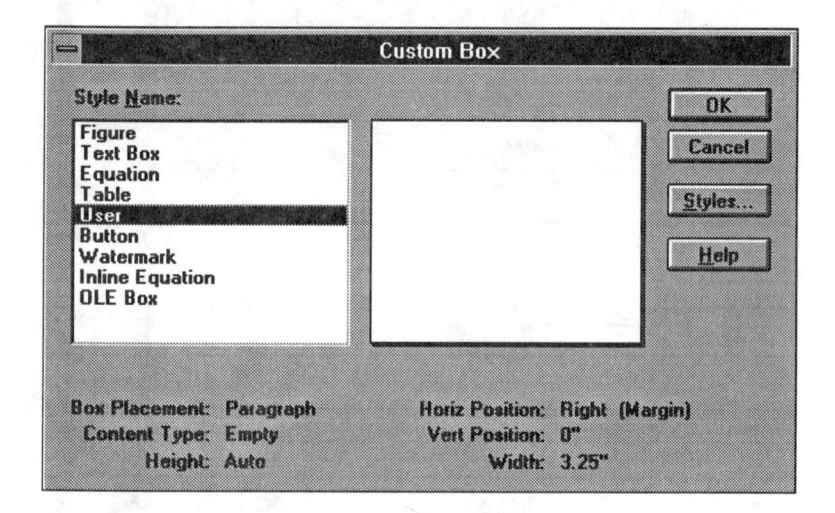

On the Graphic Box Feature Bar, click Content.

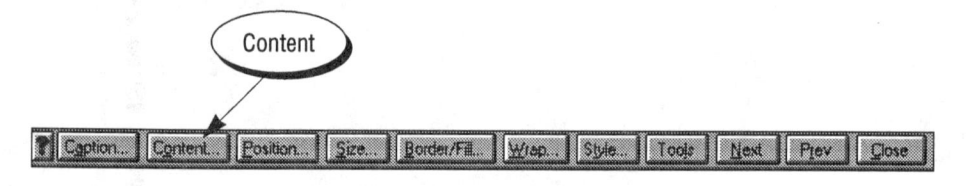

After selecting Image on Disk, you can then click on the list button to choose graphic filename.

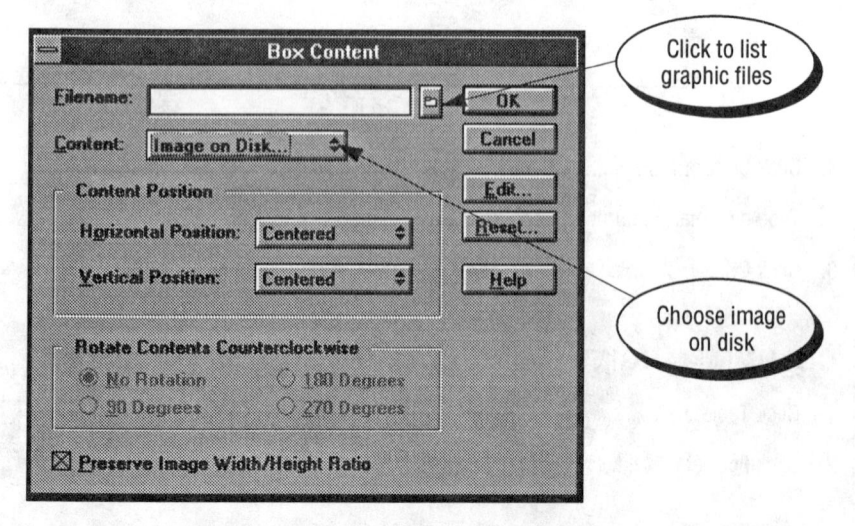

To add a graphic to a table cell:
- Click **Graphics**
- Click **Custom Box**
- Click **User Box**
- Click **Image on Disk**

Your graphic can be edited in WordPerfect Draw by choosing Content and Edit.

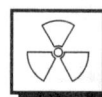

If a graphic in a table is attached to the page, it will not stay in the table if the table is moved.

- The graphic user box must be attached to a paragraph in order to move with the table.

- A graphic must be resized to fit in the table cell. It automatically comes in flush right and at the top of the cell, so the placement must be adjusted.

> In this exercise, you will add a graphic to an existing table and edit the letterspacing of selected text.

Lesson 9 ■ Exercise 69

EXERCISE DIRECTIONS:

1. Start with a clear screen.
2. Open **SUN**.
3. Change the column widths: column A to 1.75", columns B, C and D to 1.3".
4. Place insertion point in row 1.
5. Create a graphics custom user box.
   - Place the file **SUN_DSG.WPG** in the box.
   - Set the size to .75 width and height.
   - Paragraph Anchor the box and position it:

     Horizontally .1" from the left margin.

     Vertically .1" from the top of paragraph.

6. Select the title and subtitles in row 1 and change to:
   - Right align
   - Letterspacing at 130% of optimal.
7. Set the Top Line style of cell A2 to None.
8. Print one copy.
9. Close your file; save the changes.

ADD A GRAPHIC BOX TO A TABLE CELL

1. Place insertion point in cell where you want graphic to appear.
2. Choose Graphics................. Alt + G
3. Choose Custom Box........................ C
4. Select **User**
5. Choose OK............................ Enter
6. Choose Content........ Shift + Alt + O from Graphic Box Feature Bar.
7. Choose Content.......................... C

8. Select................. Alt + C, F4, D
   Image on Disk
9. Click list button...................................
10. Select a graphics file
11. Click OK.................................. Enter

POSITION GRAPHIC CUSTOM USER BOX

1. Select box.
2. Select Position............ Shift + Alt + P

3. Select.................................... U
   Put Box in Current Paragraph.
4. Select Place............................ L
5. Type number................number for horizontal offset.
6. Press Tab...................... Tab, Space to select horizontal position.
7. Select Place............................ A
8. Type number................number for vertical placement.

Sunlight Industries
SALES COMPARISON
Third and Fourth Quarters

	Third Quarter	Fourth Quarter	Percent of Change
Wanda Enrico	293,982	356,545	21.3
Jamaal Moon	314,432	309,129	-1.7
Rochelle Pollack	342,565	389,302	13.6
Tina Wong	543,987	456,893	-16.0
Ilene Fewer	165,432	217,592	31.5
Tony Nakamura	256,854	321,834	25.3
Kishna Patel	387,532	507,425	30.9
Kathleen O'Hara	198,884	278,481	40.0
Ida Nathan	407,323	492,823	20.8

Lesson 9 ▪ Tables

EXERCISE 70
TABLES WITH GRAPHICS

CONCEPTS:

- To keep the rows the same height when adding graphics,
  - set the height of the graphic.
  - set the width to *size to content* for the graphic.
  - set the wrap of the graphic to *no wrap*.
  - set the row height of the rows to fixed.

> In this exercise, you will create a table that contains graphics.

EXERCISE DIRECTIONS:

1. Start with a clear screen.
2. Center the page from top to bottom.
3. Create the table on the right using 3 columns and 10 rows.
4. Center the table horizontally.
5. Change the column widths to 1.5" for columns A and C and 2" for column B.
6. Join columns A, B and C in row 1 and center the title using a 24 point bold serif font.
7. Center the column headings over columns A and C in row 2 using a 12 point bold serif font.
8. Set the Inside Line Style for rows 1 and 2 to None and the Fill Style to 30% Fill.
9. Set the row height as follows:
   - .25" fixed for rows 4, 6, 8, 10.
   - 1" fixed for rows 3, 5, 7, 9.
10. Join cells in rows 4, 6, 8 and 10 and set the Fill Style to 30% Fill.
11. Type the table text using a 12 point serif font and insert the custom user graphic boxes:
    - **cheetah.wpg**
    - **coyote.wpg**
    - **horse_j.wpg**
    - **tiger_j.wpg**
12. Select Put Box in Current Paragraph (Paragraph Anchor) and position the graphics:
    - Horizontally 0" from the center of paragraph.
    - Vertically 0" from top of paragraph.
13. Size the graphics so the height is set at 1" and the width is sized to content.
14. Set the wrap of the graphic to *no wrap*.
15. Print one copy.
16. Save the file; name it **ANIMAL**.
17. Close the document window.

FAMOUS ANIMALS

Common Name		Latin Name
Cheetah		Acinonyx jubatus
Coyote		Canis latrans
Horse		Equus caballus
Tiger		Panthera tigris

Lesson 9 ▪ Tables

EXERCISE 71
CREATE A CHART

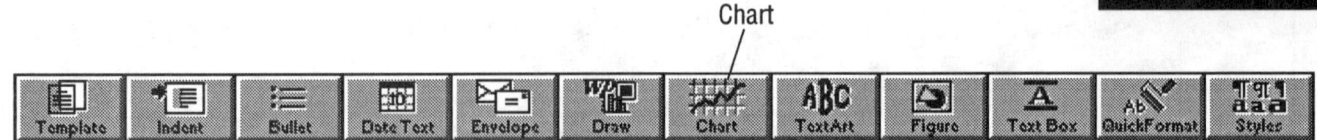

CONCEPTS:

- Using the **Chart** feature, you can create pie, bar, scatter, line, hi-lo and area charts. The chart is created within the Chart Editor from scratch, from a table, or from a spreadsheet imported from another program.

- The Chart Editor is a window in the WordPerfect Draw program where charts and created and edited.

- When the Chart Editor screen opens, you will see a sample data chart and the worksheet which contains the data that is used in the chart. This sample chart was created totally on the Chart Editor screen.

To access the chart editor:
- Click **Chart** Button

OR

- Click **Graphics**
- Click **Chart**

If the chart is selected on the document window, you will not be able to print or save your file. Click your insertion point outside the chart and then print or save.

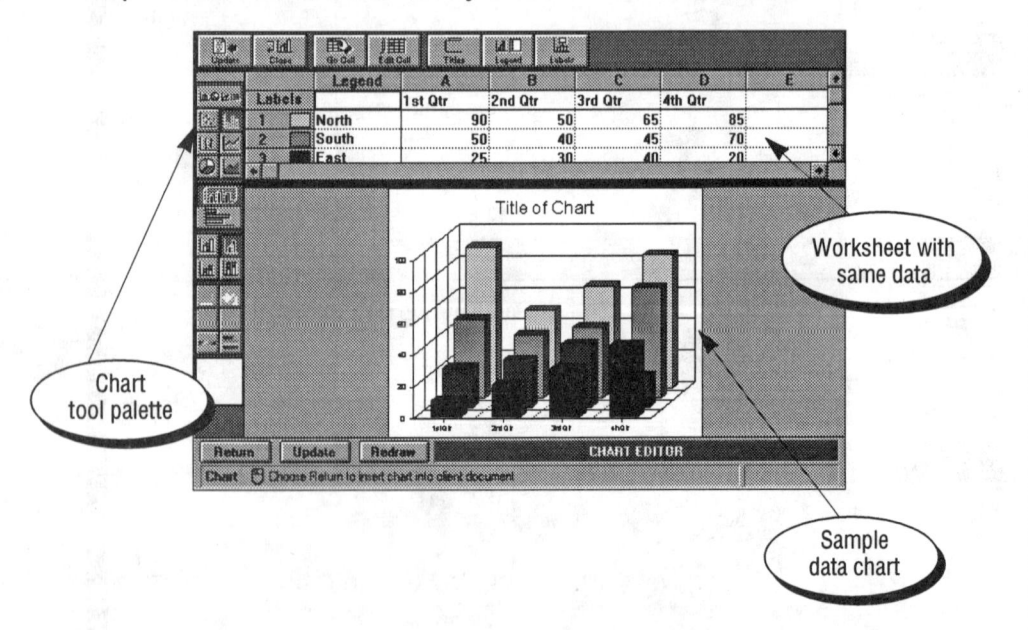

- The default chart type is a bar chart. Before creating a new chart in the Chart Editor, the type of chart must be chosen.

In this exercise, you will create a flyer that contains a chart created in the Chart Editor.

- Down the left side of the Chart Editor window is the Chart Tool Palette from which you can choose the type of chart you desire.

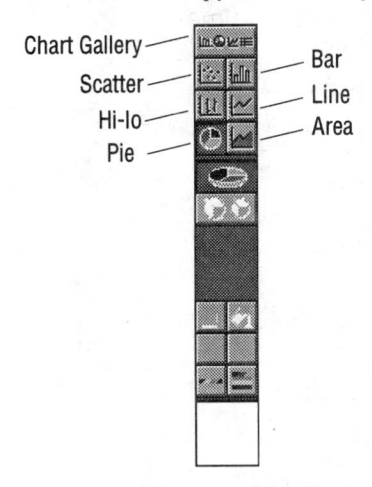

- The type of chart you choose from the Chart Tool Palette depends on what you want the chart to show:

CHART TYPE	USED TO SHOW
Scatter	interception of X and Y axis
Bar	variations between components
Hi-Lo	hi, lo, opening and closing values
Line	a change over time
Pie	proportion of parts to the whole
Area	change over time

- Once the type of chart is chosen, the chart can be further changed through the Chart Gallery which allows different variations. For example:

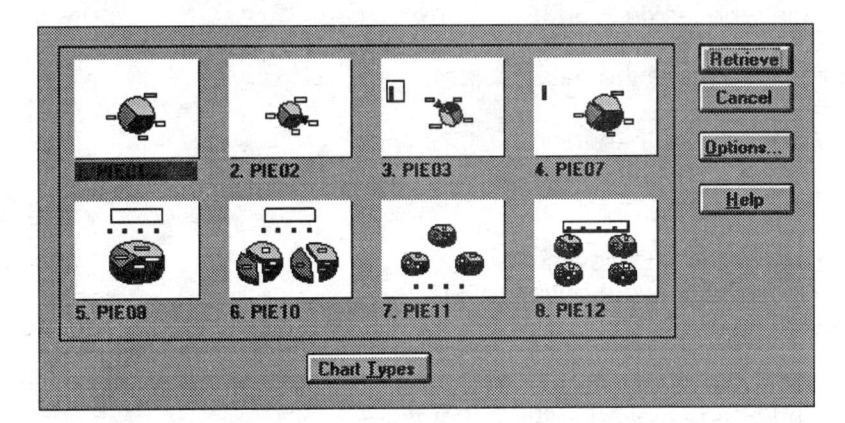

Lesson 9 ■ Exercise 71

- Each chart may contain a horizontal **x-axis** and vertical **y-axis**:

    The **x**-axis represents items or categories being compared such as time periods, products or persons. It contains the category labels that identify the data being compared. These category labels are obtained from the row or column labels.

    The **y**-axis represents the unit of measure used for comparison. The scale numbers are entered automatically based on the data being charted.

    NOTE: Pie charts do not have axes.

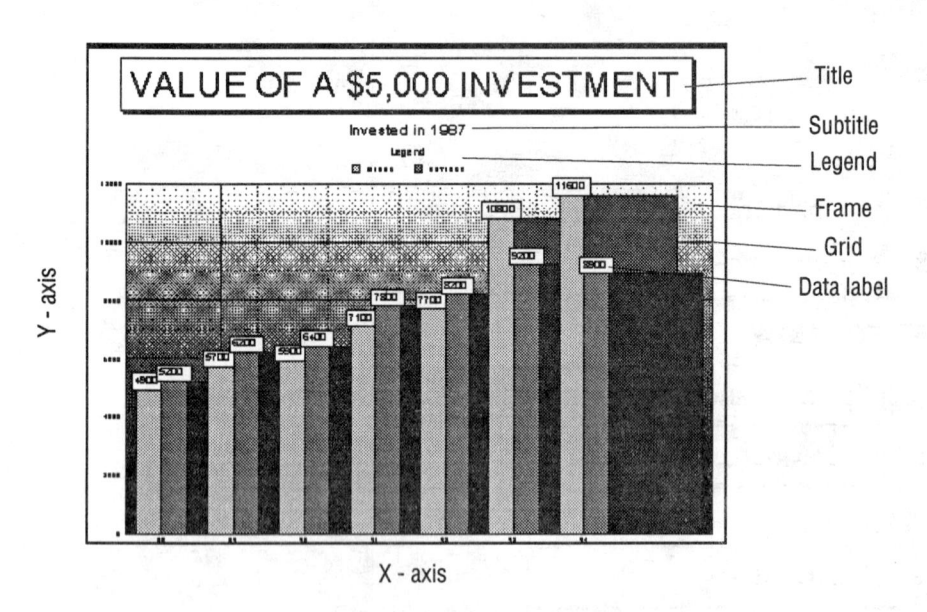

    [Chart: VALUE OF A $5,000 INVESTMENT, Invested in 1987, with labels for Title, Subtitle, Legend, Frame, Grid, Data label, Y-axis, X-axis]

- You can enhance charts using:

    - **Legends**   Contains descriptive data for the chart. Identifies the name of each row of data in your chart.

    - **Labels**   **Data labels** identify data points in a chart, and **category labels** identify the type of data represented along the x-axis.

    - **Grid/Tick**   Adds lines or ticks to make the data easier to read.

    - **Titles**   Allows you to add a title, subtitle, and axis titles.

    - **Perspective**   Allows you to adjust the 3-D viewing perspective but the 3-D Layout option must first be chosen.

    - **Frame**   Allows you to fill in the chart with a background color/pattern and/or add a base at the bottom of the chart.

- To insert a new chart into a document, you must place your insertion point where you want the chart to appear before entering the Chart Editor.

- Sample data and a chart will automatically be in the Chart Editor window and must be deleted.

- The chart type to be used must be selected before entering the chart data.

- Enter the data to be charted on the worksheet. After the data is entered the chart will appear when Redraw is selected.

- Titles, subtitles and axis titles are entered in the Titles dialog box.

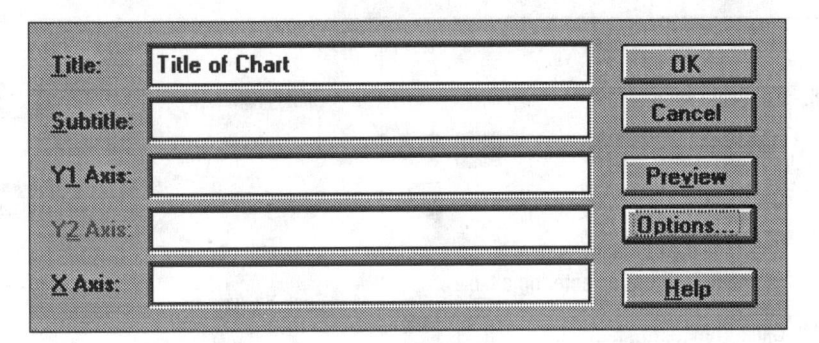

- When the chart is complete, you *return* to the document window after saving the chart to the document.

- The chart can be moved on the page by selecting it and dragging it with the mouse button.

EXERCISE DIRECTIONS:

1. Start with a clear screen.
2. Center the page from top to bottom.
3. Insert an extra double thick line.
4. Select a 14 point serif font.
5. Type the first paragraph.
6. Place an extra double thick line below the paragraph.
7. Access the Chart Editor and select a pie chart. Choose PIE 01 in the Chart Gallery.

   Enter the following information in the worksheet portion of the Chart Editor using the label and Pie 1 columns:

Perennials	$125,000
Annuals	$75,000
Pots	$25,000
Seeds	$9,500
Tools	$10,500
Accessories	$7,200

8. Redraw the chart.
9. Add the title and subtitle.
10. Insert the chart into your document.
11. Center the chart horizontally between the margins by selecting the chart and dragging it to the center.
12. Place an extra double thick line below the chart.
13. Type the final paragraph.
14. Place an extra double thick line below the final paragraph.
15. Print one copy.
16. Save the file; name it **FLOWER4**.
17. Close the document window.

Lesson 9 ■ Exercise 71

CREATE A CHART AND ADD TO DOCUMENT

1. In document window, place insertion point where you want to insert chart.
2. Choose **G**raphics .... `Alt`+`G`

   Choose Cha**r**t .... `R`

   OR

   Click the Chart button .... `Chart`
3. Click **C**hart .... `Alt`+`C`

   Select from the following:
   - **P**ie .... `P`
   - **B**ar .... `B`
   - **L**ine .... `L`
   - **A**rea .... `A`
   - **S**catter .... `S`
   - **H**i-lo .... `H`
4. Click **C**hart .... `Alt`+`C`
5. Click **G**allery .... `G`

   OR

   Click Gallery button .... on Tool Palette.
6. Click Gallery selection .... `▶`
7. Click Retrieve .... `Tab`, `Enter`

8. To delete sample text:

   Click **F**ile .... `Alt`+`F`

   Click **C**lear .... `C`
9. Enter the data on the worksheet (same techniques as entering a table).
10. Click **V**iew .... `Alt`+`V`

    Click **R**edraw .... `R`

    OR

    Click on Redraw button .... `Redraw`
11. Click **F**ile .... `Alt`+`F`

    Click **C**lose and Return .... `C`

    OR

    Click Return .... `Return`
12. Click **Y**es to save changes. .... `Y`

ADD OR CHANGE TITLES

—*WHILE IN CHART EDITOR*—

1. Click **O**ptions .... `O`

   Click **T**itles .... `T`

   OR

   Click on Titles button .... `Titles`

2. Click **T**itle .... `Alt`+`T`

   Type title.
3. Click **S**ubtitle box .... `Alt`+`S`

   Type sub title.
4. Click **Y1** Axis box .... `Alt`+`1`

   Type title.
5. Click OK .... `Enter`

POSITION CHART IN DOCUMENT WINDOW

1. Select chart.
2. Drag chart using *left* mouse button.

   OR

   Click **G**raphics .... `Alt`+`G`
3. Click **E**dit Box .... `E`
4. Click **P**osition button .. `Shift`+`Alt`+`P`
5. Click Horizontal P**l**ace .... `L`

   Select Position .... `Tab`, `Space`
6. Click Vertical Pl**a**ce .... `A`

   Select Position .... `Tab`, `Space`
7. Click OK .... `Enter`

The Perennial Pot is proud to share its June sales report with all our customers. This year has shown a large increase over last year and it is all because of you, our customers!

The Perennial Pot
June Sales

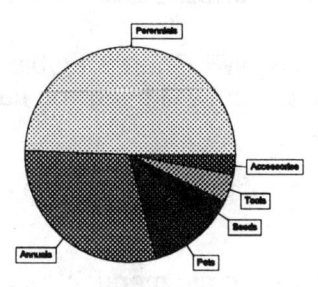

[Pie chart with segments labeled: Perennials, Accessories, Tools, Seeds, Pets, Annuals]

As a result of our analysis of our June sales, we are planning to hold a special sale in the area where we sold the least. Be at the door when our store opens on July 15 and be prepared to save money!

Lesson 9 ▪ Tables

EXERCISE 72

- **EDIT AND CHANGE THE DATA AND APPEARANCE OF A CHART**
- **EXPLODE A PIE CHART**

CONCEPTS:

- After a chart has been created, changes can be made. The data can be changed, the selected chart style can be changed (Chart Gallery) and enhanced, and the box around the chart can be modified.

- The Position, Size, and Border/Fill options can be changed once the chart is selected in the document window.

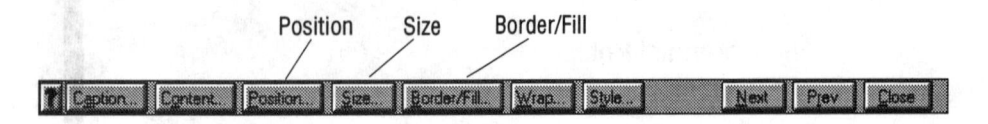

- When the chart is in a document, selecting WP Chart 2.1 Object in the Edit main menu or double clicking on the chart will bring you back into the Chart Editor in order to make changes.

- Once in the Chart Editor, the appearance of the chart and the chart data can be modified.

- The layout can be edited under the Options main menu. When a pie chart is chosen, the following layout options appear in the Layout dialog box.

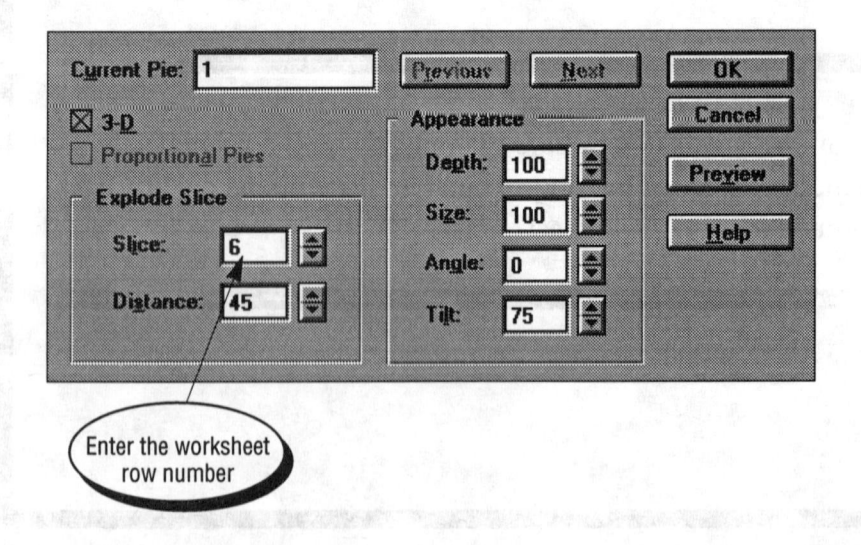

To edit a chart:
- Double click on the chart.

OR
- Click **Edit**
- Click **WP Chart 2.1 Object**

To change the border around a chart:
- Click **Graphics**
- Click **Edit Box**
- Click **Border/Fill**

If the chart is selected on the document window, you will not be able to print or save your file. Click your cursor outside the chart, and then print or save.

314

- A section of the pie chart can be **exploded** for emphasis:

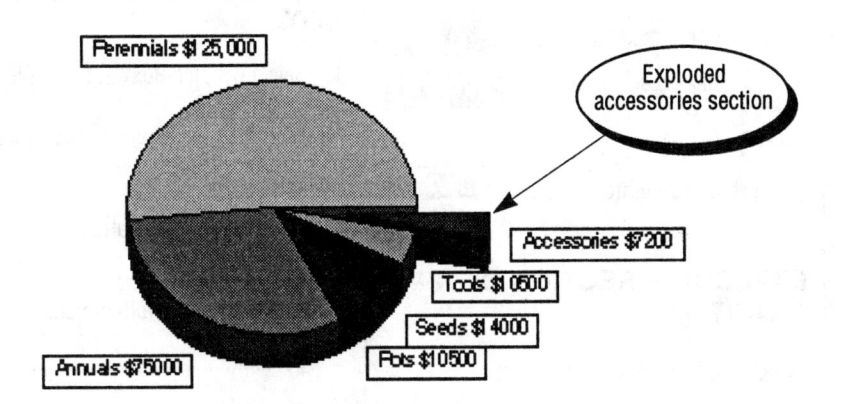

- The labels can be edited under the Options main menu. When a pie chart is chosen, the following label options appear in the label dialog box:

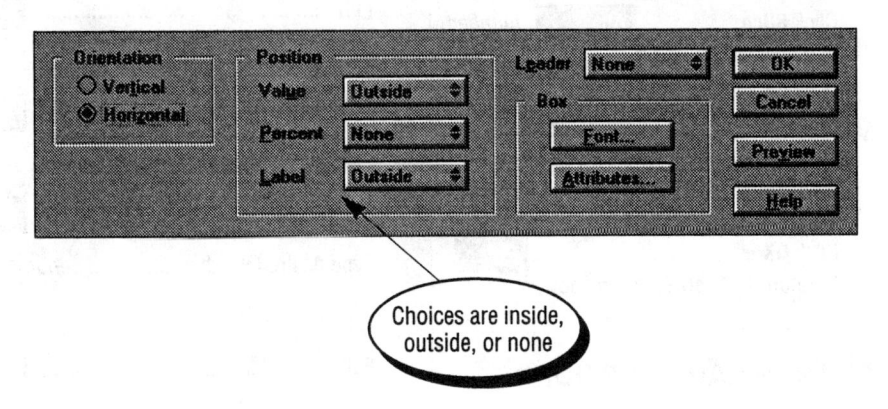

Choices are inside, outside, or none

In this exercise you will edit an existing chart by changing the chart style, enhancements, and data and the appearance of the chart box.

EXERCISE DIRECTIONS:

1. Start with a clear screen.
2. Open **FLOWER4**.
3. Delete the lines before and after each paragraph.
4. Double click the chart to enter Chart Editor.
5. In the worksheet change the seed sales to $14,000.
6. Select PIE10 from the Chart Gallery.
7. Edit the layout options so slice 6 explodes a distance of 45.
8. Edit the labels so the value and labels are on the outside and no percent is shown.
9. Return to the document windows, saving the changes.
10. Edit the graphics box by changing the size width and height to Size to Content.
11. Edit the border to add a top and bottom thick border.
12. Print one copy.
13. Close your file; save the changes.

Lesson 9 ■ Exercise 72

Lesson 9 ▪ Exercise 72

EDIT CHART FROM DOCUMENT WINDOW

1. Click **E**dit .... `Alt`+`E`

   Click **WP Chart 2.1 O**bject .... `O`

   Click **E**dit .... `E`

   OR

   Select chart by double clicking left mouse button.

EDIT DATA IN AN EXISTING CHART

—IN THE CHART EDITOR—

1. Select worksheet cell to edit.

   Click **E**dit, Go to Cell ...... `E`, `Ctrl`+`G`

   Type cell address (i.e., B1) ..... *cell address*

   Click **OK** .... `Enter`

   OR

   Click cell in worksheet.

2. Type new data .... *data*

3. Click **F**ile .... `Alt`+`F`

   Click **U**pdate .... `Shift`+`F3`

   OR

   Click Update button .... `Update`

CHOOSE A DIFFERENT FORM OF A CHART (CHART GALLERY)

—IN THE CHART EDITOR—

1. Click **C**hart .... `Alt`+`C`

   Click **G**allery .... `G`

   OR

   Click Gallery button .... `[icon]`
   on Tool Palette

2. Click selection from gallery .... `▶`

3. Click **R**etrieve .... `Tab`, `Enter`

---

4. Click **F**ile .... `Alt`+`F`

   Click **U**pdate .... `Shift`+`F3`

   OR

   Click Update button .... `Update`

EXPLODE A SECTION OF A PIE CHART

—IN THE CHART EDITOR—

1. Click **O**ptions .... `Alt`+`O`

2. Click **L**ayout .... `L`

3. Click **Sl**ice .... `Alt`+`I`, *number*
   and type slice number
   (row number of worksheet).

4. Click **D**i**s**tance .... `Alt`+`S`, *number*
   and type distance
   (experiment with numbers).

5. Click **OK** .... `Enter`
   to return to Chart Editor window.

CHANGE LABEL OPTIONS

—IN THE CHART EDITOR—

1. Click **O**ptions .... `Alt`+`O`

2. Click La**b**els .... `B`

3. Select desired **O**rientation (for Pie Chart):
   - Ver**t**ical .... `T`
   - Hori**z**ontal .... `Z`

4. Select desired Position (for Pie Chart):
   - Val**u**e .... `U`
   - **P**ercent .... `P`
   - **L**abel .... `L`

5. Click **OK** .... `Enter`
   to return to Chart Editor window.

CHANGE SIZE OF A GRAPHICS BOX

1. Select Graphic Box .... `Shift`+`F11`

2. Click **S**ize .... `Alt`+`Shift`+`S`

   OR

   Click *right* mouse button .... `S`
   and select **S**ize.

3. Select desired Width option:

   Set .... `S`

   Type desired width .... *number*

   OR

   F**u**ll .... `F`

   OR

   Si**z**e to Content .... `I`

4. Select desired Height option:

   S**e**t .... `E`

   Type desired width .... *number*

   OR

   F**u**ll .... `U`

   OR

   Si**z**e to Content .... `Z`

5. Click **OK** to return to document ... `Enter`

CHANGE BORDER OF A GRAPHICS BOX

1. Select Graphic Box .... `Shift`+`F11`

2. Click **B**order/Fill .... `Alt`+`Shift`+`B`
   on Graphics Feature Bar.

   OR

   Click *right* mouse button .... `B`
   and select **B**order/Fill

3. Click **B**order Style button .... `B`

   OR

   Click drop-down Border Style list.

4. Click desired style.

5. Click **OK** to return to document ... `Enter`

The Perennial Pot is proud to share its June sales report with all our customers. This year has shown a large increase over last year and it is all because of you, our customers!

The Perennial Pot
June Sales

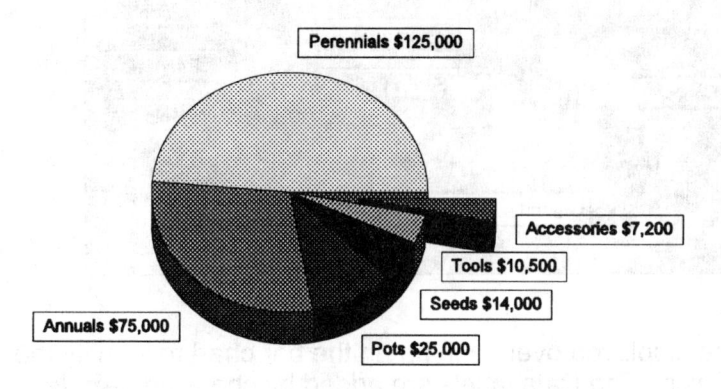

- Perennials $125,000
- Annuals $75,000
- Pots $25,000
- Seeds $14,000
- Tools $10,500
- Accessories $7,200

As a result of our analysis of our June sales, we are planning to hold a special sale in the area where we sold the least. Be at the door when our store opens on July 15 and be prepared to save money!

Lesson 9 ▪ Tables

EXERCISE 73

**CREATE A CHART FROM A TABLE ▪ PLACE CHART ON SEPARATE PAGE
▪ ADD CHART LEGEND ▪ ADD DATA LABELS**

CONCEPTS:

- The data contained in a table can be transformed into a chart. Select the data to chart on the document screen and then select **Chart** from the **G**raphics main menu to enter Chart Editor. The selected table information is transferred into the worksheet and a bar chart is automatically created.

- A **legend** is added to the chart by choosing **Legend** from the **O**ptions menu or clicking on the Legend Button and then selecting Display Legend.

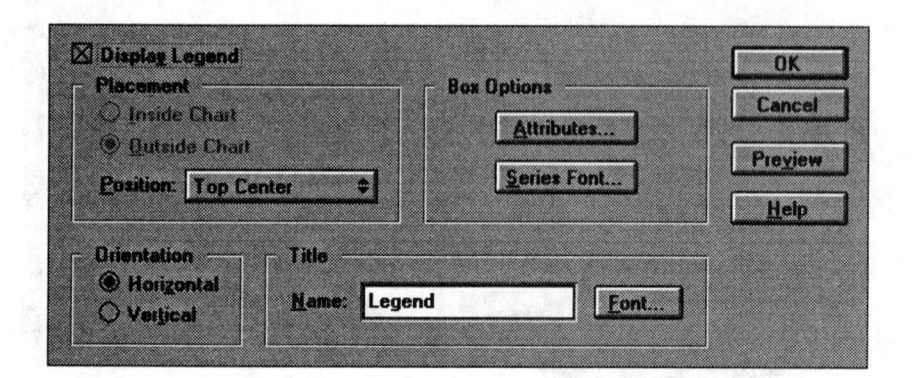

To chart table data:

Select table data to chart.
- Click Chart Button
OR
- Click **G**raphics
- Click Cha**r**t
- Click **F**ile
- Click **U**pdate
- Click **F**ile
- Click **C**lose and Return

- **Data labels** can be displayed over each bar in the bar chart to identify the amounts on the Y-axis. The Data labels are added by choosing **La**b**els** from the **O**ptions menu or clicking on the Labels Button.

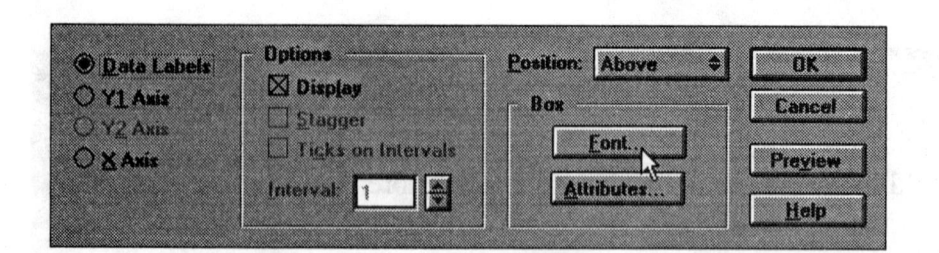

In this exercise you will select data from an existing table in order to create a bar chart.

- When Return is chosen, the chart will be inserted under the table. It can then edited by selecting **Edit Box** in the **G**raphics main menu. The Graphics Feature Bar appears.

- The location of the chart in relation to the document is selected in the Position dialog box. To have the chart appear on a page of its own, in the Position dialog box choose Put Box on Current Page (Page Anchor) as the Box Placement.

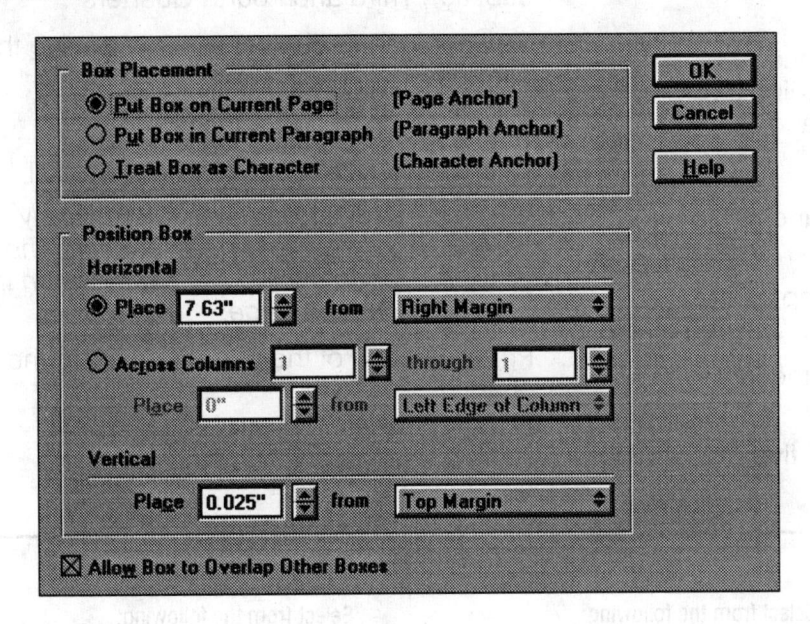

- To help differentiate between bars on a bar chart, fill patterns can be used.

Choose fill pattern for bars

Lesson 9 ▪ Exercise 73

Lesson 9 ▪ Exercise 73

EXERCISE DIRECTIONS:

1. Start with a clear screen.
2. Open **SUN**.
3. Select the names in column A and the amounts in columns B and C, including the column headings over columns B and C.
4. Enter the Chart Editor.
5. In the Chart Gallery, change the bar chart to BAR01.
6. Add a legend that appears in the top center, on the outside, with a horizontal orientation..
7. Display data labels above and set the font to 12 point.
8. Select different fill patterns for rows five through 9.
9. Add a title, SUNLIGHT INDUSTRIES, and a subtitle, "Third and Fourth Quarters".
10. Return to the document window, saving the changes.
11. Select the chart and edit the box.
12. Change the size width and height to full.
   - NOTE: The Position will automatically change to a page anchor. The chart should appear alone on the second page.
13. Print one copy of the page containing the chart.
14. Close your file; save the changes.

CREATE A CHART FROM A TABLE

1. Select table data to chart.
2. Click **G**raphics .... Alt + G
   Click Cha**r**t .... R
   OR
   Click Chart button .... [button]
3. Click **F**ile .... Alt + F
   Click **U**pdate .... U
   OR
   Click Update button .... [button]
4. Choose **F**ile .... Alt + F
   Click **C**lose and Return C
   OR
   Click Return .... [Return]

ADD A LEGEND

—IN THE CHART EDITOR—

1. Choose **O**ptions .... Alt + O
   Click L**e**gend .... E
   OR
   Click Legend button .... [button]
2. Click on Displa**y** Legend .... Y

Select from the following:

Inside Chart I
Outside Chart .... O
Position .... P
Hori**z**ontal .... Z
Ver**t**ical .... T
Attributes .... A
Series Font .... S
Font .... F

3. Click OK .... [Enter]

DISPLAY DATA LABELS

—IN THE CHART EDITOR—

1. Click **O**ptions .... Alt + O
   Click La**b**els .... B
   OR
   Click Label Button .... [button]
2. Click **D**ata Labels .... Alt + D
3. Click Disp**l**ay .... Alt + L
4. Click **P**osition .... Alt + P

Select from the following:

Above
Below

5. Click **F**ont .... Alt + F
   Click **S**ize .... Alt + S
   Select size .... *number*
6. Click OK .... [Enter]

ADD FILL PATTERNS TO BARS IN A CHART

—IN THE CHART EDITOR—

1. Select row for pattern change in Chart Editor.
2. Click pattern button .... [button]
3. Select pattern.

EDIT CHART BOX ON DOCUMENT SCREEN

1. Select chart
2. Click **G**raphics .... Alt + G
   Select **E**dit Box .... E
3. Use Graphics Box Feature Bar to edit.

Sunlight Industries

Third and Fourth Quarter Sales

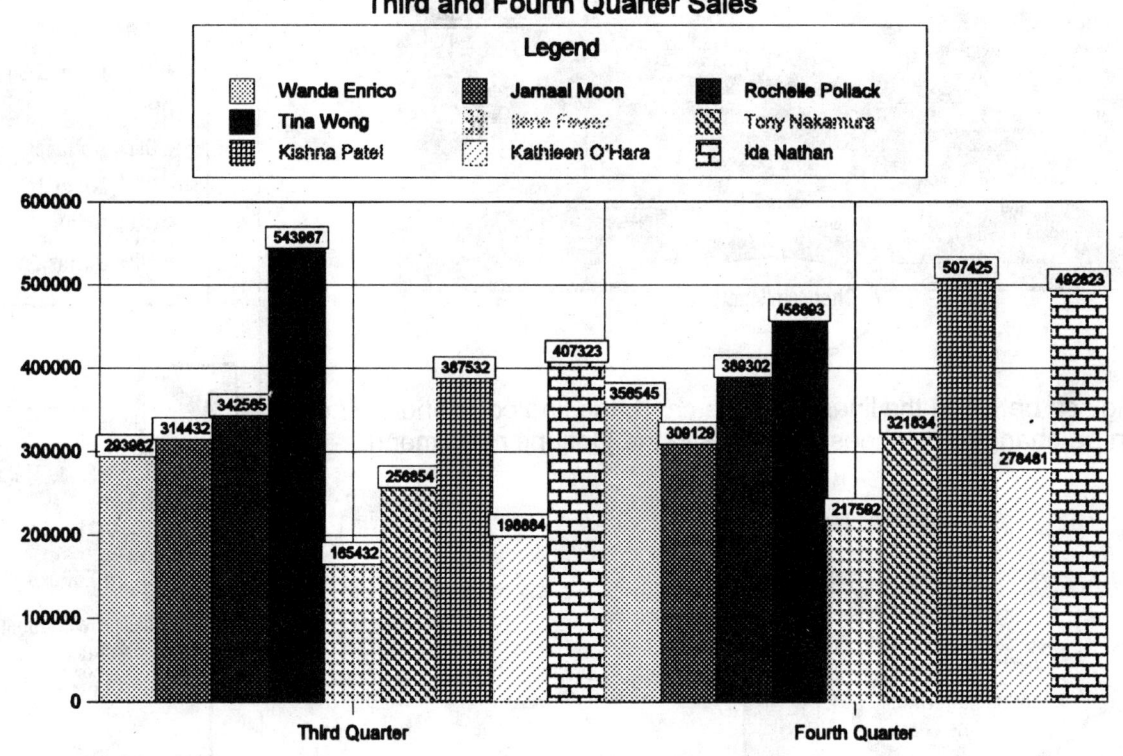

Legend
- Wanda Enrico
- Tina Wong
- Kishna Patel
- Jamaal Moon
- Ilene Fewer
- Kathleen O'Hara
- Rochelle Pollack
- Tony Nakamura
- Ida Nathan

Salesperson	Third Quarter	Fourth Quarter
Wanda Enrico	293962	309129
Tina Wong	314432	389302
Kishna Patel	342585	456893
Jamaal Moon	543987	217592
Ilene Fewer	165432	321834
Kathleen O'Hara	258854	278481
Rochelle Pollack	387532	507425
Tony Nakamura	198884	358545
Ida Nathan	407323	492823

Lesson 9 ■ Tables

EXERCISE 74

- CREATE A LINE CHART IN A DOCUMENT ■ CHANGE FONT SIZE OF LEGEND
- CHANGE COLOR AND STYLE OF CHART LINES

CONCEPTS:

- When adding a legend to a chart, the font size can be changed by selecting Options, Legends and then Series Font.

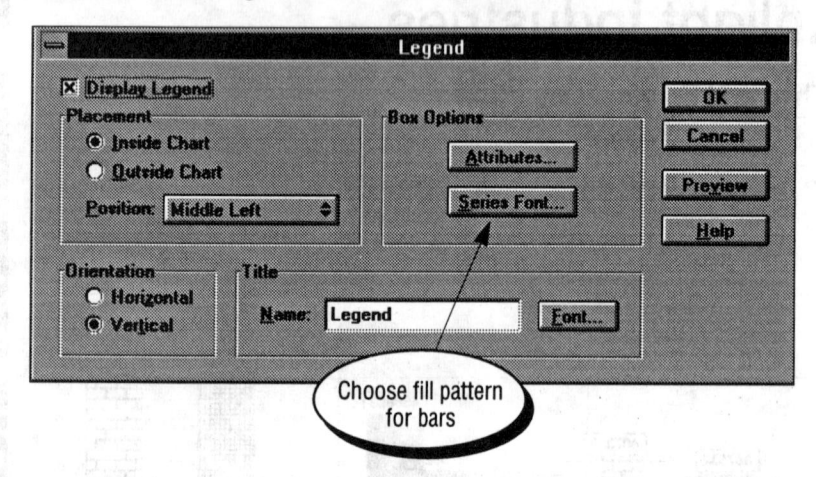

Choose fill pattern for bars

- To distinguish between the lines on a line chart, the line color and/or line style can be changed by choosing **Series** in the **O**ptions main menu.

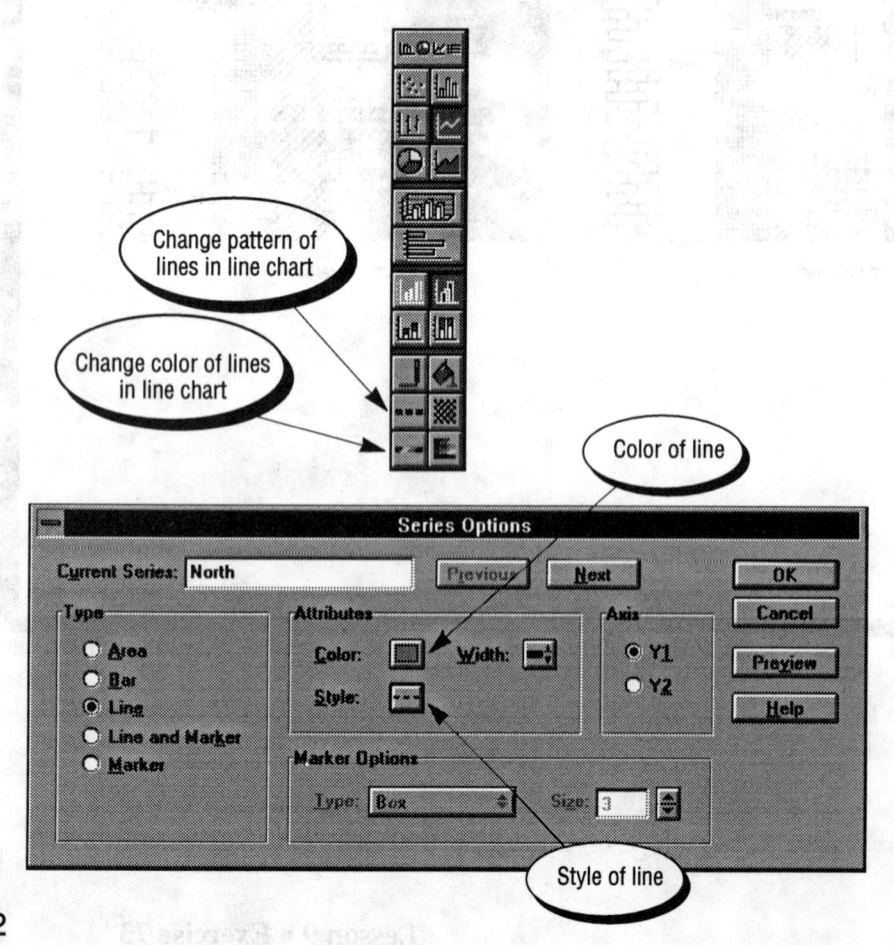

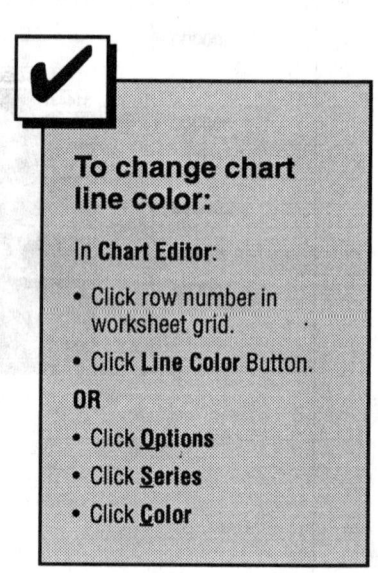

Change pattern of lines in line chart

Change color of lines in line chart

Color of line

Style of line

To change legend font size:

In **Chart Editor**:

- Click **Legend** Button

OR

- Click **O**ptions
- Click **L**egend
- Click **Display L**egend
- Click **S**eries Font

To change chart line color:

In **Chart Editor**:

- Click row number in worksheet grid.
- Click **Line Color** Button.

OR

- Click **O**ptions
- Click **S**eries
- Click **C**olor

- To have the chart appear below the paragraph, the position is changed by selecting **Edit Box** in the Graphics main menu. The Position button on the Graphics Feature Bar is chosen. In the Position dialog box, choose Put Box in Current Paragraph (Paragraph Anchor) as the Box Placement. The horizontal and vertical placement in relation to the paragraph is also chosen in the Position dialog box.

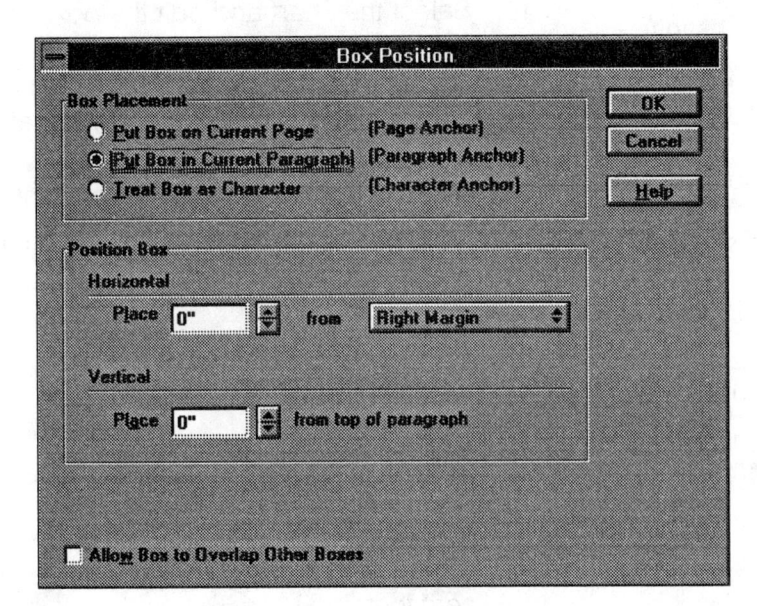

- The border and shading of the graphics box is changed by selecting **Edit Box** in the Graphics main menu. The Border/Fill button on the Graphics Feature Bar is chosen to add shading to the graphic box.

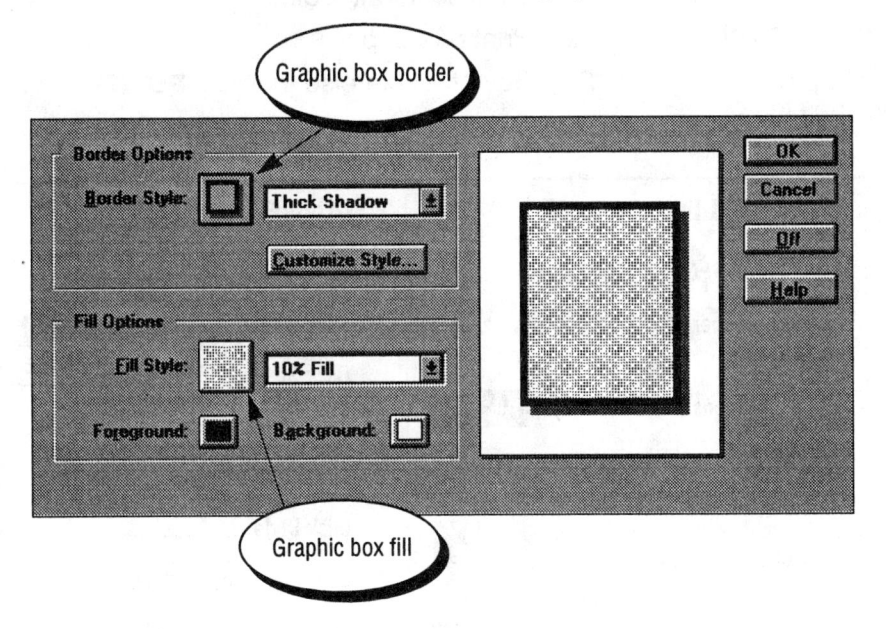

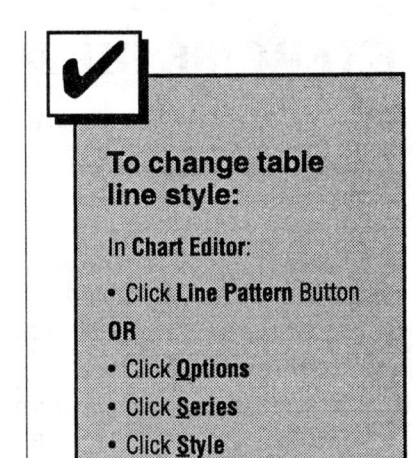

To change table line style:

In **Chart Editor**:

- Click **Line Pattern** Button

OR

- Click **Options**
- Click **Series**
- Click **Style**

In this exercise, you will create a new document containing a line chart.

Lesson 9 ■ Exercise 74   323

Lesson 9 ■ Exercise 74

EXERCISE DIRECTIONS:

1. Start with a clear screen.
2. Center the page from top to bottom.
3. Center the title in a 24 point sans serif font.
4. Type the first paragraph in a 14 point sans serif font.
5. Enter the Chart Editor and clear the sample information.
6. Enter the following information in the worksheet portion of the Chart Editor. Place the company names in the Legend section and the years in the Label section.

	'88	'89	'90	'91	'92	'93	'94
INFUND	4900	5700	5900	7100	7700	10800	11600
OUTFUND	5200	6200	6400	7800	8200	9200	8900

7. Select a line chart. Choose LINE03 in the Chart Gallery.
8. Redraw the chart.
9. Add a legend that displays on the bottom center, inside, and change the series font size to 18 point.
10. Change the color of the lines in the line chart to black.
11. Change the style of one of the lines to dotted.
12. Add a title, VALUE OF A $5,000 INVESTMENT, and subtitle, "Invested in 1987".
13. Return to the document window, saving the changes.
14. Select the chart and edit the box.
15. Position the box as a Paragraph Anchor, positioning the box horizontally 0" from the center of the paragraph and vertically .5" from the top of paragraph.
16. Size the box so it is sized to content.
17. Change the border of the box to a thick shadow.
18. Shade the box with a 10% shading.
19. Type the final paragraph in a 14 point sans serif font.
20. Change all paragraph justification to all.
21. Center the last two lines using a 24 point sans serif font, bold.
22. Print one copy.
23. Save the exercise; name it **FUND**.
24. Close the document window.

CHANGE LEGEND FONT SIZE

—IN THE CHART EDITOR—

1. Choose **O**ptions .... Alt + O
2. Click **L**egend .... E

   OR

   Click Legend button ....
3. Click Displa**y** Legend .... Y
4. Click **S**eries Font .... S
   and make font selections.
5. Click OK .... Enter

CHANGE LINE COLOR

—IN THE CHART EDITOR—

1. Click number of desired row in worksheet grid
2. Click **O**ptions .... Alt + O

   Click **S**eries .... S

   OR

   Click Line Color button ....
3. Click **C**olor C
4. Select desired color.
5. Repeat steps 2 and 3 for other lines
6. Click OK .... Enter

CHANGE LINE STYLE

—IN THE CHART EDITOR—

1. Click **O**ptions .... Alt + O

   Click **S**eries .... S

   OR

   Click Line Pattern button ....
2. Click **S**tyle .... S
3. Select desired line style.
5. Repeat steps 2 and 3 for other lines
6. Click OK .... Enter

...continued

CHANGE FILL STYLE OF GRAPHICS BOX

1. Select graphic box .... `Shift` + `F11`
2. Click **Border/Fill** .... `Alt` + `Shift` + `B`
   on Graphics Feature Bar

OR

Click *right* mouse button .... `B`
and select **B**order/Fill.

3. Click **F**ill Style button .... `F`

OR

Click drop-down Fill Style list.

4. Click desired style.
5. Click **OK** to return to document.... `Enter`

Mutual Fund Fact Sheet

If a mutual fund has a history of doing well, will it always do well? This is the most commonly asked question we get. See the answer for yourself.

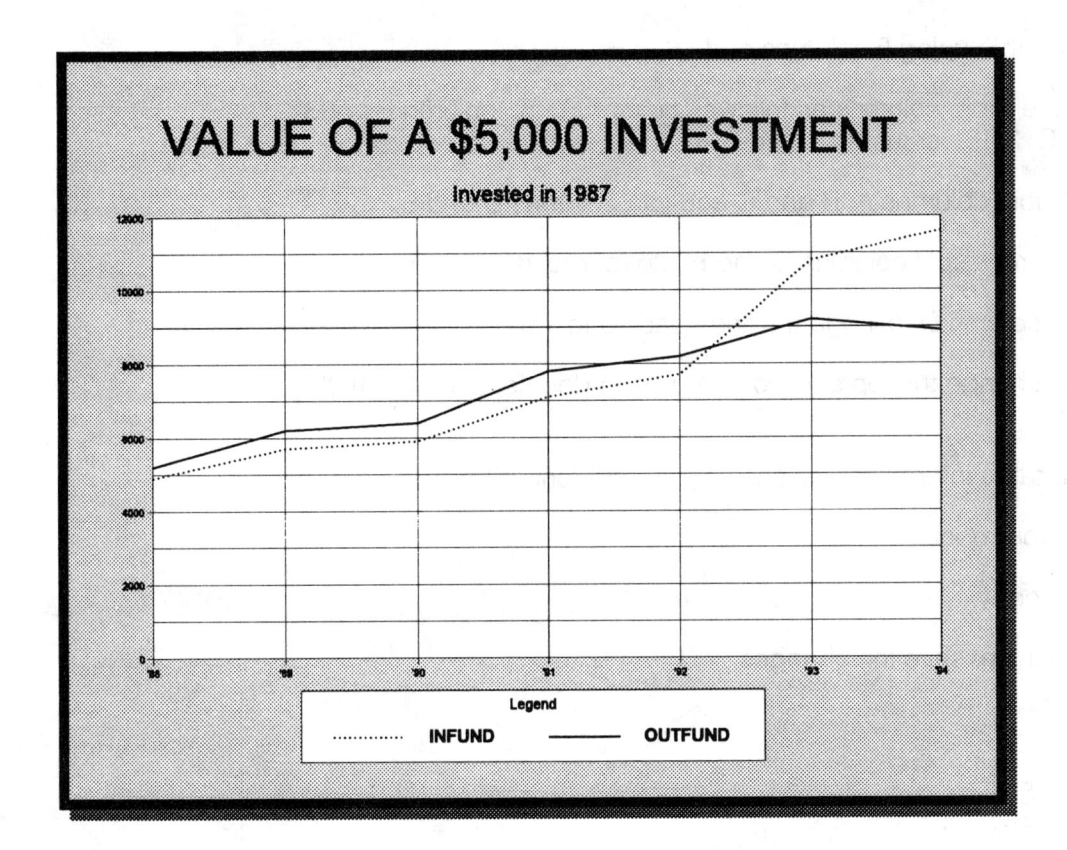

VALUE OF A $5,000 INVESTMENT
Invested in 1987

Legend: .... INFUND ——— OUTFUND

If you want expert help, call our investment advisory firm today.

SENSIBLE INVESTMENTS, INC.
1-800-STOCKUP

Lesson 9 ■ Exercise 74

LESSON 9
SUMMARY EXERCISE A

EXERCISE DIRECTIONS:

1. Start with a clear screen.
2. Open **FLOWLET**.
3. Save the file as **FLOWER5**.
4. Place cursor at end of file.
5. Set left margin to 1.75" and the right margin to .5"
6. Press the Enter key 4 times.
7. Change to a serif font, 24 point, bold and center ORDER FORM.
8. Press the Enter key 1 time.
9. Create a table using 5 columns and 16 rows.
10. Format the table columns as follows: column A, .5", column B, .563", column C, 3.13", columns D and E, 1".
11. In row 1, join columns A, B and C and join columns D and E.
12. In the last row, split columns D and E into four rows.
13. In row 1, column D, change the line spacing to 1.5.
14. In row 2, change the top and bottom lines to double, and add 10% shading.
15. Type the table information as shown in a serif font, 12 point.
16. Preview your document.
17. Print one copy.
18. Close your file; save the changes.

> In this exercise, you will add an invoice (table) to a letterhead. You will join and split cells, change lines, and add shading to cells.

The Perennial Potter

14 Highway 37
Middletown, NJ 07740
908-555-5555

ORDER FORM

SHIP TO:		Invoice #:
		Invoice Date:
		Shipping Date:
		Salesperson:
		Terms:

Qty	Item	Description	Price	Total

NO RISK GUARANTEE
If, for any reason, you are not fully satisfied with any item upon receipt, after planting, or once it grows and blooms, all you have to do is write us anytime before August 1. We will refund your money or replace the item--whichever you prefer.

Subtotal	
Tax	
Shipping	
TOTAL	

Lesson 9 ■ Exercise A

LESSON 9
SUMMARY EXERCISE B

EXERCISE DIRECTIONS:

1. Start with a clear screen.
2. Center the page from top to bottom.
3. Create the table shown on the right using 4 columns and 5 rows.
4. Place a double line border around the table.
5. Place a double line under the table title.
6. Join the cells in row 1 and add a 10% fill.
7. In row 1, center the title in a 24 point bold serif font.
8. In row 2 center and bold each column heading in a 12 point serif font.
9. Place a double line under the column titles.
10. In column 3, three different 3-D pie charts will be created from the information below. Type this information on the Chart Editor worksheet:

CELL C3:	**LEGEND**	**PIE**
	Govt. Bonds	85%
	Corporate Bonds	15%

CELL C4:	**LEGEND**	**PIE**
	Govt. Bonds	60%
	Corporate Bonds	40%

CELL C5:	**LEGEND**	**PIE**
	Govt. Bonds	68%
	Corporate Bonds	32%

    HINT: *Since the only difference in the three charts is the percentages, it is quicker to create one chart, copy and paste it into the other cells, and then place each chart individually into the Chart Editor to change the percentages.*

11. In the Label dialog box, for each pie change the orientation to horizontal and the value position on the inside.
    change the series font size to 30 point.
12. In the Legend dialog box, for each pie
    - place the legend horizontally in the top center (WordPerfect will not allow the legend to appear in a cell separate from the chart so the legend must be repeated in each cell.).
    - change the font size to 30 point.
13. Each graphic box should be treated as a Character Anchor.
14. Adjust table column widths, as desired.
15. The contents of the graphics boxes should be Sized to Contents.
16. Vertically center the cell contents in the body of the table for columns A, B, and D.
17. Preview your document.
18. Print one copy.
19. Save the exercise; name it **BOND**.
20. Close the document window.

> In this exercise, you will create a table containing 3 pie charts in 3 different cells.

BETTER BOND FUND

Bond Fund Type	Average Maturity	Asset Mix	Interest Rate Mix
Short Term	2.5 years	Govt. Bonds 85%, Corporate Bonds 15%	Low
Intermediate Term	7.4 years	Govt. Bonds 60%, Corporate Bonds 40%	Medium
Long Term	24.5 years	Govt. Bonds 68%, Corporate Bonds 32%	High

Lesson 9 ■ Exercise B

Lesson 10 ▪ Templates and Styles

EXERCISE 75
TEMPLATES

CONCEPTS:

- A **template** is a skeleton document which may contain formatting, graphics, and/or text. It may be used to create documents that are used over and over again. For example, you may create a memo form, set the word MEMO to 48 point bold, add a graphic and save it as form document. When you need to type a memo, you would use the memoform file you created previously.

- WordPerfect provides numerous predesigned templates, sometimes referred to as *ExpressDocs*. *See Appendix B for available WordPerfect templates*. These templates use a macro to prompt you for information.

- You may also fill in personal information such as your name, title, company name, address, phone and fax number in a dialog box form. When the template needs any of this information, it automatically pulls it from the personal information file it has saved for you.

A personal information dialog box appears below:

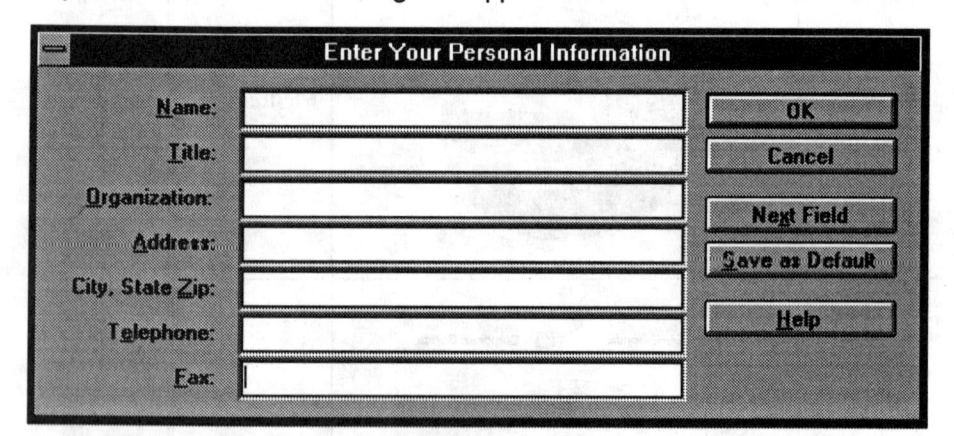

```
┌─────────── Enter Your Personal Information ───────────┐
│   Name:        [              ]              [ OK ]   │
│   Title:       [              ]              [Cancel] │
│   Organization:[              ]                       │
│   Address:     [              ]           [Next Field]│
│   City, State Zip: [          ]         [Save as Default]│
│   Telephone:   [              ]              [ Help ] │
│   Fax:         [              ]                       │
└───────────────────────────────────────────────────────┘
```

You will be prompted only to supply new information such as the recipient's name of a fax or memo, the subject or any other variable information.

Wherever a date is needed in the document, it will automatically be pulled from the computer's memory and inserted for you.

To access templates:
- Click **F**ile
- Click **T**emplates
- Select desired template

In this exercise, you will use templates to create a fax cover sheet and a memorandum. Once you insert your personal information, you need not do it again for other templates.

To quick access templates:
- Press **Ctrl + T**

EXERCISE DIRECTIONS:

Part I

1. Start with a clear screen.
2. Use the **FAX1** template to create the fax cover sheet.
3. Use the following information when prompted:

   RECIPIENT: Brittany Williams

   FAX: 777-7777

   NUMBER OF COPIES: 2

4. Fill in the Personal Information form using your own personal information.
5. Print one copy.
6. Close the document window (do not save this file).

Part II

1. Start with a clear screen.
2. Use the **MEMO4** template to create the memorandum form.
3. Use the following information when prompted:

   TO: Kristin McKay

   SUBJECT: New Product Announcement

4. Type the memo text below the square bullet as shown.

Lesson 10 ■ Exercise 75   331

Lesson 10 ▪ Exercise 75

PART I

To: Brittany Williams

Fax: (213) 777-7777

From: Your name

Date: September 9, 1994

Pages: 2, including cover sheet.

fax

From the desk of...

Your name
Your title
Your organization
Your address
Your city, state, zip

Your telephone number
Fax: Your fax number

PART II

To: Kristin McKay
From: Your name
Re: New Product Announcement
Date: January 5, 1995

- The New Product Development Committee will meet on Thursday at 10 a.m. in my office to discuss the details of the MicroForm announcement.

    We will need to prepare a press release later this month and plan for promotions. Please bring development files with you.

M·E·M·O

ACCESS TEMPLATES

Click Template Button ....

OR

1. Click **File** .... Alt + F
2. Click **Templates** .... T
3. Double-click desired template.
4. Enter information when prompted.

Lesson 10 ▪ Exercise 75

Lesson 10 ▪ Templates and Styles

EXERCISE 76
USE A STYLE

CONCEPTS:

- The **style feature** lets you combine multiple formatting commands and/or text, graphics and lines into a *style code*. This *style code* can then be applied to a word, a page, or an entire document. Using styles ensures consistency of formatting.

  For example, suppose you are working on a report and you want to format each subheading using the same font style and size. You also want to leave a specified amount of space before and after each subheading. Rather than apply the formatting each time you typed the subheading, you could create a *style,* then turn on that style for each subheading.

  If you want to change the formatting of your subheading, for example, you could edit the style. Every place where you used the style would automatically change to reflect the edit. In this example, every subheading would instantly update to include the new formatting.

- Styles are particularly useful each time you create documents such as menus, newsletters and reports, where consistency in formatting headlines, quotes, or special menu items is desired.

- You can create styles based on existing text that you have already formatted, or you can create a new style before text is typed. Or, you can use several pre-defined styles that come with the WordPerfect program.

Use WordPerfect's Pre-Defined Styles

- When Styles is accessed from the menu, a style list dialog box appears listing the pre-designed styles available.

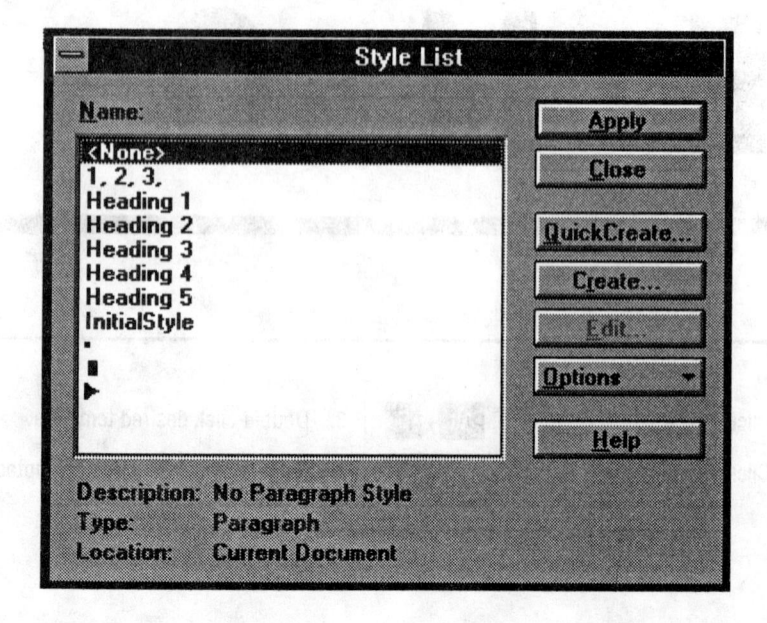

To use pre-defined styles:
- Click Styles button on the Button Bar.

OR

Press **Alt + F8**

OR

- Click **Layout**
- Click **Styles**
- Select desired style
- Click **Apply**

334

- Note that the selection bar is defaulted to <None> since none of the styles are initially applied to your text. When you wish to turn off a style, select <None> from the Style List.

- As each selection is highlighted, a description of that style is indicated at the bottom of the dialog box.

- To apply a pre-defined style, place your insertion point before the text (before typing) or on the text (after typing) where the style is to be applied. Select the style from the Style List dialog box, and click Apply.

> In this exercise, you will apply a pre-defined style to the title and subheadings of a short report.

Lesson 10 ■ Exercise 76

EXERCISE DIRECTIONS:

1. Start with a clear screen.

2. Set left and right margins to .5"

3. With your insertion point at the top of the screen,

   📁 Open **WATCH** from data disk; save as **WATCH1**.

   or

   ⌨ Type the exercise exactly as shown in illustration A.

4. Right align the title and subtitle. Press Enter 4 times after the subtitle.

5. With your insertion point to the left of the subheading, *Preparing for a Trip*, create three newspaper columns.

6. Set column widths as follows:

   column 1:   1.75"

   column 2:   2.58"

   column 3:   2.58"

   space between each column: 0.3"

7. With your insertion point to the left of the subheading, *Preparing for a Trip*, press Ctrl + Enter.

   ■ NOTE: This will force all text to the second and third columns, leaving the first column blank, as shown in the illustration of the result.

8. Using the pre-defined styles, set the title, subtitle, and subheadings as indicated in the exercise.

9. • Import the **MARSH.WPG** graphic in the first column.

   • Remove the border from around the graphic.

   • Position the graphic at the bottom of the first column.

10. Create a drop capital for the first letter in the first paragraph of the second column (use a script or Old English font).

11. Copy the graphic and position it at the bottom of the third column.

12. Create a dashed page border.

13. Preview the exercise.

14. Print one copy.

15. 📁 Close the file; save the changes.

    or

    ⌨ Save the file; name it **WATCH1**.

16. Close the document screen.

USE A PRE-DEFINED STYLE

Alt + F8

1. Place insertion point on paragraph to receive style (after typing text)

OR

Place insertion point before text to receive style (before typing text)

2. Click Layout .... Alt + L

3. Click Styles .... S

4. Highlight style to be applied.

5. Click Apply .... Alt + A

ILLUSTRATION A

Heading 1 — TRAVEL GUIDE 94 → Right Align →
       2 — Bird Watching on Cape Cod

3 — Preparing for a Trip

The Cape Code Bird Club and the Massachusetts Audubon Society have compiled a listing of birding sites on the cape entitled, *Birding on the Cape*. This booklet is available in Cape bookshops and from the Massachusetts Audubon Society, Bay Wildlife Sanctuary Society, Wellfleet, MA 02631.

4 — The Birdwatcher's Store,
Route 16A, Orleans, MA 02456, serves as an information exchange for Cape birders. This establishment offers binoculars and spotting scopes, bird books, prints and photographs, food, feeders and T-shirts of all kinds. Binoculars may be rented.

3 — Tours

4 — Wellfleet Bay Wildlife Sanctuary,
West Road, off Route 6, South Wellfleet. Admission to the sanctuary, nonmembers: $3, $2 for children 6 to 15. It offers an extensive program of sanctuary walks, children's and family programs, summer day camps and field schools for adults.

4 — Cape Cod Museum of Natural History,
Route 16A, Brewster. Admission: $4, $2 for children 6 to 14. In addition to exhibits on nature and the environment on the Cape, the museum offers walks on its 80 acres.

3 — Other Birding Sites

4 — Morris Island,
in Chatham, opposite Monomoy, houses the headquarters for the wildlife refuge but offers no direct access to the island and parking is sparse.

4 — Coast Guard Beach,
National Seashore, reached by walking or bicycle trail, 1.6 miles from Salt Pond Visitor center, has *No Trespassing* posted on its back porch and is fenced for most of the summer season, as the rangers try to guard the tern and piping plover colonies.

4 — Fame Hill,
off Route 6, National Seashore, has a trail through a grassy field that recalls the Cape's agricultural past. Many fall migrants pass this way. Fame Hill is an excellent lookout for all the shorebirds.

4 — Hiker State Park,
Route 6A, Brewster. The 1,750 acres of this recreation area include five freshwater ponds, bicycle and walking trails, a large contingent of migrating and wintering ducks, a variety of nesting land birds and notable populations of great horned and screech owls.

RESULT

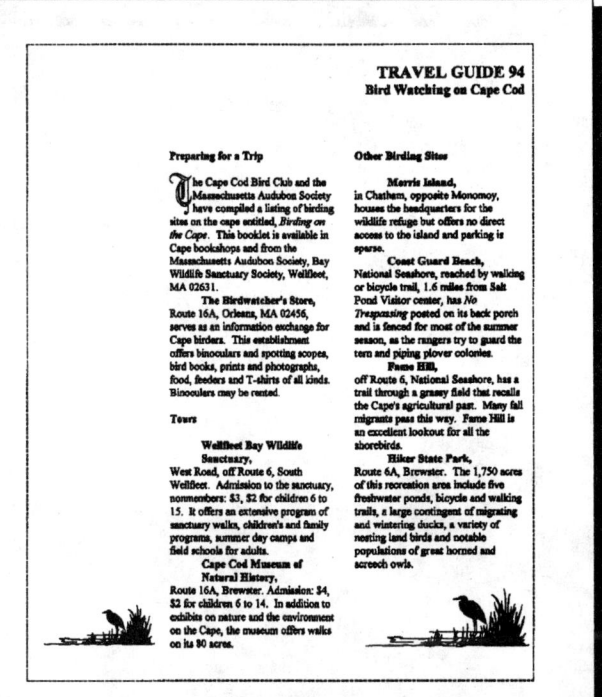

Lesson 10 ■ Exercise 76   337

Lesson 10 ▪ Templates and Styles

EXERCISE 77

CREATE AND SAVE A NEW STYLE

CONCEPTS:

- In the previous exercise you used WordPerfect's pre-defined styles. You can, however, create your own style.

- Suppose you wanted to create a contents page like the exercise shown on the right. You might create a style for each page number, a style for the article titles and a style for the description text below the article titles.

- To create a style, select <u>S</u>tyles from the <u>L</u>ayout main menu and click Create.

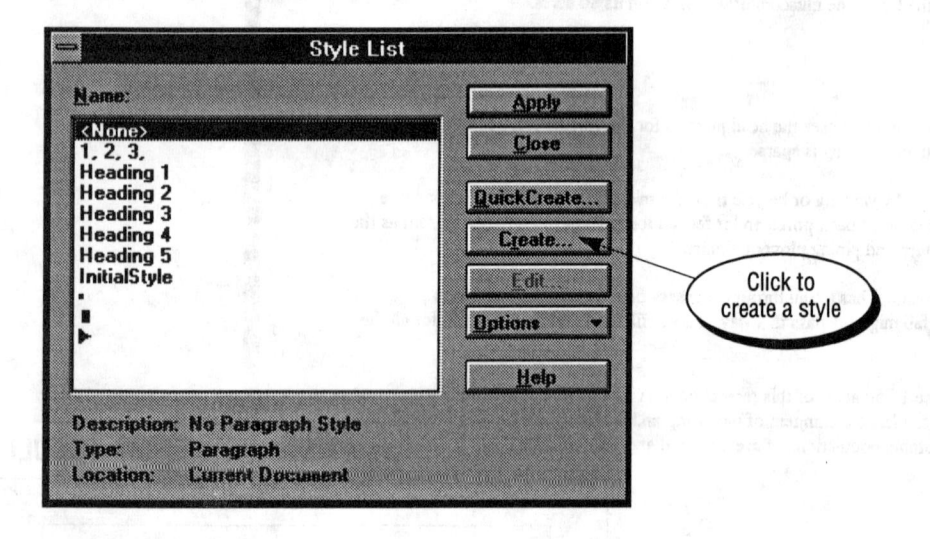

Style List dialog box shown with Name list including <None>, 1, 2, 3, Heading 1, Heading 2, Heading 3, Heading 4, Heading 5, InitialStyle. Buttons: Apply, Close, QuickCreate..., Create..., Edit..., Options, Help. Description: No Paragraph Style; Type: Paragraph; Location: Current Document. Callout: "Click to create a style"

To create a style:

- Click Styles button on Button Bar
OR
- Press **Alt + F8**
- Click **L**ayout
- Click **S**tyles
- Click **C**reate
- Type style name
- Type description (optional)
- Enter style in Contents
- Click **OK**

338

- In the Styles Editor dialog box which follows, you name, describe and create the new style.

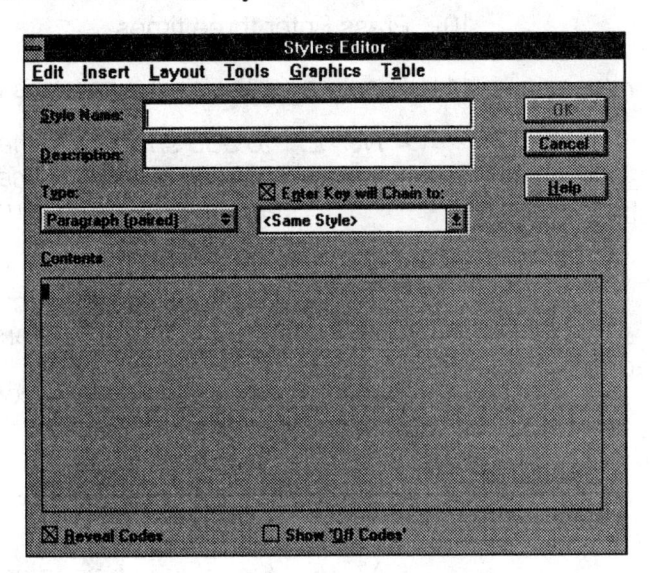

> **To apply a style:**
> - Place insertion point in paragraph to receive style
>
> OR
> - Click where style is to begin.
>
> OR
> - Select text to apply a character style
> - Press **Alt + F8**
> - Click desired style
> - Click **Apply**

Style Types

- Note the *Type* drop-down list in the Styles Editor dialog box. When you create a style, you must indicate the style type.

- There are three types of styles: character, paragraph and document. Paragraph is the default style type.

  - **Character styles** (called *paired styles* because they have a beginning code and an ending code applied to the desired text) apply the style to small blocks of selected text or text you are about to type.

  - **Paragraph styles** (also called *paired styles*) apply the style to the entire paragraph containing the insertion point.

  - **Document styles** (called *open styles* because they have a beginning code, but no ending code) affect the entire document.

- The *Enter Key will Chain to* option allows you to specify how hard returns affect the text after the style is applied. Choose what style you would like applied following this one when you press the Enter key. If you do not want any style applied, select <None>.

- To actually create the style, enter the codes for that style in the Contents box using the menus at the top of the Style Editor dialog box.

- After the style has been created, click OK and the style will be included in the Style List dialog box.

> In this exercise, you will create three styles: for the page number, for the article title and for the article description. You will link the styles so that each time you press enter, you activate another style. You will then apply the styles to create a Table of Contents magazine page.

Applying Styles

- When you want to apply a paired style (character or paragraph), either select the text you want the style applied to and choose the style from the Style list, or choose the style from the Style list and type the text.

- Styles are only available in the document in which you created them. Therefore, if you want to use the styles at another time, you need to save them. In the next exercise, you will learn how to save and retrieve styles.

EXERCISE DIRECTIONS:

1. Start with a clear screen.

2. Create the following paragraph style for the page number; name it **PN**:

   Set font to sans serif (use Swis721 BlkEx BT, if available) 24 point bold with a 60% shade.

3. Create the following style for the article title; name it **ART**:

   - Insert an indent (click Layout, Paragraph, Indent).
   - Set font to sans serif 18 point bold.

4. Create the following style for description text; name it **DT**:

   - Insert an indent (click Layout, Paragraph, Indent).
   - Set font to sans serif 12 point italic.
   - ■ NOTE: To chain one style to another, you will need to edit each style and indicate in the **Enter Key will Chain to** drop down list, to what style you wish Enter to be chained.

5. Select PN from the Style List and select Edit.
   - Chain Enter to ART.

6. Select ART from the Style List and select Edit.
   - Chain Enter to DT.

7. Select DT from the Style List and select Edit.
   - Chain Enter to PN.
   - Close the Style List.

8. Use the default margins.

9. Type and right align the magazine title in sans serif 48 point bold. Type and right align the subtitle in sans serif 14 point. Use special characters (5,115 and 5,116) between words as shown.

10. Press Enter three times.

11. Create a table using 2 columns and 2 rows.
    - ■ NOTE: To add shading to the second column, a table format, rather than a column format, is used.

12. Center INSTRUCTION in the first column and FEATURES in the second column in sans serif 14 point. Set them to reverse.

13. Place insertion point in the second row, first column.

14. Apply the PN style and type the first column of text.
    - ■ NOTE: Since you chained each style to the other, each time you press Enter, a new style will be applied for each level of text.

15. After completing the first column of text, click in the second column, second row.

16. Apply the PN style and type the second column of text.

17. Shade cell B2 10% gray.

18. Create a button page border. Remove all table lines.

19. Import **GOLFSWNG.WPG**.
    - Set the width to 1.90" and the height to 2.30".
    - Remove the border from around the graphic.
    - Position the graphic as shown.

20. Preview the file.

21. Print one copy.

22. Save the file; name it **GOLFPG**.

23. Close the document window.

GOLF JOURNAL

August 1994▲Volume 27▼Number 15

INSTRUCTION

22
Tom Water's Shortcuts
How he gets up and down so well.

38
Fast Fixes
Contact the grass first for a soft lob.

67
Which Swing Fault Do You Have?
Your follow-through answers the question.

88
Tricks of the Champs
Four PGA winners share their stroke-saving secrets.

FEATURES

50
Equipment Specials
Just in time for your next tournament, new equipment hits your golf shop.

63
Golf Is Meant For Walking
You'll derive many health benefits—from dropping weight to increasing energy.

118
Travel Destinations
Where are those golf hide-aways?

138
Robins at the U.S. Open
Read what really happened.

CREATE A STYLE:

Alt + F8

1. Click Styles button on Button Bar.

    OR

    Click **L**ayout.......................... Alt + L

    Click **S**tyles .... S

2. Click **C**reate............................ C
3. Type style name.
4. Type a description (optional).
5. Click in Contents window.
6. Type desired style (font style, size, tabs, indents, etc.)
7. Click **OK** .... Enter

LINK STYLE TO ANOTHER USING ENTER

1. In Style List dialog box,

    Click style name to be linked.

2. Click **E**dit................................. Alt + E
3. *Click Enter Key will Chain to* list box.
4. Select style to be linked *to*.

    Repeat procedure to link to another style, if desired.

5. Click **OK** .... Enter

APPLY A STYLE

1. Set insertion point or select text as follows:

    – To apply *paragraph* style:

    • place insertion point in paragraph to receive style

    OR

    • select desired paragraphs.

    – To apply *character* style:

    • select text to receive style.

    – To apply *document* style:

    • place insertion point where you want style to take effect.

2. Press **Alt + F8**....................... Alt + F8
3. Click desired style.
4. Click **A**pply............................. Alt + A

Lesson 10 ■ Exercise 77   341

Lesson 10 • Templates and Styles

EXERCISE 78

■ USE QUICKCREATE ■ SAVE STYLES

CONCEPTS:

Use QuickCreate

■ QuickCreate lets you build your style from existing text. After you have formatted a paragraph or character, place your insertion point in that paragraph, open the Style List dialog box, and click QuickCreate. In the dialog box which follows, type a style name and style description (optional).

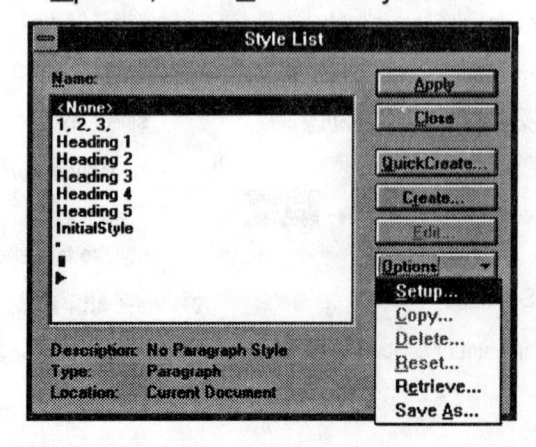

To use QuickCreate:
- Place insertion point in paragraph or text containing desired style.
- Click Styles Button on Button Bar
OR
- Press **Alt + F8**
- Click **QuickCreate**
- Type style name
- Type description (optional)
- Click **OK**

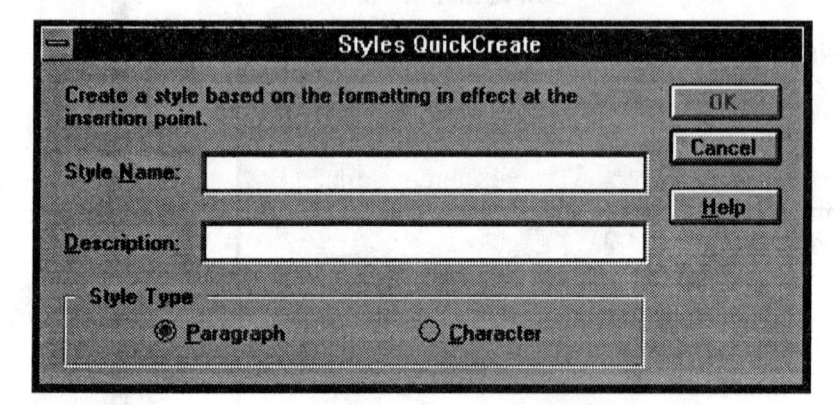

The new style you created appears on the Style List and may be applied to text as you did previously.

Save Styles

■ As indicated in the previous exercise, styles are only available in the document in which you created them. You must save the styles and retrieve them later to use them in another document. If you are creating more than one style in a document, you save the set of styles in the style list box, not each individual style.

■ To save styles, click Options, Save As in the Style list.

To save styles:
- Press **Alt + F8**
- Click **Options**
- Click **Save As**
- Type style filename
- Click **OK**

342

- You must specify the path, and filename of the styles you are saving in the Save Styles To... dialog box. If you wish to save only styles you created, select User Styles. If you used WordPerfect styles and you want to save them along with those you created, select Both. If you wish to save only WordPerfect styles, select System Styles.

- If you do not specify a path, WordPerfect will save your files in the WPWIN60\TEMPLATE subdirectory.

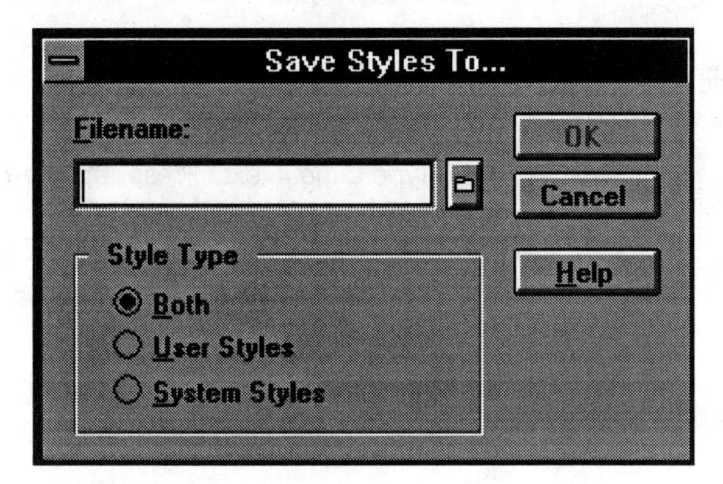

> In this exercise, you will create styles for a film festival flyer. In a later exercise, you will retrieve the styles to create another flyer.

NOTE: To avoid confusing style files with other WordPerfect files, you might give styles a .sty filename extension.

Lesson 10 ■ Exercise 78

EXERCISE DIRECTIONS:

1. Start with a clear screen.

2. Create the following style for the reverse date line; name it **DATELINE**:

   - Set font to sans serif 14 point (use OzHandicraft BT, if available).

   - Set paragraph to reverse (use a macro-- click Tools, Macro, Play, click drop down list, click REVERSE.WCM).

   - Chain to <None>

3. Create the following style for the movie description; name it **MOVDES**:

   - Insert an indent.

   - Set font to serif 12 point (use BernhardMod BT, if available).

   - Set justification to *full*.

4. Create the following style for the movie title; name it **MOVTITLE**:

   - Insert a hard return.

   - Set justification to *center*.

   - Set font to serif 18 point bold (use BernhardMod BT, if available).

5. Set top and bottom margins to .5".

6. With your insertion point at the top of the screen, type *Madri Film Festival* as shown in sans serif 48 point bold.

   - Type *June* as shown in the same font face in 18 point. (*Use OzHandicraft BT font face, if available.*)

7. Using QuickCreate, create a style for the title (Madri Film Festival); name it **FILFES**. Save the style.

8. Save the styles you have created; name it **MOVIEALL.STY**.

9. Press Enter four times.

10. Create a table using 2 columns and 8 rows. Set column 1 width to 4" and column 2 width to 2.5"

11. Join rows 1,3,5 and 7. (Highlight row, click Table, Join, Cell)

12. Position insertion point in row 1.

    - Apply the DATELINE style.

    - Type *June 4* text. Press Tab key 7 times and type the director's name.

    ■ NOTE: *In a table, the Tab key does not advance text; you must use Ctrl + Tab instead.*

13. Position insertion point in row 2, column 1.

    - Apply the MOVEDES style.

    - Type the movie description.

    - Position insertion point in row 2, column 2.

    - Apply the MOVTITLE style.

    - Type the movie title.

14. Complete the exercise, applying the remaining styles.

14. Remove the table lines; create a dotted table border.

15. Import **CAMERA.WPG** graphic (created earlier in Draw lesson) and position as shown.

16. Preview the file.

17. Print one copy.

18. Save the file name it **FILM**.

19. Close the document window.

MADRI FILM FESTIVAL

June

| June 4 | Directed by G. Toradore of Cinema Paridso |

This sentimental film centers on an aging Sicilian widower who decides to pay surprise visits to his five grown children. As he journeys from city to city to find that everybody is not fine, the film reveals a modern Italy.

EVERYBODY'S FINE

| June 11 | Directed by J. Jarmusch |

Described by Jarmusch as a "neo-bete-noir, part nightmare, part fairy tale, the two characters meet a hilariously guileless Italian tourist in jail, who leads them on a jail break inspired by American prison movies he has seen.

IT'S THE LAW

| June 18 | Directed by Elio Perti |

A thriller with Gian Voltare. A police inspector commits a murder, then plants self-incriminating evidence, thinking himself above suspicion.

EVIDENCE

| June 25 | Directed by Daren Argentio |

Now classic art-horror thriller. Jennie Harris stars as an American schoolgirl in a European ballet academy who discovers the staff is a coven of witches.

BREW

USE QUICKCREATE

Alt + F8

1. Place insertion point in paragraph or text that contains a style you desire.
2. Click Styles Button............ [Styles] on Button Bar.

   OR

   Click **L**ayout .... Alt + L

   Click **S**tyles .... S
3. Click **Q**uickCreate .... Alt + Q
4. Type style filename.
5. Type description (optional).
6. Click OK .... Enter

SAVE STYLES

Alt + F8

1. Click Styles Button............ [Styles] on Button Bar.

   OR

   Click **L**ayout .... Alt + L

   Click **S**tyles .... S
2. Click **O**ptions .... Alt + O
3. Click Save **A**s .... A
4. Type style filename.
5. Select type of style to save:
   - **B**oth .... B
   - **U**ser Styles .... U
   - **S**ystem Styles .... S
5. Click OK .... Enter

Lesson 10 ■ Exercise 78   345

Lesson 10 ▪ Templates and Styles

EXERCISE 79
EDIT STYLES

CONCEPTS:

- Suppose, after you create your style and apply it, you decide that the font size you used was too large.

- To change a feature of your style, select the style from the Style List and select <u>E</u>dit.

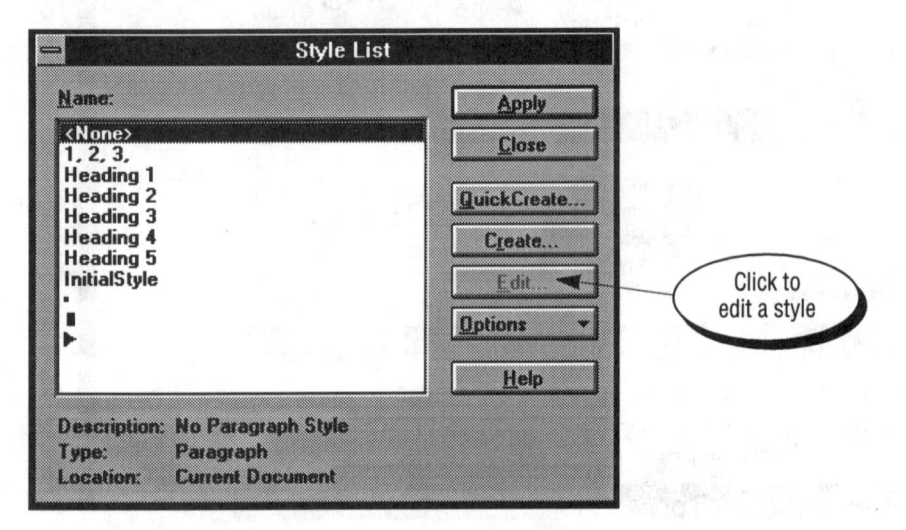

To edit a style:
- Press **Alt + F8**
- Highlight style to be edited.
- Click **Edit**
- Add or delete style elements in the Contents box.
- Click **OK**

- In the Styles Editor dialog box, you can add or delete any elements of the style. To delete an element, drag the code out of the Contents box. To add a code, click in the Contents box and use the procedures described in Exercise 77.

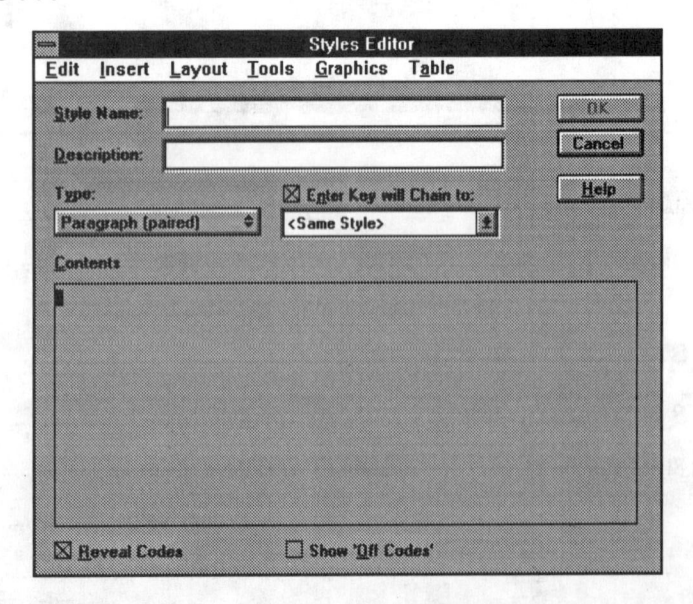

In this exercise, you will edit the style used for the Golf Journal contents page.

- After clicking OK, all text where that particular style was used will change to reflect the edited style.

346

EXERCISE DIRECTIONS:

1. Start with a clear screen.
2. Open **GOLFPG**.
3. Edit the PN (page number) style as follows:
   - change the font size to 28 points with a 40% shade.
   - remove the bold.
4. Edit the ART style by changing the font to bold italics.
5. Print one copy.
6. Save the file as **GOLFPG1**.
7. Close the document window.

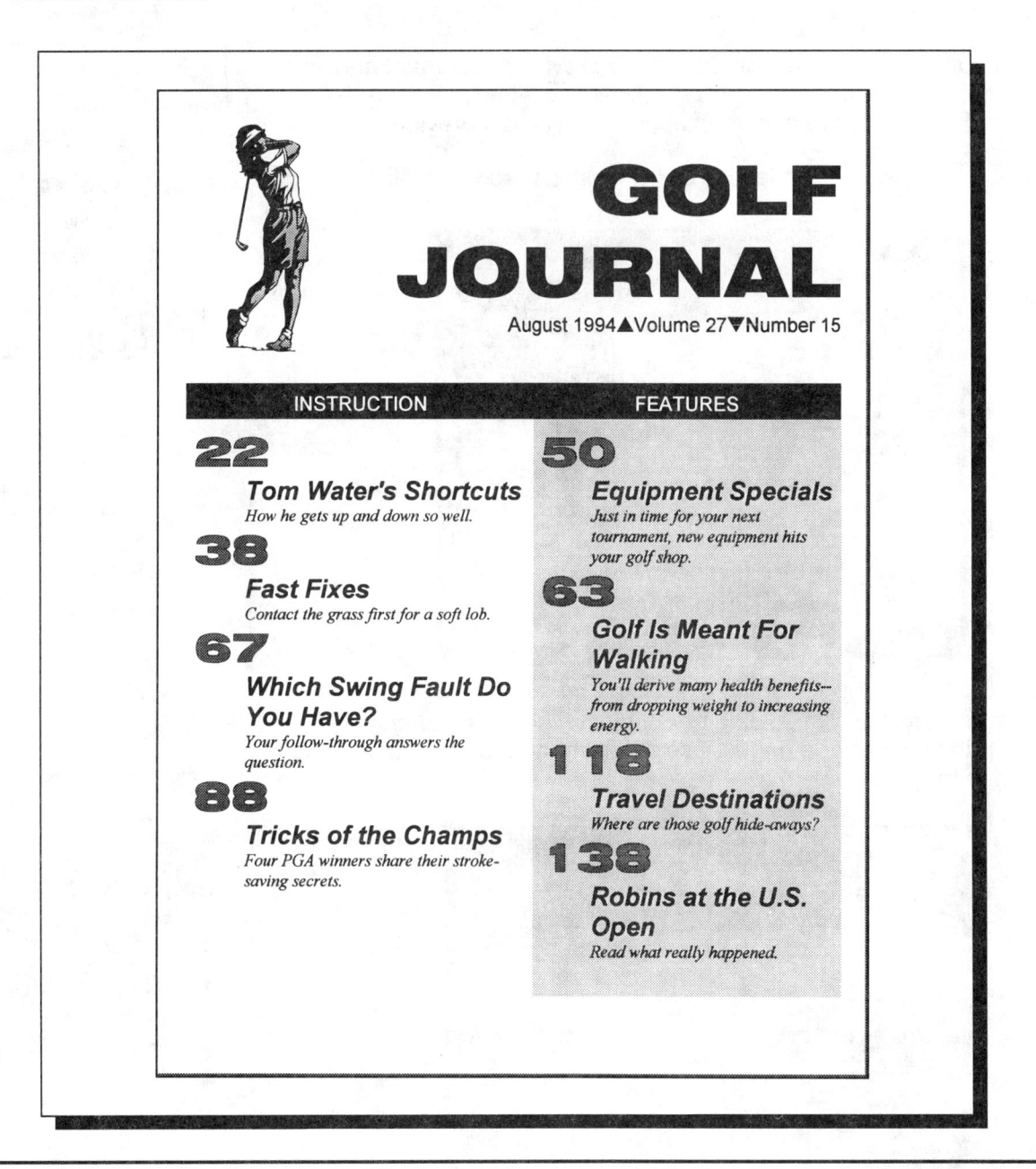

GOLF JOURNAL

August 1994▲Volume 27▼Number 15

INSTRUCTION

22 Tom Water's Shortcuts
How he gets up and down so well.

38 Fast Fixes
Contact the grass first for a soft lob.

67 Which Swing Fault Do You Have?
Your follow-through answers the question.

88 Tricks of the Champs
Four PGA winners share their stroke-saving secrets.

FEATURES

50 Equipment Specials
Just in time for your next tournament, new equipment hits your golf shop.

63 Golf Is Meant For Walking
You'll derive many health benefits— from dropping weight to increasing energy.

118 Travel Destinations
Where are those golf hide-aways?

138 Robins at the U.S. Open
Read what really happened.

EDIT A STYLE

Alt + F8

1. Open the document where style was used.
2. Click Styles Button.......... on Button Bar.

OR

Click **L**ayout .... Alt + L

Click **S**tyles .... S

3. Click **E**dit .... E
4. Click in Contents box.

5. Drag off desired code.

OR

Use menus to add new codes.

6. Click **OK** .... Enter
7. Click **A**pply .... Alt + A

Lesson 10 ■ Exercise 79   347

Lesson 10 • Templates and Styles

EXERCISE 80
RETRIEVE STYLES

CONCEPTS:

- If you want to use a style that you saved in a previous document and apply it to the current document, you must retrieve it into the current document's Style List. You may then apply it as you did previously.

- To retrieve a style, select Retrieve from the Options drop down list.

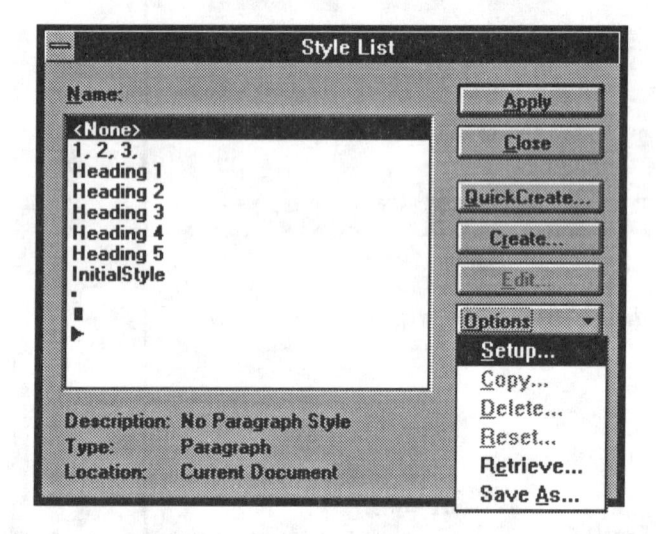

To retrieve a style:
- Press **Alt + F8**
- Click **Options**
- Click **Retrieve**
- Type filename to retrieve.
- Click **OK**

- In the *Retrieve Styles From..* dialog box, indicate the filename and style type to be retrieved (enter a path or use the list button to find the desired file) you wish to retrieve.

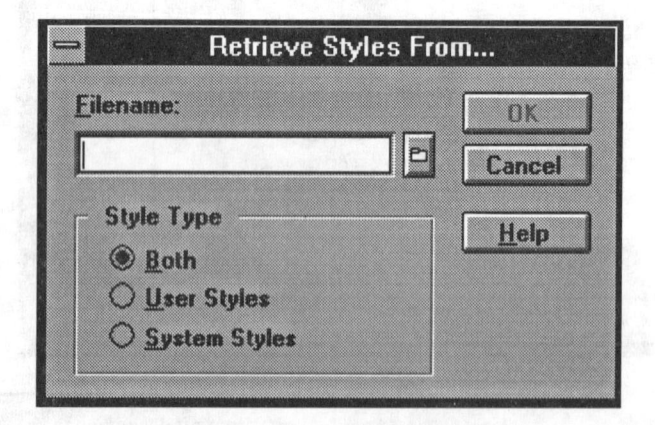

In this exercise, you will retrieve styles created earlier to create another film festival flyer.

- You might get a message that asks if you wish to overwrite current styles. This message appears if one or more styles in the current document have the same names as the styles in the file you are retrieving.

- If you overwrite a file, it will only affect the style attached to the current document.

CONTINUED...

EXERCISE DIRECTIONS:

1. Start with a clear screen.
2. Set top and bottom margins to .5".
3. Open FILM.
4. Retrieve **MOVIEALL.STY** style.
5. With your insertion point at the top of the screen, apply the FILFES style and type the heading as shown.
   - Type *July* using the same font face in 18 point.
6. Create a table using 2 columns and 8 rows. Set column 1 width to 4" and column 2 width to 2.5". Join rows 1, 3, 5 and 7.
   - NOTE: *If you saved the column format as a style in exercise 79, retrieve it.*
7. Position insertion point in row 1.
   - Apply the DATELINE style.
   - Type July 2 text. Press Ctrl + Tab three times and type the director's name.
8. Position insertion point in row 2, column 2.
   - Apply the MOVEDES style.
   - Type the movie description.
9. Position insertion point in row 2, column 2.
   - Apply the MOVTITLE style.
   - Type the movie title.
10. Compete the exercise, applying the appropriate styles.
11. Remove the table lines, create a dotted table border.
12. Import **CAMERA.WPG** and position as shown.
13. Preview the file.
14. Print one copy.
15. Save the file; name it **FILM1**.
16. Close the document window.

MADRI FILM FESTIVAL

July

July 2 — Directed by Gina Weiner

An anarchist peasant falls in love with an undesirable while plotting the assassination of the country's dictator in this fascinating view of fascism during the 1930's. Comic and tragic, a classic.

ANARCHY

July 9 — Directed by Carlos Cantini

Award winning film from director Carlos Cantini. A breathtaking thriller about a ten-year-old boy and his quest to escape from a dark world where violence has become a way of life.

THE INNOCENT

July 16 — Directed by Gino Richetti

When a single parent is arrested, a young military officer takes her two children to a home. A silent friendship develops among them. Both hard-edged and heartwarming.

THE LITTLE ONES

July 23 — Directed by Sergio Franco

This film features Barry Fondue, Claudia Cardi, and Charles Rumson. Mythic tale about the coming of the railroad and the exacting of revenge with its larger than life characters. A classic western.

THE NEW WEST

RETRIEVE STYLES

Alt + F8

1. Click Styles Button on Button Bar.

   OR

2. Click **L**ayout .... Alt + L

   Click **S**tyles .... S

   Click **O**ptions .... Alt + O

3. Click R**e**trieve .... E
4. Type style filename to retrieve.
5. Click **OK** .... Enter

Lesson 10 ■ Exercise 80

LESSON 10
SUMMARY EXERCISE A

EXERCISE DIRECTIONS:

Part I
1. Start with a clear screen.
2. Use the **CERTIF2** template the create an award.
   Use your name as the recipient when prompted.
   Use For Outstanding Achievement in Design as the award reason.
3. Update the Personal Information dialog box with your own personal information.
4. Print one copy.
5. Close the document window.

Part II
1. Start with a clear screen.
2. Use **BUSCARD1** template to create your own business card.
   - NOTE: WordPerfect will insert your personal information in the relevant places on the card.
3. Print one copy.
   - NOTE: To make business cards from this printout, give this sheet to a printer who will print it for you using high quality paper. The printer will also properly cut the cards.

In this exercise, you will create a certificate and business cards using a pre-designed templates.

PART I

Certificate of Achievement

for

Your name

For Outstanding Achievement in Design

Date _____ Signed _____

PART II

YOUR ORGANIZATION	**YOUR ORGANIZATION**
YOUR NAME YOUR TITLE	**YOUR NAME** YOUR TITLE
YOUR ADDRESS YOUR CITY, STATE AND ZIP	YOUR ADDRESS YOUR CITY, STATE AND ZIP
YOUR PHONE — FAX: YOUR FAX	YOUR PHONE — FAX: YOUR FAX
YOUR ORGANIZATION	**YOUR ORGANIZATION**
YOUR NAME YOUR TITLE	**YOUR NAME** YOUR TITLE
YOUR ADDRESS YOUR CITY, STATE AND ZIP	YOUR ADDRESS YOUR CITY, STATE AND ZIP
YOUR PHONE — FAX: YOUR FAX	YOUR PHONE — FAX: YOUR FAX
YOUR ORGANIZATION	**YOUR ORGANIZATION**
YOUR NAME YOUR TITLE	**YOUR NAME** YOUR TITLE
YOUR ADDRESS YOUR CITY, STATE AND ZIP	YOUR ADDRESS YOUR CITY, STATE AND ZIP
YOUR PHONE — FAX: YOUR FAX	YOUR PHONE — FAX: YOUR FAX
YOUR ORGANIZATION	**YOUR ORGANIZATION**
YOUR NAME YOUR TITLE	**YOUR NAME** YOUR TITLE
YOUR ADDRESS YOUR CITY, STATE AND ZIP	YOUR ADDRESS YOUR CITY, STATE AND ZIP
YOUR PHONE — FAX: YOUR FAX	YOUR PHONE — FAX: YOUR FAX
YOUR ORGANIZATION	**YOUR ORGANIZATION**
YOUR NAME YOUR TITLE	**YOUR NAME** YOUR TITLE
YOUR ADDRESS YOUR CITY, STATE AND ZIP	YOUR ADDRESS YOUR CITY, STATE AND ZIP
YOUR PHONE — FAX: YOUR FAX	YOUR PHONE — FAX: YOUR FAX

Lesson 10 ▪ Exercise A

LESSON 10
SUMMARY EXERCISE B

EXERCISE DIRECTIONS:

1. Start with a clear screen.
2. Create the following paragraph style for the food name; name it **FOOD**:
   - Center and set font to Blackletter 686 BT (if available) 22 point. If the suggested font is unavailable, use another serif font.
3. Create the following paragraph style for food description; name it **DESCR**:
   - Center and set font to serif 10 point italic
4. Create the following paragraph style for food price; name it **PRICE**:
   - Center and set font to sans serif 10 point bold.
5. Chain one style to another. (Edit each style and indicate in the **Enter Key will Chain to** drop down list, to what style you wish Enter to be chained).
6. Use the default margins.
7. Create a table using 2 columns and one row.
8. With your insertion point in the first column, press Enter enough times to expand the column to fill the page.
9. Size the first column to approximately 1.75" and shade it black.
10. Type F R E D ' S vertically as shown in Blackletter 686 BT (if available) 65 point. Shade the letters white. Center the name vertically and each letter horizontally within the column.
11. Type and center **famous fish food restaurant** in the second column as shown using the same font used for FRED'S in 48 point.
12. Create a 3" horizontal line using a 0.138" thickness and position it as shown.
13. Enter once.
14. Type the date in serif 10 point italic.
15. Enter three times.
16. Apply the FOOD style and type the first food item. Press Enter once.
    - NOTE: Since you chained each style to the other, each time you press Enter, a new style will be applied for each level of text.
17. Type the remaining menu items.
18. Apply the DESCR style to the last line of text.
19. Create an extra thick table border.
20. Preview the file.
21. Print one copy.
22. Save the file; name it **FISHFOOD**.

In this exercise, you will create and apply styles for menu.

FRED'S

Famous Fish Food Restaurant

Friday, February 14

Shrimp Scampi

Sauteed in Garlic and Oil

15.95

Flounder Lemone

Broiled in Lemon and Wine

12.00

Lobster Salad

Cold Lobster on Bed of Greens with Vinegarette Dressing

22.00

Calamari

Lighly Battered and Fried with Red Sauce

13.00

Salmon LeFred

Salmon with Dill and Caper Sauce

15.00

All entrees served with vegetable and rice.

Appendix A

TEMPLATES

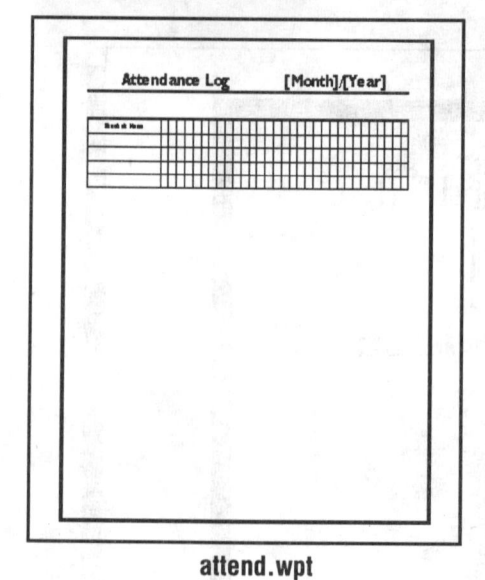

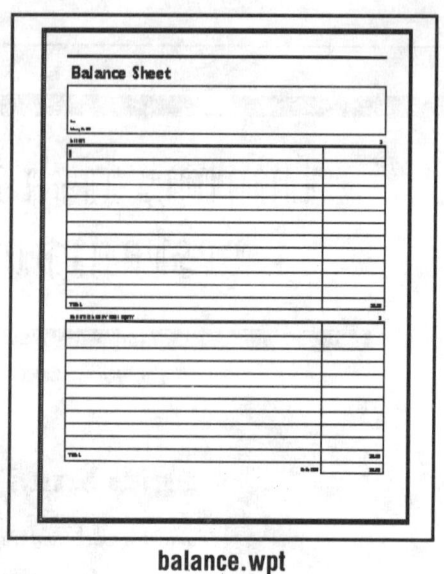

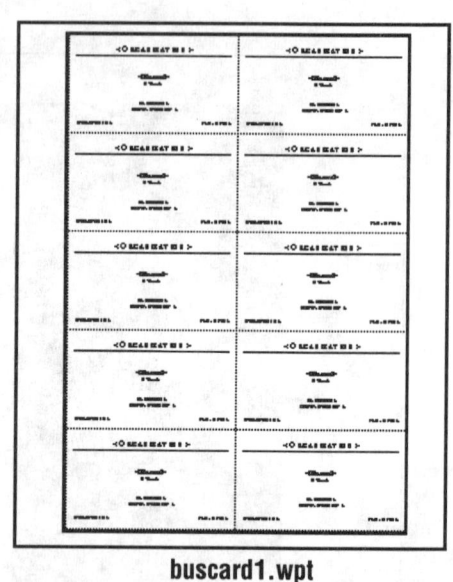

attend.wpt

balance.wpt

buscard1.wpt

buscard2.wpt

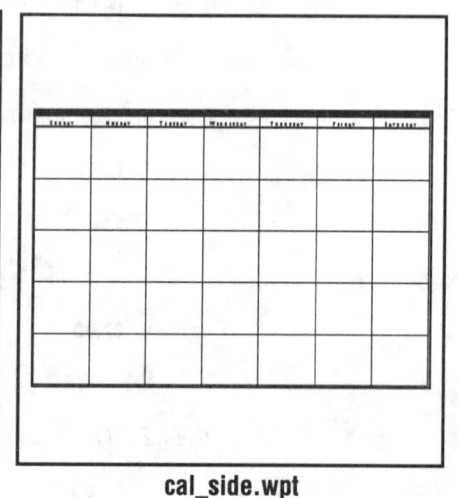

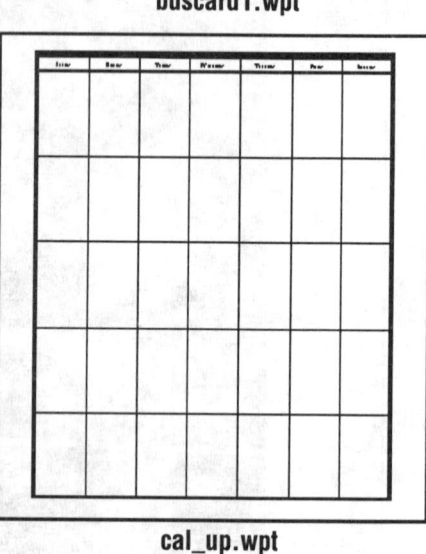

cal_side.wpt

cal_up.wpt

certif1.wpt

certif2.wpt

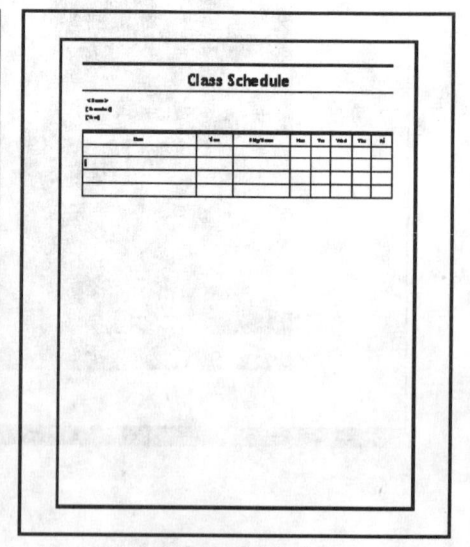

classchd.wpt

Appendix A

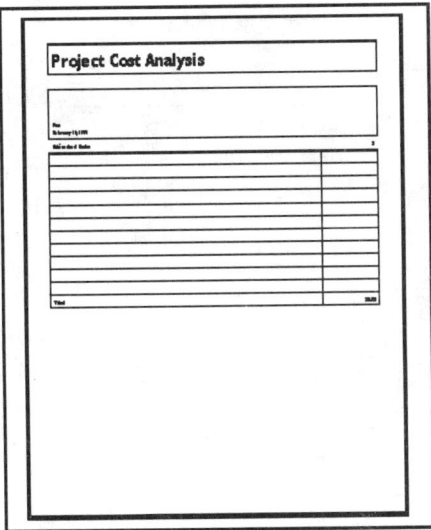

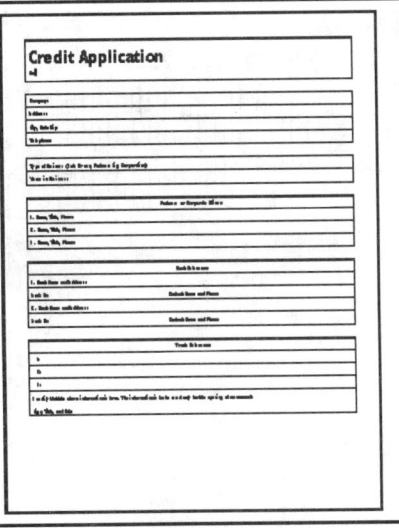

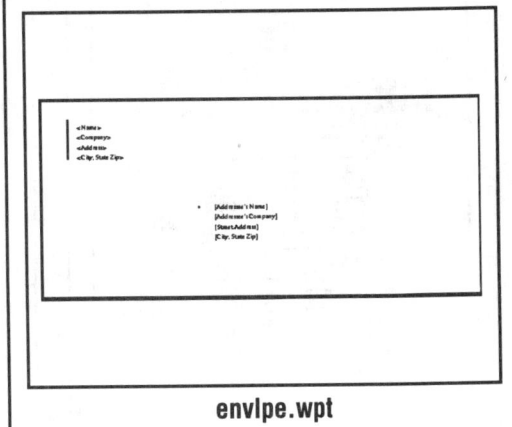

costanyl.wpt

creditap.wpt

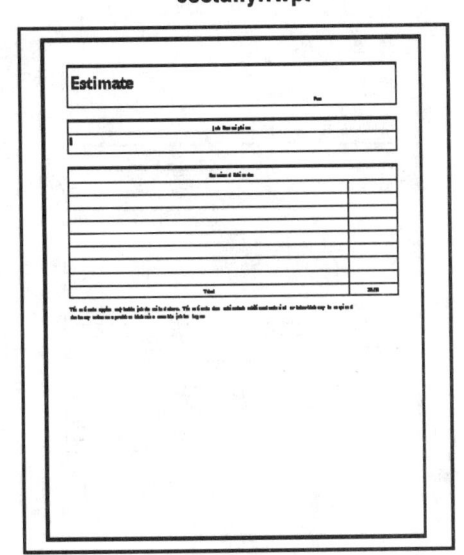

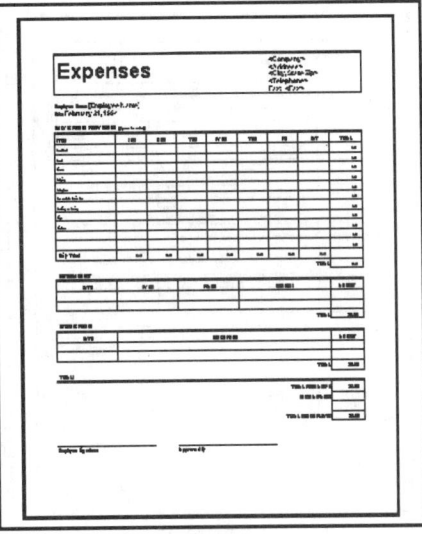

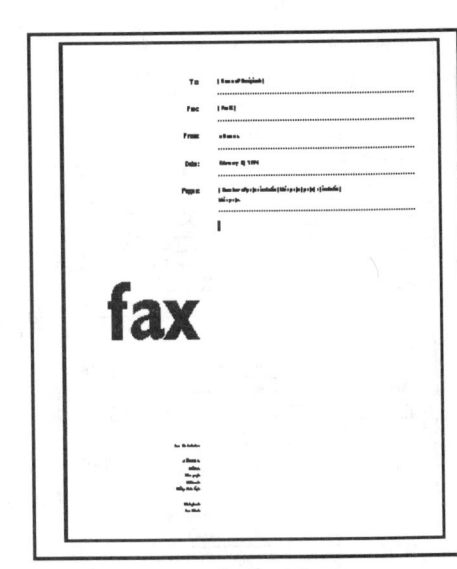

envlpe.wpt

estimate.wpt

expense.wpt

fax1.wpt

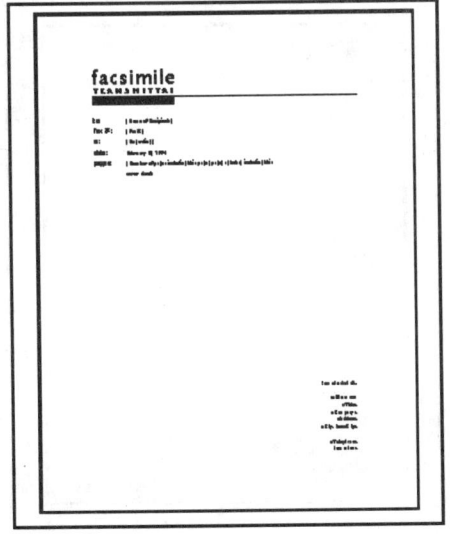

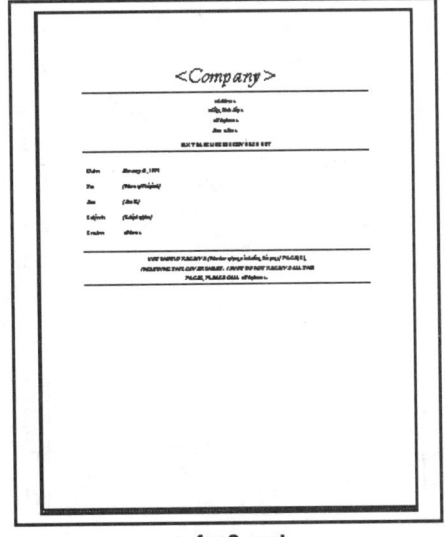

fax2.wpt

fax3.wpt

fax4.wpt

Appendix A 357

Appendix A

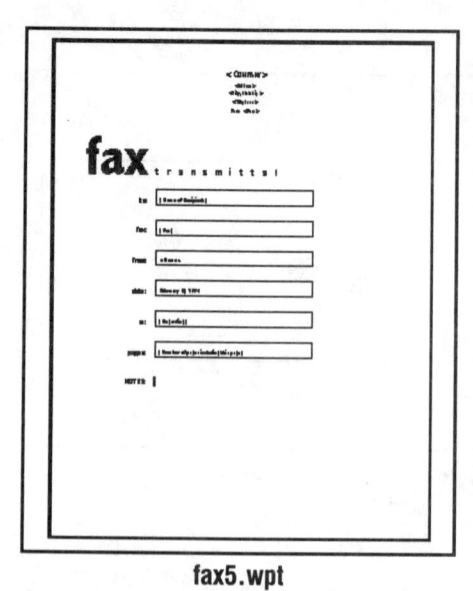

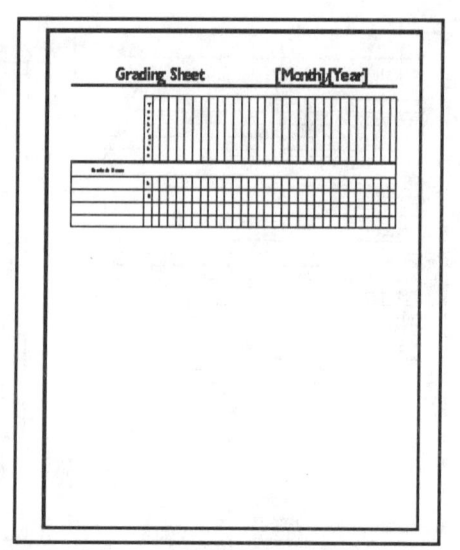

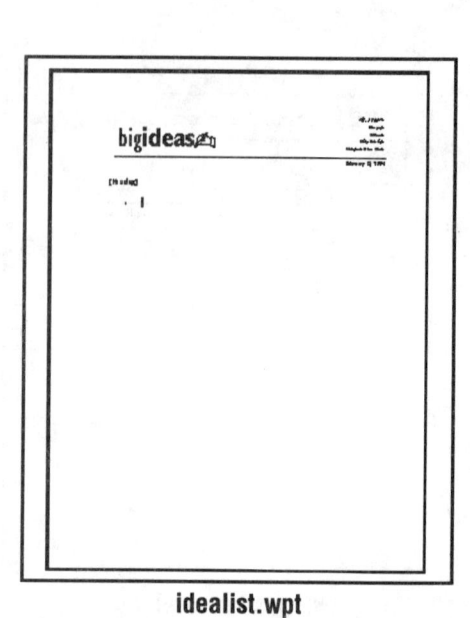

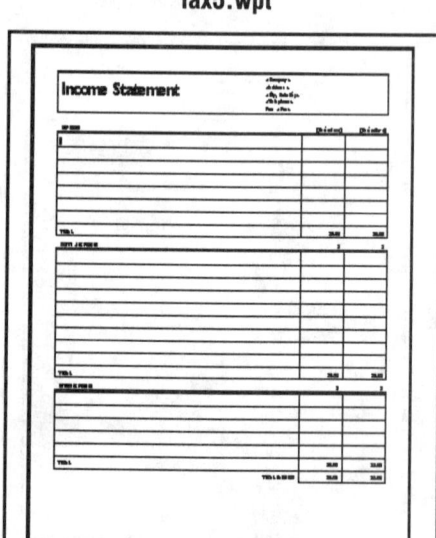

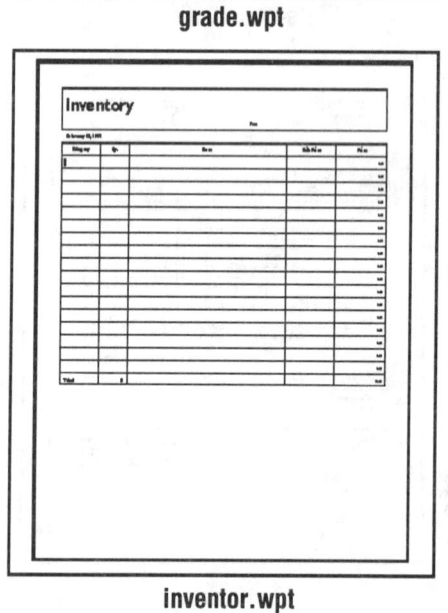

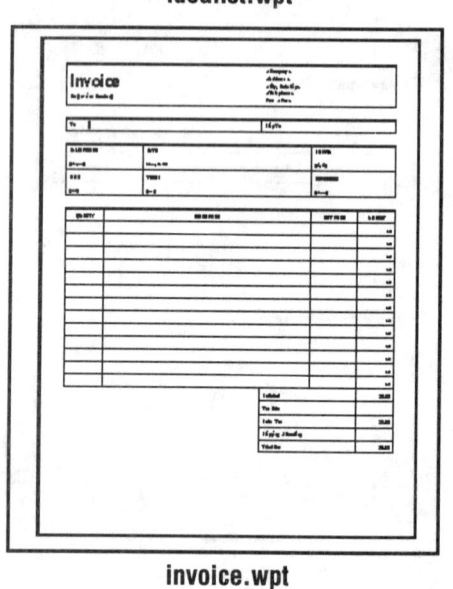

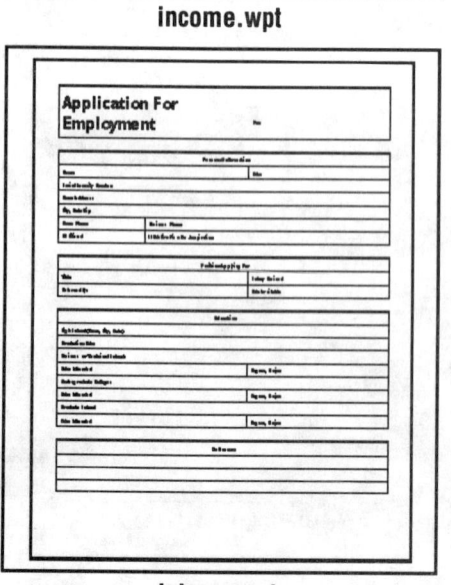

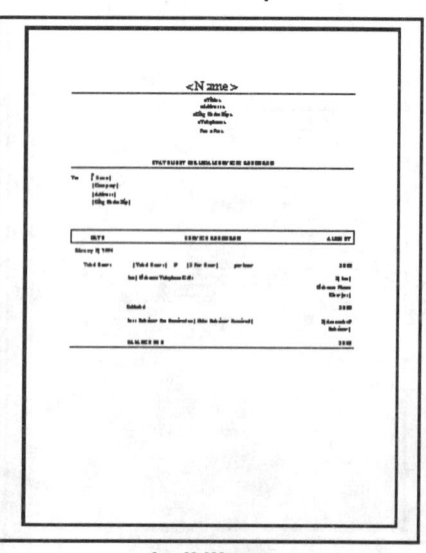

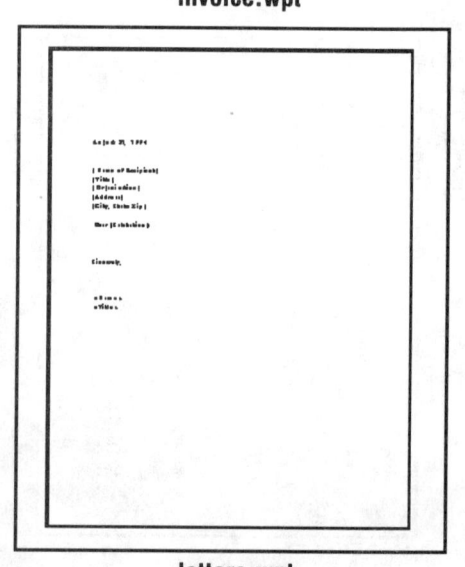

fax5.wpt

grade.wpt

idealist.wpt

income.wpt

inventor.wpt

invoice.wpt

jobapp.wpt

leglbill.wpt

lettero.wpt

Appendix A

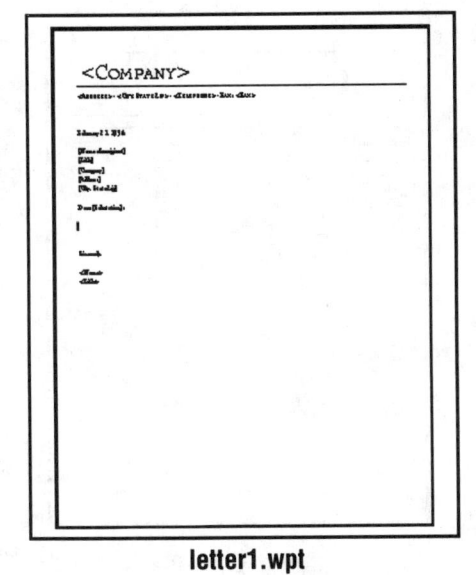

letter1.wpt

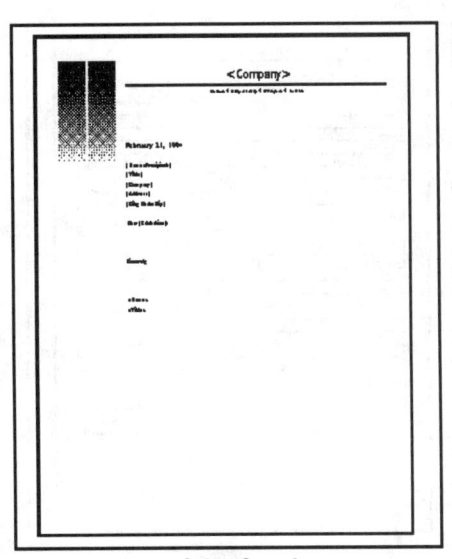

letter2.wpt

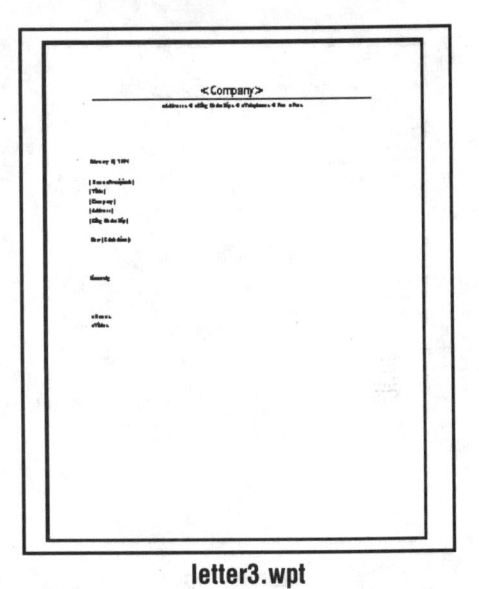

letter3.wpt

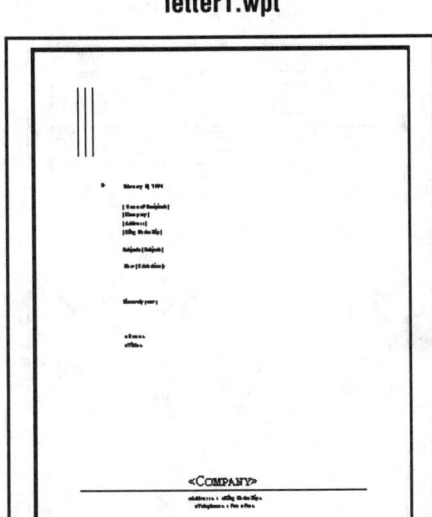

letter4.wpt

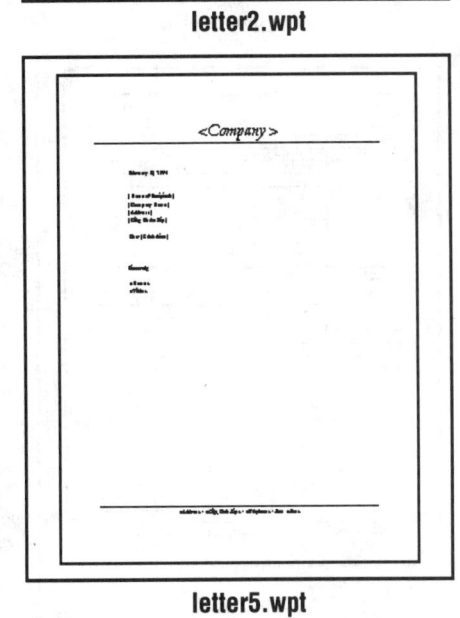

letter5.wpt

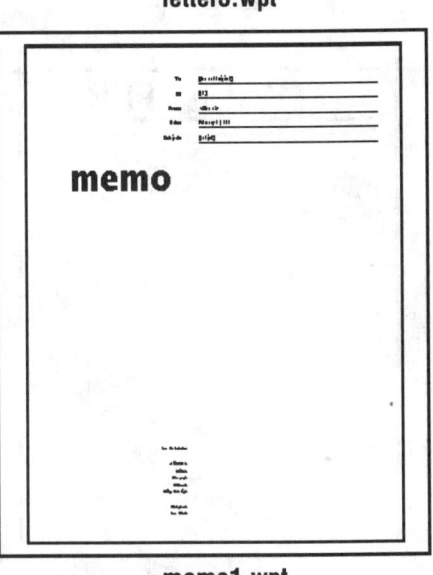

memo1.wpt

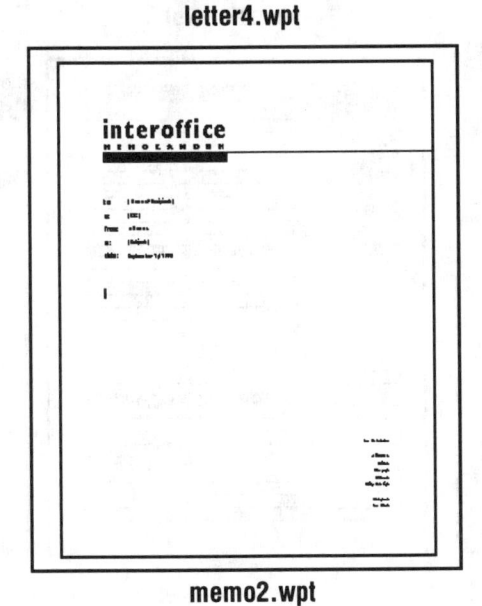

memo2.wpt

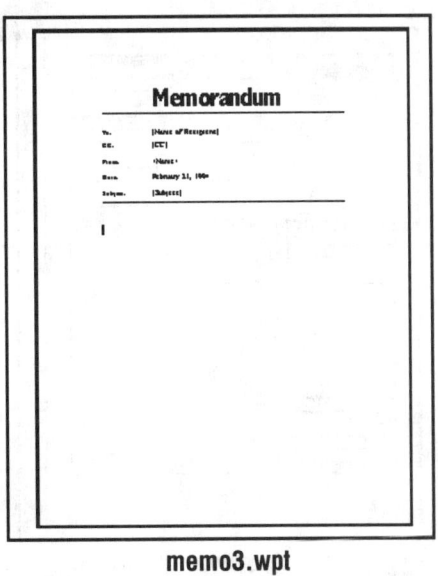

memo3.wpt

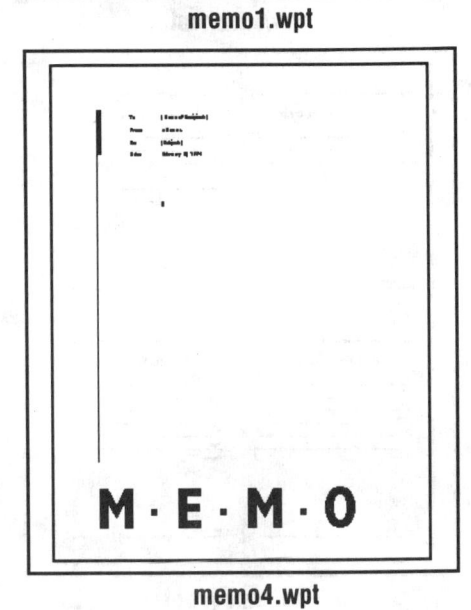

memo4.wpt

Appendix A

memo5.wpt

mileage.wpt

newsltr1.wpt

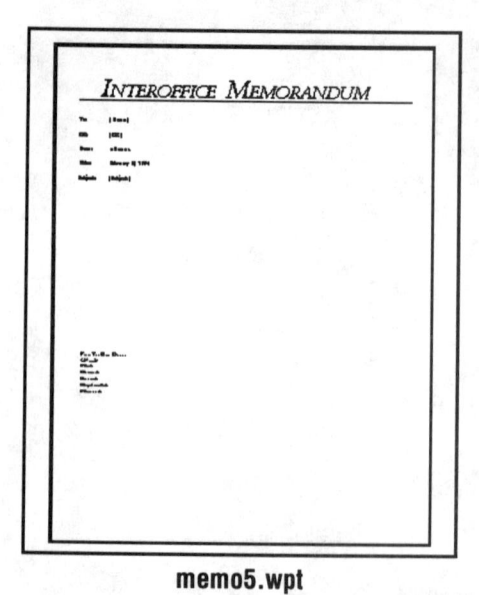

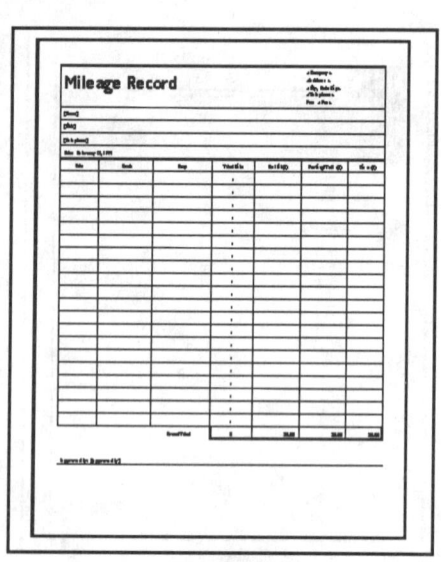

newsltr2.wpt

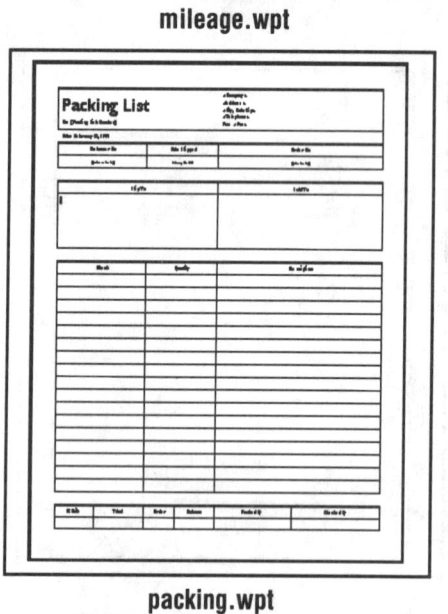

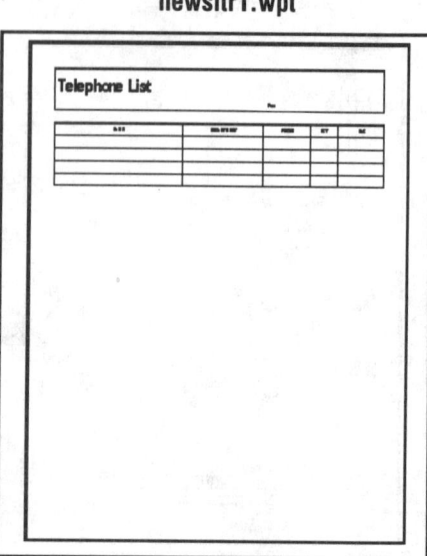

packing.wpt

phonelst.wpt

phonemsg.wpt

planday.wpt

planweek.wpt

Appendix A

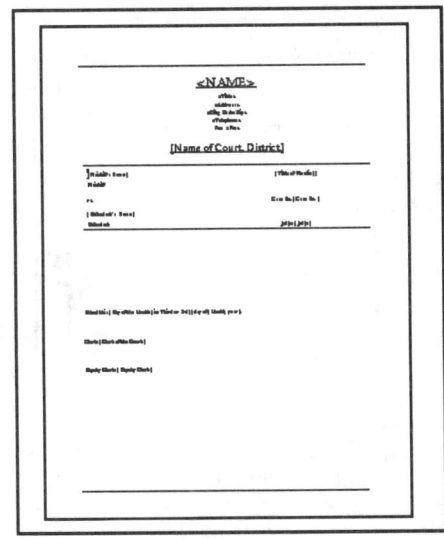

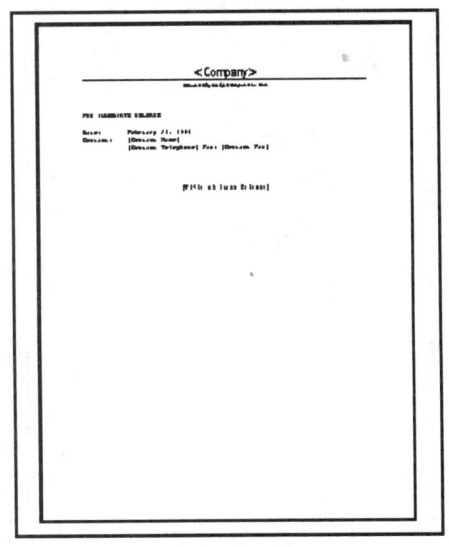

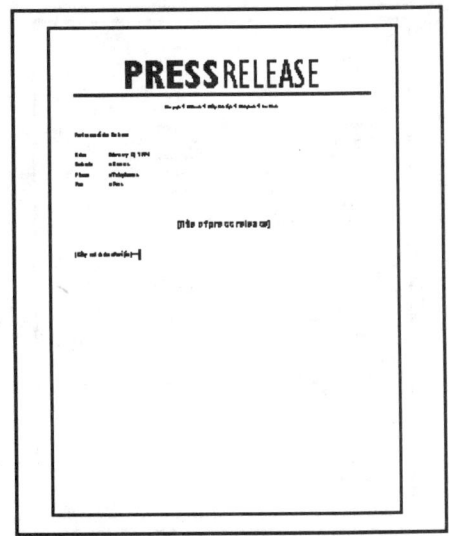

pleadcvr.wpt

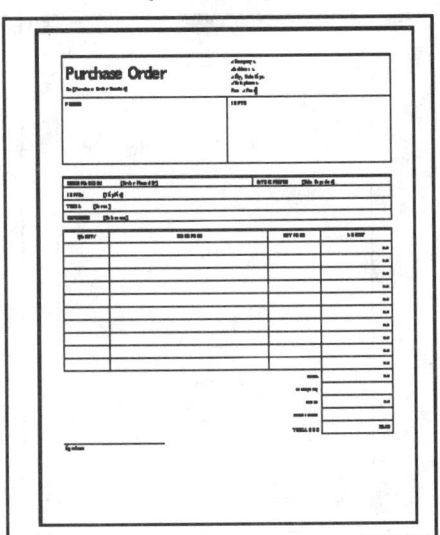

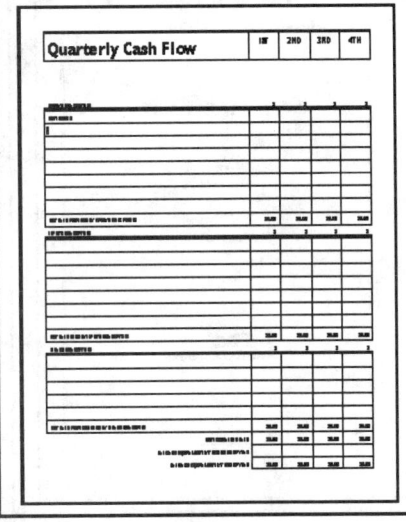

press1.wpt

press2.wpt

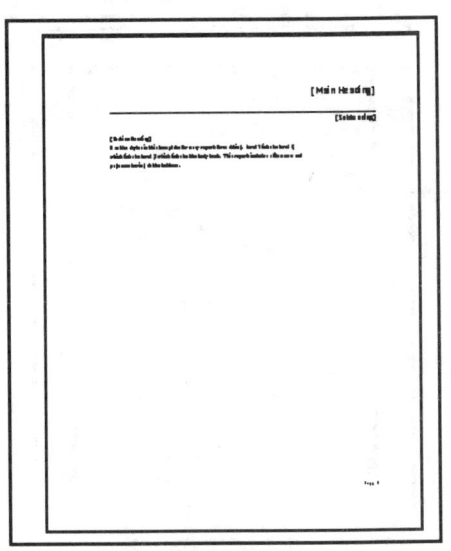

purchase.wpt

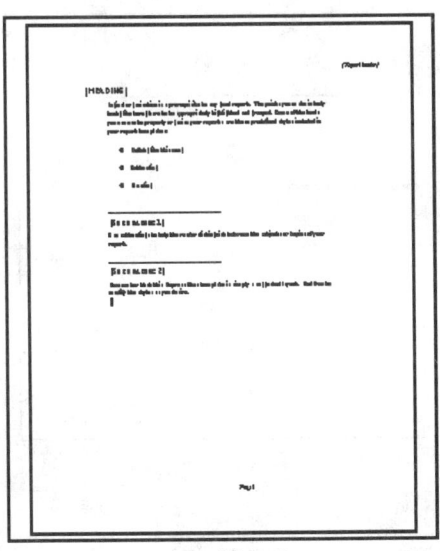

qcashflw.wpt

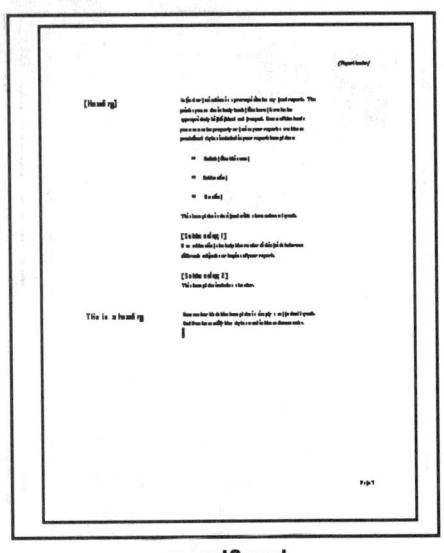

report1.wpt

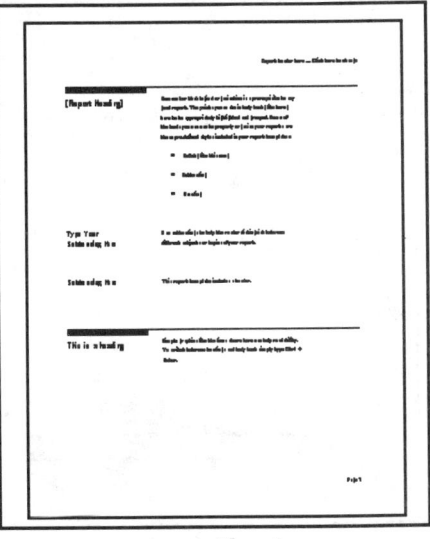

report2.wpt

report3.wpt

report4.wpt

Appendix A

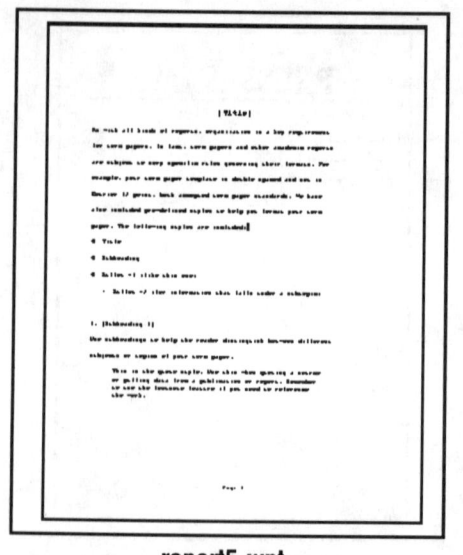

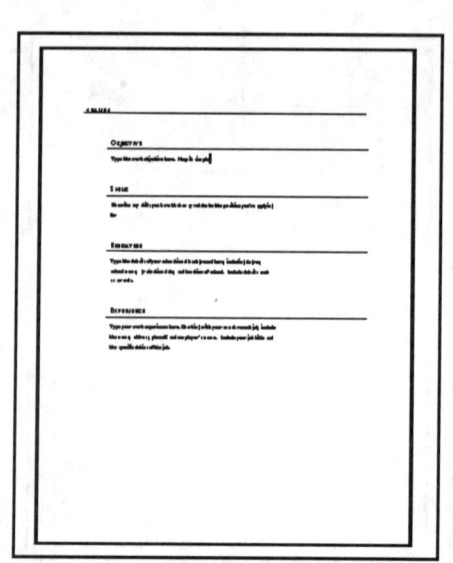

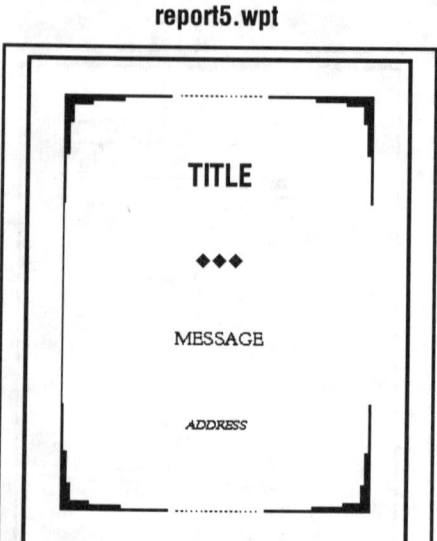

report5.wpt

resume.wpt

sign1.wpt

sign2.wpt

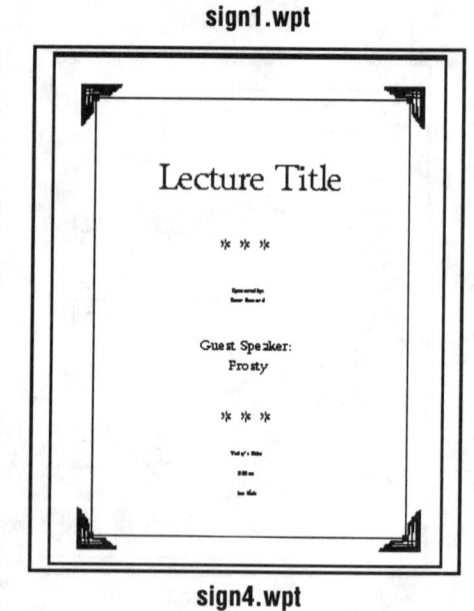

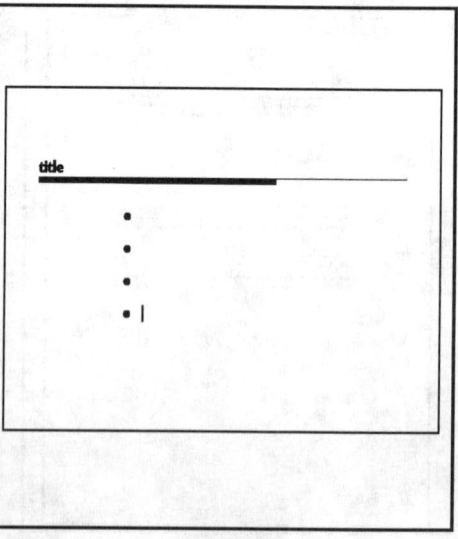

sign3.wpt

sign4.wpt

sign5.wpt

slide1.wpt

slide2.wpt

Appendix A

slide3.wpt

slide4.wpt

term.wpt

titlepg1.wpt

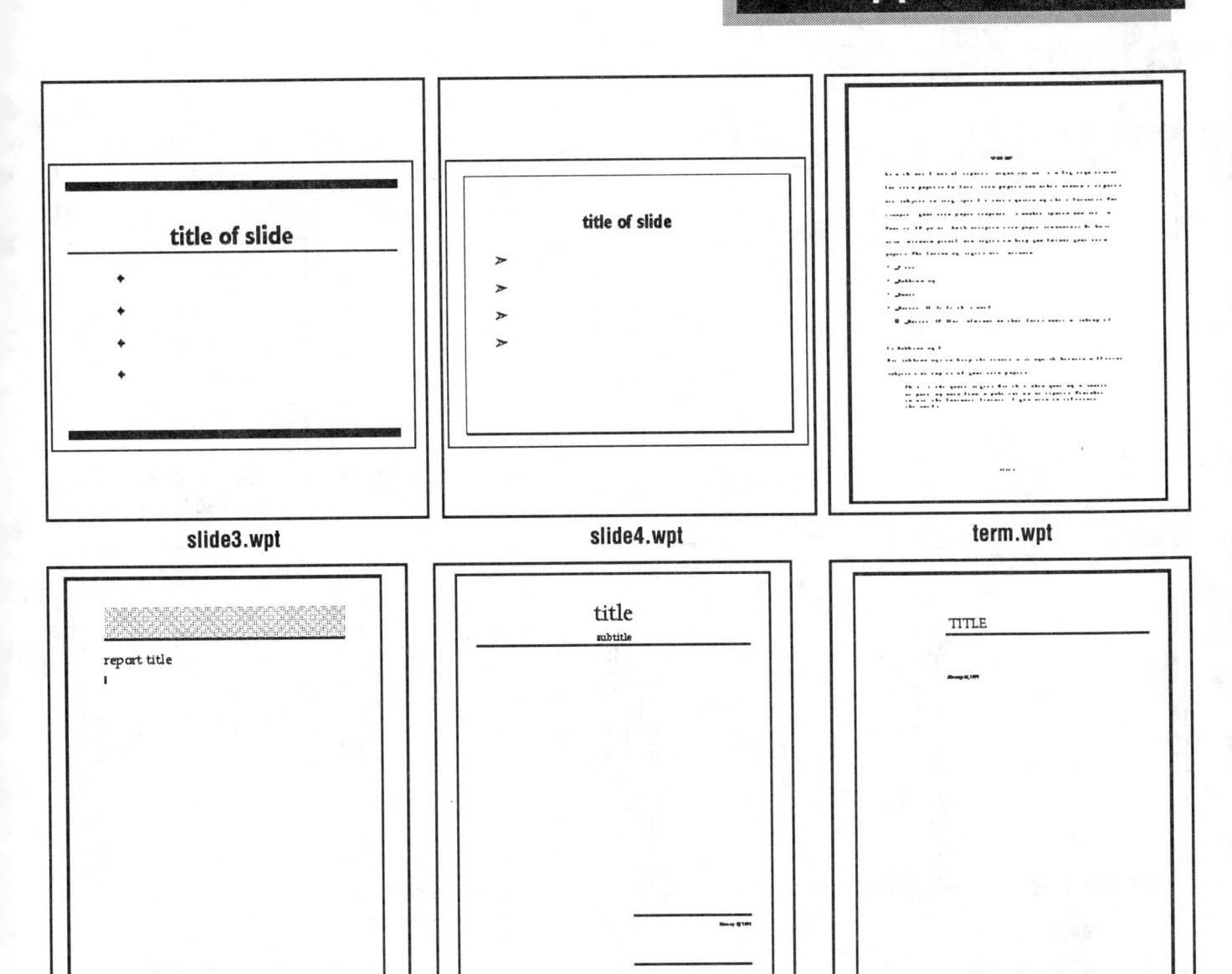

titlepg2.wpt

titlepg3.wpt

Appendix A 363

Appendix B

CLIPART GRAPHICS

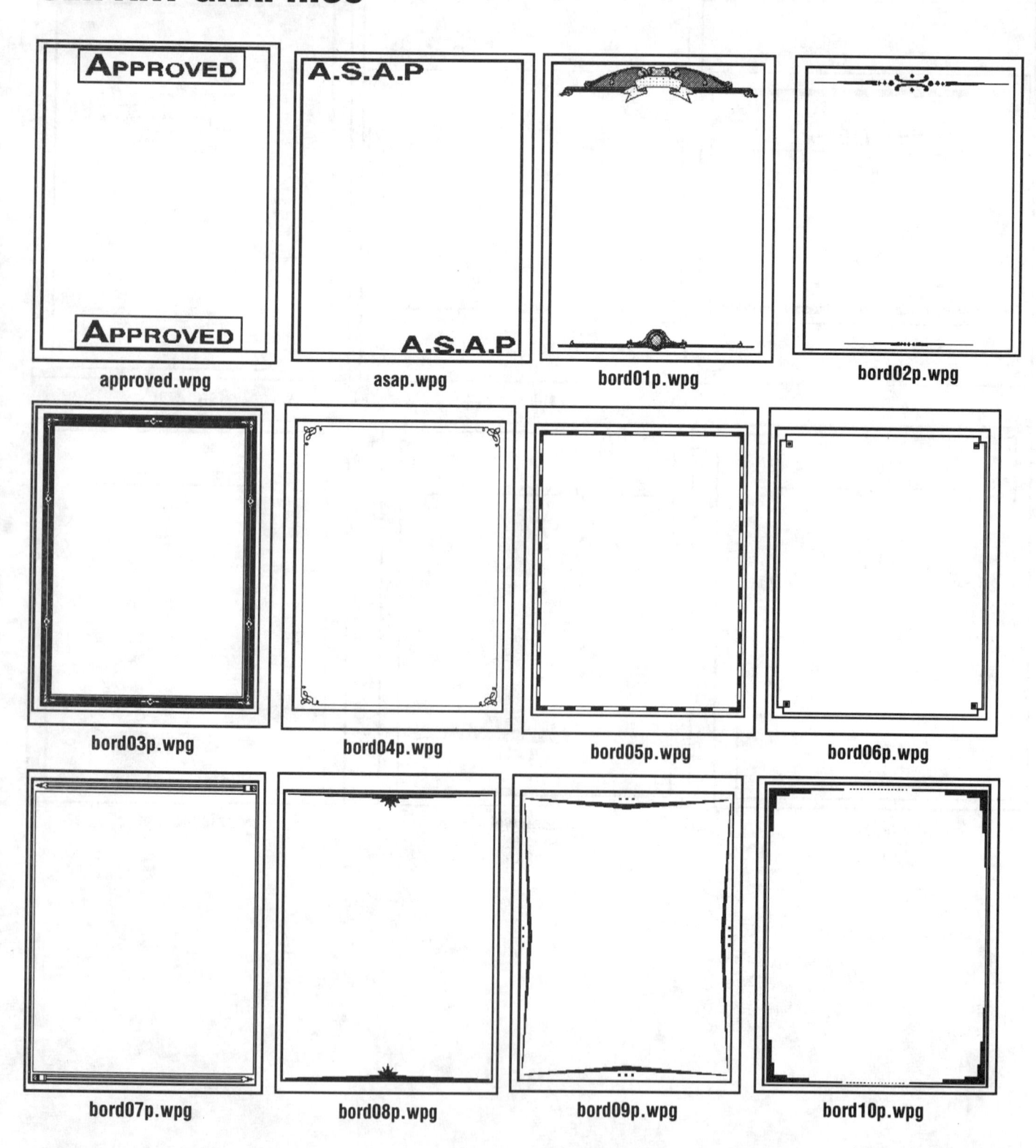

approved.wpg

asap.wpg

bord01p.wpg

bord02p.wpg

bord03p.wpg

bord04p.wpg

bord05p.wpg

bord06p.wpg

bord07p.wpg

bord08p.wpg

bord09p.wpg

bord10p.wpg

Appendix B

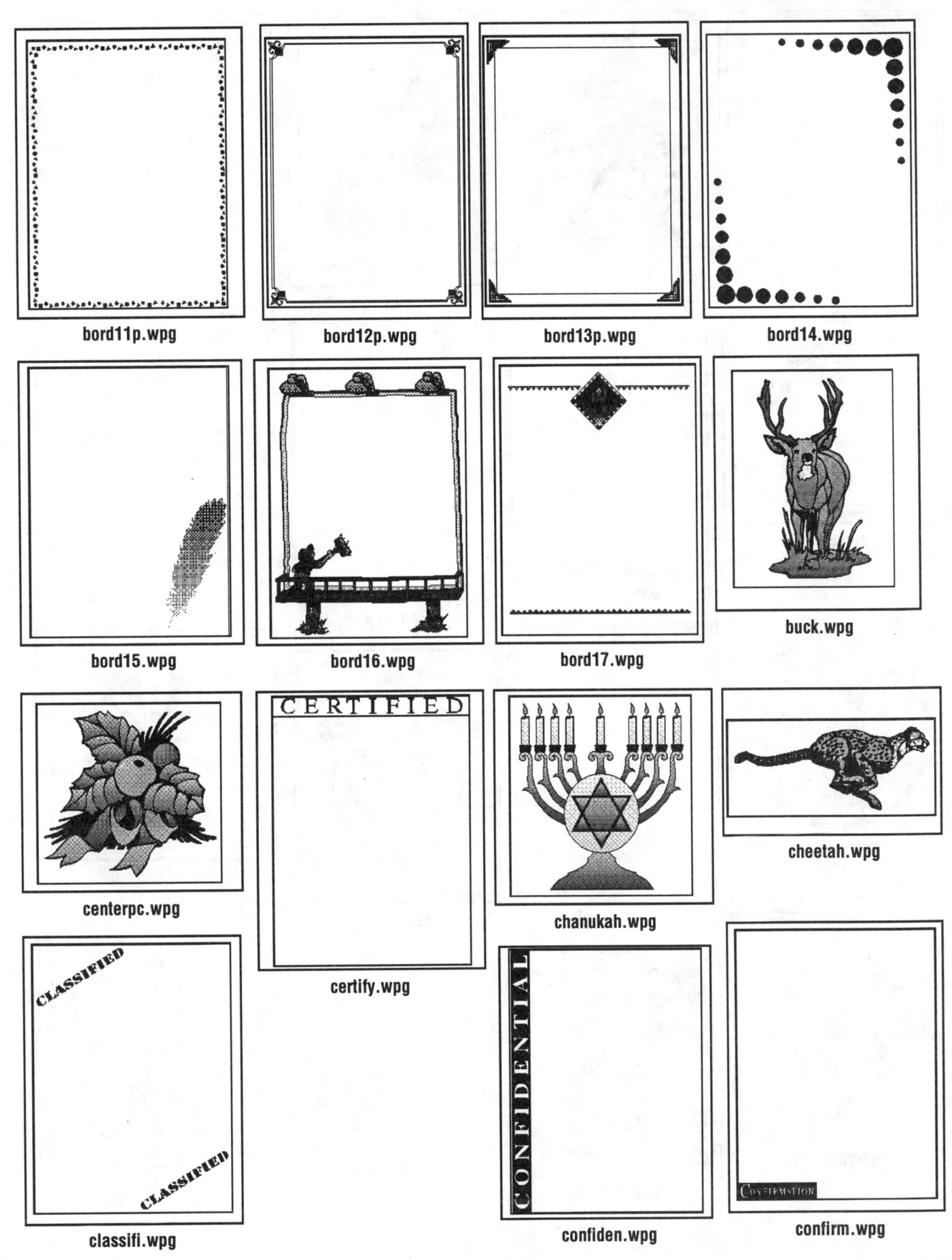

bord11p.wpg

bord12p.wpg

bord13p.wpg

bord14.wpg

bord15.wpg

bord16.wpg

bord17.wpg

buck.wpg

centerpc.wpg

certify.wpg

chanukah.wpg

cheetah.wpg

classifi.wpg

confiden.wpg

confirm.wpg

Appendix B 365

Appendix B

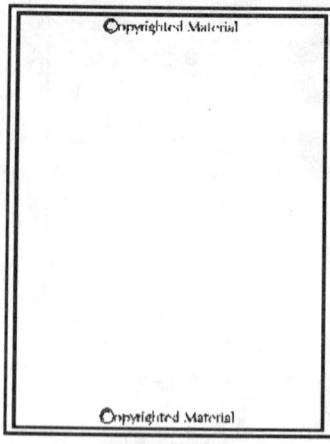

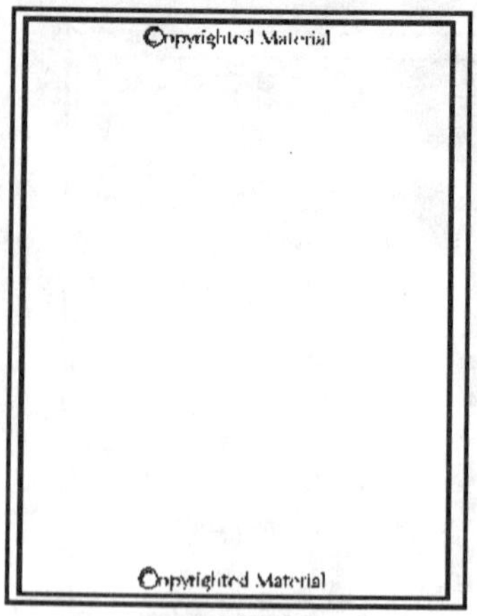

copyrite.wpg

cowboy.wpg

coyote.wpg

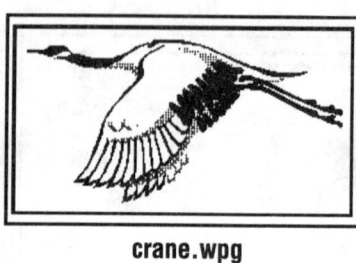

crane.wpg

crest.wpg

dontcopy.wpg

draft.wpg

dragn.wpg

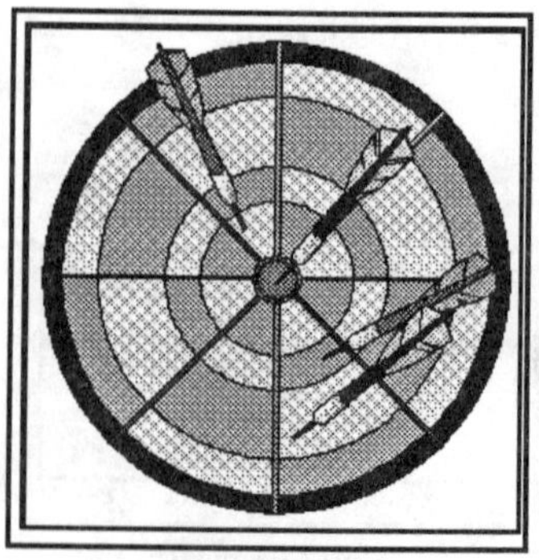

drtbord.wpg

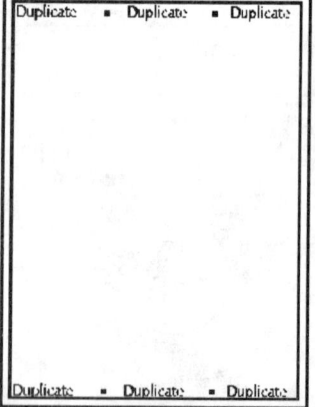

duplicat.wpg

ender01.wpg

ender02.wpg

ender03.wpg

ender04.wpg

ender05.wpg

ender06.wpg

Appendix B

ender07.wpg

ender08.wpg

ender09.wpg

ender10.wpg

ender11.wpg

estimate.wpg

eyesonly.wpg

fathrtme.wpg

file_co.wpg

final.wpg

group.wpg

horse_j.wpg

hotair.wpg

hotrod.wpg

importnt.wpg

inkgolf.wpg

inkskier.wpg

internal.wpg

Appendix B 367

Appendix B

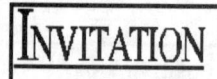

invitatn.wpg

jockey.wpg

makewish.wpg

marsh.wpg

medical1.wpg

nonegot.wpg

odori.wpg

overdue.wpg

padlock.wpg

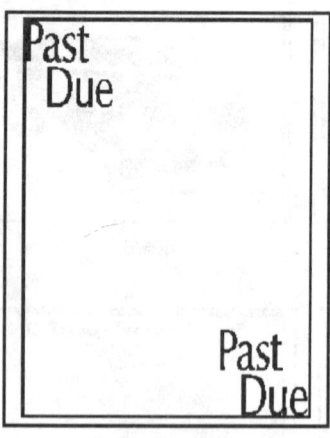

past_due.wpg

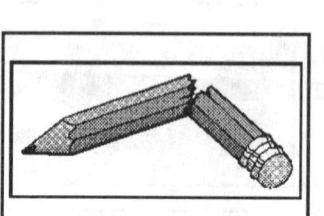

pencilbr.wpg

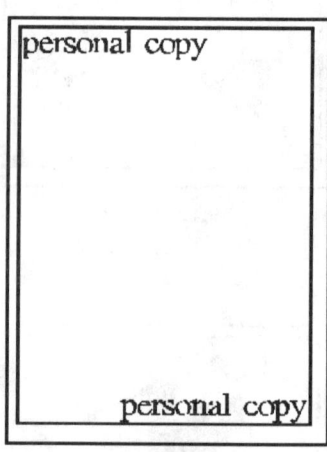

personal.wpg

piano.wpg

pointer.wpg

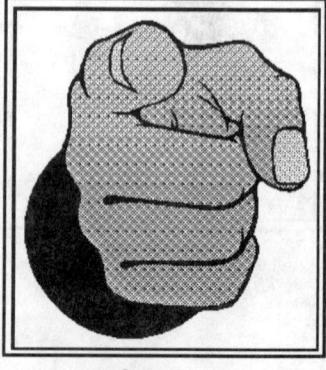

pointout.wpg

Appendix B

prohibit.wpg

proof.wpg

proposal.wpg

reply.wpg

rose.wpg

rsvp.wpg

rush.wpg

secret.wpg

silo1.wpg

silo2.wpg

silo3.wpg

skipper.wpg

skydive.wpg

sun_dsg.wpg

telerec.wpg

thanks.wpg

Appendix B

tiger_j.wpg

topsecrt.wpg

trn_cnd.wpg

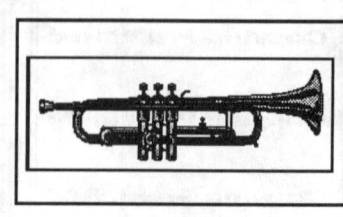

trumpt.wpg

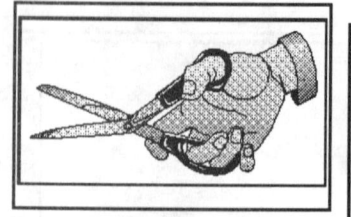

usesciss.wpg

windmill.wpg

winrace.wpg

woman02.wpg

womdesk.wpg

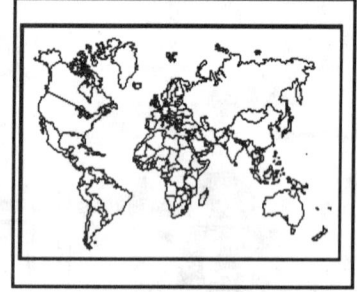

world.wpg

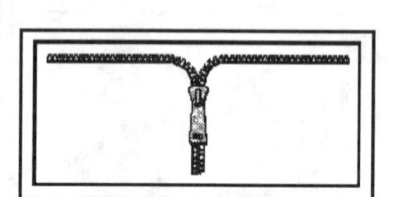

zipper.wpg

370

INDEX

A

Advance 108
Align text
   center 32
   full 32
   in tables 268-270, 272, 273
   left 32
   right (flush right) 30-31
Anchor types 116-119
Appearance of text (changing the) 46-48
Attributes, fonts 46

B

Balanced newspaper columns 92
Bold 46, 48
Border/Fill
   graphics boxes 124-127
   tables 288-292
   text 168-169
Borders
   styles 125, 127
   page 168-169
   paragraph 168-169
Bulleted lists (creating) 191-192
Bullets, special characters 190-192
Button Bar
   display 3, 5
   hide 3, 5
   select 3, 5

C

Captions (graphics) 130, 132
Cells
   align text within 268-270, 272-273
   delete contents 277-278
   join 284-286
   move between 263-264
   split 284-286
Center
   justification 32-33
   line 28-29
   vertically 28-29
Characters, special 186-188
Chart
   color 322, 324
   create 308-312
   create from table 318-320
   edit 314-316
   explode pie chart 315-316
   data labels 310, 312, 318, 320
   legends 310, 312, 318, 320
   line styles 322-324
   type 309
ClipArt 102
Codes, reveal 12-14
Columns
   balanced newspaper columns 92
   border/fill 84
   create 84-85
   custom width 88, 90
   newspaper 82-85
   moving from column to column 84
   parallel 94, 96
   vertical line between 84-85
Contour text to graphics 224-225
Cursor *(see Insertion point)*

Continued...   371

INDEX

D

Decimal tabs 272-273
Default settings 6
Desktop Publishing, defined v
Display Button/Power Bar 5
Document window
    displaying scroll bars 2
    multiple 2
    opening new 2
Double click (mouse) definition 2
Double indent 34-36
Double underline 46, 48
Drag (mouse) definition 2
Draw
    alignment guides 200-201, 205
    arranging objects 226-228
    colors 208-210
    contouring text 224-225
    editing 212-214
    editing graphic parts 223-225
    fill patterns 208-210
    grids 200-201
    grouping/ungrouping objects 226-228
    line styles 208-210
    line tools 206-207
    rulers 200-201, 205
    shape 198-199
    shape tools 198-199
    text 216-218
Drop Capitals

E

Edit
    graphics box 112-114

F

Figure box (see *Graphics*) 102-104
Fills
    graphic 124-127, 325
    paragraph 168-169
    styles 126-127
    table 288-292
First-line indent 38-41
Flip graphic 139, 142
Flush right 30-31
Fonts
    appearance 46-48, 50-53
    face 42, 43, 45
    monospaced 43
    position 54-55
    proportionally spaced 43
    relative size 54-55
    shading 62-63
    size 44-45
    style 43, 45
    Wingdings 58-60
Footers
    create 240-241, 243
    edit 241-243
    multiple 246, 248
    suppress 242-243
Full justification 32
Full page, viewing 7-10

G

Graphics
    anchor types 116-119
    border 124-127
        anchor types 116-119
        change contents 118-119

INDEX

    sizing 113-114
  user boxes
    caption 130-132
    ClipArt 102
    copy 113-114
    delete 113-114
    fills 124-127, 325
    flip 139, 142
    import 102-104
    lines 156, 159
    move within border 138-139, 142
    position 113-114
    rotate 106-108, 139-140, 142
    scale 137-138, 142
    select 112, 114
    TextArt 194-195
    text box 106-108
    wrap text 129, 132, 134

H

Hanging indent 38-41
Headers
    create 240-241, 243
    edit 241-243
    multiple 246, 248
    suppress 242-243
Help 24-26
Horizontal line (graphics) 156-159
Hyphenation 252-254

I

Images (see *Graphics*)
Import Graphic 102-104
Indent 34-36
Italics 46, 48

J

Join cells (tables) 284-286
Justification 32-33

K

Kerning 66-68

L

Landscape 20
Leading 74-75
Left align (text)
Letterspacing 70-72
Line height 76-77
Line spacing 10
Lines
    between columns 84-85
    copy 164
    create graphic 156, 159, 160-161
    custom 160-161
    delete 164
    edit 157-159
    move/size 157-159
    paragraph 168-169
    shade 164
Lists, bulleted 191-192

Continued...

INDEX

M

Mouse, terminology; using the 2
Multiple headers 246, 248
Multiple footers 246, 248

N

Newspaper columns 82-85
Numbers, page 242-243, 246, 247

O

Orientation (paper size)..............................20
Ornamental font faces...........................58-60
Orphan protection 252, 254
Outline..50-51

P

Page
  border/fill 168-169
  number 242-243, 246, 247
  view (zoom) 10
Page View...7-10
Paper Size and Orientation....................18-22
Paragraph numbering 190-192
Paragraph spacing................................39-41
Parallel columns....................................94, 96
Portrait..20
Power Bar, display/hide 3-5
Preview document 2-22
Print quality..110-111

Q

QuickCreate (styles) 342-343, 345

R

Redline...50-51
Remove font appearance.......................52-53
Reveal codes 12-14
Reverse text......................................180-182
Right align...30-31
Rotate
  graphics 106-108, 139-140, 142
  text...106, 108
Rules *(see Lines)*

S

Scale graphic 137-138, 142
Select an object 112, 114
Shade
  graphic boxes.......................124-127, 325
  lines 164
  text 62-63
Shadow..50-51
Sizing handles..103
Small Caps..50-51
Spacing, line...10
Special characters 186-188
Split cells..284-286
Strikeout..50-51
Styles
  create 338-341
  edit 346-347
  pre-defined.....................................334-336
  QuickCreate 342-343, 345
  Retrieve 348, 351
  Save 342-343, 345
Suppress, headers/footers..................242-243
Symbols show 10

INDEX

T

Tables
- align text................................268-270, 272-273
- borders..288-292
- change column width........................280-282
- column margins..................................298-301
- create..262-264
- delete..277-278
- edit..276-278
- enter text..263-264
- fills..288-292
- join cells..284-286
- lines..288-292
- move insertion point through............263-264
- position..285-286
- row margins......................................298-301
- tabs...294
- with graphics....................................302-304
- Templates..330-333

Text Box *(see Graphics)*................102, 106-108
Text, reverse..180-182
Text wrap.............................128-119, 132, 134
TextArt...194-195

U

Undelete...16-17
Undo action...16-17
Underline..46, 48

V

Vertical lines (graphics)..........................160-161
View document..7-10
View bars...3-5

W

Watermarks..144-146
Width, changing columns in tables......280-282
Widow/orphan protection....................252, 254
Wingdings..58-60
Word Spacing..70-72
Wrap text around graphics...128-129, 132, 134

Z

Zoom..10

375

Learning Desktop Publishing for WordPerfect 6 for Windows™

Solutions/Data Disk

Provides the data for each exercise in this book as well as the solution as it should appear on your screen. Reduces keyboarding time and enables the trainer to skip different exercises.

3 1/2" Disk

Cat. No.   DD-88......................................$7.50 each
Cat. No.   DD-88SL...........................$65 site license

Transparencies for Training

Selected transparencies of screens, menus and dialog boxes. Call outs define and explain as you teach.

20 Transparencies   Cat. No. T-33...........................$50

Test Yourself on Desktop Publishing WordPefect 6/Windows

Designed to measure your software skills with a suggested time frame and point scale to determine your competency level.

Can you turn *this*... into *this*...

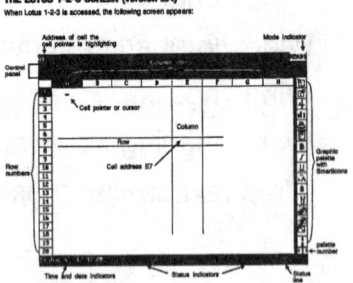

Includes booklet and 3 1/2" diskette

Cat. No.   T-WPW6D $14.95
Cat. No.   T-WPW6DSL .....$65 Site License

Teacher's Manual

Provides vocabulary, points out trouble spots, and contains other helpful information for the teacher or trainer.

Cat. No.   WD6-TM $10

SUPPORT MATERIALS

DDC Publishing (800) 528-3897   FAX (800) 528-3862